fr

DIARY OF A
WARTIME NAVAL
CONSTRUCTOR
SIR STANLEY GOODALL

Photograph by]   [Elliott & Fry, Ltd.

The official portrait of Goodall with his signature which appeared in *The Shipbuilder* in September 1936 with the announcement of his appointment as DNC.

DIARY OF A
WARTIME NAVAL CONSTRUCTOR
SIR STANLEY GOODALL

EDITED BY IAN BUXTON

Seaforth
PUBLISHING

www.seaforthpublishing.com
Email info@seaforthpublishing.com

British Library Cataloguing in Publication Data
A CIP data record for this book is available from the British Library

ISBN 978-1-3990-8270-9 (Hardback)
ISBN 978-1-3990-8271-6 (ePub)
ISBN 978-1-3990-8272-3 (Kindle)

Pen & Sword Books Limited incorporates the imprints of Atlas,
Archaeology, Aviation, Discovery, Family History, Fiction, History,
Maritime, Military, Military Classics, Politics, Select, Transport,
True Crime, Air World, Frontline Publishing, Leo Cooper,
Remember When, Seaforth Publishing, The Praetorian Press,
Wharncliffe Local History, Wharncliffe Transport, Wharncliffe True
Crime and White Owl.

Typeset and designed by Mac Style
Printed and bound in Great Britain by CPI Group (UK) Ltd,
Croydon, CR0 4YY.

Contents

Preface

David K Brown, usually known by his initials DKB, was one of the most renowned naval architects at the Admiralty, later Ministry of Defence, not least for his extensive writings from the 1970s. He combined his professional expertise with a deep interest in the Royal Navy's warships past and present, which gave him special insight into the demands of warship design. I first met him as a young warship enthusiast at meetings of the Naval Photograph Club in London. As I also became a naval architect, we continued to meet and share our interests for the next 50 years. One of his heroes was Sir Stanley Goodall, Director of Naval Construction during most of the Second World War. Although Goodall had retired before DKB joined the Royal Corps of Naval Constructors (RCNC), they knew each other through common membership of the (Royal) Institution of Naval Architects and social gatherings of past and present members of the RCNC. Goodall probably told him about his diaries, and that having no children he was leaving them to the British Library.

When DKB published his history of the RCNC, *A Century of Naval Construction*, in 1983, he was able to consult them for insights into Goodall's career and work and his designs of many of the ships that fought in the war. DKB included some pithy quotations from them, but was sparing of including names, especially of those of whom Goodall was critical, as many were then still alive. His later *Nelson to Vanguard* also drew on the diaries. Those books were enough to whet my appetite to look at these fascinating diaries myself. My retirement provided the opportunity to do so, all 15 years of diaries from 1932 to 1946. His early diaries consisted of one foolscap-sized diary each year, with a week to a page. In those Goodall summarised his work, the people he had met and the places he had visited. While the diary's main function seems to be as an aide memoire, it was also a place to vent his frustrations, especially with people who he felt were not up to the job. After he became DNC, he switched to a more compact five-year diary, with one page covering the same day for all five years, 1937–41 and 1942–6. The resulting entries are more cramped, with his handwriting more difficult to decipher and full of abbreviations. On my first visit to the British Library, it took me a full day to read and summarise a single early diary with its then brief entries, with very little transcription possible. Fortunately the BL later permitted taking digital images, so reading, deciphering and transcribing the more extensive entries of later years could be done more thoroughly at home.

The World Ship Society's quarterly journal *Warships* published a selection of my extracts from 2018 to 2020, annotated to explain what ships or classes were being discussed and who were the people he met and their positions. These were well received, with much information that was new to readers. Seaforth recognised the value of making the extracts more widely available as a unique historical record, but with more background and with a selection of photographs of ships and people mentioned. The diaries run to around 400,000 words in all, but some of the entries are routine or semi-repetitive as an action was followed through. So these extracts cover about 30 per cent of the wartime years, and then not every day nor every line of a day's entry, only the most interesting. The breadth and depth of Goodall's knowledge and experience shine through in his perceptive and frank comments. The result is a unique and revealing record of the contribution of a most distinguished naval architect to the Royal Navy's successes (and failures) in the Second World War.

Ian Buxton
Tynemouth
2021

Abbreviations

A's & A's	Alterations & Additions
A/A	anti-aircraft
AC	Aircraft carrier; Assistant Constructor
accom	accommodation
ACNS	Assistant Chief of Naval Staff (H = home, F = foreign, W = weapons)
AC(WP)	Assistant Controller (Warship Production)
Admy	Admiralty
ADNC	Assistant Director of Naval Construction
AFD	Admiralty Floating Dock
agin	against
ANCXF	Allied Naval Commander Expeditionary Force
AP	armour piercing
app'd	approved
appt	appointment
AR	air raid
armt	armament
arrgt	arrangement
AS	Admiral Superintendent
A/S	anti-submarine
ASCBS	Admiral Superintendent Contract Built Ships
ASIs	Admiralty Supply Items
BAD	British Admiralty Delegation (in USA)
BATM	British Admiralty Technical Mission (in Canada)
BC	British Corporation
BDE	British destroyer escort (US-built)
bkd	bulkhead
blr	boiler
BSRA	British Shipbuilding Research Association
C in C	Commander in Chief
C of S or COS	Chief of Staff

C'tee	Committee
CC	Chief Constructor
CCO	Chief Combined Operations
CE	Civil Establishments?
C E in C	Civil Engineer in Chief
Cl	Class
CL	Cammell Laird; Controller of Labour?
CMSR	Controller of Merchant Shipbuilding & Repair
CNC	Contact Non-Contact (torpedo)
CO	Commanding officer; Combined Operations
compt	compartment
Contr	Controller
CS	Cruiser Squadron
D of C	Director of Contracts (and Purchase)
D of D	Director of Dockyards
D of P	Director of Plans
DA/SW	Director of Anti-Submarine Warfare
DC	Damage control; depth charge
DCOM	Director Combined Operations Material
DCT	Director control tower; depth-charge thrower
DCW	Director of Contract Work
DDNC	Deputy Director of Naval Construction
DE	Destroyer escort
DEE	Director of Electrical Engineering
dept	department
destr	destroyer
DFSL	Deputy First Sea Lord
DMB	Director Merchant Shipbuilding
DMR	Director Merchant Ship Repair
DMSR	Director Merchant Shipbuilding & Repair
DMWD	Department of Miscellaneous Weapon Development
DNAD	Director of Naval Air Division
DNC	Director of Naval Construction
DNO	Director of Naval Ordnance
D of D or DoD	Director of Dockyards
D of S	Director of Stores
DSC	Deputy Superintendent of Conversions?
DSR	Director of Scientific Research
DTM	Director of Torpedoes and Mining
DTSD	Director of Training & Staff Duties
dwg	drawing
DWP	Director of Warship Production
E in C	Engineer in Chief

ECF	European cease fire
EO	Engineer overseer or officer
ERO	Emergency Repair Overseer
exptl	experimental
FAA	Fleet Air Arm
FBC	Future Building Committee
FOIC	Flag Officer in Charge
FO(S) or FOS	Flag Officer, Submarines
fwd	forward
GM	Metacentric height, distance between metacentre (imaginary point of suspension) and centre of gravity. Needs to be positive i.e. G below M
GMO	Gun mounting overseer
H & W	Harland & Wolff
HA	High angle. i.e. anti-aircraft
HA/LA	High angle/low angle i.e. dual purpose guns
HF	Home Fleet
HL	Hawthorn Leslie
HQ	Headquarters
IAC	Intermediate aircraft carrier (light fleet carrier)
INA	Institution of Naval Architects
kn	knot(s)
LCF	Landing Craft Flak (anti-aircraft)
LCG	Landing Craft Gun (M = Medium)
LCI(L)	Landing Craft Infantry (Large)
LCT	Landing Craft Tank
LFC	Light fleet carrier
LR	Lloyd's Register
LST	Landing ship tank
Lt	light
M of WT	Ministry of War Transport
MAC	Merchant aircraft carrier
machy	machinery
MBr	Military Branch (Admiralty department)
MCD	Manager Constructive Department (at a dockyard)
MGB	Motor gunboat
MMS	Motor minesweeper
mos	months
M/S	Minesweeper
M.S.	Merchant ship
MTB	Motor torpedo boat
mtg	mounting
NA	Naval Attaché; naval architect; naval assistant
NC	New construction; non cemented (armour); non-contact

NE	North-east
NO	Naval officer
No.	number
NOIC	Naval Officer in Charge
OB	Outer bottom; Ordnance Board
OF	Oil fuel
PA	Public Accounts
PBr	Priority Branch (Admiralty department)
P.M.	Prime Minister; post meridiem
Prog	Programme
PSO	Principal Ship Overseer
pts	points
RA(D)	Rear Admiral (Destroyers)
RA(S) or RAS	Rear Admiral Submarines
RCNC	Royal Corps of Naval Constructors
RDF	Radio direction finding (radar)
RNVR	Royal Naval Volunteer Reserve
RPC	Remote Power Control
RY	Royal Yacht
S of C	Superintendent of Conversions
S/M	Submarine
SCW	Superintendent of Contract Work
Sec	Secretary
SGB	Steam gunboat
SH	Swan Hunter (& Wigham Richardson)
SL	Sea Lord
SLC	Superintendent of Landing Craft
SO	Senior officer
SYDC	Shipyard Development Committee
TF	Transport ferry i.e. LST
T G	Thank God
TLC	Tank landing craft (later LCT)
USN	United States Navy
USS	United States Ship
UXB	Unexploded bomb
v	very or versus
V-A	Vickers-Armstrongs
VCNS	Vice Chief of Naval Staff
v.g.	very good
WPS	Warship Production Superintendent
wt	weight
WT	Watertight; watertube (boilers)
W/T	Wireless telegraphy

Stanley Goodall's portrait was painted by James Barraclough and presented to him in March 1938. For many years it was on display at the Royal Institution of Naval Architects offices in London but is now at University College, London.

Sir Stanley Goodall

Stanley Vernon Goodall was the Royal Navy's most successful Director of Naval Construction in the twentieth century, holding office from 1936 to 1944. Born in Limehouse, London on 18 April 1883 to parents Samuel, a fireman, and Eliza, he went to school in Islington. He was accepted as a Royal Navy engineering officer cadet in July 1899 at Keyham in Plymouth, but transferred as a cadet for the Royal Corps of Naval Constructors in 1901, whose early training was also at Keyham. Quite probably Goodall was influenced to do so by the low status and pay that naval engineer officers were then accorded compared with executive officers. Sir William White was Director of Naval Construction at the time, shortly to be succeeded by Sir Philip Watts. Goodall finished his constructor training at the RN College, Greenwich in 1907, with one of the highest marks recorded, often seen as a pointer to high office. His initial appointment as Assistant Constructor was to Devonport Dockyard, then starting to build the battleship *Collingwood*. It was at Plymouth that he met Helen Isabella Phillips, 11 years his senior, marrying her on 17 August 1908.

That year he was appointed to the Admiralty Experiment Works at Haslar, where under R E Froude, son of the pioneer of ship model testing William Froude, he appreciated the importance of predicting and minimising the resistance of ship hull forms. At the early age of 28 he was given the responsibility of designing the light cruiser *Arethusa*, the forerunner of a series of successful cruiser classes built during the First World War. The 1911 census shows him as living at 56 Earlsfield Road, Wandsworth with his wife and one servant, although they had no children. He next became a lecturer at the RN College at Greenwich, a prestigious post so early in his career.

He was recalled to the Admiralty building in Whitehall in February 1915 to work under DNC Eustace Tennyson D'Eyncourt on the battlecruisers *Repulse* and then *Glorious*. He was thus well placed to participate in post-Jutland inquiries into battle damage to RN ships and improving British projectiles. Now of Constructor rank (albeit acting) and clearly very promising, he was selected in November 1917 to be Assistant Naval Attaché in Washington to liaise with the US Navy Bureau of Construction and Repair. Armed with the plans for *Hermes*, *Eagle* and *Argus*, he helped set the USN on its path to developing their designs of aircraft carriers which proved so successful in the Second World War. He reported his experiences back to the Admiralty, including the US practice of using electric transmission (as opposed to gearing) in battleships and their use of welding, of which Goodall became a strong advocate. He wrote a well-informed critique of US and RN warships for the weekly journal *Engineering* (10 Feb, 17 and 24 Mar 1922). His work was recognised by the award of an MBE (Member of the Order of the British Empire).

Goodall returned to the Admiralty in mid-1919 to work on new capital ship designs. He was able to examine the surrendered German battleship *Baden* and was familiar with US designs. Working under Chief Constructor E L Attwood, the result was the G3 battlecruiser design with nine 16in guns, displacing 48,000 tons. However, when the G3s were cancelled in 1922 following the signing of the Washington Treaty, he switched to the design for the smaller battleships *Nelson* and *Rodney*.

His next posting was a more relaxed one, to Malta Dockyard in 1925. He was involved in battleship refits and getting *Admiralty Floating Dock VIII* into operation. This dock was part of German post-war reparations, originally a 40,000-ton lift dock for Kiel. In order to take the 860ft-long *Hood*, it had a new section built at Chatham in 1923 and was then capable of lifting 65,000 tons. It had been towed to Malta in three sections in August 1925. The sections were joined up and tested in April 1926 by lifting *Royal Oak*. Goodall wrote an account of such Admiralty floating docks published in *Engineering* (10 Aug 1928). The couple's time at Malta included a full social round and plenty of tennis, Goodall's pastime.

1927 saw him back in London and promoted to Senior Constructor in charge of destroyer design. The 'A' and 'B' classes were the result, forerunners of a succession of flotillas going up to the 'I' class. His next appointment, now as Chief Constructor (salary range £700–£850 with £25 annual increments; multiply by about 80 to get present-day values), was in charge of modernising the RN's ageing battleships which needed upgrading against the threat of new weapons. Trials were also conducted against obsolete vessels to assess the lethality of such weapons and the protection needed against them. Promoted again in 1932 as one of three Assistant Directors of Naval Construction, he took on a wider responsibility including submarines and river gunboats. That was the year he started keeping a professional diary, recording his many activities. His diaries contain little of his private life; indeed entries usually ceased when he was 'on leave'.

He and his wife, who he called Nell, had moved into a large end-of-terrace house at 50 Lyford Road, just across from Wandsworth Common (currently worth over £3 million). He could get a train into Victoria and then walk to the Admiralty in Whitehall. He was awarded an OBE, although he did not regard this as adequate for his rank. Indeed he always felt that the honours system did not give proper recognition to Admiralty technical civilian officers, uniformed officers faring much better, and later lobbied strongly for a greater number of awards.

DNC's department was responsible to the Controller or Third Sea Lord, a member of the Board of Admiralty. From now on, Goodall found himself increasingly involved in meetings and discussions with Controllers. From 1928 that was Vice Admiral R R G Backhouse, later First Sea Lord, and from March 1932 Vice Admiral C M Forbes. In April 1934, Vice Admiral R R G Henderson became Controller, who made a vital contribution to rebuilding the navy over the crucial years in the run-up to war. When DNC Sir Arthur Johns retired due to ill health in 1936, Goodall was seen as his natural successor, and indeed had been standing in for Johns for several months. He was formally appointed on 25 July, with terms of reference:

> He is the principal technical adviser to the Board of Admiralty, and the final authority on the design of warships and other vessels of H M Navy, and will be directly responsible to the Controller for all matters of design, stability, strength of construction, weights built into the hulls of ships, armour, boats, masting and all nautical apparatus for all ships whether building in H M Dockyards or by contract.

DNC was also responsible for preliminary estimates of warship costs.

The First Sea Lord was now Admiral of the Fleet Sir Alfred E M Chatfield (a previous Controller), for whom Goodall had great respect. He noted in his 1937 diary '1st SL is astonishingly good for his age (63!), keen brain, most extensive knowledge & experience, brings talk back to the point, gives decision.' Studies for a new class of battleship had been going on for some time, to be laid down as soon as Treaty limitations expired, i.e. January 1937. Goodall signed off the design of his first major project, the 35,000-ton (nominal standard displacement) *King George V* class – he had prepared the early design studies before handing over design to Herbert Pengelly. Orders for the first two were placed (without tenders) on 29 July 1936, together with contracts for their 14in gun mountings and armour plate, both on the critical path to completion planned for 1940. The two latter industries had been greatly run down since the end of the First World War, but the Treasury was able to fund rebuilding manufacturing facilities for them. Goodall was involved in procuring the large quantities of armour required for the projected battleships, aircraft carriers and cruisers. Sources from abroad were sought; the US declined to provide any but some orders were placed in Czechoslovakia in 1938.

Goodall plunged into the challenges of rearmament enthusiastically, heralding a spate of new designs, working late most days. Treaty limitations on displacement were often a handicap to a well-balanced design, so weight saving became a paramount consideration. The Navy Estimates doubled from £60 million in 1935 to £126 million in 1938, much of it for new construction. This put great pressure on DNC's staff, as few new constructors had been recruited during the lean years. Goodall persuaded the Treasury to fund some new staff, albeit still at meagre salaries, which made it difficult to recruit experienced new men – no women. One of DNC's many responsibilities was for constructor appointments, whether in design teams at headquarters or in production at dockyards at home and overseas or as overseers at shipyards. He had to weed out a few weak performers before the war but carefully considered the best appointment for his remaining staff, being rewarded in return by their loyalty.

Succeeding years saw a flurry of new classes: *Illustrious* class carriers, *Dido* and 'Colony' class cruisers, 'J', 'K' and 'L' class destroyers and 'T' and 'U' class submarines. He was invited to the Coronation Fleet Review on 20 May 1937 in his official capacity. But none of his staff who had been responsible for the design of most of the 134 British ships present were so honoured; if they wanted to attend (in the liner *Rangitiki*) they had to pay. Goodall regarded this as another slight on Admiralty technical staff. But he did get a chance to get a closer look at foreign warships attending. He commented on the German *Graf Spee* – 'a mass of gubbins' – and the Japanese cruiser *Ashigara* – 'poor workmanship'. Goodall advised Controller that he was convinced the Germans and Italians were cheating on their declared warship standard displacements, suggesting that if he was allowed to so cheat, he too could produce much better ships. The next month saw Nell launching the 'Tribal' class destroyer *Cossack* on Tyneside ('very slick launch') and in July the oiler *Aldersdale* at Birkenhead. In each case she would have been invited to choose a piece of jewellery as a memento.

On 15 February 1938 Goodall was invested as Knight Commander of the Bath, as had most of his predecessors, becoming Sir Stanley. He had already been invested as CB in February 1937. That year saw the delivery of *Ark Royal* (whose launch Goodall had attended as DNC), and several 'Town' class cruisers and 'Tribal' class destroyers, all designed under Johns. Sir Roger Backhouse was appointed First Sea Lord in September,

The party at Vickers-Armstrongs' Naval Yard on 8 June 1938 for the launch of two 'Tribal' class destroyers. On the right is Sir Charles Craven, chairman of V-A, next to him Lady Helen Goodall who launched *Cossack*, then a beaming Sir Stanley, revealing his modest height. In the centre Lord and Lady Foster who launched *Afridi*. Far left is general manager James Callander. (© *National Maritime Museum, London T0573*)

Vickers-Armstrongs' High Walker shipyard on the Tyne, known locally as Naval Yard, had the longest fitting-out quay of any British shipyard at 2,000ft. Four 'Tribal' class destroyers are alongside in March 1938, from left to right *Afridi*, *Cossack* (launched by Goodall's wife), *Eskimo* and *Mashona*. The prominent 250-ton cantilever crane which had been installed only seven years previously was invaluable for lifting heavy gun mounting and machinery components. It is still in use today, although the shipyard itself was demolished by 1988 to make way for offshore manufacturing facilities. (*Author's collection*)

succeeding Chatfield. The possibility of rebuilding *Hood*, *Nelson* and *Glorious* was considered but the resources were not there for such extensive work to be undertaken; three other capital ships were already in hand. The smaller, slower *Royal Sovereign*s were never so considered, lacking any margins for major reconstruction. In April 1938 he had to order three more *Kingfisher* class coastal sloops, which he regarded as 'useless little ships'. Designing the hull form, machinery and propellers to achieve the required 38 knots was a challenge for the three *Abdiel* class minelayers ordered in December.

War clouds were clearly looming in 1939. Backhouse was pressing for more escorts, resulting in designs for 'Hunt' class 'fast escorts' and 'Flower' class corvettes, the latter based on Smiths Dock's whaler *Southern Pride*, and even a new Royal Yacht. Plans were made to move most Admiralty technical departments to Bath in the event of war with heavy bombing of London anticipated, including DNC, Engineer in Chief (E in C) and Director of Naval Ordnance (DNO). Goodall was distressed when Henderson died on 2 May, probably brought on by overwork. He agreed with the decision that the next Controller would be Vice Admiral Bruce Fraser, previously Chief of Staff to C in C Mediterranean Fleet. Goodall had worked with Fraser when he was DNO 1933–6. The next day he was at Cammell Laird in Birkenhead for the launch of the battleship *Prince of Wales*. That yard had the submarine *Thetis* on trial when she sank in Liverpool Bay on 1 June. Both inner and outer doors of one torpedo tube had been left open, so she flooded rapidly. Among the ninety-nine who died were two constructors, which affected Goodall badly. He suspected that DNC would get the blame at the subsequent inquiry, although in the event the cause was found to be mistakes by the shipyard (see page 50).

Backhouse died from ill health on 15 July, to be succeeded by Admiral Sir Dudley Pound as First Sea Lord. Goodall was not impressed by Pound's keenness to continue building battleships rather than aircraft carriers. Indeed he often had a better vision of what ships the RN needed as the war progressed than many senior officers. Winston Churchill was appointed First Lord of the Admiralty on the outbreak of war, a position he had held at the start of the First World War. The move to Bath took place by special train on 7 September. DNC's department was moved into the Grand Pump Room Hotel, while Goodall and his wife were accommodated in the Landsdown Grove Hotel. Only senior Admiralty staff remained in London, so Goodall had to make frequent visits there by train via Paddington. Although he could travel first class (which allowed him to discuss affairs with other Admiralty officials en route in a reserved compartment), the trains were slow, frequently late and blacked out at night.

Also at Bath was Deputy Controller Rear Admiral J W S Dorling, who doubled as Director of Naval Equipment, who was able to advise the 'user's' point of view. Goodall had to arrange for his overworked staff to take part in air-raid precaution duties, not a good use of a scarce resource. He was helped by Fred Bryant, who was brought back from retirement as an Assistant Director of Naval Construction to look after RCNC administrative and personnel matters. Short-term projects included the conversion of passenger liners to armed merchant cruisers and fishing trawlers into patrol vessels.

In May 1940 Churchill became Prime Minister, with a new First Lord of the Admiralty A V Alexander, who had held the post in the 1930 Labour Government; Goodall did not rate him highly, nor indeed most politicians. June saw the fall of France and Norway which gave the Germans advanced U-boat bases nearer the vital Atlantic convoys. New battleship and cruiser designs were still being discussed despite the suspension of construction of many such ships whose completion was not imminent, while shortage of gun-mounting manufacturing capacity meant that they were unlikely ever to be built. Goodall found himself increasingly involved in peripheral projects such as armouring the Royal Train and the Maunsell anti-aircraft forts in the Thames Estuary.

He had to come into the office most Sundays to keep up with his workload, although at least it was only a short walk from his hotel. Indeed the modern term workaholic could be applied to him. Although some thought him something of an autocrat in ordering what was to be done, Goodall himself knew that his breadth of experience had showed that his judgement was nearly always right. Although impatiently rejecting impractical ideas, he was always ready to listen to the views of colleagues who he trusted.

The first 'Hunt' class *Atherstone* was inclined at Birkenhead on 4 February 1940 when her stability was found to be alarmingly deficient. Owing to a miscalculation of the position of her centre of gravity at the design stage, her beam was too narrow to carry her designed armament (see page 53). Goodall blamed himself for not picking up the error, but the destroyer design team was overworked and it had slipped through. But others of his early designs were proving themselves well in service, including the 'J' and 'K' class destroyers and *Illustrious* whose Swordfish aircraft disabled Italian battleships at Taranto in November. Frequent air-raid warnings disrupted the work of his staff. Shortages of labour and materials and late delivery of gun mountings resulted in delayed ship deliveries from shipyards.

1941 was even busier, with demand for faster escorts ('River' class) and tank landing craft. Goodall made regular visits to shipyards, where he cast an observant eye over the activities. His estimates of ships' completion dates were often more realistic than the shipyards' own optimistic figures. He confided to his diary comments, often uncomplimentary, on the companies and their senior staff: 'hopeless', 'lazy', 'a go-getter', 'in his dotage' etc. Such visits (or to ships) usually took several days, so he returned to a pile of papers on his desk, many of which he regarded as unnecessary time-wasters. He was pleased with the support Britain was getting from the USA, although it was not yet in the war. He had met some of the USN officers back in 1918 who were now in senior positions and was given permission to share RN experiences with them, e.g. on damaged ships. Serious losses included *Hood* (no surprise to Goodall who was well aware of her weak deck protection), *Barham*, *Ark Royal* (with better damage control, she should not have sunk), *Prince of Wales* and *Repulse*. For *PoW* he feared DNC would get the blame. It was only later that the main cause of her loss became apparent, an unlucky torpedo hit on a propeller shaft bracket. Britain's last battleship *Vanguard* was ordered, with the hope that by using existing 15in gun mountings she could be completed in 1944.

Although the US and Soviet Union were now allies, a degree of war weariness had set in by 1942 in both Admiralty staff and UK industry. The U-boats were still sinking many ships, although with the widespread use of radar and improving air cover, there were more effective countermeasures being introduced. With Japan a new enemy, Goodall was involved in many discussions for more aircraft carriers, fleet, light fleet and escort. In May Fraser was made second in command of the Home Fleet, and a new Controller appointed, Vice Admiral Sir W Frederic Wake-Walker, previously Flag Officer 1st Cruiser Squadron. Goodall had hoped that Rear Admiral C E B Simeon would become the new Controller (having replaced Dorling as Deputy Controller in April 1941), but now had to bring a new man up to speed in the complexities of warship design and construction. Fred Bryant had been killed in an air raid on Bath on 27 April, so Goodall had to find a new RCNC administrator. He chose L D Stansfield, who had been in charge of the destroyer group when the 'Hunt' design error was made, and recently retired. Vice Admiral Sir George Preece having retired as E in C, he also had to deal with a new man, Vice Admiral F R G Turner from March. In October 1942 Goodall was given the additional role of Assistant Controller (Warship Production), which gave him greater authority dealing with shipyards, including pressing them to do more welding. That month Controller agreed to Goodall moving back to London (and to his house in December); he had long felt sidelined from important meetings and decisions while based in Bath.

(Sir) Charles Swift Lillicrap (1887–1966) succeeded Goodall as DNC in January 1944. His training as a young constructor had included 12 months at sea in the battleship *Superb* – a valuable experience. Early in the First World War he worked on the design of the new monitors for coastal bombardment. Like several others destined for high office in the RCNC, he became lecturer (later accorded the title of Professor) at Greenwich in 1921. Much of his work over the succeeding years was involved in cruiser design, taking a special interest in the development of welding. In 1938 he was appointed an ADNC. When Goodall was appointed Assistant Controller (Warship Production) in 1942, he was confident in leaving most of the design work to Lillicrap at Bath, giving himself more time for his production duties and interacting with senior Admiralty officials in London. Lillicrap oversaw the design of ships for the postwar navy, retiring as DNC in 1951. Shipbuilders J Samuel White appointed him to their Board; he was also Prime Warden of the Worshipful Company of Shipwrights which included many senior RCNC staff among its members. (*Author's collection*)

Large numbers of 'Loch' class frigates and 'Castle' class corvettes were ordered early in 1943, to be largely prefabricated and fitted out at special bases on the Clyde and Wear. Although Goodall became 60 in April, the normal retirement age for civil servants, it was agreed that he would stay as DNC until January 1944. He left much of the design work at Bath to Deputy Director of Naval Construction Charles Lillicrap, who was to become his successor as DNC. Consideration started to be given to building up the fleet that would be needed for the fight against Japan. Some of these would need to be built in Canada e.g. Mark 3 tank landing ships. Goodall was pleased that the new Undex works at Rosyth was established for research into underwater explosions and ship structures. He was greatly upset when one of his senior staff was jailed for corruption – see diary for July 1943. Pound died on 21 October; Admiral of the Fleet Sir Andrew Cunningham succeeded him as the new First Sea Lord.

On 22 January 1944 he handed over to Lillicrap after 7½ years as DNC. He could look back on a successful record of designing so many of the RN's warships which were soon to bring the war to a close. He continued working as AC(WP), albeit now taking Sundays off, and was seen as something of an elder statesman regarding warship designs. The U-boats in the North Atlantic had been largely mastered, so orders for escorts were scaled back. He continued to be concerned at the slow progress in the shipyards, the strikes, the shortage of key trades like electricians, the complacency and the feeling after D-Day that the war was nearly over, so why make an effort. There were also delays due to the late deliveries of director control towers and gun mountings, especially for destroyers including the 'Battle' class needed for the war against Japan. Flying bomb attacks on London from June were another hazard; indeed Goodall's house was damaged twice. He had bouts of ill health; perhaps one reason why he banned smoking at meetings. The all-welded 'A' class submarines were well under way, with Vickers-Armstrongs' Barrow shipyard taking the lead. Creating the Fleet Train for the Far East put a great strain on the ship repair yards converting the merchant ship hulls, which Goodall could do little to ease. Goodall was greatly displeased to hear of the loss in August of the brand-new *Admiralty Floating Dock 23*, which collapsed at Trincomalee while raising the fully-loaded battleship *Valiant*. He had fought hard back in 1941 for this 50,000-ton lift dock to be built, albeit in India as the UK yards were all full. The loss was due to negligence; no-one including the RCNC officers on the spot had read the dock operating instructions before starting to lift such a heavy ship. On 30 November *Vanguard* was launched, although Goodall did not attend. It was hoped she would be completed in time to participate in the war against Japan, then seen as likely to last until the end of 1946.

Goodall's brother Ernest died in January 1945. In May, Germany was defeated, so the RN was able to switch the focus of its operations to its new Pacific Fleet. The first of the light fleet carriers were delivered, ships of this successful design remaining in service for the next half-century. When Japan surrendered in August, Goodall had the task of managing the cancellation of warship contracts without disrupting the shipyards too much as they switched to building merchant ships. Other wartime building contracts were deferred; indeed the cruiser *Blake* was not completed until 1961, albeit to a revised design. Wake-Walker died unexpectedly in September, but as Goodall retired the following month, he had no dealings with his successor Vice Admiral Sir Charles Daniel.

1946 was the last year of Goodall's diary, where he penned his final reviews: 'In the last War [WW1] ammunition & supply were the big failures but ships got the blame. This war high angle gunfire, torpedoes, naval aircraft, propelling machinery have all shown more weaknesses than the ships.' 'Looking through my diary made me remember what a hell of a time I had, particularly in '39, '40 & '41.' He kept himself busy in retirement by taking a greater part in the affairs of the Institution of Naval Architects, being a Vice President and member of four of its committees including its Scholarship Committee. I might well have met him there when I applied (successfully) for the Denny Scholarship in 1955. He delivered his paper to the INA on 'The Royal Navy on the Outbreak of War' in April 1946, but was disappointed when the Admiralty refused him permission to deliver its sequel 'Warship Production during the War'. No doubt that paper would have drawn on the experiences recorded in his diary. He was also on the Council of the newly formed British Shipbuilding Research Association and was supportive of the British Welding Research Association. He joined the Board of shipbuilders Cammell Laird in 1947, although it had taken the Admiralty a full year to give him permission to do so. Goodall became Prime Warden of the Worshipful Company of Shipwrights in 1950. He kept in touch with Lillicrap, his successor as DNC.

With the increasingly poor health of his wife, he was more involved in domestic duties, noting that 'Helped N with the shopping, what a time it takes'. His wife died in 1953, leaving no children. He himself died on 24 February 1965, aged 81, with fulsome obituaries noting his great contributions to warship design and naval architecture generally.

D K Brown reckoned that Sir William White was the greatest of all the DNCs (1885–1902) but I believe Goodall was his equal. Both were talented naval architects and both were workaholics. White had a greater political influence in shaping the navy of the 1890s, during a period of rapid transition in warship types. But he was overworked and had bouts of ill health which probably led to his errors over the design and construction of the Royal Yacht *Victoria & Albert* building at Pembroke Dockyard, whose stability was found to be deficient in 1900, which led to his resignation. Goodall, however, had to manage a department three times the size of White's and had to design a wider range of ships to meet the threats of submarines and aircraft, as well as challenges to his authority. His contribution to Britain's success in the war at sea has been largely overlooked, but he was the all-rounder who was in the right place at the right time.

The Royal Corps of Naval Constructors

The RCNC was formed in 1883 to provide the Royal Navy with the best ships, designed, constructed and repaired by a cadre of professional naval architects. With ever-developing technologies in hulls, machinery and weapons, all aspects of design needed to be integrated scientifically to produce well-balanced ships. Sir Nathaniel Barnaby was appointed the RCNC's first Director of Naval Construction. The Corps' members were drawn largely from within existing Admiralty institutions, often the brightest shipwrights from the Royal Dockyards. Unlike commercial shipyards where the ironworking boilermakers were king, in the dockyards shipwrights were the pre-eminent trade having made the successful transition from wood to iron in the 1860s. A rigorously competitive selection process followed by comprehensive training ensured that the highest standards were maintained. Practical training started at Devonport Dockyard and Keyham before moving to more theoretical aspects at the RN College, Greenwich, rounded off with time at sea. The successful student was graded Assistant Constructor (equivalent to a RN Lieutenant), ready to be posted to a design group at the Admiralty or to a Dockyard where warships were built or refitted. When more experienced, postings could include overseers of Admiralty contracts in shipyards or to the staff of Commanders in Chief of the main fleets.

The Naval Construction Department liaised with the Engineer in Chief's department with regard to ships' main and auxiliary machinery and fuel, with the Director of Electrical Engineering (who had been part of DNC department in its earliest days) and with the Director of Naval Ordnance for weapons and ammunition. It built up its own expertise with regard to protection (armour and subdivision) and in hydrodynamics (running the Admiralty Experiment Works at Haslar) and in materials.

It was probably this all-embracing role that persuaded the 18-year-old Goodall to switch to the RCNC in 1901. This talented and energetic young man was seen as a safe pair of hands by his superiors, as shown by the succession of challenging appointments recorded previously. He reached the peak as DNC aged 53, a rank equivalent to a Vice Admiral, the same as E in C.

DNC was directly responsible to the Controller, an ancient title accorded to the Third Sea Lord. The Controller was responsible for the Navy's materiel, as detailed later. Vice Admiral Henderson, whom he called Reggie, was Controller when Goodall became DNC in 1936. Each had a great respect for the other; both were advocates of aircraft carriers, although recognising the need for modern battleships as well.

Recruitment to the RCNC had been cut back in the 1920s and early 1930s, reflecting the reduction in new building and closure of two dockyards (Pembroke and Rosyth). With the start of rearmament, Goodall tried to increase RCNC establishment, but despite a few new recruits was left with a dearth of experienced men in their 30s, often their most productive age. At the same time, he eased out a few who he felt were not up to the job. By May 1939 the RCNC comprised only 140 men: sixteen Assistant Directors of Naval Construction and above, twenty-two Chief and Senior Constructors, sixty-nine Constructors and thirty-three Assistant Constructors. In addition there were some 340 junior overseers and some 305 draughtsmen plus about 100 clerical and support staff (including modelmakers) at Headquarters. The total staff was about 900, but expanded as the war progressed.

Constructor annual salary scales in 1939 were:

Assistant Directors of Naval Construction	£1,400
Chief Constructors	£950–£1,150
Constructors	£680–£847
Assistant Constructors	£350–£680

Goodall had long felt these did not reflect the abilities of and demands on his staff. His own salary as DNC was £2,500, above E in C (£2,263) and DEE (£1,650), but below Controller (£3,350).

Most RCNC staff fell into 'design' or 'production' categories, the former in London until war broke out, then moved to Bath. These were formed into eight main ship groups, dealing with battleships, destroyers, submarines etc. as listed on page 29. The design groups also kept an eye on ships under construction and in service. In the latter case, they ensured that 'their' ships remained capable of operating safely as well as providing feedback into new designs. 'Production' included overseers and dockyard appointments, the latter seconded to the Director of Dockyards department. In the latter case (and Fleets) while Goodall had a say in their appointments, he was no longer their line manager. Men tended to stay in one of those two main categories, so retaining their expertise and contacts as well as reinforcing their corporate memory (one of the strengths of having a specialist Corps). While no comprehensive listing of RCNC postings has been found, it is possible to build up a general picture of senior appointments. The bi-monthly Navy Lists give the names and ranks of all RCNC members, but actual appointments of only a few posted as Warship Production Superintendents or Principal Ship Overseers or to Fleets. Others can be deduced from official papers, Goodall's diary entries or D K Brown's history. The listings on pages 29–32 are reasonably accurate for RN officers, but they are inevitably tentative for many RCNC staff and their dates of tenure.

No Admiralty organisational tree has been found to show line responsibilities, so I have attempted to reconstruct one as at 1941–2; see page 24. But new posts and divisions continued to proliferate during the war, e.g. Combined Operations, all with many temporary staff. In the latter case, some were classification society surveyors seconded to RCNC (e.g. from Lloyd's Register), some promoted dockyard foremen, while others were young graduates who would not be retained after the war. Brown (1983 p 210) gave a table of 305 RCNC staff in August 1945, barely double that at the outbreak of war despite the huge growth in fleets. One hundred and seventy-two of these were permanent staff and 133 temporary; fifty-eight in total were in uniform with Fleets or at bases overseas, summarised:

Admiralty design	101
Admiralty production and dockyard department	33
WPS and overseers	35
Dockyards and repair bases, home and overseas	74
Serving with Fleets	20
Experimental establishments	11
Miscellaneous	31
Total	**305**

A committee appointed in 1946 to review the RCNC commented that the Corps was 'seriously undermanned and underpaid'. However, it did not recommend integrating the RCNC into the RN, which Goodall had long been proposing (Brown 1983 p 209).

Post-war numbers were run down but the same general structure remained. In 1959 the RCNC numbered 153, but its head Alfred J Sims was now titled Director General Ships, while the DNC under him was J H B Chapman. DG Ships' department now included marine and electrical engineering groups. These latter became members of the RCNC in 1975, now a cadre of professional engineers within the Ministry of Defence's

An official photograph of DNC's destroyer design section at Bath on 12 June 1945, full of interest, showing many of the tools of the naval architect's trade. This was one of the most overworked sections, but benefitted from the same head throughout the war, A P Cole, who may be the man standing at the back right. The constructor in the foreground, who might be A J Vosper, is using a Fuller barrel slide rule. By wrapping its logarithmic scale spirally round a sliding cylinder, its effective length was about 40ft, compared with a conventional slide rule at 10in. This enabled multiplication and division to be done to four significant figures instead of three. The result will probably be recorded in the workbook in front of him, which every constructor was required to keep. Behind him a draughtsman has laid out a flexible batten to draw what looks like a waterline on a lines plan (sheer draught in Admiralty terminology) held to shape by a series of weights. Partly visible to his left is a mechanical calculator, which could add and subtract, unlike a slide rule. On the other side of his bench is another draughtsman using an integraph. This device, which moved along a steel rail, could trace out complex shapes and measure areas and moments, useful for calculations such as longitudinal strength. On the same bench and also on the rearmost one, are two rather crude models of destroyers. These would not be used so much as a design tool as to show visiting officials what a proposed new destroyer might look like. On the back wall and on top of the cupboard to the right are half block models, used to lay out shell plating, which was better done in 3D than on a 2D drawing (although one was later prepared from it as the shell expansion plan). The one on the right shows the traditional forecastle design, but the one at the back a flush deck design, which was not used in Second World War RN destroyers. It looks rather like a US destroyer escort, which were supplied to the RN but not built in the UK. The desks are piled high with files and dockets, the latter to circulate between departments for comment. The drawing office ceiling looks reinforced with steel beams and columns. (*IWM A29267*)

Royal Naval Engineering Service. But by the 1990s the rundown of the RN with few new ships being built caused a rethink into how the Navy acquired its ships, with greater reliance placed on designs from industry, with the RCNC now more of a professional society than a procurement organisation. But that not altogether successful change is another story.

Procurement and Output

When Goodall became DNC, the Admiralty warship procurement system was much the same as it had been since 1920. The normal process for ordering British warships in the 1930s was:

- Naval Staff perceive the need for a new (class of) warship, to meet new threats or to replace old ships.
- After internal Admiralty departmental discussions coordinated by Director of Training & Staff Duties, a Staff Requirement is sent to the Director of Naval Construction to prepare sketch designs.
- Designs with estimated costs reviewed by the Controller and Staff.
- Preferred design submitted by Assistant Chief of Naval Staff to the Admiralty Board, if affordable. If accepted and with Treasury approval, detailed design prepared. Brief particulars and estimated costs included in forthcoming annual Navy Estimates presented to Parliament each March.
- Tenders issued to suitable shipbuilders on Admiralty list, together with design drawings and specifications prepared by DNC department.
- Tenders received by Admiralty (typically one to two months later), reviewed by DNC, Director of Contracts and Engineer in Chief, including a check that prices looked reasonable.
- Recommendation via Controller to Board of Admiralty on shipbuilder(s) selected.
- Hull and machinery orders placed with shipbuilder and engine builder by Director of Contracts. Sometimes phased to give a regular pattern of expenditure throughout the financial year (monies voted but not spent could not at that time be carried forward to the next year).

The contract covered the hull and machinery only, as at the same time the Admiralty placed separate orders for the armament, armour plating and other Admiralty Supply Items (ASIs) such as fire-control equipment.

As rearmament got underway, strategic considerations and the Treasury Inter-Service Committee played a greater role in priorities for defence expenditure. When it came to shipbuilding expenditure at that time, what the Admiralty was not fully aware of was that the main warship builders were operating a price-fixing scheme. A Warship Builders Committee had been formed by their trade association The Shipbuilding Conference to ensure that loss-making tenders were not submitted for British warships. This Committee reviewed the tenders which the various builders were about to submit, placed them in cost order and then added what they regarded as an adequate profit margin to each. The prices submitted were thus in a competitive order but high enough to offset some of the losses they had been making on merchant-ship contracts. By so doing they were inadvertently maintaining a core of warship-building skills and capacity which would be desperately needed once war came. This arrangement resulted in some high profit margins for some ships as discussed on page 196.

During the war, operational demands and resource limitations drove procurement rather than international politics and finance. The Admiralty Board proposed the types and numbers of vessels to be built, notionally under an annual programme, for approval by the War Cabinet and the Treasury. They had to bear in mind the limited shipbuilding manpower and materials available, which were also required for merchant ships and ship repairing. But in view of the urgency, it was more important to place the hull and machinery contracts wherever the resources existed, rather than go through a lengthy tendering process. Goodall, with input from his Director of Warship Production on current workloads and labour levels plus his own assessment of the competence of the various shipbuilders, was able to advise Controller where orders for the next batch of ships should be placed. Once Controller had given his approval, DNC would advise the selected shipbuilders of the forthcoming order, to be followed up by a formal letter from the Director of Contracts. Specifications and design drawings would be sent as soon as possible to allow shipbuilders to order materials.

A provisional price was proposed by the Admiralty to form the basis of contract stage payments. There could be a hundred or more such 'milestones' during construction, at which the specified percentage would be paid. From about 1942, the final price paid to the shipbuilder (and machinery builder) was based on the actual costs of labour, materials and overheads, plus any extras as a result of Admiralty changes during building. A profit margin would then be added, typically 7 per cent of costs, to give a final price. But negotiations of all the details and changes meant that a final figure might not be agreed until a year or more after a ship's completion. While this was essentially a 'cost plus' system, it was not a blank cheque for the shipbuilder. Not only could Admiralty accountants challenge costs which differed significantly from other shipbuilders, but a group of ships would be costed as a whole. Thus for all the destroyers of a flotilla an average cost would be worked out on which the associated profit margin was based. That price would be paid to all the builders in the group, resulting in a lower actual profit for a high-cost builder.

RCNC staff were used to progress the contracts. The Director of Warship Production was concerned with delivery of the overall programme, accelerating or deferring ships as required. The Director of Contract Work focussed on financial aspects, cost estimates and claims to determine what should be paid to contractors and sub-contractors. The Superintendent of Contract Work was concerned with progress, inspection and modifications to ships being built. Other issues concerned labour availability and transfers between shipyards, liaison with other Admiralty departments and priorities. Each region had a Warship Production Superintendent to implement the policies. Under him each warship builder had a Principal Ship Overseer as the Admiralty representative. He and his staff had to check that all the materials and equipment arriving in the yard were up to specification and tests. He was empowered to approve minor changes to the ship, but major drawings and proposed suppliers (e.g. of forgings) were sent to headquarters for approval, which also helped achieve commonality across sister ships built in other yards. His experience enabled him to clarify Admiralty intent to the contractor and he was able to advise of modifications to be incorporated. Standards of workmanship at the building berth and fitting out were checked, and compartments signed off when completed. Regular progress reports were submitted along with any problems such as shortage of particular shipyard trades. He had to check the shipyard's preparations for the launch. He could also recommend that the Admiralty finance new equipment for the shipyard, e.g. more welding plant. The Admiralty was handicapped in this respect by getting only 6 per cent of fixed capital allocated for war production, nearly all of which went to the Air Ministry, War Office and Ministry of Supply.

A recurring theme throughout the diaries is a shortage of labour for shipbuilding. Indeed the Admiralty as a whole had many fewer workers producing for it than the other services. The *Statistical Digest of the War* shows that even at its peak in 1943, the Admiralty had only about 597,000 compared with 1,678,000 for the Ministry of Aircraft Production and 1,318,000 for the Ministry of Supply (Army and munitions generally). Their share was thus only about 17 per cent out of a total of about 3.4 million. Of the Admiralty total, less than half was for shipbuilding and repair, the balance being for machinery, ordnance and other naval equipment. At its peak in September 1943, the figures showed (Buxton 1998):

Naval Vessels	Thousands
Private yards, new work	89.3
Repair & conversion	44.1
Royal Dockyard	36.7
Total naval	**170.1**
Merchant Vessels	
Private yards, new work	42.9
Repair & conversion	59.5
Total merchant	**102.4**
Total new work	135.2
Total repair	137.3
Overall total	**272.5**

Warship work constituted about 62 per cent of the total. Unlike before the war where ship repair was largely maintenance work, during the war damage repair and conversion work dominated, with repair labour now exceeding newbuilding. The UK's modest level of resources of about 270,000 workers for shipbuilding compares with about 1.6 million at its peak in the USA, six times greater. Although US productivity in tons per man was only about half that of the UK, reflecting the lower average level of skill, nevertheless its overall output was much larger. For warships it was about twice as great (1940–5 4.7 million tons displacement vs. 2.4 million) as well as being faster in production. For merchant ships the figures were about 38 million gross tons vs. 6 million, reflecting the huge output of standard ships like Liberties (Fassett 1948).

The chart shows RN naval vessel completions from 1939 to 1945, adapted from Buxton (1998). The often-overlooked landing craft made up 20 per cent of the total. Annual output peaked at half a million tons, ten times the average of interwar warship production. The peak years were about one-third higher than those of the First World War, despite fewer shipyards and fewer workers. This was due to better control of shipbuilding resources by the Government and higher productivity. These figures exclude mercantile types, built or converted, such as escort carriers, repair ships, oilers, stores vessels, tugs and dockyard craft. Nearly all the vessels were designed under Goodall as DNC so are a measure of his work. They total 7,235 vessels of 2.522 million tons standard displacement.

However they exclude 'his' ships provided by the Admiralty to Allied navies such as destroyers and corvettes. The full line shows total tonnage from the British Shipbuilding Database, which is very similar. This does include Allied vessels, but excludes small vessels under about 100 tons such as MTBs, MLs and minor landing craft, large in number but small in aggregate tonnage. That total is 2,893 vessels of 2.618 million tons.

Goodall's frequent visits to shipyards and his diary entries show that he had a much higher opinion of some warship builders than others. From his comments, I assess his ratings would have been:

Good: John Brown, Cammell Laird, Vickers Armstrongs Barrow, Yarrow.

Average: Harland & Wolff, Swan Hunter, Vickers Armstrongs Tyne, Hawthorn Leslie, Stephen, Denny, Thornycroft, White.

Poor: Fairfield, Scotts.

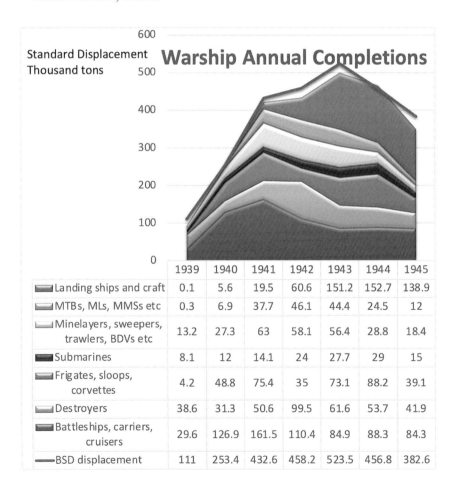

	1939	1940	1941	1942	1943	1944	1945
Landing ships and craft	0.1	5.6	19.5	60.6	151.2	152.7	138.9
MTBs, MLs, MMSs etc	0.3	6.9	37.7	46.1	44.4	24.5	12
Minelayers, sweepers, trawlers, BDVs etc	13.2	27.3	63	58.1	56.4	28.8	18.4
Submarines	8.1	12	14.1	24	27.7	29	15
Frigates, sloops, corvettes	4.2	48.8	75.4	35	73.1	88.2	39.1
Destroyers	38.6	31.3	50.6	99.5	61.6	53.7	41.9
Battleships, carriers, cruisers	29.6	126.9	161.5	110.4	84.9	88.3	84.3
BSD displacement	111	253.4	432.6	458.2	523.5	456.8	382.6

Controller's Department

By 1942 the Controller's responsibilities had expanded greatly from its core materiel departments such as Director of Naval Construction, Engineer in Chief, Director of Naval Ordnance and Director of Electrical Engineering with some twenty now reporting. This demanding workload contributed to the early death in post of two Controllers: Vice Admiral Sir Reginald Henderson and Vice Admiral Sir W Frederic Wake-Walker. They were reluctant to delegate much, despite new support positions being created. At the outbreak of war, Vice Admiral F T B Tower was Deputy Controller based in London while Rear Admiral J W S Dorling was Assistant Controller in Bath. In October 1940 Tower became Vice Controller and Dorling Deputy Controller doubling as Director of Naval Equipment. DNE's role was more advisory than procurement, representing the 'user' to DNC, although he was responsible for A's & A's (Alterations and Additions), and seamanlike equipment such as boats, anchors and cables and accommodation, having to bear in mind the ship as a whole. Retired Rear Admiral E B C Dicken was then brought in as Assistant Controller, concerned with Allied ships, overseas shipbuilding and administration at Bath. A new Deputy Controller, Rear Admiral C E B Simeon, took over from Dorling in April 1941, also becoming DNE. He was a former DNO, appropriate as in his new role his focus was on armament. Vice Controller's focus was on shipbuilding and ship repair and small craft. As well as purely technical issues, DNC had to ensure that each ship, new or in service, as a whole was safe and well balanced, in the face of ever-increasing demands from specialist departments and enemy threats.

New Assistant Controller posts were created. In October 1942, Goodall was made AC (Warship Production) in addition to remaining DNC. Having just moved to London, he delegated much of his design activities to the Deputy Director of Naval Construction at Bath, Charles Lillicrap. Scientist Charles Goodeve became AC (Research & Development). In 1943 Lord Reith, Director General of the BBC before the war, became

Vice Admiral (Sir) William Frederic Wake-Walker (1888–1945) succeeded Fraser as Controller in May 1942, although Goodall thought Simeon (Deputy Controller) would have been a better choice. He was a torpedo officer (which also covered electrical) so had a good awareness of technical matters. Ships he had commanded included the cruisers *Castor* and *Dragon*, then in 1938 the battleship *Revenge*. Between 1935 and 1938 he was Director of Torpedoes and Mining, so Goodall would have had dealings with him then. He had commanded the 1st Cruiser Squadron during the *Bismarck* action in May 1941. Goodall felt that initially he was impetuous, with a lot to learn about warship design and construction, but they got on better later. He died in September 1945, probably brought on by overwork. Behind him appears to be a scrambler telephone. (*IWM A23582*)

Naval Assistant to Controller with special responsibility for Combined Operations materiel, with the rank of Captain RNVR.

The three main departments with which Goodall interacted were E in C, DNO and DEE. The main postholders are shown on page 27 and an Admiralty organogram below. Many of the senior staff of E in C and DNO were RN officers who also had career postings to ships, thus bringing user experience, but they had little experience of design, as they relied on manufacturers far more than DNC. DEE like DNC was a civilian department, RN electrical officers being still under the Torpedo Department. It was not until 1946 that a separate Electrical Branch was formed. As the war progressed, new departments were made responsible to Controller but Goodall had few dealings with them e.g. Boom Defence, Salvage and Small Vessels Pool.

The stress of war (and the run-up thereto) resulted in the early deaths of several senior Admiralty officials. Controller Henderson had died in 1939 aged 57 and Controller Wake-Walker in 1945 also aged 57. First Sea Lord Backhouse also died in 1939 aged 60. Recently-retired Engineer in Chief Preece died in 1945 also aged 60. E in C Turner resigned on grounds of ill health in 1945. Deputy First Sea Lord Kennedy-Purvis died in 1946 aged 62 and his chief Pound in 1943 at 66, but having been in poor health for some years. Fourth Sea Lord Pegram died in 1944 aged only 53. Permanent Secretary Markham died in 1946 aged only 49. Key industrialist Sir Charles Craven of Vickers-Armstrongs died in 1944 aged 60. War took a heavy toll indeed.

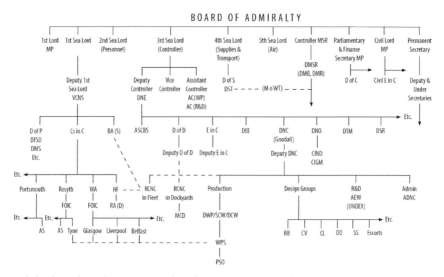

While the Admiralty never produced an organogram of its organisation during the war, it has been found useful to try to construct one to show the myriad departments and individuals that Goodall dealt with. (*Ian Buxton and Ian Johnston*)

Senior Admiralty Officials 1939–1945

Board of Admiralty

First Lord: Winston S Churchill MP (3 Sep 39); Albert V Alexander MP (12 May 40)

First Sea Lord and Chief of the Naval Staff: Admiral Sir Roger R C Backhouse (7 Sep 38); Admiral of the Fleet Sir Dudley P R Pound (12 Jun 39); Admiral of the Fleet Sir Andrew B Cunningham (15 Oct 43)

Second Sea Lord and Chief of Naval Personnel: Admiral Sir Charles J C Little (30 Sep 38); Vice Admiral Sir William J Whitworth (1 Jun 41); Vice Admiral Sir Algernon U Willis (8 Mar 44)

Third Sea Lord and Controller: Vice Admiral Sir Reginald G H Henderson (23 Apr 34); Rear (later Vice) Admiral Sir Bruce A Fraser (1 Mar 39); Vice Admiral Sir W Frederic Wake-Walker (22 May 42)

Fourth Sea Lord and Chief of Supplies and Transport: Rear Admiral Geoffrey S Arbuthnot (1 Oct 37); Vice Admiral John H D Cunningham (1 Apr 41); Vice Admiral Frank H Pegram (May 43); Vice Admiral Sir Arthur F E Palliser (20 Mar 44)

Fifth Sea Lord and Chief of Naval Air Services: Vice Admiral Sir Alexander R M Ramsay (19 Jul 38); Vice Admiral Sir Guy C C Royle (21 Nov 39); Rear Admiral Sir Arthur L StG Lyster (14 Apr 41); Rear Admiral Sir Denis W Boyd (19 Jan 43); Rear Admiral Sir Thomas H Troubridge (1 May 45)

Deputy First Sea Lord: Admiral Sir Charles E Kennedy-Purvis (19 Jul 42)

Vice Chief of the Naval Staff: Vice Admiral Tom S V Phillips (1 Jun 39); Vice Admiral Henry R Moore (21 Oct 41); Vice Admiral Sir Edward Neville Syfret (7 Jun 43).

Controller of Merchant Shipbuilding and Repair: Sir James Lithgow (1 Feb 40)

Churchill with his Board of Admiralty on 4 December 1944. Seated are Admiral of the Fleet Sir Andrew Cunningham (1st Sea Lord), WSC, A V Alexander MP (1st Lord). Standing L-R: Sir Henry Markham (Permanent Secretary), Vice Admiral Sir Neville Syfret (VCNS), Rear Admiral J E Edelsten (ACNS), Admiral Sir Charles Kennedy-Purvis (Deputy 1 SL), Vice Admiral Sir Arthur Palliser (4 SL), J P L Thomas MP (Financial Secretary), Capt R A Pilkington MP (Civil Lord), Rear Admiral W R Patterson (ACNS), Vice Admiral Sir Frederic Wake-Walker (3 SL), Sir James Lithgow (Controller Merchant Shipbuilding & Repair), Vice Admiral Sir Algernon Willis (2 SL) and Rear Admiral D W Boyd (5 SL). (*IWM A26683*)

Parliamentary & Financial Secretary: Geoffrey Shakespeare MP
(28 May 37); Sir Victor A G Warrender MP (4 Apr 40)
   Parliamentary Secretary: Lord Bruntisfield (9 Feb 42)
   Financial Secretary: G H Hall MP (9 Feb 42); J P L Thomas MP
   (28 Sep 43)

Civil Lord: Captain A U M Hudson MP (15 Jul 39); Captain R A
Pilkington MP (5 Mar 42)

Permanent Secretary: Sir R H Archibald Carter (23 Jul 36); Sir Henry V
Markham (5 Dec 40)

Principal Staff and Departments Reporting to Controller

Vice Controller: Vice Admiral F Thomas B Tower (Oct 40); Vice Admiral Henry C Phillips (Aug 44)

Deputy Controller (and Director of Naval Equipment): Rear Admiral F T B Tower (28 Aug 39); Rear Admiral James W S Dorling (Oct 40); Rear Admiral Charles E B Simeon (1 Apr 41)

Assistant Controller: Rear Admiral J W S Dorling (28 Aug 39); Rear Admiral Edward B C Dicken (17 Oct 40)

Assistant Controller (Warship Production): Sir Stanley V Goodall (1 Oct 42)

Assistant Controller (Research and Development): Dr Charles F Goodeve (1 Oct 42)

Director of Naval Construction: Sir Stanley V Goodall (25 Jul 36); Sir Charles S Lillicrap (22 Jan 44)

Engineer in Chief: Vice Admiral Sir George Preece (12 Sep 36); Vice Admiral F R G Turner (16 Mar 42); Vice Admiral John Kingcome (25 Jan 45)

Director of Naval Ordnance: Captain J C Leach (1 May 39); Captain W R Slayter (30 Jan 41); Rear Admiral O Bevir (1 Aug 41); Rear Admiral C H L Woodhouse (13 Mar 44)

Director of Electrical Engineering: Sir James S Pringle (1937); H D MacLaren (1945)

Director of Dockyards: Vice Admiral Sir Cecil P Talbot (1 May 37)

Principal Naval Staff

Commander in Chief, Home Fleet: Admiral Sir Charles M Forbes (12 Apr 38); Admiral Sir John C Tovey (2 Dec 40); Admiral Sir Bruce A Fraser (8 May 43); Admiral Sir Henry R Moore (14 Jun 44)

Rear Admiral (Destroyers) Home Fleet (RA(D)): Rear Admiral R H C Hallifax (1 May 39); Rear Admiral L H K Hamilton (28 Feb 41); Rear Admiral R L Burnett (5 Mar 42); Rear Admiral I G Glennie (12 Jan 43)

Commander in Chief, Mediterranean Fleet: Admiral Sir A B Cunningham (7 Jun 39); Admiral Sir J H D Cunningham (15 Oct 43)

Commander in Chief, Portsmouth: Admiral Sir William James (30 Jun 39); Admiral Sir Charles J C Little (1 Oct 42)

>   Admiral Superintendent, Portsmouth Dockyard: Rear Admiral M I Clarke (30 Nov 40)

Commander in Chief, Western Approaches: Admiral Sir Percy L H Noble (17 Feb 41); Admiral Sir Max K Horton (19 Nov 42)

Flag Officer in Charge, Liverpool: Rear Admiral J S M Ritchie (14 Dec 40); Rear Admiral J W S Dorling (15 Aug 44)

Flag Officer in Charge, Glasgow: Vice Admiral James A G Troup (19 Feb 40)

Flag Officer in Charge, Belfast: Rear Admiral R M King (24 Aug 39); Rear Admiral R H L Bevan (22 Oct 42)

Commander in Chief, Rosyth: Vice Admiral Sir Charles G Ramsey (25 Aug 39); Admiral Sir Wilbraham T R Ford (15 Apr 42); Admiral Sir William J Whitworth (1 Jun 44)

Admiral Superintendent, Rosyth Dockyard: Rear Admiral C Cantlie (24 Aug 39); Rear Admiral H C Bovell (15 Apr 44)

Flag Officer in Charge, Tyne: Rear Admiral Wellwood G C Maxwell (26 Aug 39)

Commander in Chief, Orkneys & Shetland: Vice Admiral Sir T Hugh Binney (22 Dec 39); Vice Admiral L V Wells (7 Jan 42); Rear Admiral P Macnamara (1 Mar 45)

Admiral Superintendent, Lyness Dockyard: Rear Admiral P Macnamara (1 Sep 40)

Chief of Combined Operations (CCO): Vice Admiral Lord Louis Mountbatten (27 Oct 41); Major General R E Laycock (Oct 43)

Rear Admiral (Submarines) (RA(S)): Rear Admiral Bertram C Watson (15 Dec 38); Vice Admiral Sir Max K Horton (1 Sep 40); Rear Admiral C B Barry (9 Nov 42); Rear Admiral George E Creasy (Oct 44)

Director of Plans (D of P): Captain Victor H Danckwerts (2 Apr 38); Captain C S Daniel (8 Mar 40); Captain C E Lambe (12 Mar 42); Captain Guy Grantham (1 Apr 44)

Director of Training and Staff Duties (DTSD): Captain W L Jackson (14 Sep 37); Captain J W Rivett-Carnac (2 Apr 40); Captain H P K Oram (4 Sep 42); Captain C L Robertson (Jun 45)

Director of Operations (Home) (DOD(H)): Captain R A B Edwards (18 Oct 39); Captain J A Eccles (12 Dec 41); Captain C T M Pizey (10 Jan 44)

Director of Trade Division (DTD): Captain M J Mansergh (23 May 39); Captain B B Schofield (15 Apr 41); Captain W D Stephens (21 Jul 43)

Director of Anti-Submarine Warfare Division (DA/SW); Captain G E Creasy (23 Sep 40); Captain A Pritchard (17 Mar 42)

Director of Torpedoes and Mining (DTM): Captain J U P Fitzgerald (28 Jan 38); Captain H C Phillips (14 Feb 40); Captain G B Middleton (Feb 42); Captain A S de Salis (1942); Captain W W Davis (29 Nov 44)

Director of Minesweeping Division (DMS): Captain H E Morse (20 Oct 39); Captain J H F Crombie (2 May 43)

Director of Naval Equipment (DNE) – see Deputy Controller

Admiral Superintendent Contract Built Ships (ASCBS): Vice Admiral St A B Wake (Dec 37); Vice Admiral H E Morse (1 Oct 44)

Principal Civilian Staff

Director of Merchant Shipbuilding and Repair (DMSR): (Sir) Amos L Ayre (1940)

Director of Merchant Shipbuilding (DMB): W McArthur Morison (1944)

Director of Merchant Ship Repair (DMR): Lawrie Edwards (1944)

Director of Contracts and Purchase (D of C): E C Jubb (c1936)

Director of Scientific Research (DSR): Charles S Wright (c1936)

Director of Sea Transport (D of ST): W G Hynard (c1936); Sir Ralph Metcalfe (c1942)

Civil Engineer in Chief: F A Whitaker (c1940)

Minister of War Transport (MoWT): Lord Leathers (1 May 41)

Director of Naval Construction Senior Staff

DDNC = Deputy Director of Naval Construction. ADNC = Assistant Director of Naval Construction. CC = Chief Constructor. SC = Senior Constructor. C = Constructor. AC = Assistant Constructor. Most appointment dates approximate.

Director of Naval Construction: Sir Stanley V Goodall (25 Jul 36); Sir Charles S Lillicrap (22 Jan 44)

DDNCs: Sidney E Boyland (Oct 38) London

William G Sanders (1940) Bath, London from 1942

Charles S Lillicrap (1942) Bath

Lawrence C Williamson (1944) Bath

Albert P Cole (1945) Bath

Design Groups Senior Staff 1940 onwards

Battleships: W G Sanders (ADNC, later DDNC); Herbert S Pengelly (CC, ADNC 1943); H Stanley (CC); V G Shepheard (ADNC 1942); F S Sutherby (C 1941); G Bryant (C 1942)

Sidney E Boyland (b1880) was one of two Deputy DNCs under Goodall when war broke out. He remained in London while Goodall moved to Bath. During the First World War he was involved in airship design, moving to Warship Production Superintendent Scotland. As an ADNC he had been in charge of the cruiser design section in the 1930s. Goodall felt that Boyland was rather set in his ways and not pulling his weight fully in representing DNC in London, with little to contribute to wartime technical demands. He was not sorry when Boyland retired in 1941, leaving the way for Lillicrap to be promoted to DDNC (the other being Sanders) and Goodall to move back to London. (*The Shipbuilder*)

Aircraft Carriers: Thomas L Mathias (ADNC); J Leslie Bartlett (CC, ADNC 1943); A Mitchell (C 1941); C E Sherwin (CC 1942); W R Perrett (C 1942)

Cruisers & Fast Minelayers: C S Lillicrap (ADNC); E G Kennett (CC); F Hickey (CC); W G John (C); W R Andrew (C 1940)

Destroyers and Sloops: L D Stansfield (ADNC); A P Cole (CC, ADNC 1943); J L Bessant (C, CC 1943); A J Vosper (C 1943)

Submarines: L C Williamson (ADNC); W A D Forbes (CC, ADNC 1944); George W Pamplin (SC, CC 1943); Alfred J Sims (CC 1944)

Escorts and Small Craft: A W Watson (ADNC); G McCloghrie (CC); W J Holt (SC); A E Kimberley (C)

Mine and Net Craft and Depot Ships: Lloyd Woollard (ADNC); H May (CC); Rowland Baker (C)

Auxiliaries and Conversions: F H Steed (ADNC); V G Shepheard (CC)

Specialists

Armour and Protection: Dudley J Offord (CC, ADNC 1943) Superintendent of UNDEX, Rosyth (1943)

Superintendent of Admiralty Experiment Works, Haslar: Richard W L Gawn (1938). Assistants: L G Stevens (C, CC 1943); S J Palmer (C)

Superintendent of Welding Development 1942: W G John (CC)

Superintendent of Landing Craft 1942: Rowland Baker (CC)

RCNC administration (ADNC): Fred Bryant (Oct 39); L D Stansfield (Jun 42)

Production Staff Based at Bath

Director of Warship Production (DWP): E D Meryon (c1940); S A McCarthy (2 Oct 42)

Director of Contract Work (DCW): Claude Hannaford (1938). Became DCW (Ships) (Oct 42)

Director of Contract Work (Supplies): C J W Hopkins (Oct 42)

Superintendent of Contract Work (SCW): E D Meryon (1936); C J Butt (c1940)

Superintendent of Labour and Materials (SLM): C W Kerridge (c1941); C J Butt (c1942)

Superintendent of Conversions (S of C): S A McCarthy (1940); K H Watkins (1942)

Warship Production Superintendents (WPS)

North West: Gilbert Bulkeley (CC 1940); A E Horley (CC 1944); W H Wallond (CC 1945?)

Belfast (and PSO Harland & Wolff): F G Bogie (SC 1936); F S Sutherby (CC 1944)

Scotland, West: F Hickey (CC 1938); G Hudson (CC 1940); J E Mathias (CC 1942)

Scotland, East: W R G Whiting (SC Nov 40)

North East: Charles J Butt (CC 1936); H Stanley (CC 1940)

London: M P Payne (CC 1941?)

Southern: C C H P Mitchell (SC 1936)

Principal Ship Overseers (PSO)

Cammell Laird, Birkenhead: D W Smithers (C 1939); H S Peake (C 1940); H J Tabb (C) (1945)

Vickers-Armstrongs, Barrow: A N Harrison (C 1939); R H Richards (C 1940); H J Fulthorpe (C 1943)

John Brown, Clydebank: H T Johnson (C 1939); D W Smithers (C 1942); W R Andrew (C 1944)

Fairfield, Glasgow: J E P Moon (C 1939); V W Hall (C 1940); H W J Chislett (C 1945)

Scotts, Greenock: R N Newton (C 1939); R K Wood (C 1943)

Swan Hunter & Wigham Richardson, Wallsend: W J Hatchard (C 1939); H W J Chislett (C 1942); A Stewart (C 1945)

Vickers-Armstrongs, Tyne: H H Palmer (C 1939); G Bryant (C 1940); F W Matthews (C 1943)

There were less senior overseers at the smaller yards such as Denny and Yarrow and at the LCT and Humber builders.

RCNC Senior Staff at Dockyards:

MCD = Manager Constructive Department, Chief Constructor rank.

Portsmouth MCD: C W Kerridge (17 Mar 37); E G Kennett (1941); R H Wright (1943)

Devonport MCD: J E Mathias (1938); S Payne (1941)

Chatham MCD: J F Walker (1930)

Sheerness: W H Wallond (CC 1939); I E King (CC 1945)

Rosyth: T Sutcliffe (CC 1939); G Hudson (CC 1941); F J A Pound (CC 1943)

Malta MCD: J C Joughin (1937); J E P Moon (1942)

There were less senior constructors at smaller dockyards including Scapa Flow, Gibraltar, Bermuda, Simonstown, Singapore and Hong Kong, and at repair bases including Oban, Alexandria, Freetown, Durban, Kilindini, Bombay and Trincomalee. There were graving or floating docks at such bases.

RCNC Senior Staff under Director of Dockyards Department

Deputy Director of Dockyards: A W A Cluett (ADNC 1935), G A Bassett (1943)

Superintendent of Repair by Contract: G A Bassett (CC 1940)

Assistant Director of Dockyards: H J Curphey (1942); C F Merchant (1943)

RCNC Senior Staff on Detached Duties

Ministry of Supply for trench-digging machinery: C J W Hopkins (CC 1940)

Air Ministry Liaison: J H B Chapman (C 1940)

British Admiralty Technical Mission, Canada: A G W Stantan (CC 1940); Constr Captain A N Harrison RCN (end 1941)

USA Lend Lease: G McCloghrie (CC 1941); J H B Chapman (CC 1942)

RCNC Senior Staff Attached to Fleets (in uniform)

Chief Constructors held the rank of Constructor Captain, and Constructors that of Constructor Commander

Home Fleet: C Cdr A J Merrington (1940); C Cdr A N Harrison (1940); C Cdr H E Skinner (1941); C Capt N G Holt (1942)

Med Fleet: C Cdr A J Merrington (1938); C Cdr H R Mann (1940); C Capt I E King (1942); C Capt D W Smithers (1944)

Flag Officer, Submarines: C Cdr A J Sims (1939); C Cdr J F Starks (1944)

Combined Operations: C Cdr A J Merrington (1942)

Allied Naval Commander Expeditionary Force: C Capt A J Merrington (1944)

Eastern Fleet: C Capt H S Pengelly (1943); C Capt F G Bogie (1944)

British Pacific Fleet: C Capt G W Pamplin (Fleet Train 1944); C Capt V W Hall (Melbourne 1944); C Cdr S J Palmer (Sydney 1944)

The Diaries 1939–1945

This selection of entries covers about a quarter of the total. I have generally omitted routine or semi-repetitive entries or those of marginal interest. While Goodall's handwriting can be difficult to decipher, being familiar with the ships and the industry of the period and naval architectural terminology and abbreviations has enabled me to transcribe all but a handful of words in the diaries. I have been able to add the position a person mentioned held, although in a few cases where there were several of the same name, e.g. Johnson, I have had to guess which one from the context. I have also corrected names where they have been misspelled. In very few cases have I withheld a person's name, even though they are now all dead. The various editions of the Navy List have been useful for identifying individuals and the positions they held at the time and abbreviations. In a few diary entries it is clear that they were not written up on the day itself but the great majority were. His Whitehall office had a steady stream of people calling: I have taken a diary entry that So-and-So 'called' to mean a visitor in his office, while assuming that 'rang' or 'phoned' meant just that, usually by scrambler phone to prevent eavesdropping. While Goodall wrote ship names in lower case, they are shown here in italic for clarity (but not ship classes). An ellipsis … is used to denote an omission. My explanations or comments are in square brackets.

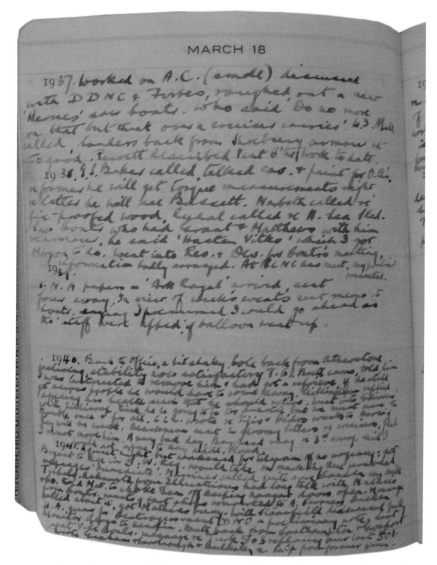

A typical page from Goodall's five-year diary 1937–41 for 18 March. His busy wartime years are reflected in the smaller handwriting needed to fit everything in. 1938 records that he was presented with his portrait, reproduced in the frontispiece and on the back of the jacket and now at University College, London.

1939

6 January: ... The talk about destroyers, he [Controller and 3rd Sea Lord Vice Admiral Sir Reginald Henderson] says single gun ships are a mistake. He wants *Repulse* [battlecruiser] ready to go back to fighting ship if balloon goes up. ...

8 January (Sunday): Contr [Controller] told me last Friday that DCNS [Deputy Chief of Naval Staff, Vice Admiral Sir A B Cunningham] when in Berlin the other day had a talk with German NO [naval officer] who was Scheer's flag lieut[enant] at Jutland; he said S[cheer's] one desire was to get out of the mess & safely home; when he found Jellicoe was across his path he said 'those destroyers haven't done much so far send them in, see what they can do'. ...

14 January: Sir J Thornycroft [Chairman of the Southampton shipbuilder] called, told him he was an old conservative on welding, he wants to get out of it for minelayer [*Latona*].

18 January: 1st SL [First Sea Lord, Admiral Sir Roger Backhouse, previously Controller 1928–32] sent for me (1) minesweepers ... (2) Contr not too good [health], he had to think of possibility of a relief, he had in mind 2 RAs [Rear Admirals] who could do the job. I said very sorry, Contr was wonderful in times such as these. I could guess

(Sir) John E Thornycroft (1872–1960) had been chairman of the family company since 1918. As a young engineer he had helped develop the diesel engine and road transport division. But Goodall felt that this urbane man in his 70s had lost his grip trying to manage a wartime shipyard, resisting pressure to use more welding, although local trade union restrictions did not help. (*The Shipbuilder*)

the name of one of the RAs, he said 'Who'. I said Fraser, he said 'Yes'. (3) R[oyal] Yacht no good getting busy without money in [Navy] estimates, sent for Seal [E A, Principal Private Secretary to First Lord] and told him this, asked me 'How much?'. I said £200,000. ...

24 January: At Walker [Vickers-Armstrongs Naval Yard, Tyne] good look at *KGV* [battleship *King George V*], then *Victorious* [aircraft carrier], 1st good, 2nd poor. Gave Hendin [A J, manager of V-A Walker] note re 1938 *Fijis* [cruisers], he gave orders to lay blocks for fast escorts [two 'Hunt' class]. Then SH [shipbuilder Swan Hunter & Wigham Richardson] for *Jellicoe* [renamed *Anson*] (poor), cruisers (good) also *Dominion Monarch* [passenger cargo liner for Shaw Savill] for tips on R Yacht.

25 January: At Hebburn [Hawthorn Leslie shipyard] *Naiad* v.g. [cruiser, very good] J's good [destroyers]. Then *Edinburgh* [SH cruiser fitting out] full up with gear. Then Blyth for 'Nets' [boom defence vessels]. Home at 1.30 a.m. train 3½ hours late thro' snow.

26 January: A shock on escort price, told Pigott [Stephen, managing director of shipbuilder John Brown] and Craven [Sir Charles, chairman of Vickers-Armstrongs] they would look into it and let me know. ['Hunt' class. Typical prices were £276,000 for hull and machinery, but with a high profit margin included, as the Warship Builders Committee of main shipbuilders was fixing prices to reduce competition and rebuild finances after the Depression.]

27 January: ... Craven rang up re battleship prices [3rd and 4th *Lion*s?] and escorts, re latter he will phone me tomorrow. [Goodall and Craven had been sharing confidences before the war.] ...

28 January: Craven rang re escort price, told SCW [Superintendent of Contract Work E D Meryon] to send wires to 5 firms. [Telegrams to five shipbuilders building two each of first batch of 'Hunts'.] ...

1 February: Signed papers re tenders for Escorts. Saw DNE [Director of Naval Equipment then Vice Admiral F T B Tower] who agreed then D of D [Director of Dockyards Vice Admiral Sir Cecil P Talbot, appointed in 1937] re 2 or more of the second batch being built at Devonport or other [dock]yard. ... [None of the dockyards actually ever built 'Hunts'; they would have had to get their machinery from private firms.]

9 February: ... Got Sanders [W G, Assistant Director of Naval Construction ADNC] and Pengelly [H S, Chief Constructor, head of battleship design] busy on capital ship for Australia. ... Looked into escort stability with new hull wts [weights] not good enough, with no margin now but must accept it ...

10 February: ~~Wrote~~ the 5 firms re watching Escort's stability. I intended to write but held back the letters. Stansfield [L D, ADNC, destroyer designer] now convinced the beam should be increased, phoned Clydebank but they had all gone [home]. Yarrow called, told him the stability of escorts not enough but at that time I had not decided to increase beam ... Dealt with 15,000 ton Greek cruiser. A thick day.

14 February: With Stansfield & Bessant [J L, destroyer constructor] decided 29-0 [ft in] extreme beam for escorts. [But even this breadth increase was not enough to give adequate stability. See 7 and 9 February 1940.] ... 1st SL sent for me re Roy Sovs [*Royal Sovereign* class battleships]: I said to send them (ex *R[oyal] Oak*) to fight up to date capital ships would be murder; he agreed.

17 February: ... FO [Foreign Office] note re Germans bagging Vitko[vice – Czech manufacturers of non-cemented armour for Admiralty], dictated yarn & took to Contr, saying we ought to spend [£]1 million to keep Vitko from Germans ...

20 February: ... With St[ansfield] and Bes[sant] worked on 2nd 10 escorts ['Hunts'] & signed sketch design docket [file]. ... Mountbatten [Captain Lord Louis] called, very pleased with J's, he is going out in *Jersey*.

Like Goodall, Wilfred George Sanders (1884–c1967) had started as an engineering cadet but one year behind him. He was Constructor Commander in *Repulse* in 1923. He was appointed Warship Production Superintendent North East in 1929. He brought this wide experience to the battleship design group in 1935, where he remained during much of the war. Goodall relied heavily on him to get the *King George V*s completed as well as preparing the many battleship design studies being pursued throughout the war. He had been promoted to Deputy DNC in 1940, moving from Bath to London in 1942. (*The Shipbuilder*)

21 February: At Newcastle, launch of *KGV* perfect. After this 1st SL took me up to Queen who was very pleasant & said she was thrilled. King asked me if this was 2nd ship launched by a man. I said 'Yes' but 1st SL broke in 'No, 3rd, KEVII [King Edward VII] launched *Dreadnought*.' King's speech hesitation makes one feel nervous when talking to him. Home midnight.

1 March: Announced today that Fraser [Rear Admiral Bruce] is Contr. Poor Reggie [Henderson] ... Saw new Contr, told him my two disagreements with Reggie i.e. on [dry]dock for capital ships on E[ast] coast & that I thought him too much pro Scott Paine [British Power Boat MTBs]. ...

9 March: ... Attended 1st SL meeting on reconstruction [of battleships]. E in C [Engineer in Chief Vice Admiral Sir George Preece] upset the cart by saying *Hood*'s machinery was falling to bits. ...

10 March: At sea in *Jersey* [destroyer from J Samuel White]. Ship did well ... she's a little beauty, spoilt by galley funnel. ... Absence of vibration impressed me & I thought the ship looked small owing to the one funnel. Heeled very little on turning.

13 March: Parl Sec [Parliamentary and Financial Secretary to the Admiralty Geoffrey Shakespeare MP] asked me a question re HA [high angle gunfire] for his speech [on Navy Estimates] he is woefully ignorant of principles. ...

15 March: 4th SL [Sea Lord, Rear Admiral G S Arbuthnot, Chief of Supplies & Transport] gave me the tip that the coal advocates will get at HM [His Majesty] & have the new yacht coal burning; told Lillicrap [Charles S, ADNC, notable cruiser designer] to look into this & told E in C. ...

24 March: Pigott called, wants to get repeat K's ['N' class destroyers, Clydebank got *Nerissa* and *Nizam*], said he doubted if Vickers [-Armstrongs]

Vice Admiral Sir George Preece (1884–1945) was appointed Engineer in Chief in 1936, the same year as Goodall became DNC. As head of the RN engineering branch, he was responsible for both personnel and machinery. He had been a high flier throughout his career, including becoming professor of marine engineering at Greenwich in 1923. Goodall and he had to work closely on the big new construction programmes of the late 1930s. Their relationship was a little prickly at times, Goodall feeling that Preece was insufficiently forward-looking, for example resisting the move to higher steam pressures and temperatures in steam turbines which the US Navy was successfully pursuing. Preece stuck with lower steam conditions on the grounds of reliability and familiarity to personnel and industry. But RN warships suffered the handicap of having much higher fuel consumption and shorter endurance than comparable USN ships throughout the war. (*The Shipbuilder*)

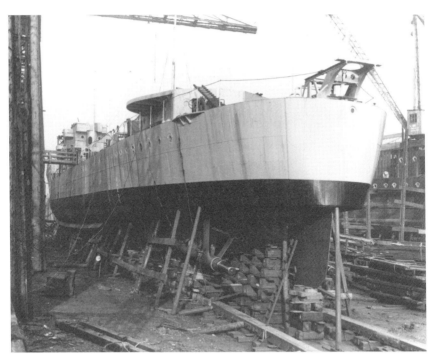

'J' class destroyer *Janus* the day before her launch on 10 November 1938 from Swan Hunter's No 5 berth. Shafts and rudder are in place but not her propellers. Launch weight was 730 tons, under half her light displacement as completed, as machinery, armament and most fittings had yet to be installed. Her steam turbine machinery from sister company Wallsend Slipway would be fitted after launch. (*Author's collection*)

using to the full the country's engineering capacity for gun manufacture. [V-A was subcontracting some parts of gun mountings, but not to the extent that was used during the war with more companies making medium and small calibre gun mountings]. ...

25 March: ... Controller's meeting. ... I spoke against Guillemots [coastal patrol vessels] & for whale catchers ['Flower' class corvettes]. ... Armour situation was tight but all right ...

1 April: ... then saw new Contr, he is for moving D'port [Devonport] or P'mouth [Portsmouth] fl[oating] dock to Alex[andria]. [32,000-ton lift *AFD.5* was moved in July]. I still think it a crime not to use the S'ton [Southampton] dock. [This 60,000-ton lift dock had been superseded by the King George V graving dock for the liners *Queen Mary* and *Queen Elizabeth* in 1933. The Admiralty did acquire it in 1940 to become *AFD.11*].

5 April: On leave. At Barrow launch of *Illustrious*. Good show. Lovely weather. Ship looks small compared to *Ark Royal*. [Understandable as depth from keel to flight deck 67ft versus 82ft 9in.]

19 April: ... *Implacable* ... amphibians [Walrus] cannot be carried if hangar height is reduced. ...

21 April: Pigott called, told him *Jackal* was criticised adversely [finish bad]. ... 14ft hangar height was all right for *Implacable* [became a handicap later with larger US aircraft]. ... Reed of Smith's Dock [William, managing director of Tees shipbuilder, designer of 'Flower' class] called, told him Contr had app'd [approved] 20 M/S [*Bangor* minesweepers] & 25 A/S [anti-submarine, 'Flowers'] tenders. ...

2 May: ... Sir R H [Henderson] died at 10.40 ... better than living on helpless but tragic he should go before his labours' fruit has fully appeared.

3 May: At Birkenhead for launch of *P of W* [battleship *Prince of Wales*]. Hichens [W Lionel, chairman of Cammell Laird] in speech at lunch gave RCNC a boost. ...

9 May: Contr's NC [new construction] meeting, gun mtgs [mountings] a terrible picture again, urged Contr to do something. Afterwards DNE, E in C & I stayed to discuss MTBs' engines [motor torpedo boats. Britain lacked a suitable powerful engine], I was for the R[olls] Royce. ...

17 May: Watson [A W, ADNC, escort designer] back from Smiths Dock who are now in a cleft stick re whale-catchers ['Flowers'] v[ersus] Prince liners [four ships ordered in April], told Contr who will approach Lord Essendon [chairman of parent company Furness Withy]. ...

19 May: ... Reed of Smiths Dock phoned, Essendon wants £2500 per ship from them if delay of 3-4 mos [months]. I told Reed he couldn't expect to get £10,000 from Admy [Admiralty]. ...

20 May: Bailey [F, submarine constructor] back from 300ft diving trials of *Triumph*, some leaky rivets & seams otherwise v.good. ...

22 May: Discussed with Lillicrap auxiliary rudder [there was concern over vulnerability of battleships with a single rudder to non-contact torpedoes]. ...

23 May: Contr discussed 40,000 ton German b'ship [battleship *Bismarck*]. I said I was puzzled it seemed to be contrary to all our ideas. Then docks, he thinks I am extravagant I stuck to 1200 × 150ft. ...

31 May: At Glasgow. With Sir J Lithgow [James, chairman of the Lithgow group] visited Moss End [steelworks] they could do 2500 tons/year more

within their size & thickness limit (N.C.) [non-cemented armour, much used as deck armour but limited UK production capacity] then Dalmuir, they with P'head [Beardmore's Parkhead works] think they can do 5000/yr more. At launch *Fiji* [cruiser at Clydebank] thought welding bad [Goodall was an advocate of using welding more widely]. Looked at *D[uke] of York* [battleship] getting on well. ...

1 June: At Fairfield [shipyard] talk re strike which shows signs of spreading. Saw *Beatty* [battleship renamed *Howe*] doubt if launch Oct[ober. Actual 9 Apr 40] then *Phoebe* [cruiser] ... *Implacable* coming on, some armour there already. *Juno* [destroyer] with galley funnel inside the main funnel looks a great improvement. To Stephens [shipyard] saw *Manxman* [fast minelayer] coming on well, *Kenya* [cruiser] welding good. ...

2 June: *Thetis* down, Hill [A A F, ship overseer] & Bailey on board, with W'son [L C Williamson, ADNC, submarine designer] saw Contr, he thought W'son should go, told him to fly, & recommending sending signal to cut hole in exposed tail, reply not enough tail out of water. [The submarine on trial from Cammell Laird had flooded forward with her bows touching the bottom of Liverpool Bay, with part of the stern exposed, but that last 20ft was a tank, not crew space.] ...

3 June: *Thetis* looks a loss, still faint hope so did not write Mrs Bailey & Hill. ...

7 June: Attended *Thetis* Mem[orial] Serv[ice] at St Martins [in the Field, nearest church to the Admiralty building]. ... DTM [Director of Torpedoes & Mining, Captain J U P Fitzgerald] wanted me to look at

While Alexander Stephen & Sons Ltd at Linthouse, Glasgow, had built many destroyers, *Kenya* was the first cruiser they completed, seen at launch on 18 August 1939 (Yard No 566). From order to completion she took 33 months. Her 4½in side armour belt is clearly seen. The timber from the sliding launchways and poppets will be collected and re-used. (*Author's collection*)

[torpedo] bow cap indicator & tube empty indicator dwgs [drawings]. The game of blaming the disaster on DNC has started. [The flooding had resulted from opening the inner door of torpedo tube No 5 while the outer door was still open, although the indicator showed wrongly that the bow cap was closed.]

10 June: W'son back from CL [Cammell Laird]. Johnson [Robert S, managing director of CL] will make model. Salvage dead lift to be attempted again. ... Evident from Richards [R H, constructor] talk [with Rear Admiral (Submarines) B C Watson] that we are going to be blamed. Such is the lot of the materialist.

13 June: ... Johnson rang up, said Admy lawyer was with him, taking statements but men would not sign them unless I said I had no obj[ection], he read them, they put the onus on us which is right for design, fittings we supply, inclining etc, made memo & showed Contr. ...

20 June: Nearly all day with Lillicrap & W'son drafting yarns for *Thetis* court. ...

21 June: Critchley [G R, general manager Liverpool & Glasgow Salvage Association], Thomas, Robb [A M, consultant], Hall called re salvage

Thetis sank on trials in Liverpool Bay on 1 June 1939, due to a torpedo tube bow cap having been left open. Only four men were able to escape, ninety-nine being trapped in the submarine with its bow on the bottom but part of the stern in the air. Goodall was distressed that two of his small team of submarine designers were lost. She was salvaged by the London & Glasgow Salvage Association and brought inshore on 3 September and beached at Traeth Bychan on Anglesey. She was taken back to her builders Cammell Laird at Birkenhead and rebuilt as *Thunderbolt*. (*Author's collection*)

Thetis. W'son had a go result nearly an impasse; talked with Contr who thought we ought to take the risks. They all came to my room, I signed dwg & dictated memo. [The agreed plan was to sling wires from the cargo ship *Zelo* and use a tidal lift to bring the submarine inshore, as described in the 1940 *Transactions of the Institution of Naval Architects*.] ... Johnson called, told him to watch his step, my experience was that such a disaster was always blamed on the materialist, in this case him or me.

23 June: ... Craven called said Warne [Lt Cdr R S Warne] 1st CO *Triton* said 'What a pity they are lovely S/Ms [submarines] ... Bad result FB [Firth Brown, armour maker] 15″ plate for *P of Wales*. ESC's [English Steel Corporation] for *Beatty* v.g. [side armour over magazines].

26 June: ... *Thetis* model arrived, had it altered to cut out secret items ... Left for Liverpool; read *Thetis* spec[ification] on way.

27 June: At Cammell Lairds. ... Looked at *P of Wales* progress slow, armour setback (failure in FB plate) is going to be serious. Called on Mrs Hill [widow of constructor lost in *Thetis*].

28 June: 1st Lord [A V Alexander] sent for RY [royal yacht] model & dwgs yesterday & went thro' them with Lillicrap, sent for them again today & took them to B[uckingham] Palace. ...

29 June: King has kept model & dwgs of RY. ...

30 June: ... Saw Attorney General [Sir Donald Somervell], he did not impress me very favourably but I thought better of him at last than at first. I got in my bit that I hope Court will bring out one truth i.e. that *Thetis* was a very safe satisfactory S/M, this necessary as Navy must not have confidence in their material shaken & country must feel money for rearmament is being wisely spent. ...

1 July: ... With Lillicrap & W'son went thro' yarns on salvage & safety of contractors' diving trials & had them typed.

5 July: ... go to Law Courts. Att Gen wanted to know if possible for a mechanical failure to result in bow cap to be open; said not impossible but inconceivable. ... Only salvage will show if material failed or Woods [Lieutenant F G Woods, *Thetis*' torpedo officer, a survivor] was mistaken.

8 July: ... Had White of McT.Sc [MacTaggart Scott, hydraulic engineers in Edinburgh], Lillicrap, W'son, & Harrison [A N, submarine overseer at Barrow] & flagged out bow cap & indicator gear with view to W'son's & Harrison's evidence next Monday. I feel satisfied with both gears but made 2 pts [points] to be further investigated i.e. test pressure & an indicator

worked from side of cap remote from hinge. [The gear was intended not only to show whether bow cap and inner door were open but also to prevent both being open at the same time. See also 8 Nov.]

10 July: Lillicrap says *Fiji* coming out heavy with appreciably less GM [metacentric height and measure of a ship's initial stability and ability to return upright after heeling] than estimated, ship safe but we must now set our faces against all additions. ...

12 July: Went with Contr & 1st Lord to B Palace. Lillicrap & Kennett [E G, constructor] had set up models etc & marked out areas. King & Queen discussed Yacht for nearly 1 hour & seemed pleased. ...

13 July: ... Asked Wall [A T managing director of Cowes shipbuilder White] about MTB 101 [an experimental hydrofoil boat] he still sticks to it that he can deliver the goods, also RY he says he wants to tender [as did several other shipbuilders including John Brown, Fairfield and Stephen].

25 July: 3 years as DNC. *Triton* & J cl successful, Fiji's going to be a worry. A bad year owing to loss of *Thetis* with Hill & Bailey & the deaths of RB [Backhouse] and Reggie [Henderson]. Good effect of change in training for RCNC is already apparent.

8 August: Returned from Leave. Saw Contr who is worried about prices from repair firms for re-arming destroyers [probably converting 'W' class to air defence] he has had to give the work to dockyards. Met Amos Ayre [chairman of the Shipbuilding Conference, the shipbuilders' trade association] in the corridor, he, SCW and I had a talk, he says D of C [Director of Contracts E C Jubb] is not fair to the firms, he cuts down their profit when he finds they have made a profit but will not listen when he finds they have made a loss. Hence I gather next time firms boost their prices, ...

9 August: Contr signed RY tender papers, got it to D of C. ... [This yacht was never built, overtaken by the outbreak of war.]

16 August: At Belfast. *Formidable* [carrier] looked all right. *Adamant* [submarine depot ship] is behind & firm has not realised the magnitude of the job they have in *Unicorn* [maintenance carrier]. ... In my opinion it is too risky to dock *Formidable* in the Thompson [graving] dock unless it was imperative to take the risk. [Goodall was quite right. Not only was *Formidable*'s waterline breadth 95ft 9in and the dock entrance only 96ft, but the width in the body of the dock was only about 3ft wider than the hull each side, with little room for staging or painting.]

17 August: *Formidable* launch nearly a disaster, apparently hot weather caused grease to be extra greasy, as ship was set up from aft [ship weight

transferred from building blocks to launching ways] she settled down there but not fwd [forward] so many of blocks still being in place, cradle [sliding ways attached to ship] parted abaft triggers [which held ship in place on slipway until ready to slide] & ship began to move [about 20 minutes before scheduled time] triggers were released but ship went down ways leaving fwd poppets behind [the wooden structure that transferred the hull weight forward to the sliding ways] luckily fore foot did not get seriously struck by slip[way], fore peak full of water & next compt [compartment] leaking, plating & framing bulkhead at 52 station where upthrust was taken [as the stern entered the water and became buoyant, the hull would pivot about its fore end, normally via the fore poppet but now on the hull itself]. ...

24 August: Contr said AMCs [Armed Merchant Cruisers] & trawlers would be requisitioned tonight. ...

28 August: Batchelor from Vitko[vice] came in, told Hannaford [Claude, Director of Contract Work, previously chief constructor at Gibraltar Dockyard] to try & get the 250 tons now in Poland out. [This was probably not completed before the outbreak of war.] ... On Contr's instructions placed orders for 30 patrols (whale-catchers) [second batch of 'Flowers'] 10 [*Bangor*] minesweepers & told D of C to order the oilers [probably 'Rangers']. ... A good day, arranged [DNC] staff on outbreak of war.

1 September: ... Ordered replace Vitko [non-cemented] armour ...

3 September (Sunday): Came in re more merchant ship conversions. ... [War declared; Churchill became First Lord of Admiralty].

5 September: ... Brazil destroyers requisitioned [six 'H' class under construction in UK yards]. ...

7 September: ... Contr said evacuation [of DNC Department from London to Bath] has now been decided on, I said Shall I stay because of Winston & he said No, I must be with my staff. He told me to take the next weekend off: a brick he is [Goodall had clearly been overworking].

8 September: ... Winston [W S Churchill] sent for me, stalked about working & signs with his coat off very pot belly. Sketched what he wanted, I went to pocket it but he grabbed it and burnt it. ...

11 September: ... WSC wanted to know condition of *Thetis*, said cannot be given until ship is docked [she had been brought inshore on 3 September, then refloated with compressed air and beached on the east coast of Anglesey. She was brought back to Birkenhead on 18 November

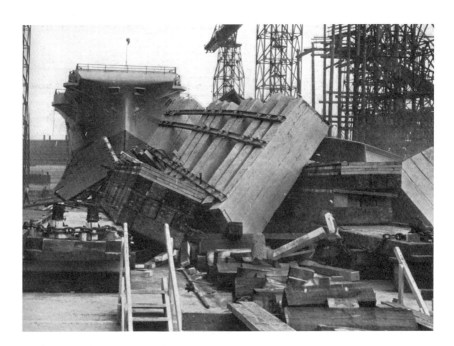

Above & Opposite: Goodall attended the launch of *Formidable* at Belfast on 17 August 1939 which was a near disaster. The slipway was No 14, which had been enlarged to allow the White Star liner *Oceanic* to be built – but cancelled in 1929. Hot weather caused the after portion of the launching cradle to detach from the forward portion, allowing the hull to slip into the water prematurely without the support of the forward poppets. Those structures and the forward siding ways were pulled apart, sending debris flying into the watching crowd, killing one woman and injuring twenty-two other people – surprisingly not more given how close the crowd was to the slipway (not allowed today at dynamic launches). The worthies on the launch platform are horror struck: Goodall at left behind the shipyard manager holding his head (probably John Morrison), chairman of Harland & Wolff Frederick Rebbeck pointing and launch sponsor Lady Wood, wife of the Secretary of State for Air. (*Shipbuilding & Shipping Record 24.8.39*)

for inspection, then rebuilt as *Thunderbolt*.] ... WSC sent for me at 11.30 [pm] I was home in bed [house near Wandsworth Common].

13 September: ... left for home at 6.40 the earliest for weeks.

14 September: Crease [Captain T E, an official of the Shipbuilding Conference] called & we fixed up what could be done if 16″ ships [*Lion* and *Temeraire* ordered in February] stopped for 18 mos.

15 September: ... I reported to Contr how to place 8 dest[royers] if L & T are kept back 12 mos.

18 September: ... heard that *Courageous* had sunk, 2 torp[edoe]s went down in 9 min[ute]s, this worried me as she should not have gone down as quickly, heard later this not so. ...

23 September: ... Trouble at G'wich [Greenwich, RN college which trained constructors] Army threatens to call up ACs [Assistant Constructors. Goodall's protests must have been listened to as there are no more diary entries on the subject.]

24 September: Left home [in London] 8.15 a.m. arrived Bath 12.00 [probably by car]. ... Went to my billet, not impressed said Thank you but I was staying with my wife at L.G. Hotel [Lansdown Grove, still in business]. ...

5 October: ... at Admy ... Dined with Contr at 1st Lord's, admit he is an inspires [sic] phone went, it was Pres Roosevelt re *Iroquois* [an American steamer that Germans might sink], Winston said you must publish 'How's Baruch' [? Bernard Baruch was an adviser to President Roosevelt and a friend of Churchill's].

9 October: ... Denny [Maurice, chairman of Dumbarton shipbuilders] rang, can't do B[arrage] Balloon in [destroyer] *Kandahar*, switched this over to *Kimberley*.

10 October: With Sanders, Pengelly, Watkins [K H, constructor], Hopkins [C J W, chief constructor, previously at Devonport Dockyard] decided *Warspite*, *Malaya*, *Val[iant]* alterations and drew up points for letter re *Malaya*. ... Panic from 1st L re delays in new constr[uction]. ...

12 October: In London. All morning on Turk[ish] Requirements, a dreadful waste of time. All afternoon on increased HA [high angle] arm[mamen]t &c including Glen Line [fast cargo liners being requisitioned] & AM ships. ... A thick day. RDF [radar] is to be speeded up.

13 October: ... Saw McNeill [James, John Brown's naval architect] re omitting welding from *Indefat[igable]*, said I was fed up with Cl'bank [Clydebank].

16 October: ... DEE [Director of Electrical Engineering J S Pringle] rang that *R[oyal] Oak* [torpedoed at Scapa Flow 14 October] inquiry is at Rosyth, we are to send somebody, got Pengelly to [at?] hotel & told him to go. ...

(Sir) James M McNeill (1892–1964) was apprenticed at John Brown's in 1908. Unusually for the time, he took a BSc at Glasgow University. He received a Military Cross during his time with the Royal Horse Artillery in the First World War. Appointed Clydebank's chief naval architect in 1928, he had responsibility for the design and successful launching of the *Queen Mary*, the heaviest ship launched from a slipway to date. Goodall had a great respect for McNeill's abilities as a naval architect, frequently consulting him. He became managing director of John Brown 1948–59, which included the building of the Royal Yacht *Britannia* for which he was duly honoured. (*The Shipbuilder*)

5 November: Hill [S I, constructor] from D'port [Devonport] to discuss *Roy Sov[eign]* bulging [planned for Operation 'Catherine', a proposed Baltic Sea offensive]. …

8 November: At Admy. Johnson called, Birkenhead rang thro' *Thetis* inspection results, as we expected Gear OK & Wood's evidence wrong.

Fiji's four triple 6in Mark XXIII mountings were the first for the class, Registered Numbers 9-12, from Vickers-Armstrongs' Elswick works. 'B' mounting was shipped from the Tyne in the coaster *Shoal Fisher*, arriving at Clydebank on 11 September 1939. John Brown's recently uprated 200-ton cantilever crane lifted the 120-ton mounting into place; the three guns and cradles (weighing 12 tons each) and the 9-ton roof plates were installed shortly afterwards. Across the basin *Queen Elizabeth* still has her Cunard colour scheme. When she left on 26 February 1940, she was painted grey; two days later the newly-launched battleship *Duke of York* took her place. (*UCS*)

[The cause of the flooding was found to be an indicator that showed a torpedo bow cap was closed when it was actually open, the connecting pipe opening having been blocked by paint so was ineffective, i.e. the shipbuilder's fault] ... 1st Lord's meeting decided bulge QE [*Queen Elizabeth* modernising at Portsmouth] if possible in time [no bulging in addition to that existing appears to have been added], new *Marshal Soult* [monitor *Roberts*], rearmoured *Erebus* & *Terror* [added deck protection]. ... 1st L in better form tonight very pleased at reception of his afternoon speech in H of C [House of Commons].

14 November: ... NC meeting then QE & fleet tender & WT [watertight] door *Kelly* (re latter Contr said No, Mount B[atten] must learn to be a better seaman). ...

24 November: At D'port. Inspected *Valiant*, nearly finished, *Vindictive* [converting to a repair ship] all right but mach[iner]y shop vulnerable, *Carlisle* [cruiser] poor old thing, new caisson good [for widened entrance to Basin 5], *Vega* looking well [destroyer conversion to air defence], *Fearless* [destroyer] shaft brackets not too good but not as bad as I thought. ...

11 December: ... DNO [Director of Naval Ordnance Capt J C Leach, who became the first CO of *Prince of Wales*] sent over remarks re *Belfast* [6in] turrets for Fijis – cannot accept top weight [*Belfast*'s gunhouses had thicker protection than the *Fiji*s. She had been mined on 21 November and would be out of action for a long time. In 1941 her 'Y' mounting was used to replace 'A' mounting destined for *Trinidad* lost on the ship carrying it from Barrow to Devonport].

14 December: ... *Graf Spee* fight announced this a.m. expect a spate of hot air about little weakly armed ships being able to knock out a heavy ship: must wait for official details before drawing conclusions. ...

Memoranda 1939

A most distressing year. Reggie & RB died. *Thetis* lost Bailey & Hill. Then the war. Bright spots Fraser Controller, our war organisation functioned well but Treasury is spoiling all by being niggardly over salaries. J's very successful. My *Ark Royal* INA [Institution of Naval Architects] paper went well. The move to Bath worked better than I expected but puts a great strain on me [continual travelling between London and Bath].

1940

2 January: … With 1st L[ord] from 4.30 to 6.45, he is mad keen on the cultivator [a trench-digging machine] very pleased with *Barham* [battleship] which he said had received 2 torpedoes [28 December off west coast of Scotland, repaired on the Mersey] … He took me down to see the basement protection which he said was due to me!

8 January: … With Lillicrap and John [W G, cruiser designer] drew up military characteristics for 8″ cruiser and looked at turret design & subdivided shell room. …

12 January: Discussed with Sanders & Pengelly 15″ b'ship [which became *Vanguard*] dictated notes … then discussed *Repulse* re-armouring, phoned DNO, I was agin [against] it and will send him a yarn … With Lillicrap discussed lessons of *Graf Spee* action. …

23 January: To Admy [from Bath to Admiralty Building in Whitehall] discussed with Contr, Dep[uty] Contr [Rear Adm F T B Tower] & Hannaford new constr[uction] prog[ramme]. Contr agreed we could not do the 5 cap[ital] ships [four *Lions* and *Vanguard*].

24 January: At Admy. 1st SL [1st Sea Lord, now Admiral of the Fleet Sir Dudley Pound] meeting at 10 a.m. to discuss new constr. I was horrified that 1st SL wants still more cap[ital] ships: he is willing to give up anything to get them. …

25 January: At Admy. … At 5.30 attended 1st L meeting with 1st SL, Contr, DCNS [Deputy Chief of Naval Staff, now Vice Admiral Tom Phillips, later lost in *Prince of Wales*], D of P [Director of Plans Capt V H Danckwerts] & Sec [Permanent Secretary Sir R H A Carter] re New Constr. 1st L adamant in his opposition to big prog[ramme] of new cap ships. Finally said Prepare me tables of rel[ative] strength. [Note that civilians Churchill and Goodall were sometimes more in tune with the Navy's real needs than the seagoing officers.] Later 10.15 he sent for me

& Contr, said he wants Roy Sovs bulged & deck armour added. Contr said he couldn't see how it could be done without stopping other work. ... Left at 11.45 p.m. [presumably for home].

7 February: ... Cole [Albert P, constructor in charge of destroyer design since 1934; friendly with Mountbatten] came in with *Atherstone* inclining result. [An inclining experiment heels (inclines) a ship to determine its centre of gravity and metacentric height.] GM 1' less than calculated [for destroyers typically 2–3ft, so 1ft reduction seriously compromises the ship's safety], bad error in calculations, shall have to do something drastic. Stansfield & Bessant to return at once [from Birkenhead] to decide what is to be done, meanwhile told Cole to phone CL [Cammell Laird, *Atherstone*'s builder] not to put in guns till they hear from us, calcs to be made leaving out gun & ballasting, also giving more beam. ...

9 February: ... Asked Lillicrap if *Abdiel*'s stability [minelayer] is all right, he said 'Yes'. With Stansfield, Cole, Bessant and Patterson [A P, constructor] went into *Atherstone* inclining result & agreed to proposed modifications.

An error was made in the design calculations of the first group of 'Hunt' class escort destroyers, resulting in too narrow a breadth and inadequate stability. Topweight had to be removed and permanent ballast added to lower the vertical centre of gravity. This view of *Cattistock* in July 1941 shows the third (superfiring) twin 4in Mark XIX mounting was replaced by a quadruple 2pdr Mark VII, saving 6 tons in weight plus less ammunition. (*Blackman collection*)

[The superimposed third twin 4in mounting aft was removed, some other weights shaved off and 50 tons of permanent ballast added. The next batch of 'Hunts' had beam increased from 29ft to 31ft 6in, a measure of how far deficient the Type 1 'Hunts' were. There was a serious error in the original weight and centre of gravity calculations which despite the system of checking was not picked up. When D K Brown analysed the case 50 years later, he concluded that the weight of the main deck had been placed at 10ft below its true position, as well as other weights being heavier than estimated. Yarrow's naval architect told me in 1968 that they advised the Admiralty that the stability of the 'Hunts' was deficient but the latter would not listen.] Phoned Contr who said 'Go to bed & stay there' [Goodall was suffering from a bad cold]. I love him, said I was not as bad as I sounded. He gave me approval to tell firms [other 'Hunt' builders]. Kept Bessant back [the constructor who had not picked up the error of his draughtsmen in wrongly calculating the position of the centre of gravity], poor devil he is very contrite, owned he should have put hull CG higher, went thro' his workbook [record of a constructor's calculations]. I still think these ships could have been built, our hull wt [weight] seems excessive, then machy [machinery] wt & ammo [ammunition] wts have all gone up a lot. [Weight estimating is still something of an art in the early stages of design, relying largely on previous experience rather than detailed plans, so can go badly wrong with a new or different ship type – the 'Hunts' were much smaller than regular fleet destroyers.]

11 February (Sunday): In evening Stansfield, Cole & Bessant came to [my] hotel with Hunt modifications & GZ curves [showing a ship's stability at large angles of heel]. Altered them & agreed to action which they promised to have ready for tomorrow midday.

15 February: ... DNO phoned they have put *Arethusa* turret into *Ajax* which means heavier *Ajax* turret might go one day into *Arethusa*, said 'Can do'. [*Ajax* was refitting at Chatham after the Battle of the River Plate. Her 'X' twin 6in Mark XXI mounting had been damaged. But as *Arethusa* was with the Home Fleet at the time, one of the spare mountings for the class was probably used. The mountings for both ships had been made by Vickers-Armstrongs at Barrow in 1934.]

1 March: Much time spent phoning London re Purvis [M K, assistant constructor] to go to *Graf Spee* [at Montevideo]. ... Am concluding destroyers are too flimsy for the rough work which they are being employed in this war.

6 March: Arrived Glasgow, went to Greenock & aboard *Rodney* about 10.00. [Presumably he had got the sleeper train from London]. C in C

[Admiral Sir Charles Forbes] very cheery & pleasant, explained my views ... After lunch went to *Woolwich* [destroyer depot ship] & had long talk with RA D [Rear Admiral Destroyers, R H C Hallifax], he is not worried about stability, went on board a Tribal & a K [class destroyer]. ... Then visited Scotts looked at *Tyne* [destroyer depot ship being built] and *Glenroy* [stores ship being converted from fast cargo liner]. ...

7 March: Breakfast with Winston [aboard *Rodney*?] had a talk in his dressing room, he first in vest & pants, long key chain, & round tummy, gold watch & chain, oil for hair, scent for hankie. ... Long talk with Troup the snob [Vice Admiral J A G, Flag Officer in Charge, Glasgow. He was also in effect the local Shipyard Controller] re Kicks [?] ... To Clydebank, feel we do not get decisions to firms properly as in repeat Ks ['N' class destroyers] have not got the extra stiffening fwd [forward]. ... Then to Fairfield not enough men there [a perennial problem for shipbuilders during the war]. Then to Stephen *Kenya* [cruiser] looks good, had talk about escorts ['Hunts']. [Evidently a busy day for Goodall, who probably got the sleeper back to London as he was in the Admiralty next day.]

14 March: ... Agreed with Hannaford re allocation of orders for 1940 prog[ramme].

15 March: ... Discussed *Edinboro'* [cruiser *Edinburgh* built by Swan Hunter but under repair for seven months at Middle Dock on the Tyne to strengthen highly stressed area where forecastle deck stepped down to upper deck and replace some armour] with Lillicrap, he thinks termination of armour (deck) is cause of trouble [presumably cracking]. I think the nasty corner of the sheerstrake is the reason. ... Discussed OBE & MBE recommendations with D & ADNCs [Deputy and Assistant DNCs]

18 March: ... Cole back from *Atherstone* inclining stability now satisfactory T.G. [Thank God] ...

25 March (Bank Holiday): Left 9.18 for London, then on 1.10 from Euston with Contr to Preston; motored in Vickers car to Abbey House [Vickers-Armstrongs guest house in Barrow]. Talk with Contr re *Edinboro'* & *Fiji*. ... Fraser seems very keen to know who I should make my heir [as DNC] if I died. I think today Sanders, next month Lillicrap, 5 years Forbes! [W A D, chief constructor]

26 March: At Barrow with 1st L & Contr; 1st L worried about Merlin [petrol] engines for Cultivator [designed to have Davey-Paxman diesel engines, presume he did not want to divert Merlins from aircraft production]. He went round at a great pace, men gave him a wonderful reception, he clambered up straight ladders on *Illustrious*, then made a

grand speech after lunch. In the train he went to bed then did some work, dressed for dinner when he was in high fettle then went to Admy to work till about 2 a.m.; he said he takes sleeping tablets before a train journey. A wonderful man. I hope he lasts.

27 March: Back in Bath. ... Capt Chaliopin French Navy called with dwgs of *Richelieu* &c. [battleship building at Brest, left for Dakar Jun 1940] ...

9 April: ... heap of papers mainly tripe, it seems hopeless to keep people from making paperwork that doesn't help a little bit towards winning the war. NOs [naval officers] the worst sinners. ...

11 April: At sea in *Fiji* [trials from John Brown] weather good. Ship very free of vibration, congested of course, stern wave as Haslar expts showed [experiments in towing tank near Portsmouth with first cruiser transom stern] shortly after reaching 80,000 SHP [her maximum power] bearings gave trouble & trial abandoned. Fired off all guns except 6″ which Benn [W G, Captain of *Fiji*] would not do, he is nervy [?] & has not recovered from *R Oak* [he was CO of *Royal Oak* when torpedoed in Scapa Flow on 14 Oct 39], he grumbled at bridge draught which really was not bad, told him about Merrington [A J, Constructor Commander attached to Home Fleet] he said 'OK'. Regret I have never been on trials where I have sensed [?] such a feeling of estrangement between ship's officers and Firm's men.

22 April: ... With Andrew [W R, constructor] & Lillicrap discussed AA [anti-aircraft] cruiser with Russian machinery, then worked on the design. [The Soviets had ordered some sets of destroyer turbines in the UK before the war but these had probably not been delivered. Lacking boilers, auxiliaries and the hulls, there was little advantage in Britain trying to use them.]

24 April: Attended Asst Contr [Assistant Controller Rear Admiral J W S Dorling] conf[erence] on R Plate lessons, useful but more work & all lessons mean weight & cost. ...

3 May: Went by air from Bristol to Lincoln. My first flight, noisy & I got bored. Disappointed with the C[ultivator] success depends on nature of soil, evidently clay will beat us. Looked over Rushton works [Ruston & Hornsby making diesel engines] very good & well organised.

17 May: Cole back from *Kelly*, good show getting that ship back [torpedoed on 8 May]. ...

18 May to 1 June: On leave. [No diary entries. Churchill had become Prime Minister on 10 May.]

(Sir) James Callander (1877–1952) was general manager and director at Vickers-Armstrongs' Barrow works during the Second World War, having been appointed in 1931. A Scot, he had joined Vickers' engine works about 1903 as a draughtsman. He oversaw Barrow's impressive wartime output of submarines, making a practice of entertaining the crews of newly-commissioned boats at his home before they departed. Barrow moved to all-welded submarine construction in 1943, somewhat later than it should have done, given the example of the captured German *U 570* examined at Barrow in 1941 and the advocacy of a young V-A manager Len Redshaw (J S Redshaw's son) who had seen such boats under construction before the war. Quoted in his biography (*Vickers Master Shipbuilder*) Redshaw blamed the slow adoption of welding on the Admiralty. But both Goodall and Lillicrap were strong advocates; the slowness was due more to shortages of men and equipment and a general reluctance among shipyard managers. (*The Shipbuilder*)

(Sir) Stephen J Pigott (1880–1955) was a talented American engineer who came to John Brown in 1908 to help them build the Curtis steam turbine, marketed as the Brown-Curtis. He rose to the position of chief engineering designer in 1920. Following the retirement of Sir Thomas Bell, he became managing director at Clydebank in 1935, responsible for the completion of both *Queen Mary* and *Queen Elizabeth*. Goodall regarded Clydebank as his 'go to' shipyard during the Second World War, where Pigott could be relied upon to assist in every way, from loaning draughtsmen to the Admiralty, finishing incomplete hulls from other shipbuilders to becoming lead shipyard for the big aircraft carrier *Malta* (although she was cancelled after the war). (*The Shipbuilder*)

4 June: In London. Contr wants AA cruisers & *Vanguard* [named for first time] designs proceeded with. He said pig iron situation so serious that we must not use it for ballast unless absolutely essential. [Adding 50 tons of pig iron ballast to the twenty-three 29ft beam 'Hunts' would have taken 1,150 tons.] ...

6 June: Spent most of the day visiting DNO, E in C, Asst Contr, DEE, & D of D on (a) Contr shadow dept [department] in Canada [in case of invasion] (b) evacuation if Bath raided or threatened by landing parties. Found differing views. ... Talked MTB engines with E in C & told Watson [A W] to get busy.

8 June: Wrote Johnson [Cammell Laird], Rebbeck [F E, chairman of Harland & Wolff], Swan [Charles S, chairman of Swan Hunter & Wigham Richardson], Pigott [John Brown] & Callander [J, managing director of Vickers-Armstrongs, Barrow] to see if we could get mass production of hulls. ...

16 June: ... Note from Dorling re finishing *Jean Bart* & *Richelieu* here [the unfinished battleship *Jean Bart* left St Nazaire for Casablanca on 19 Jun]. ...

18 June: Discussed with Hannaford remaining 1940 orders. ... Discussed with Lillicrap & Jackman [W H, *Dido* class designer] trouble with *Naiad*'s 'A' turret (apparently her support is elliptical) ... [*Naiad* was the first *Dido* class cruiser to get all five twin 5.25in mountings, from V-A's Elswick works on Tyneside.]

19 June: Looked carefully into gun supports of *Naiad* not too happy, discussed with Lillicrap & Jackman, told latter to tour [?] to H Leslie [Hawthorn Leslie, *Naiad*'s builders] find out true situation. CL & Fair[field] & Scott to see they make sure all is well before they ship 'A' mtg, put my money on *Bonaventure* [Scotts] being all right on gun trials but in later ships might stiffen up so better to be safe than sorry. ...

28 June: Went into MLCs [motor landing craft, which became tank landing craft (LCT) Mark 1] with heavy tanks with Woollard [L, ADNC mine etc craft] & Baker [R, minesweeper constructor] latter's design looks all right, but impressed on him we ought to use Turk ferries if possible [Swan Hunter was building eight 180ft tank ferries for Turkey]. Arranged for Baker & Whittock to see Maund [Captain L E H, Combined Operations, Admiralty] & Contr today. ...

3 July: ... Rang Leach (DNO) re old *M Soult* [First World War monitor *Marshal Soult*] & getting her to Glasgow with reconditioned [15in] turret. [A new hull had been ordered from John Brown in March, which became

the monitor *Roberts*. The mounting was refurbished at Portsmouth before dismantling for shipping to Glasgow.] ... Wrote Johnson re 1940 Hunts [Type 2 with 31ft 6in beam] accepting his offer of help in design; I will send 2 men to B'head [Birkenhead] to decide on spot & thus avoid delays due to AR [air raid] warnings here. Boyland [Sidney E, Deputy DNC] rang re depth ch[arges] to put *Richelieu* out for a year, said it must be under the counter preferably just before rudder post. ...

6 July: ... Jackman back from Newcastle we <u>must</u> take on more splinter protection somehow ... Jackman has not found any explanation for *Naiad* 'A' turret trouble. Signed docket re UPs [unrotated projectiles, i.e. rockets] in *KGV* & *P of W*, adding 'no delay to completion'. ...

8 July: ... Read report on Italian destroyers sold to Sweden don't know what to do with them. [*Romulus* & *Remus* had been seized by the British on 20 June en route to Sweden but were later released.] ... Went thro' 'large MLCs', signed dwgs & docket. [The first twenty LCTs Mark 1 were ordered on 27 Jul.]

11 July: ... Contr said *Blyskawica* should be re-armed; [British-built Polish destroyer which had escaped in 1939; ammunition supply was an issue] French [destroyers] not yet. ...

25 July: 4 years as DNC. A very trying year. Our war organisation worked well & I got staff salaries after tremendous fight. Corps [RCNC] stock went up with Winston as 1st L, going down with Alexander. Cruisers most disappointing (Boyland & Kennett [cruiser designer] the sinners). These and destroyers got a tremendous hammering during winter. Destrs trouble not serious but cruiser trouble is. I am not in the picture enough at Bath, difficult to get to firms as I go to London once a week & out of touch with [Admiralty] Board & staff. At Newcastle long talk with Rowell [H B R, chairman of Hawthorn Leslie] must do something. *Naiad* 'A' turret jambed, bad show. Then to Middle Docks to see *Edinboro*' a big job. Then to SH [Swan Hunter] talk with Swan re Hatchard [W J, overseer], good go at *Holderness*, CO happy ['Hunt' completing].

26 July: Good go at *KGV*, getting on, *Victorious* almost stopped. Douglas (CO *Nigeria*) is happy & ship is well on. To Middlesbrough, Smith's [Dock] welding v.g., heavy teak in corvettes looks a sin [shortage of hardwoods was a problem]. Whiting doing well [W R G, overseer]. Then to Furness not impressed they had a shake up by bomb but are not counting their blessings, pity we gave them *Erne* & *Ibis* [sloops ordered in Jun 1939]. Left by train for Darlington AR warning there at 23.45 train left at 23.55 & 1h 30 mins late at Kings X [Cross station].

This view from the top of Vickers-Armstrongs Naval Yard crane in mid-August 1940 shows the forward part of *King George V*, the carrier *Victorious* and the cruiser *Nigeria*. 'B' turret's roof plates have yet to be fitted. *Victorious* is out of reach of the quayside cranes so a travelling crane has been erected on her flight deck. Note the extensive workshops to the left and the large volume of fittings and materials waiting on the quayside to be lifted on board these ships. (*Author's collection*)

28 July: Sunday. AR warning 00.00-03.00. I was very tired & slept thro' it. In office. Accumulation of papers in 3 days, vile. ...

29 July: ... Sent Contr a statement re relative time for building T, S & U S/Ms [submarines]. Harrison [A N, now Constructor Commander with Home Fleet] called says people are pleased with Hunts. RA D[estroyers] wants *Le Triomphant* now & then only [Free French destroyer].

31 July: ... Barnaby called [Kenneth C, Thornycroft's naval architect, and grandson of Sir Nathaniel, the first DNC] told him not to run our Hunt at NPL [towing tank at National Physical Laboratory, Teddington]. He bet me 2/6 [2 shillings and 6 pence = 12.5p say £10 today] their [hull] form was worse than ours; he has a weird form for dry foc'sle [forecastle]. [Their two Type 4 'Hunts' were ordered on 27 Jul with a heavily flared knuckled forebody.] We should be howled down for costly ships if we took it on. ...

6 August: In London. Roped in without warning to attend P.M's meeting re munitions & armour for tanks (with Lithgow) [Sir James, now Controller of Merchant Shipbuilding & Repair] P.M. looked well, not impressed by Beaverbrook [Lord, Minister for Aircraft Production] or Morrison [Herbert, Minister of Supply] (particularly M.) said our armour production had gone over to guns & aircraft engines, if we

(Sir) James Lithgow (1883–1952) was the son of William Lithgow, one of the founders of the large Russell shipyard in Port Glasgow. He had earned a Military Cross when a Lieutenant Colonel in the Royal Garrison Artillery in the First World War before joining the Merchant Shipbuilding Directorate. The company became Lithgows Ltd in 1918; after the war it was run by James and his brother Henry. Seen as a safe pair of hands, he was called upon by the Government in the 1930s to help rationalise the Scottish steel and shipbuilding industries, becoming chairman of National Shipbuilders Security Ltd. He became chairman of many weaker companies including Fairfield, Beardmore, Steel Company of Scotland, shipbuilder Hamilton, engine builder Rowan and engine builder Rankin & Blackmore. Not surprisingly, he was called upon in 1940 to join the Board of Admiralty as Controller of Merchant Shipbuilding and Repairs. Goodall was pleased that the Board now included a technical man (a position which he had hankered after himself), and had a high respect for Lithgow, though sometimes feeling that he favoured merchant shipbuilding at the expense of warship building. But actually the amount of labour allocated to the latter was roughly double that of the former. After the war he returned to run the Lithgow businesses. (*The Shipbuilder*)

got it back all armour required could be produced, promised P.M. figures later. Lithgow said he would get these from Iron & Steel Control. [Most of the armour for the *KGV* battleships had already been rolled, freeing up alloy steel production for other uses, especially tank production.] ...

16 August: ... Forest [Lt Cdr F X], Craig & Wilson USN here, told Forest what we wanted of their expts & gave instructions that there were no restrictions on what he could be shown of damage [to RN ships]. ...

17 August: ... Our wedding day 32 years ago [1908]. ...

29 August: ... At Liverpool. ... After lunch to CL, King & Queen had been there in morning pleased everybody. Had good look at *P. of Wales* don't think she will finish this year [completed Mar 1941]. ...

30 August: ... Inspected *Dido*, *Thunderbolt* [rebuild of salvaged *Thetis*], *Charybdis* [cruiser] & *Springbank* [conversion of cargo liner to anti-

Cammell Laird's fitting out basin at Birkenhead is given over entirely to naval vessels in September 1940. The two cruisers at right reveal the problems of late delivery of 5.25in gun mountings. On the nearly-completed *Dido* (outboard) 'Q' turret is replaced by a token 4in, while on the newly-launched *Charybdis*, the forward superstructure has been rebuilt to take two twin 4.5in Mark III mountings. The vessel at left is the former Bank liner *Springbank*, being converted to an auxiliary anti-aircraft ship, with 4in and 2pdrs equivalent to a cruiser's AA armament. On the far wall with the engine shop behind, the battleship *Prince of Wales* is about to have her twin 14in 'B' turret shipped, using the 150-ton floating crane to lift the components out of the coaster *Sea Fisher* which had brought them from Vickers-Armstrongs' Barrow works. (*Author's collection*)

aircraft ship] D. all right, T. also, *Springbank* backward. Downhearted by enormous amt. [amount] of electrical work which is behind. [A continuing problem throughout the war.]

2 September: ... *P. of W.* damaged by near miss, phoned Johnson I would send Offord [Dudley, armour specialist constructor] if he wished but John[son] said they were getting on all right. ...

4 September: ... In London got thro' a lot with Contr viz suspended Fijis & Didos, Contr said I could go ahead. Bigger lifts in carrier must send to VA Barrow re *Indom[itable]*. ... giving up P'mouth & Rosyth dock limitations for *Lion* & *Vanguard*, shells with bigger bursters ...

10 September: ... Dido [class] gun mtgs all appear to be giving trouble except *Bonaventure*, can only wait & see. ... With Sanders & Pengelly went into *Lion* & *Vanguard* if beam increased to 108' [it was], told them to examine tumble home [inwards sloping of side of ship towards deck]. ...

11 September: ... Got ready for NC meeting, DDNC will <u>not</u> shed his peace routine mentality [not working Goodall's punishing hours?] ... Looked into Thornycroft Hunt design, they are now wisely increasing size but cutting scantlings [size of structural members] severely. ...

12 September: ... NC meeting not too bad. Short discussion on anti E-boat design [to become steam gunboats], Tower for his Fairmiles, later I asked him not to crab [find fault with?] the anti-E design, told him the estimated cost vy [very] high (£100,000) he says no intention to crab but do <u>not</u> stop Fairmiles, I agreed. ...

16 September: ... Watson back discussed anti E-boat with him & W J Holt [Bill, small craft constructor] went into Ad Fullerton's [Admiral E J A, at minesweeper base Yarmouth] criticisms of 105' wood [motor] minesweepers. [The first to be completed was *MMS.1* on 19 Nov.] ...

18 September: ... Boyland phoned Contr wants particulars & dates of S/Ms building for Turks, may be taken over. [At Barrow, two were taken over by RN, two delivered to Turkey.]

21 September: ... More trouble with Dido class turrets [Vickers-Armstrongs were well behind the delivery schedule for 5.25in mountings]. *Kenya* machy not accepted. *Adventure* mine rails all wrong. ...

23 September: ... John back from *Kenya* trials all right except power and steampipe joints. Agreed to increase depth of corvette bilge keels. [The 'Flowers' rolled badly.]

27 September: AR warnings during night, several during day over Bath, one caused all staff to go to shelters (time 2 mins). In London, arrived during air raid, 2 more later last causing staff to go underground, train 1 hour late at Padd[ington] 1¾ hrs at Bath. ...[saw] Contr re anti E-boat, 10,000 ton cruisers & minesweepers. Morse (DMS) [Captain H E, Director of Minesweeping] present for minesweeper talk, he gave me good information re acoustic mines, LL sweep [against magnetic mines] & MS requirements generally.

29 September: ... Cole back, *Ivanhoe* a sad story, ship's co[mpany] badly trained & ship prematurely abandoned. [Destroyer mined off Texel 1 Sep.]

1 October: ... Americans came. Cochrane was in Philadelphia N[avy] Yd when I was there [1918], he knows his job & was very frank, so I ditto. [Edward L Cochrane (1898–1955) Philadelphia N Y in the First World War with Construction Corps. Chief of Bureau of Ships Nov 42–Nov 46. After the war Massachusetts Institute of Technology.]

4 October: ... [in London] Contr said TLC [tank landing craft] model too big for 1st L's car. ... Left in 1st L's car about 5.55 p.m., AR warning just after 6. Arrived Chequers about 7.30. No talk before dinner. After dinner talk & walk in garden to see gunfire over London. P.M. & Fraser [now a Vice Admiral] had great argument over non-offensive spirit of Navy. P.M. v. sick about Dakar & started work 11.30 p.m. P.M. very tired & chucked his hand in after 1 a.m. ...

5 October: 1st L, Contr & I started work about 10.15. P.M. came down in siren suit about 10.45. Discussion mainly about new cruisers, battleship programme & building dest[royer]s more quickly, a little about anti E-boats. Left at 11.45. ...

8 October: ... NC meeting went tamely, afterwards new programme discussed, go on with Fijis & Didos, 10 anti-Es [only nine SGBs were ordered due to shortage of steam turbine capacity, two of which were later cancelled] ... DNO to say how long to produce three 8″ like *London*. [Vickers-Armstrongs were so short of gun mounting capacity that building 8in mountings as well as all their other orders was quite impracticable.] Talk with Maund re TLCs.

9 October: ... Got Sanders busy on bulging & armouring *Reso[lution]*. ... D of D will do *Reso* at P'mouth. [She was actually refitted at Philadelphia from Apr 1941.] Told Watson E in C will order anti E-boat machy at once. [Twin screw with Metrovick 8,000 shp lightweight steam turbines.]

Woollard said Baker was doing a gantry on merchant oilers to carry LC [landing craft] for Maund. [Ennerdales]

11 October: ... Talk to Watson & Kimberley [A E, escort constructor] on corvettes, much grumbling about them, I think real reason is lack of amenities.

15 October: ... Worked on Town cl[ass] destroyers [US destroyers of First World War vintage supplied under Lend-Lease] stability & strength & drafted yarn. ... Kimberley back from L'pool [Liverpool, escort base] with Contr's instruction re corvettes, decided to get full records of ship with & ship without deep bilge keels.

19 October: ... Got ready for 1st L. He arrived about 12.15, introduced 3 officers then came to my room & talked with Meryon and me on slow progress of new constr[uction]. We said 'LABOUR', he said dilute especially more women, I said women were not suitable for shipyards, put them into shops & aircraft work so release men for ships, ...

22 October: ... Contr rang re corvettes, says they are 'useless'. Sent Watson to L'pool to do something at once. Gawn [Richard W L, Superintendent of Admiralty Experiment Works AEW since 1938] came says singing propeller problem solved ... [Rough finish of 'U' class submarine propellers was causing noise. Sharpening blade edges helped cure the problem.] Conference re anti E-boats from 14.30-15.00. [Goodall seemed to use 12-hour and 24-hour clock times interchangeably.] Thorny[croft] is going to lie low & rat [? – their two SGBs were cancelled], Wall [of White's] butted in to offer too much. Russell [E W, managing director] of Denny most helpful, E in C wants Denny Yarrow combination to do dwgs. Russell thinks we are too optimistic on wts & stability. [These were the four SGB builders plus Hawthorn Leslie.] ...

25 October: ... Contr & VCNS [Vice Chief of Naval Staff, Phillips, formerly DCNS] tackled me over corvettes, I consider I came thro' with flying colours being the only fellow to point out they were slow. We have to design 20 knotters. [The first suggestion of what became 'River' class frigates.]

7 November: ... Wrote Office of Works re protection to Cabinet War Room [Goodall was probably regarded as an expert on armoured deck protection against bombs]. ...

8 November: ... With Cole discussed stability of Town class which for the latest bigger ships is dangerously low. [D K Brown claimed that the RN had never lost an intact ship through poor stability, unlike the US Navy.] ...

The early tank landing craft were built by regular shipbuilders, but at the expense of the more important destroyers and escort vessels. Seen alongside Swan Hunter & Wigham Richardson's Wallsend yard on 13 May 1941 is *TLC 35*, later renumbered *LCT 104*, outboard of two 'Hunt' class fast escorts *Heythrop* and *Lamerton*. The covered berths behind had been erected in 1904 to build Cunard's *Mauretania*, then more recently the battleship *Anson*. (*Author's collection*)

11 November: … Reed called & went into corvette business, he will send a sketch design of a 20 knotter. …

12 November: … In afternoon discussion re TLCs, Sheffer [A T S, seconded from Lloyd's Register as Principal Ship Overseer, Tees, where many LCTs were to be built] dangerous tho' keen, shipbldrs to do 15, rest by structural firms. [Regular shipbuilders actually did sixteen LCT Mark 2, numbers 100–115.]

14 November: … Bevir CO *Resolution* [O, Captain, DNO in 1941] when torpedoed [25 Sep at Dakar] called described what happened, left his report. …

15 November: … DNO & party came to discuss American 5″ HA/LA [high angle/low angle gun] in 'D' class [cruisers] decided 5 singles, said would not do anything in destroyers. [*Delhi* was so fitted at Brooklyn Navy Yard in 1941.]

16 November: ... Agreed to *Sussex* 4½″ armour [machinery space sides, after being bombed Sep 40 on Clyde]. Turner [F R G, Engineer Rear Admiral, Deputy Engineer in Chief] rang can't get Paxmans [diesels] for more than 7 TLCs, said I would accept 4 shaft arrgt [arrangement] [Most LCT 2s had triple-screw petrol engines.] ...

'J' class destroyer *Jervis* was in collision with Swedish cargo ship *Tor* on 19 March 1940. The substantial damage was repaired in Swan Hunter's No 1 drydock at Wallsend until 23 June; an example of the increased workload ship repairers faced during the war. (*Author's collection*)

21 November: ... I am more worried about *Kenya*, hear Denny [Captain M M, her CO] has written Stephens [her builders] a letter that indicates bad workmanship, sending John [W G] to Scapa to take passage to D'port [Devonport] if possible & let us know from Scapa what the trouble is. ... Sims [A J, Constructor Commander with RA Submarines] called says my S/Ms got many UBs [U-boats] from Lorient but now Huns all more wily. ...

22 November: ... Went thro' Offord's Lessons of 1st Year of War.

2 December: ... John back from *Kenya*, not so bad, must write Merrington to keep him sane. ... Cole back from D'port *Javelin* a miracle but why didn't we hit the Hun as hard! [She received torpedo hits, one forward and one aft on 29 Nov. She spent 1941 under repair at Devonport.] ...

4 December: ... With Woollard & Williamson discussed Maunsell's fort [anti-aircraft towers for Thames Estuary] & sent on docket. ... Strafed Stephen for bad work in *Kenya* [buckled bulkheads]. ...

13 December: ... Contr wanted to know if we could get an armour plate from *Graf Spee*: I said 'Not a hope'.

16 December: ... With Offord saw Creasy [Captain G E, Director of Anti-Submarine Warfare DA/SW] & discussed cast iron, he was very reasonable but E in C should have taken strenuous steps to eliminate cast iron years ago & [previous] DNC ought to have kept him up to it. [Cast iron is brittle, so a shock from an explosion, e.g. a mine, could fracture castings such as used in machinery items. *Belfast* suffered badly from this effect when mined in Nov 39. One solution was to use welded material, but a better one was to shock-proof equipment using resilient mountings.] ... Contr now says TLCs to be built by structural engineers in Clyde area & Sheffer has signed order to Davies [W J A, Deputy Warship Production Superintendent, Scotland] 'for DNC'. I must tackle Contr even if it means a big row; present position intolerable. [Goodall was very sensitive to any challenge to his authority.] ... [Using structural engineers to build LCTs was an obvious solution to limited shipbuilding capacity; the structural engineers were under employed without export orders during the war and could easily work with straight frame craft.]

18 December: Worked on 20 kn corvettes, not very happy they look too complicated, told Watson to have a go, also I should like to keep turbine & recip. machy ships the same. ... *Branlebas* [Free French destroyer foundered 14 Dec] lost, trouble for me ahead. ...

19 December: ... Saw Tower re *Branlebas* apparently ship broke in two, told Cole to send Dunstan [M C, assistant constructor] to interview the

Mine damage on 1 November 1940 to the sloop *Black Swan* caused fractures in both low pressure turbines. Forward end of starboard one looking inboard. (*Admiralty*)

3 survivors & to incline the other 2 [*Boucliere* & *La Cordeliere* were refitting] at P'mouth. ...

20 December: ... Discussed Winettes with Woollard & Baker told DCW [Hannaford] to order 3. [LST Mark 1, *Boxer* class] ...

21 December: ... Dunstan back from interview of 3 survivors from *Branlebas*, ship broke at after end of fwd engine room when sagging. [French warships were designed to higher stresses than British, hence smaller margin of safety in heavy weather.] ...

28 December: Message from Contr to meet him at Ascot Monday to discuss giving up my staff to D of D made me furious. D of D rang said 'Fine'. I said I should fight like Hell. ...

29 December (Sunday): ... In office a.m. DNO called re 5″ U.S. guns in destroyers he does not want to move so long as Whyham [S C, Engineer Rear Admiral, Chief Inspector of Gun Mountings CIGM] is certain he can get the mtgs in time, agreed to lie low for 4 months, then if 55° mtgs going to be late there is time to order 40° for the 5th E Flotilla. [5th Emergency Flotilla i.e. 'S' class destroyers. The single Mark XVIII 4.7in mountings in the 'R' class could only elevate to 40° whereas the 55° Mark XXII was better for anti-aircraft fire and was actually fitted in the 'S' class.]

31 December: At Admy. Contr very sick I would not give up any more staff to D of D. I said latter had had no vision & was now in trouble. I had helped all I could but had reached the limit. Contr said I could employ Gunning [M, Dutch naval architect] & any other allied nav[al] architects I could get. I said if I could I would release a constr[uctor]. ... [Goodall was quite right to resist giving up any of his already overloaded constructors.]

Memoranda 1940

Have settled down to Bath & the war. Southampton class cruisers very disappointing mainly due to badly designed details. *Nelson, Barham & Resolution* stood underwater damage well. Fijis are better than I feared. Hunt class stability my first big mistake which was overcome without spilling much gravy. A dead set against corvettes which they don't deserve. [They were not designed as ocean escorts but were so used.] Moral is don't try to force cheap ships on the Navy which as Winston says 'always travels first class'. *KGV* got thro' her trials well. Bombing [air raids] has not upset us as much as I thought it might. Transport is the greatest trouble. *Illustrious* a great success.

1941

1 January: … Gave Lillicrap instructions re RDF in small ships, he attended Dorling's [now Deputy Controller] conference, destroyers the most difficult, masts not strong enough to carry coil [antenna]. … Davies, Stanley [H, Warship Production Superintendent, North East], Sheffer had to confer with DCW about TLCs building by structural engineers. [The Clyde and North East England were the two principal regions building LCTs.] Davies says Troup (the snob) is insufferable. …

3 January: … Leach called to say he is going [appointed CO of *Prince of Wales*], good for him but bad for me, we had a heart to heart talk about gun mtgs [a bottleneck in building ships], he agreed with me that his crowd wanted improving. AR warning, whistle about 18.50. IBs [incendiary bombs?] near Bath. … Discussion with Cole & Lillicrap about a fair weather certificate for *L'Incomprise* [French destroyer, sister to lost *Branlebas*].

4 January: … Paper arrived on *L'Incomprise* & sent Cole with yarn to Dorling who put up to keep these ships on care and maintenance. … Discussed organisation for salvaging of papers if hotel [Grand Pump Room where DNC staff worked] burnt down, gave lines on which to proceed.

7 January: NC meeting. Hannaford talked too much & gave E in C chance to air off on matters outside the scope of the meeting thus wasting time of the majority of people there. Conversion [meeting] afterwards served a useful purpose, told McCarthy [S A, Superintendent of Conversions] to think out better liaison with Bath.

8 January: … Then Leach and I had a talk with Contr and Dep[uty] Contr about CIGM & his party. I said it sounded brutal but Whyham sick should go [he died in July]. Leach said I had put my foot in it properly. Contr didn't like it but I feel you cannot win a war by being nice. …

11 January: ... Haslar [AEW] got a severe blitz, phoned to ask if we could help. Some men have not turned up. Material damage mainly glass. ...

14 January: Discussed with DDNC [Sanders], Lillicrap, Offord, Bartlett [J L, aircraft carrier chief constructor] loss of S'ton [cruiser *Southampton* bombed on 11 Jan 41 in Med] & damage to *Illustrious* [dive bombed in Med 10 Jan 41]. Former sounds a sorry business but we must apparently give more fire-fighting facilities. ...

15 January: ... DNO [Leach] called to say Au Revoir, he is not replacing Whyham. ... Decided *Vanguard* barbette armour. Discussed *L'Incomprise* and asked for stresses with oil [fuel] out, could not think of her going to sea as she is. Stothert & Pitt [engineers in Bath] called with model of landing bridge, looks straightforward [extending ramp to bridge gap between bow of LST Mark 1 and shore].

16 January: ... Watson back from looking at Canadian corvettes ['Flower' class building in Canada] said 'Good & Canadian officers full of beans' ... With Mathias [Thomas L, ADNC aircraft carriers], Bartlett & Mitchell [A, constructor] looked into *Emp[ire] Audacity* [captured German cargo vessel being converted at Blyth into an escort carrier] very annoyed I thought it half baked & was being brought in prematurely. [Because of no hangar?] ... Lobnitz [Clyde shipbuilder building eight reciprocating engine *Bangor* class minesweepers] has sent in a minesweeper design with annoying letter. ...

Frederick Bryant (1878–1942) had retired as Deputy DNC in 1938, having held the fort during DNC Johns' illness in 1936. Although senior to Goodall, he stood aside; a factor may have been that his wife had just died. He served Goodall loyally, so Goodall brought him back as an ADNC in 1939 to manage RCNC administration – policy, staffing and accommodation – taking a load off Goodall's shoulders. He had taken charge of the aircraft carrier section as an ADNC in 1928, becoming DDNC in 1932. He had been instrumental in getting better recognition for the RCNC within the Civil Service, with improved pay and additional senior posts. Goodall was greatly saddened when he was killed fire-watching during an air raid on Bath in April 1942. (*The Shipbuilder*)

23 January: D of D rang re repairs organisation in US said he thought there should be 'Design' RCNC man not a dockyard [man], he spoke of

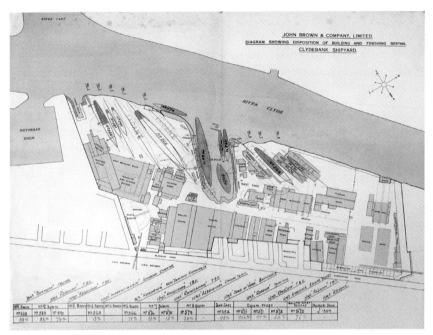

John Brown was one of the most productive shipyards during the war, and was also Goodall's 'go to' yard for difficult jobs. The monthly situation report for August 1941 shows thirteen ships under construction, eight on the berth and five fitting out; eight of the total being destroyers. On Berth No 1 (the easternmost) *Bermuda* is shown as 53 per cent complete, *Indefatigable* only 13 per cent on No 4 with *Vanguard* yet to be laid down on No 3, from which both *Duke of York* and the monitor *Roberts* had been launched, now both in the fitting out basin, 98 per cent and 95 per cent complete. The former Clan liner *Athene* is noted as completing conversion (to an aircraft transport) at nearby Dalmuir basin. The Admiralty priorities in May 1942 were: Naval repairs; Destroyers on Berths 7 and 8; *Bermuda*; *Indefatigable*. (UCS)

Eng RA being head! [Engineer Rear Admiral]. Called in Bryant [Fred, ADNC, RCNC administrator].

26 January: ... An anon[ymous] letter from draughtsmen's wives against female fire watchers sleeping in [Bath] hotel at night. [!]

30 January: ... Told McNeill [Clydebank] they could <u>not</u> start *Vanguard* yet. ... Reed of Smiths Dock here, will do 20kn corvettes instead of commercial trawlers.

31 January: With Watson, W J Holt & March discussed SGB [steam gunboat] development, drew up statement & drafted yarn to Contr, Denny & Yarrow. ...

11 February: Contr's meeting. Gloomy dates going back. Dictated notes. Contr said Japan will be in the war in about a month's time. 1st SL [Pound] thanks Bath [i.e. DNC] and calls for more. Since Hunts have been on East Coast convoys his [enemy's] attacks have become much less serious. ...

17 February: Pengelly back from visiting b'ships [battleships], says *D of Y* can't keep her date. *Howe* [building at Fairfield] could if men available. ... With Stansfield and Cole discussed Canadians building destr[oyers] to US designs. ...

19 February: Slayter [Captain W R, new DNO, previously Deputy Director] called re protection of 5.25 [in] gunhouses in *Vanguard*, wanted more, said I would do what I could. [She ended up with 90lb (2.25in) non-cemented armour vs 40lb in *KGV* class.] ...

21 February: ... To Admy with DCW. Contr would not open out on what is going on re labour for shipyards but sounds like another job for an Admiral. ... Contr lukewarm about Canadians building in Can. destroyers to US designs. Preece came in & said the US N A [US Naval Attaché] had said that 3 flotillas are coming here & will convoy US ships ... 1st SL at his meeting down on us re *Lion* & *Tem[eraire]*. I said we wanted 5000 more bodies in the industry. In talk at end of meeting 1st SL went to sleep [Pound's hip degeneration caused him to lose sleep but to doze off more].

24 February: ... Slayter came in, lost *Trinidad* 'B' mtg [in coaster *Shoal Fisher* mined 23 Feb en route Barrow to Devonport] said better finish her as a 3 turret ship (Question may arise of *Belfast* mtg, which will be difficult as it is 30 ton heavier). [Thicker gunhouse protection.]

25 February: John back from Scapa inspected *Nigeria* & *Edinburgh*. *Nigeria* not bad *Edinboro'* worries me rather. DNO back from London said *Trinidad*'s lost turret was 'A'. Can we use *Belfast*'s if lighter shield (but not lighter floor plate) is fitted, I said 'Yes'. [*Belfast* 'Y' mounting was transferred, and a new one ordered.] ... Whitaker [F A, Civil Engineer in Chief] called re Maunsell fort ... [Goodall was consulted about many subjects outside his formal remit.] ...

27 February: ... Went thro' Winette dwgs with Woollard & Baker & signed. ... Saw Dep Contr re my responsibility for collecting data on damage to ships & left docket with him (only ½ hearted I fear, both he & Contr). ...

28 February: ... Question of big dock in East Med. [*AFD.5* at Alexandria could not take *KGV* battleships]. I favour a fl. dock. ... DCW back from London talk, merchant ship repairs to have priority till end March, a

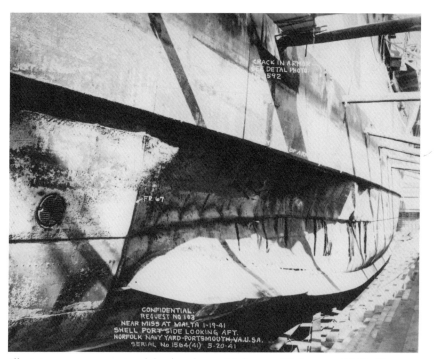

Illustrious was near-missed by bombs at Malta on 19 January 1941. She was repaired at Norfolk Navy Yard from 12 May to 12 December. This drydock view of her port side looking aft on 20 May 1941 shows the hull damage but the 4.5in side armour looks almost intact. (*Admiralty*)

further blow to new construction. [Losses from U-boats and immobilised damaged merchant ships were causing a severe shortage of shipping capacity.] ... Difficulty over new side armour plate for *Illustrious*, said get it anyhow. [She was further damaged by bombing while under repair at Malta on 16 and 19 Jan 41 with damage to port side armour. Full repairs were carried out at Norfolk Navy Yard 12 May–12 Dec 41.] ...

1 March: Staff want a new monitor vice *Terror*, went into this with Hannaford. [Bombed off Libya 23 Feb.] Rang Clark & Standfield [floating dock designers], Salmon [Dr E H, managing director] will come here on Monday to discuss fl. dock in Med. ...

2 March: Simeon (to be Dep Contr) [Rear Admiral C E B, previously CO of *Renown*] called looks all 2 years older but full of buck. ... German shells rotten. *Renown* all right except fore ends of bulge; I hope he shakes Bath up. Salmon ... called, made notes. Phoned Swan [whose company had built many floating docks] who couldn't or wouldn't help. ... Agreed to extra dynamo in *Roberts* [60kW diesel generator?] ... Decided to put

3″ on Bangors bilge keels [to reduce rolling]. Wrote firms re OBEs & MBEs [recommendations for honours].

4 March: ... With Stansfield and Bessant discussed 'O' cl[ass destroyers] as minelayers & gave instructions [too late for the first (*Oribi*) which had just been launched, fitted in last four].

5 March: ... Wrote to Evans-Lombe [Captain E M, Naval Assistant to 3rd Sea Lord] re stability of Town cl[ass destroyers from US].

6 March: Finished apologia re Bangors. Turner rang, told him what I am doing & will send him a copy, he will send me a copy of his remarks, he intends to blame bad performance of Diesel on the propellers. [Only four of the British-built *Bangor*s had diesel engines. It is more difficult to match propeller design to the torque characteristics of a diesel engine than steam.] Rang Craven & Hendin re monitor at Walker. [*Abercrombie* ordered 4 Apr 41.] *Terror* lost all her power (steam & electric) filled up and sank. ...

7 March: ... Telford [of Clark & Standfield?] with Humphreys & Taylor of Braithwaite [civil engineers] here re floating dock [to be] built in India, they sounded hopeful, priority machinery [pumping] the snag. [AFD.23 of 50,000 tons lift was ordered 7 Jul 41 built by Braithwaite, Burn & Jessop at Bombay. See 15 August 1944 re her loss.]

8 March: ... N class (2) for Dutch [*Noble* and *Nonpareil*] told Stansfield to get the list A's & A's [Alterations & Additions] for service in E Indies. ...

9 March (Sunday): ... Usborne, Scantlebury & Cooper came re new Fairmiles [Fairmile was a private company that procured coastal craft like motor launches for the Admiralty. Retired Rear Admiral C V Usborne was a director, the other two presumably on his staff], accepted form, & strengthening but said new form would mean 5 mos [months] delay; then if we could supply 6 dr'men [draughtsmen] for 10 weeks & they could take Solent Yard this could be shortened. ... *Dido* cracked plate, sent Kennett (more damned square vent holes in strength members). [Not only reduced cross section of continuous structural material but sharp corners caused cracks.] ...

12 March: ... Contr here all morning most interesting discussion on how to carry fighter aircraft [on merchant ships?] & 8″ cruiser.

13 March: ... Dorling & Simeon came to inspect *Vanguard* model, they are all for Dorling's bridge but wait & see! Simeon told me *Renown* lost *Scharnhorst* because Whitworth [Vice Admiral W J, in *Renown*] insisted on turning to starb'd to get wind on port bow & they thus lost about 5000 yards. [Action off Norway 9 Apr 40.]

14 March: ... Offord back from anti S/M meeting 30lbs charge agreed on. [For Hedgehog A/S mortar bombs?] Milne of Cowes [J A, new managing director of shipbuilders J Samuel White. He had been manager of the Dunkirk shipyard before the war] called, said Dunkirk was a disorganised flop, brigadiers & privates all shook up, their only concern was to get away; he agreed *Branlebas* was over-engined. *[Le] Triomphant*'s shaft brackets were the wrong stuff, thinks welded were good in his opinion [later used in RN ships due to shortage of forging capacity]. Lost ML.501 [Camper & Nicholson MGB] in the blitz last Monday [10 March] a sad thing for me personally, this was my pet ... Worked on destroyer stability & gave decisions, I will keep off solid ballast as long as I dare [it lowered the centre of gravity but at the expense of increased draft and reduced freeboard]. Cluett [A W A, Deputy Director of Dockyards] called re *Reso[lution]* refitting at USA port [Philadelphia Navy Yard 22 Apr– 16 Sep 41] ...

15 March: ... LNER [London & North Eastern Railway] dr'man called re armoured railway carriage for H.M. [King] put him wise. [Another example of the wide range of people consulting Goodall.] ... Hannaford brought in letter from Grant [Allan J, director of John Brown] saying that Lithgow has stopped all armour work in order to get on with merchant ships [his company was a partner in Firth-Brown armour makers at Sheffield]. ...

16 March: ... Dictated letter to Craven re using [Vickers-Armstrongs] St Albans [towing] tank [the two Admiralty ones at Haslar were overloaded]. ...

17 March: AR warnings long noisy night, enemy machines all appeared to approach Bristol via Bath, many bombs but a long way off altho' houses shook often. ... Inspected 8″ cruiser design a big ship with 8 – 4″ twins but they don't look too many. ...

18 March: ... Marriner [W W, of Yarrow now in Canada] called quite sure Canada can build Tribals [destroyers, two were ordered shortly from Halifax Shipyards]. Ackworth [Lieut Cdr H W] from *Illustrious* had long talk with Mathias [T L] & Co, told Mat. to choke them off keeping hangar doors open. Message from Contr wants 9 fast ships converted to A. Carriers. Dicken [Rear Admiral E B C, now Assistant Controller] called about it, got Mathias busy. ...

19 March: ... Agreed to Hannaford's minute re no overtime at H & W [Harland & Wolff] on merchant ships building for private owners.

22 March: ... Contr wants to put deck armour on *Malaya*, he will not say anything to US about it yet. [She was refitted at Brooklyn Navy Yard

6 Apr–9 Jul 41] … Blackman [F T, chief constructor] phoned re *Viscount* [converting to long-range escort at Devonport] must have 10 DC [depth charge] pattern …

24 March: … Arranged Baker should attend oiling at sea conference on Tuesday [to give escorts longer range] then go to Belfast, then to minelayers who have cracked top deck. *Abdiel* [fast minelayer completed by White 15 Apr 41] a mystery apparently sent from trials on an operation & got damaged. [Laying mines off Brest 22 Mar.]

25 March: N G Holt [Neville, senior constructor, younger brother of W J] described difficulties of 2 aircraft in *Maplin* [ex-refrigerated cargo vessel then ocean boarding vessel, fitted with one Sea Hurricane as catapult armed merchantman] … Discussed with Bartlett, Mathias, Mitchell US ships as A. carrier conversions, dictated draft to US Mission & took to London. [The genesis of the CVE escort carrier?] A v. thick day.

26 March: At Admy. Prelim[inary] talk with Contr on conflicting claims of merchant and naval programmes, then full conference. Lithgow trying to get away with it, pulled up a little by Board (concluded vested shipowning interests are after Lillicrap where we don't get that trouble). …

27 March: … Letters from Merrington *Rodney* wants refit badly. [Done at Boston Navy Yard 13 Jun–27 Aug 41] … Went into bows of *Formidable* with Mathias & Bartlett … Told D of S [Director of Stores, E S Wood] to get *Malaya* armour to USA. …

31 March: … Looked at *Havock* (couldn't torpedo *Littorio* [Italian battleship] as all torps gone) she had 2 sets of tubes. Lunched Dorling (this his last day as Dep Contr). …

2 April: … P.m. long & useless discussion re men for merchant ship repairs, having said he wanted 4000 men & we agreeing [presumably taken off naval ship construction] Lithgow now says he couldn't use them because no docks nor berths. He disappointed me. Craven present said 'Make Johnson [R S, managing director of Cammell Laird] king of L'pool [Liverpool] repairs'. I supported this. … Contr said *Bonaventure* sunk quickly [on 31 Mar] after 2 torps, I said couldn't expect ship to stand 2.

3 April: … From 10.30 to 17.00 interviewing university candidates for RCNC, a poor lot on the whole, selected 2 from Cambridge & 2 to take entrance exam to Greenwich [new constructors' course]. …

4 April: … With Parham [Captain F R, Deputy Director of Naval Ordnance] agreed to final version of yarn re fully HA [high angle, i.e. anti-aircraft] guns in destroyers. Told Cole, Bessant & Modeller to make

a rough mock-up of [?] 80° 4.7″ mtg so that it can be rocked about. ... M Denny called, with him Woollard & Cole discussed stabilisers [Denny-Brown fins], dictated notes, then his hydrofoil boat [planned 55-knot *MTB.109*] showed him letter I had written to Tower asking for loan of engine, then SGB he said machy will be late, then general situation he said men are working 'fairly' if we diluted to increase labour by 40% we might increase output by 5%, industry had warned Govt [Government] of this years ago.

15 April: With Mathias, Kennett, Sanders & constructors went into arrgts [arrangements] for sending dwgs & materials to USA for *Illust, Delhi* [cruiser being re-armed at Brooklyn Navy Yard 3 May 41–12 Jan 42], *L'pool* [cruiser *Liverpool* torpedoed in Med 14 Oct 40, repaired at Mare Island Navy Yard 16 Jun–3 Nov 41], *Reso* & *Malaya*, everything in order except that May [H, chief constructor] was passing the buck to D of D, told him to withdraw this & issued instructions that he must take the responsibility. ...

17 April: At Haslar. Told Gawn to take & give good leave. Cathode

(Sir) Robert S Johnson (c1872–1951) was appointed managing director of Cammell Laird at Birkenhead in 1922, having been a director of Belfast shipbuilders Workman, Clark. He modernised the shipyard, enabling them to build *Ark Royal* with extensive welding and Cunard's second *Mauretania* in the late 1930s. Becoming chairman in 1940, he managed an extensive business comprising the shipyard, engine works and repair yard, employing about 12,000 without major labour troubles. Goodall had a high respect for him, his yard causing few problems, so readily accepted an invitation to join the Board after the war. (*Cammell Laird*)

Ray Oscilloscope apparatus most promising for pressure measurements on propeller blades. ... At Portsmouth lunch with Admiral Clarke [Rear Admiral M I, Admiral Superintendent, Portsmouth Dockyard] who impressed me favourably. With Hickey [F, senior constructor] & King [I E, constructor] looked at *Antonia* [Cunarder being converted to repair ship *Wayland*]. ... 3 alerts during day P'mouth badly knocked about. ...

19 April: ... Talk with Bessant re his visit to Haslar next Monday on wetness of destroyers. Heliston propellers in *Abdiel* eroded badly [by cavitation, propeller design by J Stone]. Rec'd *Liverpool* damage report

of Court of Inquiry a very sorry tale, no precautions after smelling petrol whole fwd end full of petrol vapour [from aviation fuel tank] blew up 20 mins after torpedo hit, yet 1st L went for me on weaknesses, can't stand a torp hit without fore end falling off & I knew nothing of facts; also poor constructor scapegoat. [She had been torpedoed 14 Oct 40. Temporary repairs at Alexandria. Damage Control handbook was amended to advise switching off electrical equipment if petrol vapour present to prevent sparks.]

23 April: ... At Admy. Discussed with Contr wetness of destroyers of J cl[ass] he brought in VCNS who was annoying and silly, insisting that Tribal raked stem made ship dry, sent Cole instructions. ...

24 April: Visited Cleveland [Bridge], Whessoe [Foundry] [both LCT fabricators at Darlington] & old yards of Raylton Dixon & Craig Taylor [formerly closed shipyards on the Tees being used to erect LCTs]: structural work good. Whessoe most impressive & go ahead. But they have not yet got to grips with fitting out. [The first LCT Mark 2 from the Tees was launched on 28 May.] At Furness looked at *Ibis*. Boardman [R, assistant managing director] unimpressive, worried about sabotage. On to Hebburn, Rowell very against costing [Admiralty scheme of contract payments?] an inveterate grumbler. ... Firm not doing badly. *Cleopatra* [cruiser fitting out] had a knock but not badly. Saw FOIC [Rear Admiral W G C Maxwell, Flag Officer in Charge, Tyne] who was very pleased with my staff.

25 April: At Swan Hunter, Swan said they made too much profit on Hunts. [The Type 1s averaged £55,000 profit on a price of £275,000 or 20 per cent, but dropped below 10 per cent on the Type 2 'Hunts'.] Not very worried over costing, wants a new scheme something like the *Nelson* contract to limit profit but still give the more efficient firms the greater profit. [The Admiralty did bring in such a scheme later.] Looked at *Ennerdale* [oiler being completed as landing ship gantry] OK must do something about armour for *Anson* [presumably side plates delayed by priority for tank armour.] At Walker [Vickers-Armstrongs] Hendin really wants to go on with *Lion* [her keel was lying on Berth No 2 with 'Hunt' class destroyers building on either side]. *Misoa* OK [former tanker converting to tank landing ship] two 400 kilo AP [armour piercing] bombs just missed *Victorious*. [Left Tyne 16 Apr for drydocking at Rosyth.] At Blyth, minesweeper vibration bad [four *Bangor*s building] (White's marine engine) [White's Marine Engineering of Hebburn was building the triple expansion engines; they had a patent four-cylinder compound engine fitted to merchant ships before the war]. *Empire Audacity* getting on, said give an optimistic date. Talk with ASCBS re shifting men. [Vice

Admiral St A B Wake, Admiral Superintendent Contract Built Ships based in Newcastle; he had previously been a Director of Naval Equipment.]

26 April: Arrived Kings X 07.00. Looked round damaged London (Jermyn St) before breakfast. At Admy saw Contr & told him firms really doing well. He is still of opinion too many men on new construction. He is thinking of calling a meeting to push repairs. Really he should put somebody like N G Holt as repairs boss. Back in Bath 16.00.

30 April: ... Dep Contr very depressing over damage to Portsmouth & Devonport yards, he said rightly that we are now going to do what should have been done a year ago viz. scatter yards, not concentrate at the yards. My view entirely, lack of vision of D of D has been deplorable.

1 May: ... Harrison [A N] called, a long talk on destroyers, Tribals are going wavy under the bottom fwd [slamming pressures on transverse framing?] he seemed not too sure that J's are very wet. *Erne* damaged. [Delivered 26 Apr. Bombed 30 Apr, serious damage to main and auxiliary machinery.] What a pity after waiting for her so long. ... Gave Boyland view on using Oerlikons [20mm AA gun] in QE [*Queen Elizabeth*], *Gloster* [*Gloucester*] & *Ark* [*Royal*].

6 May: ... Told Bryant to give WPS's [Warship Production Superintendents] a lead on what to destroy if area invaded.

9 May: ... Rude docket from D of D [Talbot] re stability of foreign ships, drafted rude reply & decided to sleep on it. [D of D was based in the Pulteney Hotel, Bath.] ... Sent Watson up to Admy to discuss building new corvettes in USA. ... Chadburns blitzed [ship telegraph manufacturers, Liverpool] & we had had paper on alternative factory for months!

10 May: ... Watson back [from Admiralty] fear result of conference will be that we shall have forced on us more American ships. [Fifty destroyer escorts were ordered in US in August.] ...

12 May: ... Had talk with Pringle [DEE] & DCW re supplying power to a blitzed shipyard. ... Liaison officer with Free French called with CO [*Le*] *Triomphant*, said I could not advise as this ship was theirs but her stability was below our standards. [Some Free French ships were French manned, others British.]

13 May: NC meeting not bad. At Repairs chucked off my chest my dissatisfaction at US arrgts but Contr said Operations [Division] will never give a programme. [Goodall was probably concerned that last-minute decisions to send ships to USA gave little opportunity to prepare refit plans, e.g. to compensate for reduced stability.] At Conversion meeting E

in C put all the onus of taking over a ship with defective mach[iner]y on to DNC! Moral DNC is the senior tech[nical] adviser on machy [sarcasm]. I had a go at E in C about this & comforted McCarthy. ...

15 May: ... With Woollard & Baker discussed taking topweight off Bangors & putting in ballast to reduce heel when turning. Discussed with Bryant & Offord how to deal with DNE's plagiarism in labelling our damage reports & dwgs as the work of DNE [now Simeon, who was also Deputy Controller]. ...

16 May: ... Davies called, LCTs on Clyde not doing well. [First launch July from structural engineers, two months after Tees.] ...

18 May: Sunday. Took the whole day off. Lovely. [His first for months.]

19 May: ... Sent Contr reply that oil, air & wood did not prove an enemy S/M was destroyed.

21 May: Agreed to US firing at *Illustrious* damaged [armour] plate. Butt [C J, Superintendent of Contract Work] begged off [going to] Devonport [Dockyard] (I hated giving in but his point that Mrs B would hate going back to the scene of her dead boys' life moved me). With Stansfield & Bessant went into *Oribi*'s stability, as minelayers these ships start life with no stability margin. [Sixty mines with sinkers weighing 75 tons were a large weight to be carried on the main deck.] ...

The 'O' and 'P' class destroyer flotillas were ordered on the outbreak of war as AA rather than fleet destroyers. Four 'Os' were fitted out a minelayers carrying sixty mines on rails (just visible) on the main deck with sponsons on each quarter. *Obdurate* seen here in Clyde in September 1942 had just been completed at Denny as Yard No 1352, Engine No 1102, with a light displacement of 1,530 tons, load 2,310 tons. (*Blackman collection*)

22 May: Wrote Dewar D S/V D [Director of Salvage, Rear Admiral A R Dewar] about consulting me before starting action for orders. [Presumably for new salvage ships.] ... Brooking [Captain P W B, Deputy Director Signal Dept] called re [Type] 271 in corvettes. [The first surface-search radar had recently been fitted in the 'Flower' class *Orchis*.] ... Patterson [A P] called re *Lion* armour for *Vanguard*. [Much of *Lion*'s armour would have already been ordered as the battleship was ordered in Feb 39.]

23 May: ... Wrote Narbeth [J H, retired constructor, designer of *Dreadnought*, whose son was now constructor at Auckland Dockyard] to cut out of his paper all the stuff about *V & A* [royal yacht *Victoria & Albert*] & her stability. [Pity, as Narbeth knew the inside story of her overweight building at Pembroke Dockyard, but this did not feature in his 1941 paper to the Institution of Naval Architects on his practical experience.] ... Wrote FO(S) [Flag Officer (Submarines) Admiral Sir Max Horton] re more fuel in S's & U's [submarine classes.] ...

24 May: ... Boyland phoned for speed of *KGV* on trials [28 knots with paravanes streamed], gathered *Hood* sunk. *Fiji* sunk also 2 hrs [actually 5 hrs, bombed 22 May off Crete] a bad day. Later heard *P of W* damaged. Came in after dinner, went to Dockyd Dept re sending *P of W* to USA, said I hoped not, heard later from D of D. With DDNC & DCW decided to send message to Hudson [G, Warship Production Superintendent, West Scotland] to get Johnson [H T, overseer at Clydebank] & Hall [V W, overseer at Fairfield] to discuss accelerating *D of Y* at expense of *Howe*.

25 May (Sunday): Dep Contr held meeting re accelerating *D of Y,* all depends on gun mtgs, he will see Contr this p.m. [Only her aft 14in mounting had been fitted.] ... Contr wanted to know what *Hood*'s protection would do v. 15″ at 26000 yds, told him. I had already had our records searched. DNO in 1932 said *Hood*'s mag[azine]s were not immune, she was last on list for reconstruction & war came too soon. ...

27 May: ... At lunch met Thursfield [retired Rear Admiral H G, naval correspondent of *The Times*], told him I didn't like Times leading article Monday 26th. He should rub in *Hood* today fighting *Bismarck* was like old *Majestic* at Jutland against latest German Dreadnought ... [The passage to which Goodall probably took exception read '... She [*Hood*] is stated to have blown up and sunk, undoubtedly through the explosion of a magazine. The same swift and total destruction befell three of our battle-cruisers at Jutland. After that experience British naval architects determined to make future battle-cruisers invulnerable to that kind of danger; and with the *Hood*, which was completed shortly after the last War, it was believed that they had succeeded. ...' It was poor

Prince of Wales took seven hits during her action with *Bismarck* and *Prinz Eugen* on 24 May 1941 which resulted in the loss of *Hood*. This photo shows the result of the third hit (15in) which exploded by the after funnel after hitting her starboard aircraft/boat crane. Her fighting efficiency was seriously impaired, requiring six weeks of repairs at Rosyth. (*Admiralty*)

ammunition-handling practices that caused the Jutland losses, rather than poor magazine protection.]

28 May: Sweated up history of *Hood* & drafted report to Controller. ... Offord back, says flame from *Hood* came up between after funnel &

mainmast, ship sank in 3-4 mins (sounds mysterious if magazine blew up). ...

29 May: ... Went thro' my *Hood* yarn to Contr, who showed me 1st SL proposal for c'tee [committee] of inquiry, I said I was all for it, Admy had nothing to hide, I was agin Dreyer [retired Admiral Sir F C] as Chairman, Contr then suggested Renouf [Rear Admiral E de F] or Willis [Rear Admiral A U] I was for W, said a naval architect & a scientist should be on. Told Contr about upper deck torp. tubes [in *Hood*] ...

30 May: ... With Bryant, Sanders & Lillicrap discussed *Hood* c'tee, if I am asked I shall suggest W S Abell [formerly of Lloyd's Register and Newcastle University]. Then interrogation of *Bismarck* prisoners, sent this to Boyland. Denny & Wallace [William, managing director of Brown Brothers, Edinburgh] called re stabilisers, fixed up for fully HA destroyer [eventually became 'Battle' class]. ... Talk with DCW re *D of Y* and labour on Clyde. Letter from Grant re giving OB [Ordnance Board] particulars of armour research. ...

2 June: ... Letter from Swan offering N Hunter [Norman, shipyard manager at Swan Hunter] for India fl dock. ... Mason [H R, constructor] back from *P of W*, *Hood* more of a mystery than ever, range roughly 16,500 not 22,000 [yards] & German shells in *P of W* were nothing wonderful.

3 June: ... Report re vulnerability of Barrow [shipyard] must send copy to DEE as report states supply of electric power not satisfactory. With Shepheard [V G, chief constructor] discussed US plastic antifouling composition [paint] decided to try it in *Liverpool*. ... C in C [now Admiral Sir J C Tovey] wants Mark Ms [multiple 2pdr pom poms] in *KGV* & *P of W* on turrets instead of UPs [ineffective rockets].

4 June: Pengelly back from *Hood* inquiry not very satisfactory finding *Hood*'s mag. blew up but without reason and thro' shell penetrating to it. Told Pengelly to report protection to mags. Of all the old 15″ ships (*Roy[al] Sov[ereign]*s hopeless without big reconstruction). ...

5 June: ... With Bryant saw Pringle re Treasury circular to work 51 hr. week, we [RCNC] approach this & I don't think I should increase output by working longer hours ... Lillicrap back, says slacking on Clyde is bad & Pigott & Stephen [Sir A M, chairman of shipbuilder Stephen] are scared. ...

11 June: ... Long talk on *Hood*. Simeon rather insisting that 'X' mag went up, Contr seemed to think torp. tubes a possibility. I have to prepare statement on the existing ships & *Bismarck* with view to discussion by Staff on Tactics of the Gun. [Goodall was well qualified to do this,

having been the senior constructor in charge of modernising battleships in the early 1930s.] E in C on *KGV* endurance. [Although it met the Staff Requirement, it was found to be too low for wartime requirements, e.g. *KGV* having to break off the *Bismarck* engagement owing to being low on fuel.] ... Off on Leave [well deserved, until 18 Jun.]

22 June: ... With Stansfield & Cole discussed stability of old destroyers & gave decisions, accepting strength & stability margins I don't like but extra topwt. [top weight] essential to win war. ...

23 June: At Admy. Contr conference on more S/Ms produced little: Vickers promise 12 U's. After lunch went to Northways [submarine headquarters]. FO(S) turned down our simplified design – too slow we will have another go: FO(S) wants to know why Hun does so much on 500 tons [displacement]. I believe his battery is lighter, engines run to death more, welding saves more than we do, reserve buoyancy less & perhaps

(Sir) A Murray Stephen (1892–1974) continued the family tradition of shipbuilding at their Linthouse, Glasgow shipyard. He succeeded his father as chairman in 1932, nursing the company through the Depression between the wars. Having a ship-repairing division as well as the shipyard and engine works helped the company survive. Goodall respected his hands-on approach to wartime demands. (*The Shipbuilder*)

500 tons is understatement [true, the Type VII was about 750 tons]. ...

26 June: ... Harrison called says Fleet destroyer circles favour 4″ gun for HA/LA, described loss of *Mashona* [bombed on 28 May] (full from fwd to aft bkd [bulkhead] of No.2 blr [boiler] room) took over 2 hrs to turn over. Annoyed by Home Fleet screed about *KGV* bow & wetness. [Lack of freeboard forward was due to Staff Requirement on 14in firing arcs forward at low elevation, not DNC's fault.]

27 June: Harcourt [Captain C H J] CO *Duke of York* called told him about plastic prot.[ection] & *Bismarck*. ...

30 June: Worked on *Hood* Court of Inquiry, more doubtful than ever that after mags blew up; why did ship heel to port if she was turning to port to open 'A' arcs? ...

3 July: ... Mt.Batten [Mountbatten] called said *Kelly* [lost off Crete 23 May] was turned over dynamically, he wants J's but with after gun a twin 4″ HA/LA & ship drier. Contr got DTM [now Captain H C Phillips] in re *Hood*, DTM is certain not more than 1 torpedo head could go up [presumably no countermining]. Contr seemed to have made up his mind mags. went up. [Modern analysis suggests one 15in hit by *Bismarck* caused a fire in a 4in magazine, which spread to the after 15in magazine with the detonation pressure spreading to the engine rooms, destroying all that area of the hull.]

J Maurice Ormston (c1886–1971) became Craven's right-hand man at Barrow in the 1920s. Following Hendin's ill health, he took charge of Vickers-Armstrongs' Tyneside shipyard in 1943; he was also made a director of the company. Goodall felt he was not getting the best out of the labour force there, where productivity was markedly lower than at Barrow. In the 1950s he became managing director of the Austin & Pickersgill shipyard in Sunderland. (*The Shipbuilder*)

11 July: At Admy. First called to see Craven at Thames House, told him shipbuilders should be quick to appoint his successor, he said I should speak [to] Ormston [J Maurice, manager of Vickers-Armstrongs' shipyards and former student on Constructor's course at Greenwich] & Denny: hit him up about Hunt prices. ...

12 July: ... Offord described Hedgehog trials [in destroyer *Westcott*]. Capt [at] Fairlie [Anti-submarine Experimental Establishment] is not above dirty tricks; got him [Offord] busy on OB & USA armour [penetration] formula. A bon mot re Ordnance Board 'Never did so many know so little about so much'. [OB membership included Goodall (ex officio) and about 70 from the other services and civilians.]

21 July: ... He [Captain J F W Mudford, Deputy DTM] showed me innards of German Mag[netic] mine. Lovely work but we should have said too intricate to be practicable. ...

22 July: At Barrow. Long talk with Callander & Ormston re labour, much departmental criticism there. [Barrow was the site of both the V-A shipyard and the engineering works.] O. says he is all right but engine side's premium bonus scheme is rotten. C. says bound to have trouble when demand for labour exceeds supply. O. said 'Men working well'.

Went over *Indomitable* thought she could keep her date [completed 10 Oct] & more men could be working on ship. O. said 'Yes but he hadn't got them'. [Barrow was then employing about 20,000 in total.]

23 July: At Barrow. Went over *Jamaica* with Tozer [R E, overseer at Barrow]. Then S/Ms with Richards [R H, Principal Ship Overseer PSO]. Looked at *Montgomery*'s rotten shaft brackets [ex-US destroyer refitting as escort at Barrow]. Idling not very bad so far as I could see but it is worse than it should be in war. [This was a function both of poor planning (with men waiting for materials and instructions) and a lazy attitude.] Left by road for Liverpool. ...

24 July: At Birkenhead. Long talk with Johnson. Later Hamilton [James, shipyard manager] & Humphreys [H R, director Cammell Laird] they all claim that with piecework men are working well. ... Then with Peake [H S, PSO] only went over *Charybdis*, *Badsworth* ['Hunt'] & slips [building berths]. Idling bad. Told Johnson. Must admit hot & close afternoon & the previous night had been very disturbed [from air raids]. At both Barrow & Birkenhead failed with my appeal that shipbuilders should work together.

25 July: 5 years as DNC. We have now settled down to war organisation. Calls for Corps men more than can be met. *Illustrious* very successful & *KGV* all right so far. Destroyers are now doing well (L. Class a worry when designing appear satisfactory). Hunts have now got over their troubles also corvettes. LCTs a good show. Fraser getting tiresome, scientists & other stunt mongers have his ear & I do not. Left Birkenhead for Clumber Park [near Worksop]. Trial of Nellie [Cultivator trench-digging machine] not bad but she isn't good enough. Arrived King's X 9.30 p.m.

29 July: ... DNO wants to put US 5″ twins into *Orion*. [Repaired at Mare Island 5 Sep 41–27 Jan 42 after bomb damage including 6in turrets 29 May 41 off Crete.] I said it could be done, sounded Simeon who thought it a good idea. ... Saw D of D re repair party at Scapa having a promoted foreman to deal with stability &c he said he was doing nothing. I said I should object. [This was not jealousy on Goodall's part, more a concern that a dockyard foreman's training would not cover the naval architectural principles and practice regarding ship stability and associated weights and centres of gravity, critical to maintaining ship safety.]

30 July: ... DNO [Slayter] came to say 'Au Revoir' [appointed CO *Liverpool*]. With DDNC & Offord went into immunity diagrams of *Tirpitz* &c. Letter from E in C kicking at Fairmile VP propellers [variable pitch, good for matching engine torque to propeller thrust] (an obstructor or dept. jealousy). ...

31 July: To Bristol. Examined drawing work [of constructor students] which was good. Took V.V. [viva voce oral exam] 1st year Daniel good [R J, went on to become Director General Ships and later wrote his autobiography *The End of an Era*] rest indifferent to poor. ...

4 August: Bank Holiday. At Glasgow long talk with Troup fussed over labour & repairs. Then with Sir J Lithgow & Butterwick [W T, Assistant Director Merchant Shipbuilding & Repair] promised to do something re Oerlikons in DEMS [Defensively Equipped Merchant Ships]. To Clydebank had talk with Pigott re labour; then look at *D of Y*. To Finlay's [Alex Findlay & Co Ltd] yard [at Old Kilpatrick] & saw TLCs. To Denny & had long talk with him and Russell. To Yarrow & pressed Harold [Sir H E, chairman] to take on Craven's job [Craven was involved in both the Ministry of Aircraft Production and Ministry of Production as well as maintaining his links with Vickers-Armstrongs]. SGBs look nice. ...

5 August: To Stephen, had long talk with Murray [Stephen] they say labour a little better. *Sussex* [major repair of bomb-damaged cruiser Dec 1940–Aug 1942] is a brick round their necks. Then to Fairfield [adjacent shipyard] to launch of [destroyer] *Partridge*, ship went down very slowly, a bolt in the ways? Sabotage or carelessness. Speeches after launch too long. Whitworth [now 2nd Sea Lord] not good & Wake awful. Long talk with Barr [G W, managing director of Fairfield] who is very against essential works order. [EWOs applied to men in key industries reserving them from being conscripted for armed forces.] *Howe* looked not too bad [launched 9 Apr 40]. To Scotts [at Greenock; so Goodall's driver was

(Sir) George W Barr (1881–1956) was the son of John Barr, general manager of National Shipbuilders Security Ltd, the body set up in the 1930s to rationalise the shipbuilding industry. Starting as an apprentice at Vickers Barrow shipyard, he became shipyard manager in the 1920s. He was appointed deputy managing director of Fairfield in 1933 and was effectively managing director throughout the war, receiving a CBE in 1945. The company tended to be too optimistic to the Admiralty on delivery dates, then claiming that labour shortages were responsible for delays. Goodall had his doubts about Barr before the war when he objected violently to the longitudinal framing in the 'J' class destroyers – 'I don't trust him'. During the war Goodall felt that Barr was not managing the labour force that he did have most effectively, especially the outfit trades. (*The Shipbuilder*)

busy] talk with Greig [K E, managing director], Hutchinson J B, [director] & Colin Scott [Chairman] who was also hot against EW order. They are getting over the Blitz [7 May] but are bothered by repairs e.g. *Roy Sov* at Tail of the Bank [Clyde anchorage off Greenock]. Dined with Pigott, McNeill, Harcourt of *D of Y* & Smithers [D W, overseer at Clydebank] most interesting talk.

6 August: To Rosyth with Davies, Cantlie [Rear Admiral C, Admiral Superintendent Rosyth Dockyard] a fusser. Saw *Kenya* [in No 3 drydock], *Sheffield* [undocked that day, after repairs to outer bottom] & *Malaya* [just back from US refit]. Coppinger [Captain C, CO] anxious he should be justified in coming away from New York before RDF was done, said would tell Contr. Shipwrt [shipwright on the battleship] said US wanted to weld everything. They worked 3 – 8hr shifts & did well. Denny [CO] happy in *Kenya*. On to Robb [shipbuilder at Leith] who wants to build NZ [New Zealand] merchant ships, said I would let him know what I thought but held out no hope. [Robb were building corvettes, minesweepers and trawlers.] They are a live crowd but also against EW order. Dined with Whiting [W R G, now WPS, East Scotland] who seemed to be going strong.

7 August: Back to London. Saw Contr who councils [counsels] more patience before having another go at EW order. I offered to see Bevan [*sic*, but more likely Ernest Bevin, Minister of Labour]. ...

11 August: ... With Woollard went into Maunsell Fort & shallow draft TLCs [tank landing craft Mark 4] told Baker to attend conference on latter. ...

14 August: NC Conversions & Repairs meetings, cruiser situation & minesweepers are bad. Contr grumbles but will not grasp the labour nettle. ... Dealt with *Vanguard* protection abreast 5.25″ mags. (*P of W* dud shells lesson). ... Read story of UB.110 & examined photos & drawings. [Captured 9 May, cipher equipment recovered but sank on tow.]

16 August: At Admiralty. Long talk with Ad Nellis CNS Ottawa [Vice Admiral P W, Chief of Naval Staff]. I agreed to their stability &c proposals pro tem to be reconsidered as soon as they have a RCNCC[anada]. He asked me for one good constr. captain's rank directly responsible to him & 1 overseer (lieut cdr), 1 draughtsman (lieut.). I agreed to do what I could. ...

18 August: At Admy for fully HA destroyer: present Contr, Vice C [Tower], Dep C [Simeon] 4th SL [Vice Admiral J H D Cunningham], VCNS [Phillips]. Ads Power [Rear Admiral A J, ACNS (Home)] & Harwood [Rear Admiral H H, ACNS (Foreign)] &c &c: about as many different

opinions as admirals: finally we are to go on as already app'd [approved]. Harwood wanted a bigger ship with a 4.7″ twin aft & would accept less speed. RA(D). [Rear Admiral (Destroyers) now L H K Hamilton] wanted 4″ guns & less complication. Screed from P.M. agin aircraft in *KGV*, quite wrong, wrote reply. ...

19 August: At Admy. Did some paperwork. Dock conference, still more Admirals Contr, Vice, Dep, FOIC's Glasgow & Greenock, SDG [?], D of D, 2 Eng Rear Admirals everybody but the poor blighters who will have to work the dock. I tried to get all the docks manned by D of D, he will do this for 3 small docks but no more. Then I pressed that a company (repairing) should be formed to run the big dock. Troup will look into this, he means to tap Clydebank. [*AFD.4* (32,000-ton lift) arrived in the Clyde 26 Aug from Devonport.] ...

20 August: ... Worked on screed replying to Winston's criticism of aircraft in *KGV* and progress of *Lion* & *Tem*. (DCW says he can do the armour for one and might manage 2 but doubtful). ... Vosper's MTB trial failed (engine trouble). [Probably *MTB.73*.]

21 August: Dep Contr called re after pom-poms &c in *Vanguard*, he persuaded staff to raise the question of removing aircraft. ... Cole brought in Cdr. King of *Kashmir* who described how his ship was bombed & sunk. [Destroyer off Crete 23 May.] ...

26 August: ... With Cole discussed close range A/S ahead weapons & gave instructions to faster [sinking?] DC and spigot mortar. ...

27 August: Worked on *Bismarck* report revision & dictated draft. Got Mason busy on revised immunity diagrams which he did in the day: good work [*Tirpitz* remained a threat]. ... Discussed with Bessant mod[ified destroyer] designs viz 1 J twin [4.7in] & 2 BD's [between decks twin 4.5in mounting] & 2 quad tubes; 3 BD's & 1 quad tube. Agreed to USN HT [high tensile] steel for Canadian Tribals, subject to extensometer tests. ...

28 August: Finished *Bismarck* draft. NID's [Naval Intelligence Division] book on prisoners arrived. [*Bismarck* survivor interrogations?] ... Cole back from Ahead weapons meeting, more waste of time, saw Dep Contr & said I proposed to see Contr tomorrow to suggest this meeting packs up and Dep Contr bosses the show. ... Williamson [L C] at Fl Dock meeting financial pundits need squaring, Mitchell [E H, a consulting engineer for the dock] has to produce more dope. Discussed with Baker US minesweepers, said stick out for Oropesa, LL & SA [types of minesweeping devices] & no Asdics [sonar] or DCs.

29 August: At Admy. All morning in fruitless talk new construction v[ersus] naval repairs, brought out that small vessels of SVP [Small Vessels Pool] are a wasteful drain & that southern yards are doing very small proportion of repairs [few ships were sent there for fear of bombing] which are going mainly to USA, abroad & new construction areas. ... P.m. talk on new programme hope I got in 2 AC's [aircraft carriers] instead of *Lion* & 1 AC. Contr agreed to alter *Furious* bulge if possible [she was at Philadelphia Navy Yard 7 Oct 41–14 Mar 42] said he thought fully HA destroyer settled as mock-up all right, he is for aircraft somehow in *Vanguard*.

1 September: ... Dictated letter to D of D on his charge that I favoured Corps men here [in Bath] relative to those in yards. ...

2 September: Hannaford back from Contr's meeting with Greig of Scotts, consider a cruiser for them in Dec. [*Defence* so ordered.] ... Hall and Stamp [from Fairfield] came with model of new bow of *Implacable* [less flare]. Agreed with minor modifications. Bassett-Lowke called [model-making company]. DDNC sent his docket on armour in which he agreed with DSR's [C S Wright, Director of Scientific Research & Experiment] yarn that everybody but DNC had to do with armour! ... With Williamson went into docket from DA/SW [Creasy] re attack from air on U Boats with contact bombs. ...

3 September: Inspected H.G. [Home Guard] contingent going to Tank Parade. ... Message from P.M. who wants to compare *KGV* with US contemporary design. ... DDNC [Sanders] gave me a moan against going to London vice Boyland [who was retiring]. Cole back from spigot mortar trial a window-dressed show, showed me report of c'tee & his amendments, I agreed but still feel dubious about the fuse. Discussed Tribals stability with Cole, fear we shall come to ballast. ...

6 September: *U.570* [captured 27 Aug] at Iceland, sending Pamplin [George W, senior constructor submarines]. Stirred up DDNC re *D of Y* rudder [needed stiffening during drydocking at Rosyth] & received only chits in reply. Got Cole busy on preparing ships for ice conditions. [The first Arctic convoy had started in August.] ...

8 September: Saw Instructional Films Lofoten [Raid 4 Mar] ALCs good [assault landing craft]. *Scharnhorst* bow looked no good. [New Atlantic bow fitted 1942; could have been done in *KGV*s.] Air war on Poland disgraceful as propaganda effect on public here would be to increase war effort. Wake called re *Roberts*, *Indomitable* & *D of York*. DDNC's attitude no concern of his that *Roberts* lacks accommodation! ...

9 September: NC, Conversions & Repairs meetings. At end Contr raised accommodation question generally. I have to start a docket re provision for a higher percentage of supernumeraries. ... DTM called & with him & Lillicrap I discussed Ship Noises. He promised to give us all the information he had & to run any ships we wanted over the sound range. Annoying note from 1st Lord about wetness of 'L' Class, his only comment to DNC after his visit North! A nice way to inspire war effort. ...

10 September: ... Afterwards D of D and I had another heart to heart talk, we agreed to bury the hatchet. Talbot said 'Trust me not to let the Corps down'. With Woollard & Baker went into TL Craft, signed docket & gave instructions what to do next. [The first Mark 4 orders were placed on 5 Dec.] ... Dealt with DNO's docket re starting 16" triple mtgs. Spoke Sanders re going to London vice Boyland, he very upset, but I said he must think of the side, I was quite sure I would lose a Deputy if I proposed to drop the one in London. [There were two DDNCs, one in London (Boyland) and one in Bath (Sanders).] ...

11 September: Merrington talk: he said C in C [Home Fleet] would like me to visit Fleet. I said the move must start with him, I should be delighted. [Goodall was always keen to get feedback from the ships and their crews.] ... With Pengelly went into N[orth] Carolina [US battleship] and sent report to Contr for 1st SL [comparison with KGV].

13 September: ... Went into 4 screw Fairmiles to see if we are likely to get MTB.73 trouble [first of Vosper boats with three Packard petrol engines]. it looks possible. Hefty kick in the rear from 1st SL re London [presume the cruiser not headquarters], I have to see Controller.

17 September: Gawn called discussed MA/SB 22 noise. Vosper MTB.73 bad result, Abdiel expts [experiments, on propellers?] in USA. ...

18 September: At Admy. Saw Contr re London, described fully what was done & the risk we took. [After her cruiser modernisation at Chatham was finally completed in Feb 41, her displacement had increased by 1,300 tons. She apparently suffered leaky structure and was refitted and stiffened at Palmers, Hebburn from 30 Oct 41 to 27 Jan 42.]

19 September: ... Saw 1st SL & explained London he went to sleep. He agreed to my scheme re countering German propaganda. ...

23 September: At Admy: travelled up with Cotton [G F, Under Secretary at the Admiralty, Bath] who spoke of Cluett & the future of the Corps. I told him I had come to the conclusion that the Corps ought to go into the Navy [as in US]. ...

Cruiser *London* entering the largest drydock at Middle Docks, South Shields. The cruiser outboard of the unidentified CAM ship is *Kenya* who has just completed her refit in December 1942. If the passing cruiser is *Uganda* that dates the photo to 31 December, the day she left the Tyne after completion by Vickers-Armstrongs' Walker yard. Before the war Middle Docks only repaired merchant ships, but its 630ft graving dock meant it was suitable for cruiser refits after it had been lengthened 10ft. (*Author's collection*)

24 September: ... With Sanders, Pengelly & Sutherby [Frank S, battleship constructor] discussed more oil for *Vanguard* & drafted yarn. ... Dictated letter to Johnson of CL re designing a salvage vessel for us. [It became *Salveda*.] ...

25 September: ... Had a sniff round, dept. wants ginger, these small rooms are bad for supervision. ... Contr sent note the *E[mpire] Audacity* had brought down her first F[ocke] Wolf. ...

27 September: Lady Goodall came in to Q.M. [Queen Mary] rehearsal which was an absolute fizzle. Read Riot Act. Saw red when Dep Contr [Simeon] sent note that I was to be No. 3 when introduced to Q.M. Phoned him, he said the order was 'anyhow'. I pointed out I was Princ[ipal] Tech[nical] Adviser to Board (funny that 'Anyhow' always brings E in C to the top); phoned Cotton; then suggested to Simeon I should not go to Spa [Hotel where E in C based]. He wanted me to come & said he would put me first. Always having to fight for our position! [Engineers on tap, never on top.]

28–29 September and 1–4 October: On leave.

30 September: Came to office for visit of Queen Mary. Went round and everything all right. At Spa the order of introduction was DNC, DEE, DAS [Director of Armament Supply R W Wharhirst] (then NOs.). Afterwards Pringle came in & said 'How was it done'. I told him I made a fuss. Q.M. arrived punctually & left do. [ditto] 20 minutes here. Inclined to get bored at the technical stuff, interested in *Bismarck* damage, boats, integraph [an instrument for making naval architectural calculations]. Insisted on car being moved back so that she could be photographed, asked to have a photo with her.

6 October: Ate way thro' paper accumulation. Asked DDNC if extra protection to capital ships as result of *Hood* loss had gone out as an A. & A. He didn't know! Must watch this for *Nelson*. Got busy on New Years [honours] sent Contr his list [presumably Fraser submitted names from all his departments] asked Bryant to prepare Secs. list. Looked at *Vanguard* without aircraft & *Vanguard*'s bow, put down former for discussion with Contr next week & got together other items for discussion. W'son [Williamson] back from inspection of captured UB, ship apparently designed at outset for attacking a convoy at night.

Queen Mary and a beaming Goodall on the steps of the Grand Pump Room Hotel, Bath on 30 September 1941, where DNC Department was based. The man on the Queen's right might be Under Secretary G F Cotton. (*D K Brown*)

7 October: ... Contr phoned re *Roy Sov.* protection, I said it was worth doing, later he phoned Do *Ram[illies]* & order armour for other three, also phoned why not bigger lifts aft in *Ill[ustrious]* & *Indom[itable]*. I explained. Discussed with Mathias & Bartlett launching of *Implac[able]*: said I would not go below 7 tons/sq ft W.E. [launch way end] Press[ure]. [While launch preparations were a shipbuilder's responsibility, the Admiralty overseer had to check.] Discussed with Lillicrap rearrgt. [re-arrangement] of Mark M's in Mod. Fijis. Contr phoned me re *S'ton* [*Southampton*] or *Fiji* in this coming prog[ramme]. I said Mod. Fiji & posted him reasons. Sent OBE proposals to Contr Sec[retary].

10 October: ... Sent on *Hood* report also docket saying Australians will capsize their destroyers if not careful. ...

11 October: At Barrow. Had a good go at *UB.570* [Type VIIC]. Very interesting. A clean hull & welding good. But why such a thick pressure hull in association with comparatively flimsy frames. They are not bothered about getting thro' net obstructions! Very congested because they mix up internal & external main ballast tanks. Really she is a commerce destroyer that can hide underwater. Engine room small for [her] power.

13 October: ... Commander of *London* called to say what a fine job the conversion was! ...

23 October: Finished yarn on beam of ships & decided to propose re-introduction of Board Margin. [Margins in warship design are important to allow for increases in weights and centres of gravity etc during construction and in service to be made safely.] Boyland phoned ACNS(W) [Assistant Chief of Naval Staff (Weapons) Rear Admiral R R McGrigor] & has conference tomorrow on taking out torp. tubes of *Nelson*. ...

27 October: ... Pringle called re Firms' [shipbuilders] meeting with Sec. on profits & prices, said I was keeping out of it.

29 October: P.m. big meeting with DA/SW, DMWD [Captain G O C Davies, Director of Miscellaneous Weapons Development DMWD], DTM, DSR &c on expts. against *UB.570* model, Goodeve [Commander C F] a piffler.

30 October: ... Went to Stot[hert] & Pitt's demonstration of Winette [LST Mark 1] landing platform: good show. ...

1 November: With Whiting saw a Fairmile [motor launch] & went to St Monance & Anstruther (E. Fife) [boatbuilder W Reekie] to see MMS [Motor Minesweepers 63 & 64] very interesting & looks a good solid

job. Went to Rosyth met Contr walked thro' [work]shops, then on board *Renown*. Embarked in *D of Y* 18.00. Solberg (USN) [Cdr T A, Bureau of Ships, later Captain, who had developed a boiler cleaning compound] at dinner very interesting.

2 November: At sea. Gun trials progressed. Weather calm. A hitch on FP [full power] prelim[inary trial] due to a leaky turbo condenser, & inexperienced officer in charge not reporting this till salt water was present thro'out the whole system. Vent[ilatio]n of LP room [low power electrics] bad, action machy space not good, otherwise all right. A lot of water in 'A' mag[azine] (hyd[raulic] leak).

3 November: At sea. 4 gun packed back [over-pressurising the recuperator to test gun recoil and run-out] salvo from 'Y' shook ship & hotted up one propeller shaft due to clearance being insufficient. This put off FP trial to Tuesday. Ship went well when at FP vibration very little, foc'sle wet, must alter *Vanguard*. *KGV* was leaving as we arrived [at Scapa] so I missed C in C. Contr & I & N G Holt stayed with ACOS [Admiral Commanding Orkneys & Shetland, Vice Admiral T H Binney] Moon [J E P, constructor at Scapa repair base] with others came to dinner.

4 November: With Contr inspected Lyness Yard [repair base on Island of Hoy]: Moon doing well under very trying conditions. With him went to Fl. Dock [*AFD.12*, 2,750 tons lift] (Rogers dockmaster v.g.). Then to RA(D) & had a talk about wetness, top weight & Denny-Brown roll reducer [stabiliser]. After lunch to Stanger Head & Admiralty settlement &c on Flotta, Adm. Prickett [C B, retired Rear Admiral] came to dinner & started very interesting talk about Board [of Admiralty] responsibility. Contr had rather a rough journey.

5 November: Left ACOS at 11.15. Moon came with me to landing place for Hentest [probably Hatston naval air station] aerodrome & we had a good talk. Fancourt [Captain H L S, Naval Air Division] very nice, took me round & lunched me. Left at 14.45 landed at Inverness 15.50, left 16.30 (¼ hr late) Contr didn't turn up at Perth, train got in 10 mins early & I just got the 09.05.

6 November: Left Paddington 09.15, breakfast in buffet car, arrived office [Bath] 12.40 (less than 21 hrs from Scapa v.g.). Found everything ticking over. ...

8–13 November: Influenza.

14 November: ... *Ark Royal* sunk, no particulars yet except newspaper report that she was torpedoed, taken in tow, heavy list increased.

17 November: Some particulars of *Ark R.* loss came during weekend. Went into calculations made, thick bkd evidently failed, no action taken to counterflood: unknown why ship lost all power [no diesel generators, boilers shut down]; must look into repeat *Implac.* Letter from Barr re delay due to latest A. & A. work [Continuing competition between newbuilding and repair demands.] ...

18 November: More particulars of *Ark R.* Looks now as thro' thick bkd did not collapse but generally shake up caused many bkds to leak and ship being without power she gradually filled up & turned over. Talk with DEE re Diesels [generators] & switchboards. Dep Contr came here with Dep E in C [Turner] & (late Cdr E of *Ark R.*) [Cdr F E Clemitson?], Engrs thought No.3 blr room port had shut down: ...

19 November: ... Press Div. rang D[aily] Express wants to interview me 'the designer of *Ark Royal*', said I was not [his predecessor as DNC Sir Arthur Johns was] & couldn't be interviewed, not knowing what had happened.

21 November: ... Bartlett saw Power (late CO *Ark Royal*) who said they were caught with trousers down (boiler cleaning). ...

22 November: 1st SL here, told him *Ark R.* had shaken us to the core, he didn't seem worried. ...

24 November: ... SGB is not doing too well, boiler trouble & loss p.c. [propulsive coefficient or efficiency. The La Mont boiler could not produce enough steam for the turbines.] Dep Contr held long meeting here re Diesels in aircraft carriers, Bamford took notes [F O, his confidential clerk]. ...

26 November: At Admy. With Sanders saw Contr (Vice Contr present) re *Ark Royal*, he agreed to modify boiler room vents & fit ballast to *Illustrious*. He said 'Put forward short new docket to build new designs for repeat *Indefat.* & 1942 Carrier'. We discussed 8″ cruiser which I said seemed a mistake in the light of *Ark Royal* exp[erience?]. Contr said 'Go ahead with it'. Contr insists on Dam[age] Cont[rol] going to DNE. I think Vice Contr agreed with me that it should be with DNC. [The argument might have discussed analysing what needed to be done and how to carry out the procedures.] Saw Mt.Batten [now Chief of Combined Operations, Vice Admiral The Lord Louis Mountbatten] who wants a younger man than Nicholls [A, senior constructor].

28 November: ... The report [on *Ark Royal*] shows 3 blr room arrgt weaknesses. [She had three shafts.] Actually Maund [Captain L E H, her CO] made an error (Contr thinks) in calling up everybody from below to

abandon ship & then bringing some back (key ratings were thus out of ship for 2 hours or so). ...

4 December: With Bartlett & Perrett [W R, aircraft carrier constructor] went again into machy. spaces for new carrier; said 'Go ahead as already decided but see if we could arrange alternate blr room, eng[ine] room, blr room, eng room, as I should like to separate & also avoid concentration of uptakes under hangar with downtakes [ducts supplying air to boilers] close to them. Lillicrap agreed to 6-7 ft GM [metacentric height] but suggested 300 tons at fl[ight] deck [level] instead of 600 at upper hangar deck. [Probably assumptions on distribution of aircraft weight.] ... Long talk with Harrison about his Canada job [A N, to be Constructor Captain with Royal Canadian Navy].

5 December: ... With Hickey, Forbes & John discussed new Fijis, decided to increase beam & bilge keel depth, dictated notes. Then 8″ cruiser, dictated notes, put up GM & put down stress. Worked on fully HA destroyer, look as tho' we shall be tight on speed.

10 December: At Admy. Saw Tower re Denny's hydroplane [*MTB.109*], also Evans-Lombe re Baker & BASR [?]. Just commenced talk with Contr when news came of sinking of *P of Wales* & *Repulse*. I was dumbfounded over *P of W*. Fraser was splendid, he was called away to comfort 1st L then came back to comfort me. ...

12 December: *Ark R.* officers arrived, later Mackay [D C, Instructor Commander] the commander a bit shaken still. Did not get much extra from them tho' Mackay said they did think ship was gradually going over & would not stop. Still a mystery whether it was a contact or non-contact [torpedo] shot. ... Dep Contr gave interesting talk of *Renown* going into Narvik, he persuaded Whitworth to transfer to *Warspite* & not [stay] with *Renown*; also Cork [Admiral Lord Cork & Orrery] was sent out to inquire why Somerville [Vice Admiral J] did not pursue Italians [at Cape Spartivento 27 Nov 40].

19 December: ... Worked on new AC design, studied American triple bottom. I don't think this is a solution of the NC torpedo danger; [non contact torpedoes could explode under a ship's bottom and break its back] am moving towards funnels [possibly shafts to vent the explosion gases] & welding inner bottom. ...

20 December: ... Dealt with USA wood salvage vessel design, saying criticism 'with flowers'. [ARS.13 class?]

23 December: Davies [W J A] back from Turkey [delivering a Barrow-built submarine?]. Turks not too bright over construction & dockyards. ...

Letter from Pigott he is running to Contr with yarn we are wrong in frowning on counterflooding, luckily I have already taken action. McNeill hasn't taken everything into account. ...

25 December: [Christmas Day] In office a.m. Nothing of importance in.

26 December: Very nice letter from Contr saying I had [the] confidence of the Board. ... Went into *D of Y* vent report & agreed to docket.

29 December: Milne of J S White called, could do a Q Cl [destroyer] in 6 months less than the fully HA destroyer [Battle]. ... Told Cole <u>not</u> to invite Min of War Trans[port] to join Shock C'tee. ...

30 December: At Admy. With Pigott, DCW & Sanders discussed acceleration of *Vang[uard]*. Contr will not cancel 2 sloops but will suspend *Bellerophon* [became *Tiger* building at John Brown, the sloops *Snipe* and *Sparrow* were transferred to Denny in 1942]. Contr & ACNS(W) [McGrigor] agreed to bow with more sheer & accept reduced elevation from 'A' turret guns. [A long-overdue change.] ... Contr wants a Woolworth carrier, said I would get a private firm busy in order to get merchant ship practice. [The genesis of the light fleet carrier design from Vickers-Armstrongs.] Syfret [Rear Admiral E N, 18th Cruiser Squadron] came in, I was very disappointed he came across ultra-nervous & has most heretic ideas about stability, said I would fly somebody out to Gib to lecture Force H. [Syfret took command in January.] ...

(Sir) James A Milne (1896–1966) was appointed managing director, later becoming chairman, of Cowes shipbuilder J Samuel White early in 1941, after the unexpected death of Arthur Wall. After training at Vickers at Barrow, he had moved to the Société des Ateliers & Chantiers de France at Dunkirk for 20 years, rising from draughtsman to managing director, until the German invasion of France in May 1940. Bomb damage at Cowes in 1942 allowed the East Cowes yard to be rebuilt for welded construction of its speciality destroyers; Goodall kept a close eye on the first such, *Contest*. (*The Shipbuilder*)

Memoranda 1941

A year that started well for the RCNC & ended very badly. *Illustrious* took a terrific hammering splendidly. Fijis & L Cl are doing well as are Ts & Us [submarines] & Hunts. But *Hood* tho' not unexpected was a blow, *Ark Royal* worse tho' she should not have been lost. *P. of Wales* the worst blow conceivable.

The RN wanted a largely power-operated twin 4.7in HA/LA mounting for its 'L' and 'M' class destroyers which, compared with the twin 4.7in CP.XIX mountings in the 'J' and 'K' class, had an elevation of 50° vs 40°, but a weight of 38 tons vs 25 tons. Twenty-eight (four spares) were ordered for the first flotilla from Vickers-Armstrongs at Barrow in October 1937 at a final cost of £30,000 each excluding guns (Contract 345G). Delivery was due by March 1940, but inevitably there were delays due to other priorities and shortages of materials and labour, so four 'L' class were completed with four twin 4in Mark XIX rather than three twin 4.7in Mark XX. Scotts' *Loyal* was the last 'L' to complete, seen here in the Clyde on 30 October 1942. (*Blackman collection*)

E in C after clever subterranean work has come into the open in his attempt to put the marine engineer into our place as principal technicians of the Navy. Started move to get RCNC into Navy but Contr won't bite. Sorely handicapped by lack of constructors, and no. [number] of old men compared with those between 35 & 45 the right age with a war on. The senior officers particularly Sanders & T L Mathias reacted badly to my efforts to reorganise & get younger men into higher positions.

1942

1 January: Honours List out. Merrington [A J, Constructor Commander, Home Fleet] OBE, otherwise RCNC & shipbuilders draw a blank. ... Williamson back from talk on 2 man S/M, we await instructions. Holt [W J] back from SGB.3 our propellers OK, E in C's boiler NBG [no bloody good].

2 January: Had long talk with Dep[uty] Contr[oller], he knew of damage to *Val[iant]* & *QE* [*Queen Elizabeth*, both badly damaged by Italian frogmen at Alexandria 19 Dec 41] & told me *Barham* sunk by torpedo which touched off magazine, we ought not to be kept in the dark about this. ... He is for a *Courageous* with 2 – twin 13.5 or 14″ turrets [a gunnery officer's take on US battlecruiser *Alaska*?] ... Dep Contr thought it impracticable to move fl. dock [*AFD.9*] from Singapore. [True, lifting moorings, separating into three parts for towing, finding tugs etc would be a major operation.]

5 January: ... Letter from Callander, will do Woolworth AC design [light fleet carrier]. ...

6 January: With Watson [A W], W J Holt & Sears [F H, small craft constructor] went thro' larger MMS design, agreed with only a few modifications [126ft design]. ... Halsey [?Captain T E] called, back from USA. U.S. tank LC [landing craft] carrier is much like a Winette but also slow therefore less draft. [Probably LST Mark 2.]

7 January: ... With Williamson & Hickey [floating dock constructor] discussed towing Bombay dock to K[ilindini], said get some more information from D of N [Director of Navigation, Rear Admiral W G Benn] & Hydrographer [Vice Admiral Sir J A Edgell]. [Depth of water was critical, the 50,000-ton dock needing about 70ft to submerge.]

8 January: ... With Pengelly discussed Oerlikons in *KGV* & gave instructions.

9 January: Lillicrap [now DDNC at Bath] back. 1st L & Contr turned up to his meeting yesterday. He couldn't get the stability stuff into Contr's head. Contr says C in C HF [Tovey] is worried & it looks as tho' I may have to go to Scapa. ... *Abdiel* & *Latona* propeller erosion reports which substantiate Gawn's views handsomely. ...

10 January: With Williamson & Dowding [possibly Vice Admiral A N Dowding, Admiral Superintendent Devonport Dockyard] went into site of dock building at Bombay & backed B. against Kilindini. Less than a year ago I had a great fight to get this dock at all, now everybody wants it tomorrow.

12 January: ... Wake [ASCBS] called, fussed over stern anchor of *Abercrombie* [monitor]. With DDNC [Sanders], Forbes [W A D, brilliant aircraft carrier designer], Rayner [L W A, constructor] & Lofft [R F, constructor] went into *Ark Royal* list due to flooding, agreed on results & sent docket to Danckwerts [Rear Admiral V H, Admiralty]. Longley Cooke [Captain E W L Longley-Cook, Deputy Director Training & Staff Duties Division DTSD] wanted displacement of a 2 – twin 8″ turret cruiser, told Hickey to phone 11500 tons [as large as *County*s with eight 8in]. Dep Contr rang re sending somebody to *Ill[ustrious]* & *Form[idable]* with *Ark R.* lessons I kicked, the AC people being bows under. A v. thick day.

13 January: NC meeting went not badly, repairs in USA are falling off, I suggested keeping them up. Went into Woolworth AC design with Redshaw [J S, Vickers-Armstrongs' naval architect], Bartlett & Mitchell [A] all right if not allowed to grow, but can only be built at expense of something else. ...

14 January: ... E in C wasted an awful lot of time [at Contr's meeting] on piffling pts [points] & actually said Diesel dynamo bedplates cannot be changed from cast iron to fabricated steel for years! Actually the latter is specified but I thought it better to keep quiet. DNO's [Director of Naval Ordnance, now Rear Admiral O Bevir] part came re fully HA destr, said we would not object to 4.5″ guns & would not back Ls [class destroyer], he said he could do all 1942 prog[ramme] with 4.5″ but not with Bofors & H control, told DCW [Hannaford]. [The 1942 'Battles' actually had the Dutch twin 40mm Hazemeyer gun mountings.] ...

15 January: ... 1st Lieut *Audacity* [Lt Cdr W E Higham?] called, 1st torp[edo] hit aft & eng[ine] room flooded thro' [shaft] tunnel, other two 1 hour later. Air personnel very good, accommodation congested. ...

16 January: ... D of D [Talbot] now proposes to move the floating docks from Singapore (I proposed this a week or more ago to Dep Contr &

was told it was not practicable) now paper is marked all round the world ... Parham [Deputy DNO] rang to add to docket about L cl destroyers not being much quicker to build than full HA, I agreed. Discussed with Hannaford yards to build Woolworth carriers.

17 January: Forbes back, Danckwerts wants to say COs are told <u>not</u> to counterflood, told Forbes to go to London Monday & take with him dwgs showing instructions to counterflood if heel exceeded 6°, also yarn given me by Pringle that there was neglect in not re-making ring main connections, he should tell D[anckwerts] that he ought to have an 'electrical' adviser. ...

18 January (Sunday): In office a.m. a very busy morning. Skimmed thro' *P of W* report, can't believe extensive damage port was caused by only one torp[edo]. [While there was definitely one hit abreast 'Y' engine room, there was another close to the port outer shaft bracket. The damage to that distorted propeller shaft damaged the bulkheads through which it passed and into the port outer engine room, opening up large areas of the ship to flooding, which with later progressive flooding through hatches and vents was the primary cause of her loss.] ...

19 January: ... Told W'son [Williamson] to sound Stoth[ert] & Pitt re 2-man [submarine].

20 January: Worked on *P of W* loss, the reports don't read well from our point of view. Sent Contr report on draught over Hunt's bridges. ... Told DDNC to make *Vanguard*'s turret supports good for supercharges [bigger gun recoil forces]. ... H[enry] Main of Caledon [Dundee shipbuilder] & Alfred Holt's man called re converted aux. carrier. [Blue Funnel's cargo liner *Telemachus* became *Activity*.]

22 January: ... Looked at *P of W* damage drawings which look like 2 torpedoes instead of 5. ... Looked at moving forward screws of *Vanguard* [to reduce vulnerability if aft propellers damaged].

23 January: At Admy. Filthy day, raining & thawing after much snow. In morning Woolworth Carrier design discussed, everybody added something in spite of my repeated warning that this meant more work & getting the ships later. Left to DCW & E in C to decide where 2 shall be built. At Thetis Relief Fund meeting, businesslike as usual; C Lairds to be told not to give any more £50 dowries to widows remarrying. [The Fund had received donations of about £150,000.] ...

26 January: Sick. Didn't succeed in shaking off the cold I picked up going to London on Friday, waiting about on Paddington platform for late train, then v. stuffy carriage due to black-out. ...

(Sir) Maurice E Denny (1886–1955) was a grandson of Peter Denny, one of the founders of the Dumbarton shipyard. Study abroad widened his experience before becoming a partner in the family firm in 1911, renowned for its fast turbine-powered cross-Channel ships. He succeeded to the chairmanship of the now William Denny & Brothers Ltd in 1922, stepping down in 1952. Forward-looking technically, he supported the development of the Denny-Brown stabiliser, which was fitted in the *Black Swan* class sloops, of which Denny built fourteen 1936–46. Goodall maintained a steady correspondence with him, each giving the other helpful advice. (*The Shipbuilder*)

29 January: Discussed with Hannaford Woolworths, agreed to leave out Stephens. ... Wake rang he was taking torp tubes out of Denny's SGB [*SGB.7* and *8*]. I said 'Good'.

1 February: Looked up E in C's instructions to counter his claim that he is the word on machinery types. [Choice of machinery has a major effect on the design of warships, weight, space, fuel, cost etc.]

3 February: ... *Delhi* [re-armed cruiser] stability not too good, signed paper to add ballast later. ...

4 February: 1st L's statement T.G. With Bartlett went into raising boats in *Indef[atigable]*. ... SGB at Denny in trouble, torsion-meters [to measure shaft horsepower] look wrong but Sir M[aurice Denny] is harping on propellers. ...

7 February: Hannaford back from Admy. Ineffective meeting (as usual) about Labour. Contr seems satisfied that new naval construction must be the Cinderella. Then discussion of '42 prog[ramme], 8″ cruiser comes out. *Lion* to go on. ...

8 February (Sunday): In office. Dealt with Woollard's stability screed, will do fine. Letter from CO *D. of York* [Harcourt] on his experience in bad weather [Atlantic crossing Dec 1941 with Churchill and return in Jan 1942] & *P of W* lessons, sent message to C in C suggesting N G Holt should join *D of Y* pro tem. ... Batch of *Hood* papers, 1st SL wants lessons & how we have applied them, phoned DNO: very annoyed as both 1st SL & 1st L say *P of W* went down after 2 torps while *Bismarck* didn't after 5 (*B.* 41,200 *P of W* 36,750 tons torps in former 5 × 440lbs in latter 7-8 × 850lbs) [Goodall got the warheads wrong: *Dorsetshire* 21in 750lb, Japanese aerial 18in 330lb].

9 February: ... Forbes back from *Ark R.* C.M. [court martial] Maund Guilty of negligence & reprimanded. He F[orbes] seemed rather worked up. ... Dr Cowan from *Vernon* [torpedo and mining school] called re shock, doesn't understand talk about '120g' [1g = acceleration due to gravity, 32 ft/sec^2]; didn't know we had vetoed cast iron years ago. ...

11 February: At Contr's meeting re loss of *P of W* he took a lot of convincing before agreeing she was hit by 3-4 torps. during the first attack. My suggestion re no side scuttles below weather deck was received with a frown; also when I raised the question of 5.25s being independent of electric power nobody was keen. Re *Lion* I said why I wanted to re-design. I have to put up a short paper. ...

12 February: S Payne [Stephen, Manager Constructive Dept (MCD) at Devonport, youngest of three RCNC brothers, Owen A (died 1943) and M P, retired Superintendent of AEW] of D[evon]port called v. pleased with himself as usual. Walker [J F, MCD] of Chatham [Dockyard] called.

Cameron was one of fifty elderly US destroyers transferred to the RN in 1940. Several were in poor condition, requiring refits in the UK to make them fully operational. She was under refit at Portsmouth when she was damaged during an air raid on 6 December 1940 and blown off the blocks in No 8 drydock. She was never fully repaired but used for damage control investigations and shock trials before being scrapped in 1944. (*Blackman collection*)

Both are v. perturbed about poor quality of shipwright apprentices entering. Both say they have good young ACs [assistant constructors] on S/Ms [submarines – both dockyards were building them]. Kennett [E G, now Portsmouth MCD] called, all hands on *Antonia* [Cunard liner being converted to repair ship], S/Ms nearly stopped & fl. dock [*AFD.18*] stopped, *Cameron* ['Town' class destroyer bombed in drydock at Portsmouth 5 Dec 40, never fully repaired, used for shock trials] going back. ...

13 February: ... Dunstan called, had short talk on destroyers; he said finish of last 2 of J. Brown's was bad [*Onslow* and *Paladin*].

14 February: To Haslar, arrived 12.00, looked at Cav[itation] tunnel [for testing propellers], short talk on steering tank & Palmer [S J, constructor, later at Portsmouth Dockyard]. ...

16 February: At Haslar. ... Looked at *Lion* with propellers for[war]d. Horrid is the first impression. [The plan was to have about 25 per cent of the total power forward. There would be an awkward run of shafting from the engine room and smaller diameter, less efficient propellers.] Had a brief look round. Saw *MTB.73*'s propeller in tunnel, air cavities seem to collapse abaft the blade, is this a reason why we don't get erosion trouble in these craft? ... Saw fully HA destroyer rolling at full speed. Left 13.15. Arrived Bath 17.45 [presumably by car].

17 February: E H Mitchell called, said everything going well in USA [US was supplying equipment for dock], told Bryant to get him air passage to India [*AFD.23* was building there] told Mitchell to contact Adml Turner. ... Message from 1st Sea Lord wanting strength of *Graph* [ex-*U 570*] steel, he has told Winston the wrong yarn. ... Dep Contr said Fraser is going & Wake-Walker is to be Contr [Vice Admiral W F, previously FO 1st Cruiser Squadron]. Saw Kingcome [Rear Admiral J, Deputy E in C] re new mach[iner]y for *Lion*.

19 February: At Admy. Saw film of loss of *Barham* [torpedoed 25 Nov 41] certainly when ship had turned/heeled thro' 90° mag[azine] aft blew up. Why?? Oil fuel fire Contr says shake up like that might send charges off. Then *Nigeria* with bow gone steaming at 25 knots v. good. Saw Contr re *Graph* steel he sent for DTM [now Captain G B Middleton] who said 'Not guilty' to charge that he had told 1st SL *Graph* steel was 'wunderbar': Contr told Sanders to see [Lord] Cherwell [Frederick Lindemann, Churchill's scientific adviser]. At 3 p.m. described to 1st L, 1st SL rest of Sea Lords and a host of Naval staff damage to *P of W* & why we think there may have been 8 torps in her certainly 7: a little heckling but I must have convinced as 1st SL now wants me to give same talk to

C in C HF. [Probably two torpedoes port in first attack, four starboard in second attack.] Talk with Contr over dam[age] control: *Lion* re-design & Woolworth.

20 February: Baker [R, landing craft constructor] back from Washington, his account of US procedure is very interesting. Much red tape, dept. [department] jealousy, long time in preparation but after those rocks have been safely negotiated full speed ahead at a great pace. ... Agreed to Gibbons [A J T, constructor] & Matthews [F W, constructor] having lessons of 2 years of war (secret & personal).

21 February: Wake-Walker's app[ointment]t as Contr has become known. Got in touch with Cotton who tho' still sick is getting about, said that for the Country's sake Wake W & Simeon must pull together & we can't afford to lose S. from Bath. I thought that on the Board of A[dmiralty] the Contr's side [materiel] was too few compared to Staff side. What about Simeon being on the Board. Cotton thought it a good idea but nothing could be done till W-W is well in the saddle. ...

23 February: ... V A Usborne [retired Rear Admiral C V, of Fairmile] called re making AMCs [Armed Merchant Cruisers] &c more difficult to sink, agreed our buoyancy drum scheme as good as anything practical. Found from him that DA/SW [Creasy] was responsible for yarn that *Graph* steel was wunderbar. He & Holt [W J] were in Fairmile D [MTB/MGB] yesterday & fairly well pleased. Worked on new AC Sketch Design. Letter from Contr about damage to *Scharnhorst* or *Gneisenau* by mines [on 12 February in escape from Brest] wants estimate of time for repair, got Offord busy. Sent on docket re torp prot[ection] of capital ships. Read yarn from C in C HF criticising our cap[ital] ships.

24 February: ... Redshaw came with Woolworth Legend [warship characteristics] & dwgs, passed him to Johnson [H T] & Mitchell [A], later these 3 with Bartlett came in, I agreed to their actions & dictated docket. ... I consulted Lillicrap re welding thick inner bottom ... Bartlett & Perrett are a bit raw & rather nervous about welding but their hearts are in the right place. ...

25 February: ... Yapp [Frederick, director of Vickers-Armstrongs] phoned me estimate of cost for former [Woolworth carrier] which checks with Dippy's [J W, costing constructor]. DCW up in arms this is no longer 'simple'. I am now giving 27 mos as time to build. [The first, *Colossus*, took 30 months.] Think US study of *Bismarck* agrees very much with ours. Asked Callander if he can reconstruct Jap small S/M. Saw Dep Contr re *Scharnhorst* yarn, he agreed & I sent it to Contr (6 mos to repair): also left with him Stability Book & dwgs of Jap small S/M. ...

26 February: Lt. Cdr. [C W] McMullen late Gunnery Officer of *P of W* called, said Leach's son was <u>not</u> in the ship [midshipman in cruiser *Mauritius*], he thought the first attack scored only 1 hit altho' he felt 2 or 3 shocks all about the same time, he was in DCT [director control tower]. He held strong & definite views on damage control with which I agree. ... Yesterday Rowell (H.L.) rang re P Cl [destroyers], said if disorganisation resulted he should not alter armt [armament].

27 February: ... FO(S) & Sims called, lunched them then very successful meeting of Dep Contrs. On Job 82 [Varley's design of midget submarine *X.3*]; wrote Callander for help. ... A long but good day.

28 February: Pigott kicking over 'R' Cl stern [destroyers *Rotherham* and *Racehorse*, stern slightly wider than 'N' class], replied insisting politely. ... With Lillicrap went thro' steam v[ersus] Diesel dynamos & signed, copies to E in C & DEE. ...

2 March: At Admy. Had a go at Contr about the c'tee to investigate vulnerability. Said I objected to such terms of reference which prejudged the issue. If c'tee was only to examine *P of W* it was unfair, they should also examine *Illustr[ious]*, *Kelly*, *Javelin* &c which had done very well. Said I didn't mind [Maurice] Denny but was he an 'independent' shipbuilder? Also [if] W-W [Wake-Walker] ex DTM if [is?] on a c'tee to discuss torps, I should be on a c'tee to discuss ships. Contr promised to send me terms of ref. I said announcement of 'vulnerability' was a grave political error handing out on a plateful to Goebbels.

5 March: ... Gunner Luxton & Shipwright Murch of *P of W* here. Worked on *P of W* report, don't like the part about evacuating 5.25's mags & shell rooms port, too much of a hurry to get out leaving doors open. This clears up the mystery of flooding to M.L. [middle line]. Survivors seem to put length of damage port down to shafts which I cannot believe. They do the same for the hit aft of Y.

8 March: ... Cole came in re *Campbeltown* [ex-US destroyer modified at Devonport for raid on St Nazaire] & *Burza* [Polish destroyer], I agreed. ...

11 March: Arrived Inverness about 11.00 [sleeper from Euston]. ... Left [by car] about 12.45 & arrived Thurso about 16.15. Had tea with NOIC [Naval Officer in Charge] Thurso (Capt Hurcombe) very pleasant. Left in Hunt Cl. *Wilton*. [Completed 18 Feb.] Bridge is really draughty; must stir up Cole. Arrived *KGV* about 6 p.m. Some talk with C in C [Tovey] just back from *Tirpitz* hunt, he missed her. He is having a barging match with CNS [Chief of Naval Staff was 1st Sea Lord, Pound] who wants him to go too near Norway to screen Russian convoys.

12 March: In *KGV*. Gave talk to C in C & about 50 Admirals, captains &c on loss of *P of W* & then a short talk about loss of *Ark R[oyal]*. Discussions & questions afterwards which roamed over every conceivable topic made me very tired as I had to keep alert on all sorts of things [but who better than Goodall?]. C in C doesn't want Mastodons nor speed. Curteis [Vice Admiral A T B, Flag Officer *Renown*] & Daniel [Captain C S, Chief Staff Officer] said we must have speed. C in C wants ships in self-contained subdivisions. After lunch had a go at ship with Holt [N G], Sutherby, Eng[ineer] & Spwt [shipwright]. We <u>must</u> do something about the 5.25 supply. Had tea with Capt Patterson [W R, CO of *KGV*] & went thro' WT.ness [watertightness] & dam[age] control. Left *P of W* report with him & one with CO *Duke of York*.

13 March: To *Victorious*. Saw her smashed boat. Went thro' *P of W* & *Ark R.* & left *Ark R.* report with Capt. Bovell [H C, CO *Victorious*]. Looked at his proposed WT.ness alt[eratio]ns. He is nervous about not ventilating store rooms as he has sweating troubles. Went to see one & left problem with Holt. To *Renown* & had talk with Curteis on X general grounds, he is a sensible stick. Lunch with CS 10 [10th Cruiser Squadron] (Burrough) [Rear Admiral H M, in *Nigeria*] very cheerful & then went into *Fiji* pts. which were well considered but I did not agree to two of them. Then to RA(D) [Rear Admiral Destroyers, now Rear Admiral R L Burnett]; his engineer a most awful groaner. Tribals cracking everywhere &c &c but Ad. Burnett a cheerful philosophic soul. CS 10 (Bonham Carter) very cheerful from *Sheffield*.

14 March: CS 10 said *Sheffield* can steer & steam but damage pretty extensive [mined 4 Mar]. Went to Lyness & had talk with Ad. H F Namara [Rear Admiral P Macnamara, Admiral Superintendent, Lyness Dockyard], he said Moon doing very well but lacks tact. ... Went to see underground oil tanks. Had lunch with ACOS (Admiral Commanding Orkneys & Shetland, now Vice Admiral L V Wells) very pleasant. After tea long discussion with C in C, C of S [Chief of Staff, Commodore M M Denny], C of F [Chief of Fleet], FCO [Fleet Communications Officer?], FEO [Fleet Engineer Officer, Captain D C Ford], Flag Capt [Captain P J Mack] & Sutherby re pts raised by C in C & the work I had done during my visit. ...

15 March (Sunday): Too thick to fly. Long talk with C in C & COS. They asked if I had been depressed by my visit, I said 'No' but certainly 'not elevated'. Summing up I feel that tails are not up as stiff & erect as they should be. Ford the FEO is a carping critic, if he would only give his attention to engines and get them improved, we would have better

ships. Left in *Ashanti* at about 11.00, landed Thurso 12.45, a wild drive to Inverness going 80-90 occasionally I was car sick 3 times. We got to platform as train was moving 15.40 & hurled ourselves in.

19 March: Cleared up paper accumulation at last. Preece called to say 'Goodbye' he retires next Sunday, he opened the ball & we had it out: I spoke of electric cooking, turbos [generators] v. Diesels, variable pitch propellers when he side-tracked me or turned down our schemes also Diesels for Bangors [minesweepers]; he wouldn't say where he is going. [He later joined the Board of boilermakers Foster Wheeler.] DCW back from Glasgow very perturbed about *Implac.* at Fairfields [ordered Oct 1938, suspended 1940, launched Dec 1942] ... [Mr Justice A T] Bucknill C'tee is going to *Anson* [*P of W* sister building by Swan Hunter] tomorrow.

20 March: Message from *Nelson*, wanting A's & A's as one boiler room could flood over to the other if severely damaged, we ought to have had our eyes open to this, trouble is as much deeper than originally. [Design draft was often a low figure that took little account of all the loads likely to be carried in service, possibly chosen to show that the 'design' speed had been obtained at a low displacement – 'speed' was another design figure much higher than actual service experience.] ... Read Report on

Steam turbine-powered gunboats of 8,000 shp to be capable of 35 knots were the Admiralty response to the E-boat threat in late 1940. Fifty were planned until it was found that there was insufficient manufacturing capacity; only seven were completed. Operations showed that they needed additional armament, protection and fuel, adding 50 per cent to their fully-loaded displacement (260 tons). This plus an inadequate boiler reduced their speed to 30 knots. *SGB.5* seen here in April 1942 was completed by Hawthorn Leslie (Yard No 647); she was renamed *Grey Owl* in 1943. (*Author's collection*)

loss of *Barham* (A/S inefficient) 4 torps about eng. room to X turret. Signed paper about Oerlikons in *Gambia*.

21 March: ... W J Holt back from SGBs who have broken fore ends of their bilge keels, he thinks Fairmile D superior [as anti E-boat?]; tho' form of SGB is good, ship depends on <u>one</u> boiler, <u>one</u> fuel pump, to make move in harbour, she is towed to save raising steam in big boiler.

22 March (Sunday): Yesterday E in C beat DNC 3-1 in soccer Final, I saw part of match too cold to hang about. ... Went into welded TLCs with Hannaford & agreed. [Whessoe built the first all-welded LCT Mark 4 in 1943.] ...

25 March: With Hickish [J R, assistant constructor] by car to Portsmouth. Arrived about 11.10. Saw C in C [James] who told me Little [Admiral Sir C J C] was relieving him: C in C very keen that Admy should delegate more to Cs in C (administration not technical matters) I told him RCNC should be Naval, he agreed. With Kennett, Wright, Hickish, Brooking, Lister & Mr E [?] went into *Sirius* [cruiser fitting out], Yard promised to do quite a lot, cable passages the nut we left uncracked. Lunch with A[dmiral[Sup[erintenden]t [Clarke], Kennett, Gawn there. Saw *Antonia*, Yard has a huge job to finish by time [completed August as *Wayland*]. I am still certain that this Depot Ship policy (Depot & warship & W/T ship) is all wrong. Looked at *Cameron* & T Cl. S/Ms [*Tireless* and *Token* were building in No.15 drydock]. To Haslar. ... Saw Italian 2 man S/M & explosive 2 step boat. ...

26 March: ... Attended INA Council Meeting [Goodall was a Vice President of the Institution of Naval Architects], then lunch. I sat between Chatfield [President of INA, former First Sea Lord and Controller who would have had many dealings with Goodall] and Pigott, former very pleasant, latter anxious to tell me that McNeill not he, had put Aberconway [Lord, chairman of John Brown] up to make a stir. [Not sure what about.] At General Meeting gave P.M.L. [Parsons Memorial Lecture, an annual prestigious occasion delivered to each of the marine technical institutions in turn. Goodall's title was 'Sir Charles Parsons and the Royal Navy'] from about 15.10 to 16.00, audience bigger than I expected, some went to sleep, the older men who had worked with Parsons (S S Cook, Col. Smith) very pleasant in talk afterwards. ...

27 March: A thick day, getting my head above water. Letter from Bucknill committee calling me to attend on Tuesday. ... Chislett [H W J, overseer at Swan Hunter] phoned that C'tee had seen *Anson*: Wake-W. went off on hatches & trunks being weak. ...

30 March: Most of day on *P of W*. Trying to get to the bottom of what happened is a head-aching job; even today I have modified my views. Dep Contr came over & was a great help. Must try & clarify my views in the train tomorrow [Bath to London]. ... Inspected drawings that will be sent to C[ammell] Laird tomorrow to start new aircraft carrier [*Ark Royal*]. ...

31 March: To Bucknill C'tee. In morning I gave my reasons for at least 7 torps, & damage in neighbourhood of 5.25's. In afternoon other damage. Wake-Walker seemed to dominate c'tee Bucknill was very quiet, taking notes, asked 1 or 2 leading questions. I got the impression he feels submerged at present but is taking it all in & will finish more strongly. Denny has his staff on the job, I think he is going to take the line that he could have designed a better ship. [Unlikely, Denny had no experience of larger warships.] ...

1 April: ... With DDNC [Sanders] & Nancarrow [G C, constructor] went into 5.25″ hoists' WT.ness in KGVs & wrote DNO. Agreed to Williamson's yarn re test depths of S/Ms [typically collapse depth about 80 per cent over design diving depth]. ... DCW says Urch (WPS London) has got 12 mos for bribery; bad show. [Possibly for placing repair contracts with favoured firms.]

3 April: AA gunfire last night. With Mathias [T L] & Bessant discussed new destroyer design, dealt with E in C's proposal to use Yarrow's Yugo-Slav machy [ordered from Yarrow in 1938 for destroyer *Split* building at Split] & with statement that Germans have four 5.9″ guns in destroyers. Nice letter from M.M. Denny re *Kenya*, sent extract to M[urray] Stephen. ... 'S' Class dived to 350' & stood it well [design diving depth 300ft]. ...

6 April: Easter Monday but no holiday for me. In office all day getting ready for Bucknill C'tee. Lessons of *P of W* & *Bismarck*, helped by Offord & Sutherby. Dealt only with urgent papers.

7 April: In London at Bucknill C'tee. Atmosphere much more free & easy. I gave lessons of *P of W*. Wake-W. & Denny much more interested in details than policy, tho' Wake-W agreed there should be a constructor in every big ship. Went on to *Bismarck* & took (with success I think) Simeon's tip 'She was a big ship & naturally had in much that we couldn't put into *P of W*. Not so us'. [KGV deep load displacement 42,000 tons, *Bismarck* 49,000 tons.] Then I got in my bleat about the way Civil Lord [Captain A U M Hudson MP] had announced this c'tee & the Judge took it well. We finished with tea & a general chat on the type of ship for the Navy of the future.

9 April: Visited St[othert] & Pitt to see Chariot [two-man mini-submarine], Winette & their telemotor pump. ... *Dorsetshire* & C[orn]wall* sunk [cruisers 5 Apr off Ceylon].

10 April: ... Turner [Vice Admiral Sir F R G, new E in C] at Bucknill C'tee apparently said extensive flooding could be caused by shaft (this doesn't gee as list not then enough). ... *Hermes* sunk [aircraft carrier 9 Apr off Ceylon]. Guess these sinkings are making P.M. [Churchill] revive the Seadrome [a floating airfield] heresy. ...

11 April: ... told Bryant to issue instruction that in future all invention papers are to go straight to Senior Officer first. ... Discussed Priority with Hannaford, he is a bit too full of objections.

13 April: ... Talk with McCarthy re *Montclare* at H & W, Southampton, he agrees it is a very big job for this firm but he cannot put the ship elsewhere. [P&O liner to convert to depot ship.] ... Baker [now Superintendent of Landing Craft SLC] back from talk re simplifying TLCs: result a lemon. ...

15 April: Contr here a.m. fully HA destroyer, he kicked out stabilizer [for more oil], phoned DNO who must say this is all right. ... Hannaford said Curtis of Looe [prolific builder of wooden motor minesweepers] had shut up thanks to Jubb & Treasury [possibly due to delayed progress payments]. Dep Contr will take up. I got pushed a bit further towards filling OF [oil fuel] tanks with water [to improve stability after fuel consumed]. ... Hannaford says Coxwell [C B, Principal Assistant Secretary, Admiralty] & Treasury are climbing down over Curtis.

16 April: ... Offord back from Special Bomb trial (Cherwell's) bomb did extraordinarily well. [Tallboy?]

17 April: Contr wants conference on *Graph* applications to a new design, saw Dep Contr. He will father, also talked to him of *P of W* he is toning down a bit, got DDNC to look into whirling of shaft. Also talked re kicking out stabiliser from new design destroyers, he agreed it was too much a snap decision, he thinks Bofors want ship stabilisation also. [The twin 40mm Hazemeyer was a tri-axial mounting.]

19 April: ... Got Cole in to get busy on endurance of Hunts if D[enny] Br[own] stabiliser removed. [Already done in *Brissenden* but not sister *Brecon*.]

21 April: Amended costing screed & sent to Cotton. Miller [?E J, Admiralty Secretariat] came over with it. C. suggested omitting that we didn't know establishment charges in 1936, I agreed reluctantly. [The Public Accounts Committee reported on warship prices to Parliament in 1943 – see 28 October 1943.] ... Brinton [L J, assistant constructor] told me what he had done for draught over Hunt bridges, a good lad. ...

22 April: At Admy. Contr & W-W. listened to my D[enny] B[rown] stabilisers proposals, said we didn't want them if gunnery was satisfactory

(Sir) Amos L Ayre (1885–1952) was an eminent shipbuilder called upon first in 1939 to take on the role of Director of Merchant Shipbuilding at the Ministry of Shipping, then the wider role of Deputy Controller of Merchant Shipbuilding & Repairs at the Admiralty in 1940. With his younger brother Wilfred, they had set up the new Burntisland shipyard in 1918, making it the most efficient British shipyard building cargo ships in the 1930s. It featured in the wartime shipbuilding film 'Steel Goes to Sea'. In 1936 Ayre became Chairman of the newly-formed Shipbuilding Conference, the shipbuilders' trade association formed to represent the industry to government. Goodall respected Ayre's wide experience and technical abilities; they had many discussions and correspondence, especially concerned with resources. Ayre returned to the Conference in 1944 to tackle the problems of post-war shipbuilding. (*The Shipbuilder*)

without. ... D [Sir Charles G Darwin, Director of National Physical Laboratory] wants shipbuilding industry more research-minded, told A Ayre [Sir Amos L, now Deputy Controller of Merchant Shipbuilding & Repair] who said 21 millions to turn over from riveting to welding.

23 April: Seal [E A, Deputy Secretary, British Admiralty Delegation in America] called, said USA sinkings off East Coast are going on because 'US will do nothing till everything is planned'.

25 April: ... Air Raid about 23.00-00.15, heavy bomb near Lansdown Grove Hotel [where Goodall stayed in Bath], our windows all out; ceilings in hotel down but not ours.

26 April (Sunday): ... took in some of DEE's staff as he has UXB [unexploded bomb] outside Tech. School. Dealt with St Nazaire raid, annoying remark about a 'a man from Bath' caused 24 hrs delay. With DDNC discussed *Suffolk* stability & altered docket, then Board Margin & decided to recommend 2% [of standard displacement to allow for future changes].

27 April: Air raid about 01.20-05.00. Many bombs & fires in Bath. F[red] Bryant killed, a very heavy loss especially to me personally. ... Franklin of St. & Pitt called, Chariot destroyed thinks 1 month delay but Pamplin thinks only days. ... Sampson [C P, constructor] killed at Malta,

wrote Mrs S. ... Worked on beam of new design *Lion* as compared with *Bismarck* & drafted remarks.

28 April: ... Paper from 1st SL re converting Q[ueen] M[ary] & Q[ueen] E[lizabeth] into aux[iliary] ACs, wrote Pigott. ... Panic about our bomb showing signs of going off at about 15.30 & all the staff without orders

Like so many other larger gun mountings, the twin 5.25in Mark II for the *Dido* class cruisers were delayed. 'A' mounting (Reg No 43) for *Sirius* is seen at Vickers-Armstrongs' Scotswood works on 14 January 1942 shortly before shipment to Portsmouth Dockyard. (*Author's collection*)

from me climbed out; disgraceful; however the military did rope off the road opposite. Discussed with DDNC the *Bismarck* & 1st SL's minute saying 'we knew her length/beam ratio gave good results', sent two alternative yarns with letter to Contr: told DDNC to get out a docket re rolling periods of cap[ital] ships.

29 April: Another quiet night T.G. AR warning about 11.40 to 12.10. We are all now out of the Gr[and] Pump Room [former hotel now DNC offices] & scattered. Main body with me in the Pump Room. DDNC [Lillicrap] & Williamson doing well, but there are an awful lot of scare orders flying about which seem to come from nowhere in particular & are <u>not</u> sent to me.

1 May: Our UXB was dug up last night; about 5ft long so I should say 500 kilos. ... Spoke T L M[athias, who had survived the same bomb hit] about Bryant's job, for the present he & Lillicrap will carry on between them. Talked with Hickey preparatory to *Sirius* turret trouble meeting. ... Attended public funeral. R[oman] C[atholic] part too long. ...

2 May: ... Drafted yarn on Lithgow's docket re financing firms for welding. Contr likes G Bryant's [battleship constructor, Fred's nephew] yarn re re-design *Lion* & *Bismarck*'s beam, had typed & signed. ... Went on leave.

10 May (Sunday): Returned to Bath [presumably from his house in London] after a grand week. T.G. I needed it.

11 May: ... *Sirius* trouble has blown over. Much cogitation over [F] Bryant's successor. FO(S) wants to weld pressure hulls of S/Ms, I think Vickers is playing up to him. [Redshaw's son Leonard at Barrow was a great advocate of welding, after the war managing director there.] *Q Mary* conversion doesn't look nice to me. [Not surprising, converting a liner with many decks to an aircraft carrier with hangars and flight deck would be a massive job.] Stability of *Dunnottar Castle* [Union Castle liner to be converted] & *Avenger* [US-built escort carrier] not too good, but *Furious* is now much better.

12 May: At Admy. W-W. took NC, Repairs & Conversions meetings. I made a bloomer over pumping arr[angemen]ts for TLCs. Confusion over Office Acquaint to accelerate Naval prog[ramme] by 30%. I said it was 'hot air' but it was explained this only meant keeping present dates which generally went back 30%. ... Spoke Hopkins & fixed up his coming as SCW (TLC) [Superintendent of Contract Work, Tank Landing Craft. He had been seconded to the Ministry of Supply.]

14 May: ... Interview of University candidates [for RCNC], Cambridge sent 2 poor specimens, London good, Sheffield & Belfast moderate. [Why

none from Newcastle (Durham) or Glasgow, shipbuilding areas?] Packed up to move to Warminster Rd. Dealt with *Dunnottar Castle* conversion to Aux[iliary] AC & agreed stability. [She was actually converted to a troopship, while *Pretoria Castle* was converted.] ...

15 May: ... Moved out of Lansdown Grove Hotel to Hopecote Combe Down. Absolutely lovely end of day.

16 May: ... Fairly straight at Warminster Road, thanks to Bamford, Carter & Miss Mayhew. ... Dealt with Williamson points re Varley [retired Commander C, designer of X craft midget submarine] & Chariots. ...

17 May (Sunday): In office a.m. N G Holt called: with DDNC discussed damage to *KGV* when she rammed *Punjabi* [destroyer lost 1 May], turning of *Washington* with twin rudders [US battleship]. ... *London* [cruiser] leaks; destroyer foc'sle plating & vent trunking, *Victorious* bow framing. ...

18 May: ... Attended Dep Contr's meeting on organisation in event of invasion, he will send draft & we are to send instructions. Dealt with twin rudders. *Trinidad* lost, fire according to report [bombed 14 May]. ... Pigott re *QM*'s conversion, answered. Woollard doesn't want Prof[essor] of NA [Naval Architecture] at Newcastle [the post had been vacant since Abell left] & I said I could not now spare him. Dealt with 1st Lord's paper about Mrs Kock's allegation that all my staff took gifts. [More than a bottle of whisky at Christmas?]

20 May: ... Chatten [H R P, constructor] called, he was in *Trinidad* when she was bombed & ultimately sunk, a bit shaken, didn't sound a very good show to me. Sent on *Colombo* [cruiser] rearmament paper. ... Fraser called to say 'Goodbye' made a nice little speech to ADNC's & Chiefs. I said it had been a pleasure to serve under him. [Fraser had been appointed Flag Officer 2nd Battle Squadron.]

21 May: ... With Lillicrap went thro' spaces in *KGV* where more OF might be stowed. ... Read O. Bellasis [Captain R Oliver-Bellasis, Deputy Director Training & Staff Duties] on new cap. ship, roughed out schemes for large & small, thought over various ideas for a ship of a new type but nothing good occurred to me. ...

23 May: With Johnson & Mitchell discussed Pigott's letters & new dwgs showing improved arrgts for converting *QM* & *E*. Drafted letter (signed later after J. had agreed) saying before I put fwd, I should like to be sure 3 lifts practicable also 45' × 45' also time not affected. Johnson to phone McNeill. Looked into Wilf[red] Ayre's [Amos' brother, chairman of Burntisland Shipbuilding who had started the business together in 1918]

Vice Admiral (Sir) Bruce Fraser (1888–1981) was Third Sea Lord and Controller from 1939 to 1942, halfway through Goodall's time as DNC. He was a gunnery officer, a frequent route to top roles in the RN. He was gunnery officer in the battleship *Resolution* in 1916, on the staff of the gunnery school HMS *Excellent*, in the Naval Ordnance Department in 1922, and Mediterranean Fleet gunnery officer (as a Commander) in 1924. Seagoing commands included the cruiser *Effingham* in 1929 and the carrier *Glorious* in 1936. In between he was Director of Naval Ordnance 1933–6. These postings plus being Chief of Staff to the C in C Mediterranean Fleet in 1938 put him on the shortlist when a new Controller was hurriedly sought after Henderson's death in 1939. Goodall had a high regard for Fraser and his awareness of the Navy's materiel needs, considering that as a civilian that he could speak his mind more freely than if he was a (subordinate) naval officer. However, he sometimes thought that Fraser listened more to uniformed officers and scientists than to himself, who was the Board's principal technical adviser. Fraser went on to become C in C Home Fleet in *Duke of York* (seen on board here) at the sinking of the German battleship *Scharnhorst* in December 1943. He was an obvious choice to take command of the new British Pacific Fleet in 1944, so was the British representative at the Japanese surrender in September 1945. After the war he was C in C Portsmouth before being promoted to Admiral of the Fleet and First Sea Lord in 1948. Showered with honours, he retired in 1951, dying unmarried 30 years later. (© *National Maritime Museum, London AD15345*)

grain carrier as fighter carrier [MAC ship, merchant aircraft carriers]. Talk with Offord on armour v. shaped charge. ...

26 May: ... With DCW discussed ACs. at H & W and Sw H [Swan Hunter] & agreed, former want plant latter should put off Port line ship. [*Port Sydney*, later converted to escort carrier *Vindex*.]

27 May: ... Wrote to DSR [Wright] to see if he can provide a chap to run X ray apparatus for testing welds during building of ACs. ...

29 May: In London. ... Saw Vice Contr [Tower] who is fussed over engines for MTBs &c really this work should be at Bath. Saw Contr [now formally Wake-Walker] over Future Cap. ship, he had not thought deeply, neither had ACNS(W) [McGrigor] but Vice Contr said the day of the big gun capital ship had gone. Contr agreed I should put up a yarn that RCNC should be in RN. Saw DSR about advisory panel going into underwater exp[erimen]t organisation (Goodeve [of DMWD] back as thorn in our side). [Goodeve, a Canadian, was a Fellow of the Royal Society who helped develop counters to magnetic mines and the manufacture of 20mm guns and was successfully applying scientific methods to operational problems.] Saw [Rear Admiral H B] Rawlings ACNS(F) [Assistant Chief of Naval Staff (Foreign)] who said the big gun capital ship is <u>not</u> dead. Told US converting their new cruisers & cap. ships into ACs. [*Independence* class.]

31 May: ... Reports from USN re damage to *Saratoga* & *Enterprise*.

1 June: Skinner [H E, Constructor Commander with Home Fleet] called, described end of *Edinburgh* & *Trinidad* both ships did well, *Edinburgh* particularly. He seemed a bit shaken, asked him if he <u>wanted</u> to be relieved, he said 'No, but he had done 2 years & he was 40!' Mt.Batten wants 2 constructors [now Chief of Combined Operations]. ... discussed with DDNC welding flight deck, he suggested welding OB [outer bottom] butts [transverse joints] but I haven't the courage yet. ...

2 June: At Admy to attend Shipyard Labour meeting. 1st L opened mainly Guff & then left. Contr kept to 3 pts. dilution, female labour & piecework, 2700 skilled (sic) men to come within next 3 mos. Fin[ancial] Sec[retary] [G H Hall MP] said Shipyard management was under suspicion & more could be done. ... Lithgow said shipyard practices are obsolete, I told him afterwards Satan was rebuking sin. After lunch FOICs mainly had a go at Trade Union unhelpfulness but 1st L & Fin. Sec. were not there. ...

3 June: Sent Contr our information re *Washington*'s machy w[eigh]t, also results of comparative tests of British & foreign [hull] forms. [The latest US battleships had more advanced steam conditions, so lower fuel consumption and a longer endurance than RN.] ... With DDNC & Bryant [G] discussed re-design of *Lion* & dictated notes, gave instructions for design with 2-triple 16″, having checked agreed that 3 twin 16″ give too big a ship.

9 June: At Admy. NC, repairs & conversions meetings dull. Wake-W looked ill & worried said he had a cold. Wanted to know how to cut these meetings down, I said 'Leave small stuff to Dep Contr.' *Ramillies* torpedoed near 'A' turret [30 May at Diego Suarez]. Had talk with Ayre

about efficiency of shipbuilding industry, he says on his side output per man is good. Had talk with Fowler [? Prof R H, Gunnery & Anti-Aircraft Warfare Division] & Wright [R H, constructor] on ACs of future (jet propulsion of aircraft may help us). 50° v. 80° elevation for HA guns. ...

10 June: ... Wrote DNI [Director of Naval Intelligence, Rear Admiral J H Godfrey] re QE [Queen Elizabeth] & Val[iant] getting more information from Ital[ian] prisoners re size & position of charges.

11 June: Birthday Honours out, RCNC & Shipbuilding get very little. Wrote Fin Sec, VCNS [Vice Chief of Naval Staff, now Vice Admiral H R Moore], Johnson, Cotton & others. Discussed RCNC into RN with Lillicrap who is opposed, redrafted yarn. ...

17 June: At Admy for Bucknill C'tee. Told Judge he had made a mistake in his first report & asked him to correct it. I pointed out where, he didn't like it. On Ark Royal I said contact torpedo low down would have flooded the length flooded but would have meant nobody escaping from S[tarboard] Blr [boiler] room; I believed it was a non-contact torpedo, agreed we had been optimistic in new D.C. [damage control] instructions about effect of one torpedo. ...

18 June: ... Morrison [John, shipyard manager] of H & W Belfast called for Unicorn [maintenance carrier] conference, he said H & W men doing fine but hampered by repairs: I phoned Contr. ...

19 June: ... Read Haslar report on bow rudder for Ark R. Not very impressed, shall we go to twin rudders aft as well? [Twin were indeed fitted, but not bow.] ...

22 June: ... Read Jackman's [W H, constructor] notes on last days at Singapore, looks as tho' place was left fairly intact. ...

23 June: ... With Hannaford, Watson & Holt [W J] discussed letter from men at Curtis's Totnes saying MMS work is a scandal, decided to write Montgomery [possibly an Admiralty financial man] & send Scott [? C, constructor], Holt & Lloyds [Register] man there. ...

24 June: G Bryant back from Anson, this is the 4th of KGV Cl. that has gone thro' trials without a hitch, a v.g. record even in peace time. Wallace [Brown Brothers] called, talked twin rudders & stabilizers, he is sure he can manage the former & that the latter in the fully HA would be a great improvement on present position. With Bartlett & Perrett discussed Ark R's Flight Deck where armour stops at sides & ends, agreed to their proposals tho' this means hangar armour will depend on riveted structure only. ...

29 June: At Birkenhead. In morning went round ships with Peake & Perrett. In spite of what Johnson [R S, managing director of Cammell Laird] said I thought there was plenty of slacking. *Argonaut* full of gilguys & gadgets I only hope all this RDF is of real value. S Cl. [submarine *P.216*] backwards because of Paxman engine. Looked at scheme for altering yard to take new *Ark R*, firm is doing well, saw [welded] test pieces for OB butts, biggest discussion was flight deck, finally agreed firm should weld 1½″ to see if we could take on single thickness with welded butts & edges.

30 June: In morning at Birkenhead for conference with CL & Vickers on welding submarines, dictated note. Neither Firm showed great enthusiasm to enlarge in order to produce more S/Ms of the simplified type. Must think of scheme for building complete pieces. In afternoon saw Bulkeley [G, Warship Production Superintendent, North West] on Grayson Rollo [Birkenhead ship repairers] scandal [the company had paid a subcontractor F H Porter Ltd £750,000 for fictitious employees], then with Leddra [C H, constructor] had a look at *KGV* [refitting at Liverpool]. Mack the CO [Captain P J] was very pleased, they have certainly done a lot of the improved WT.ness work but I was not happy over the 5.25″ supply. Had a look at *Aurora* [mine damage repairs at Liverpool], left by midnight.

2 July: Told Bartlett to tell Staff that *Em[erald]* & *Ent[erprise]* could be converted to AC as already described but a Fiji only to a fighter support ship as already described: better to start from scratch if a Fiji is to be built as an AC. Wrestled with paper accumulation, in particular dealt with semi-anonymous letter re Curtis & the Grayson Rollo &c scandals in NW area. Dealt with Soviet mission papers. ...

3 July: DCW back from Belfast where he was impressed. ... D of P [Director of Plans, Captain C E Lambe] has to go into the pros & cons of converting *Vanguard* (I to send him my part of the picture). ... Bartlett brought in dwg of No. 577 J. Br's conversion [refrigerated ship *Port Victor* converting to escort carrier *Nairana*], we can get in more A.C. [aircraft] than in *Activity* if we go to a lower hangar than *Act.* ...

4 July: Cdr. (E) Jameson [E W S] ANA [Assistant Naval Attaché] Washington called with a lot of information about US Naval Construction, which I went thro'. ...

5 July: ... Annoyed by paper from D of P rubbing in *S[outh] Dakota* [US battleship] endurance & *Lexington*'s [aircraft carrier] resistance to torpedo attack.

Destroyer *Gallant* had her bows blown off by a mine off Pantelleria on 10 January 1941 and was towed to Malta, but was irreparable and later sunk as a blockship. Relentless bombing of Malta damaged or sank many more ships in harbour. (*Blackman collection*)

7 July: Trevan [S N, Deputy WPS, North East] called, rubbed in necessity to see his staff is not open to bribery in any form (vide Mersey district scandal), he said Urch case & Blyth [see 24 July 1943] had made them all very careful. ... *Vanguard* to carry on as a battleship. Read letter from Joughin [J C, MCD, Malta Dockyard] to Bartlett, Malta a graveyard of ships [from bombing]. ...

8 July: ... Signed docket for new ADNC (Offord). ... Lillicrap's long absence is a trial.

9 July: At Admy. In train with Simeon talked of O.B. also he asked me to suggest a meeting on Sat 11th with FO(S) on X craft. ... Talk with D of P I did not agree to a constructor on Naval Staff [might go native?] ... At M[inistry] of Supply C'tee on armament development I got hot over Ordnance Board. Back to Admy but could not see Contr till 5.45 so I had no time to be diplomatic but blurted out I was against Fowler on the UW [Underwater] C'tee, he mumbled. I said I wanted Offord to go to USA in uniform, he said 'No'. I asked if Bucknill C'tee report was to be referred to me, he said it had gone to Board [of Admiralty] with my (sic) remarks (they are Dep Contr's not mine). A storm is brewing.

10 July: Lillicrap back T.G. He has been far North. *Washington* is a fine ship with good & bad features: former are endurance & quick turning. [US battleship temporarily based at Scapa Flow.] ... Long talk with

Hannaford about his worries from Contr. H. does <u>not</u> want to go back to London: I said 'Then you must be patient with this jumpy new broom'. …

11 July: Talk with Kingcome (E in C away) re endurance & heat in machy spaces: he told me what they were doing in *Vanguard* & *Ark R.* & thinks it better they should take on the wt. to make spaces cooler. …

15 July: Discussed Corvettes with Watson & Kimberley: then S/Ms at Scotts with Williamson: then 5th SL's letter [Rear Admiral A L St G Lyster, Chief of Naval Air Service] re armour on carriers' flight deck, then IAC's 17′ 6″ hangar [intermediate aircraft carrier, or light fleet carrier] with Bartlett, re latter said 'No. Effect on production would be too serious'. (Later Contr. agreed), then MTB forms with W J Holt. …

19 July (Sunday): In office a.m. …Went thro' *Dido* & *Fiji* 1st of class reports & drafted yarn to Dep Contr. Played for RCNC (Bath) v. Wills Hall students at Lawn Tennis; Wills Hall [Bristol] a lovely place & weather grand, won 6-3. [Goodall was a keen tennis player.] …

20 July: … Newnham [H E, constructor] from Singapore called, asked him to write yarn for Corps annals, he didn't think much of Army or Australians, eventually yard & docks were left practically intact. [The new 250 ton cantilever crane was toppled into the harbour.] … Agreed to put prot[ective] plating on SGBs.

22 July: … Fraser wants somebody to visit *Avenger* with a view to A's & A's & stability. I suggested Rayner but Bartlett wanted Johnson [H T] to go & I gave in: but it is curious that the men of 50 won't trust the youngsters. …

24 July: At Admy. Meeting of Advisory Panel 09.30: DTM held forth that Admy should do the work for everybody or at least be consulted, I agreed: I rubbed in that I wanted an Underwater Protection exp[erimen]t station at Portsmouth, DNC to provide the sup[erintenden]t, DTM the deputy, make their own structures except the full size, make up their own charges, have a hulk to fasten 1/3 scale models to & carry the recording instruments. Afterwards talked with DTM & G I Taylor [fluid flow scientist, Professor at Cambridge] re Unit & brought away notes, also *Niger* [mined 5 Jul]. Lunch with A Ayre, aired off to Lithgow about Bucknill, Ayre warned me of Tutin [J, naval architect]. Wright from USA very impressed, and said I was sending Offord. Saw Contr who brushed *Niger* aside (after I had spent a lot of time) agreed to Skinner for Syfret. Waited in Parl. Sec's room during Board meeting which broke up without discussing beam. Damn. [Goodall had probably put up a paper discussing the need for wider-beam capital ships, limited by present drydocks and Panama Canal.]

'D' class cruiser *Despatch* fresh from refit on the Tyne in late 1942. At 21 years old her draft has increased to about 18in deeper than as built, representing about 500 tons of extra weight and ballast. Goodall was reluctant to expend significant resources refitting such elderly ships, but the final decision was not his. (*Author's collection*)

25 July: ... Chinese Nav Attaché called with 2 men who want to learn submarines. ... 6 years as DNC and fed up. ...

29 July: ... Signed 'D' class [cruisers] reconstruction & gingered up Forbes re ballast in *Despatch*. Worked on Lobnitz simplification [builder of *Algerine* minesweepers]. ...

30 July: Adam of BC [J L, Chief Surveyor of British Corporation classification society], interesting talk on welding in USA he is not smitten by Unionmelt [type of automatic welding equipment] or 50 ton lifts [prefabricated units] & favours Mechanised Hand & 10 to 15 ton lifts. ...

31 July: ... Dunstan called, Denny-Brown stab[iliser] is not popular, mainly upkeep & fact that we have not trained the people in its peculiarities, told him to write to Wallace. Screed from Contr re IACs not lasting beyond 1946! Should be built accordingly [several light fleet carriers had lives of over 50 years], discussed with Bartlett & Mitchell & gave instructions. ...

1 August: John [W G] here after starting work as Sup[intenden]t of Welding D[evelop]ment, a treat to see a keen man who knows his job getting busy in the right way: told Stansfield [L D, now RCNC administrator] to get a 1st Cl. dr[aughts]man for him: rang E in C & DEE whom John saw. ...

2 August: ... Wrote FO(S) re Newton [R N, overseer at Scotts] sending an ass[istan]t to help with S/M film. ... After dinner Mrs XYZ called, said

her husband (under Steed) was leaving her, he had committed misconduct with ZYX (typist under Baker), hinted that more such went on in the dep[artmen]t.

3 August: Bank Holiday. In office a.m. Discussed XYZ with Stansfield & Lillicrap, both agreed that as long as a man does his job I can't interfere in his private affairs. ... Contr on his hind legs about action Hannaford took re *Implac.* & *Indef.* dates (Lithgow found out & butted in).

4 August: Steed [F H, ADNC] said XYZ good at his job, Stansfield reported ZYX a good typist, saw Cotton said I was doing nothing, he agreed. Later XYZ came to see me, asked if I could move him & he would then stop being a weak fool, thought this might get over my difficulty with C.E. [Civil Establishments?] re Vosper [A J, assistant constructor] for RACF [Rear Admiral Coastal Forces, Rear Admiral P K Kekewich], consulted Lillicrap, Steed & Watson who agreed & got XYZ to sign a paper that he would not disgrace the RCNC, started action to appoint him. ...

5 August: ... Russian Admiral, Commodore, 3 Captains & 1 Lieut. called with interpreter: had a talk on general Admiralty procedure, they seemed most anxious to know who got shot when anything went wrong: I said 'I did', they seemed to think the Firm [shipbuilder] should. ...

6 August: ... Talk with Contr re simplification I said I was <u>not</u> going to hold the baby as I was left to do for the corvettes, he said 'I'll do that'. I said then you will have to be very firm afterwards re A's & A's. ...

11 August: To Admy. Contr wanted to see me re McCarthy being king of corvettes &c (not MMS & Fairmiles) said I would go into this & let him know but I should have to find an ass[istan]t for McC. I said I didn't want Tutin. He discussed loss of *Naiad* [torpedoed in Med 11 Mar] & *Hermione* [torpedoed in Med 16 Jun]. ... Lunch with Brind [Rear Admiral E J P, now Assistant Chief of Naval Staff (Home)] & met Air M[arshal] Joubert de la Ferte [Air Officer Commanding Coastal Command]. Brind had Preece sized up well. ... Met K.P. [Admiral Sir C E Kennedy-Purvis, just appointed Deputy 1st Sea Lord] & later had a talk with him, he said (Dep 1st SL) will take all 1st SL's papers <u>not</u> operational & DNC will be on Building Planning C'tee. Craven [Sir Charles, now part-time adviser to Ministry of Production but also working for Vickers-Armstrongs] called, rather optimistic but he thinks we can do more warships at expense of merchant ships.

12 August: ... Letter from Capt. [B B] Schofield (Trade Div[ision]) re observations of ships of convoy in a storm, wrote Kent [J L, National

Physical Laboratory, expert on seakeeping]. With Watson dealt with aux[iliary] engine for SGBs [for manoeuvring in harbour]. Capt Morse [H E, now Naval Equipment Dept] called with new CO Dam[age] Control School (not impressed). ... Must get DDNC busy on spares for new ships coming from USA with American equipment. [Not strictly his job but he probably felt little was being done.] ...

13 August: ... Fuss at Repairs meeting over *Fame* [destroyer rebuilt at Chatham after running aground 17 Oct 40] & *Belfast* [cruiser reconstructing at Devonport after being mined 21 Nov 39]. Must keep my people up to scratch re A's & A's. Fuss at Conversions Meeting over *Montclare*. Discussion on ordering IACs & Cruisers showed 2 Cruisers possible, afterwards I examined with Butt [C J, now Superintendent of Labour & Materials] only possibility for 2 more appears to be Royal [Dock]yards. ... Callander rang he can make IAC hangar 17′ 6″ in all IACs without delay, I said 'Go Ahead'. [A good decision which enabled the light fleet carriers to have extended lives.]

14 August: Dentist. Spoke Dunlop [Rear Admiral S H, Deputy Director of Dockyards] & Bassett [G A, also a Deputy Director of Dockyards] re 2 cruisers one at P[orts]mouth, one at D[evon[port. ... Barlow report mainly hot air. [R Barlow of Metal Box was advising the Ministry of Production.] I said I would write R Rowell re riveting on ground [of prefabricated components]. Went thro' pts. of IAC: rubbed in they were merchant ships of 4 compt. standard [i.e. could withstand

(Sir) Charles W Craven (1884–1944) was a former RN Commander who came fully to Vickers in 1916 to manage their submarine building programme at Barrow. He succeeded James McKechnie as general manager there in 1923. After the merger to form Vickers-Armstrongs in 1928, he was called upon not only to run the company's shipyards but also its subsidiary, English Steel Corporation. At the outbreak of war he was chairman of V-A, but was called upon to fulfil a succession of Government roles, being Controller General of the Ministry of Aircraft Production in 1941. A part-time role at the new Ministry of Production allowed him to spend more time on V-A business. Goodall and he shared many confidences. Overwork contributed to the early death of this energetic man at 60. (*The Shipbuilder*)

flooding of four adjacent compartments but lacked warship protection, pumping & flooding]. Useful discussion on interchange of information

'F' class destroyer *Fame* and the 'Tribal' *Ashanti* were preparing to escort *King George V* from the Tyne to Rosyth when they ran aground at Whitburn on 17 October 1940; navigational marks had been changed. Temporarily repaired at Sunderland, *Fame* was towed to Chatham for rebuilding to September 1942 as an escort destroyer. *Ashanti* also required substantial rebuilding at Swan Hunter's Wallsend drydocks until 28 August 1941. (*Blackman collection*)

with US. I must get busy with McCloghrie [G, ADNC based in US]. Contr brushed aside *Argonaut*, evidently he had not read reports but would not admit L.C. [?] had sold him a gold brick. Described to him & ACNS(W) effect of damage on *Hermione*. Bassett said *London*, *Rod*[*ney*, bombed in Med 12 Aug] & *Nigeria* [torpedoed in Med 12 Aug, repaired at Charleston USA Oct 42–Jul 43] damaged.

15 August: ... Wrote Bassett to get more ships sent to USA. ...

16 August (Sunday): In office a.m. Read Battle of Matapan report, no new material lessons, aircraft in capital ships proved useful: apparently star shell do <u>not</u> make searchlights unnecessary.

17 August: Contr fussing about A's & A's (*Implac*. & letter from Barr re bomb room): while sympathizing with builders don't see any remedy, can't tell Staff that [a] ship completing 18 mos hence can't carry new type bombs. ... With Hickey & Hickish went into Didos WT.ness & *Euryalus* cracked plate aft, gave instructions. With Bartlett & Perrett went into rudders for *Ark R.* nothing in Haslar reports to give clear lead but single rudder not sufficiently good to back in face of opposition, decided on twins but asked Gawn for more expts.

19 August: ... Lunch with Craven who told me of Contr's meeting tomorrow with Firms, saw A Ayre who was in a white heat over Percy Mills [Controller General of Machine Tools] & Bentham another travelling circus. [Cecil Bentham was the chairman of Simon Engineering, commissioned to report on the shipyards' needs for new equipment.] I rang Contr who agreed I should be at meeting with Mills: Ayre rather pumped himself up too much, however we got Mills to understand he is not to tell yards how to build welded ships but to obtain for them the plant they want. ... Saw Contr, said I was being kept in ignorance, he smoothed me down & mentioned Bucknill, I took the opportunity to tell him how I felt about the Bucknill C'tee – an insult to me: he let out that C'tee had had the tip that all they had to investigate was whether DNC should be hanged.

20 August: ... Sent Dreyer, DNAD [Director Naval Air Division, Captain A R M Bridge], Dep Contr, DTSD 'Loss of *Yorktown*'. Also Dep Contr proposal to correct wrong acc[oun]t of loss of *P of W* in W.I.R. [?]

21 August: Worked on New Cruiser Design: a big ship for 9 – 6″ guns. Capt. Agar [A W S] called re *Unicorn*, interesting on end of *Dorsetshire*. ... Agar is all for the cafeteria system [for crew meals centrally rather than eating in their own messes]. ...

23 August: ... Reply from Rowell about riveting on ground, unhelpful & verbose, looks as tho' he is agin welding. ...

24 August: Visited Chinese on S/Ms they said they were getting what they wanted. Told W'son I did not agree to floating crane going from USA to Freetown in Fl. Dock. [*AFD.25* sank en route 15 Aug] ... Letter from Slayter CO *Liverpool* [W R, former DNO] saying his ship's stability is all right, answered. Wrote Merrington re experience of LCTs on Dieppe raid. ...

25 August: ... Signed docket for *Durban* [cruiser] to carry another 100 tons of ballast: Damn.

26 August: ... FO(S) [Horton] called, cheery as usual. Went on to Stothert & Pitts with W'son who said he was pleased with what he saw but gingered them up [on Chariots?]. Dep Contr read screed re A's & A's, not bad but too rosy a picture from shipbuilders' standpoint. SOs [senior RCNC officers] meeting, quite useful, dictated notes for DDNC & ADNCs & DCW, truth is every-body has been overworked for more than 6 years & calling for still further effort hasn't the response it had 6 years ago.

27 August: ... Inspected dept. a lot of space (Get Patterson [A P, constructor] or Baker here?) dwgs too elaborate, doing a lot of work

that normally would be farmed out to yards, doing a lot of production & yard dwgs.

31 August: … John [F O] of CL [Cammell Laird] phoned re time to fit sloops [*Cygnet* and *Kite*] for Arctic, said I would send somebody to cut down the work so that it could be done in time necessary for important operation. …

2 September: At H[awthorn] Leslie's, Rowell not there. Stephenson [C, shipyard general manager] said he could do no more riveting on the ground, this yard is being re-equipped well, space too restricted for much alteration. To Crowns Sunderland a small yard that cannot do much. To Palmers Hebburn, inspected Salvage Lifting Craft [*LC.17–22*]. Went on board *Kenya*, torpedo hit right forward, no petrol in tank, CO quite pleased with himself & keen on cutting out topweight. Called on FOIC [Maxwell] 1st thing, he is threatened with a strike because 50 electricians from London insist on Sunday work [to get overtime pay?].

3 September: To Smiths Dock Middlesbrough. Inspected models of corvettes, told Reed to give plenty of beam to new single screw corvettes

Three 'Hunt' class fitting out at Hawthorn Leslie's Hebburn shipyard in March 1942: (L-R) Polish *Slazak* (ex-*Bedale*), *Blean*, *Bicester*. Astern are the recently-launched tanker *Nicania* and destroyer *Quadrant* with the fast minelayer *Welshman* fresh from laying mines in the English Channel. Across the river fitting out at Swan Hunter can be seen the bow of the battleship *Anson*. No photographs have been found of her building or fitting out. (*Author's collection*)

[the first 'Castles' were ordered in December], good bilge keels but not a bar keel: we were wrong to resist jetty scheme. Sir T Edwards [Tristram, managing director, Smith's Dock] sore that we thought Co[mpany] wanted this for post-war, also very sore at getting no payment for the French corvettes. [Four 'Flowers' had been ordered before the war.] This yard is doing well but fitting out facilities are not sufficient. At Cleveland Bridge & other Tees yards building LCTs, didn't like propeller guard, these shallow draft craft are very flimsy [the Mark 4 was less robust than the Mark 3]; Lascelles [R, Principal Ship Overseer, ex Lloyd's Register] doing well. Phoned Hannaford re bottle-necks. Met Bentham who agrees to a [fitting-out] jetty for Smiths Dock, told him to visit Blyth.

4 September: To Swan Hunter, plenty of good welding there. *Newfoundland* [cruiser] cannot be finished this year in my opinion [completed 20 Jan 43]; trouble with ovality of after turret support. Looked at *Pretoria Castle* [converting to escort carrier]. This yard is very congested. Swan [C S] said Chislett [H W J, overseer] was doing well. Stanley [WPS North East] wants Chislett to give up Hawthorns. To V-A. Walker, Hendin very dickey A.D. I fear [Anno Domini i.e. age]. Craven phoned re mother ship for X craft [*Bonaventure*, converted Clan liner]. This yard could do more if fitting out were organised with more labour. At Blyth met the new manager Turnbull [William] who seemed all right, this is an old-equipped yard really cut in two by [dry]docks &c, but things are improving. [Later shipbreakers Hughes Bolckow were brought in for fitting out their escort hulls.] Bentham was there this morning.

6 September: ... I was called to Board Meeting last Thursday but could not go, serve 'em right. ...

8 September: With Lillicrap & Bartlett examined dwgs of US 45,000 ton carrier; neither L nor I had seen them before [presume *Midway* class]. ... Hickey said *Welshman* is to carry petrol on mining deck, phoned Dep Contr told Hickey to phone ERO [Emergency Repair Overseer] &c work not conforming to petrol regulations. ...

9 September: With Mathias & Bessant went into stability of US destroyers compared to ours, latter are superior in this respect & if we started off with [stability cross] curves like the Americans we should be in trouble early owing to all topweight that gets added in our service. [No RN-designed destroyer was lost due to poor stability in bad weather unlike several USN destroyers.]

11 September: ... Wrote Contr & Edwards re *La Malouine* [presumably about getting the Admiralty to pay Smiths Dock for the French 'Flowers'

'Flower' class corvette *La Malouine* was the first of four ordered by France in July 1939. Completed in May 1940, just as France was being overrun by Germany, she served in the Free French Navy. She is seen here later in the war with her forecastle extended aft, Type 271 radar and 20mm Oerlikons on the bridge wings. At first the Admiralty refused to pay Smith's Docks the final instalments, claiming that was a matter between the builders and the French Government (now Vichy) until Goodall pushed the Contracts Branch into taking a more sensible view now that the Admiralty had control of the vessel. She was scrapped in 1947 after target trials. (*Blackman collection*)

completed after the Germans invaded]. ... Dealt with Hedgehog [A/S mortar] on Fairmiles.

12 September: ... Contr phoned me re loan of overseer from Scotts for FO(S)'s film, I groaned but gave in & wrote FO(S). [Scotts were well behind on their building programme, with destroyers *Milne* and *Roebuck* having to be sent to Clydebank for completion.] Wrote Pigott re Clydebank being agin welding. [John Brown had increased their number of welders from less than 100 before the war to 220 by mid-1941, the same number as journeymen riveters, plus 280 holders-on and boys.] ... Sir T Edwards wrote he had received some money for [corvette] *La Bastiase*, told Contr. [The full cost would be about £85,000 each. The other two French 'Flowers' were completed as *Nasturtium* and *Fleur de Lys*, presumably paid for by the Admiralty.]

14 September: ... To Admy by car to attend Dep 1st SL's future building c'tee, it was decided the carrier should be the core of the Fleet of the future. Hurrah. I said a carrier could be given static protection as good

as a battleship except against heavy gunfire. I spoke of tractor screws [at fore end]. Afterwards had talk with DNAD on aircraft of the future, he is all for the 2-seater fighter.

17 September: Told Watson to take up with McCarthy building & wiring W/T office [wireless telegraphy] on ground. [This was also done for radar offices, lifted on board complete.] ... DC [depth charge] stowages for twin screw corvettes [later called frigates, 'River' class]. Wrestled with Honours recommendations; wrote Contr re paucity of honours to RCNC & backed Joughin. [He later got an OBE.] ... Lillicrap gave me his draft for *Vanguard*. L showed me rough dwg of *Vanguard* as a carrier, prepared for Sanders. Mathias [J E, WPS West Scotland, younger brother of T L Mathias (Bath) and L T J Mathias, managing the temporary dockyard at Corpach near Oban] showed me Stephens welded shaft bracket model which looked good. Told DDNC to get busy.

18 September: Andrew back from loss of *Manchester* [torpedoed in Mediterranean 13 Aug] inquiry, sounds a lamentable exhibition. Meeting with DEE, E in C, DTM re electrical power in new ships, dictated notes & sent copies. Talk with DEE & E in C on Contr's views of reorganisation which horrify me. ... Skimmed thro' Wilfred Ayre's report on small craft, made notes in margin & sent to DCW. A v. thick day. Sent out about 100 letters re MBEs & BEMs [British Empire Medal]. Discussed tractor prop[eller] scheme for N[ew] C[onstruction] with E in C.

20–27 September: On leave

1 October: ... Discussed with Bartlett bows of [USS] *Essex* & *Indefatigable* [the latter plated up to the flight deck, the former only to hangar deck]. Watson brought in Reed's S[ingle] S[crew] Corvette design ['Castle'] ... Dep Contr said *Avenger* did well with Russian Convoy [QP.14]. ...

2 October: ... Saw Contr who wanted my Production side entirely reorganised, I to go to London as Asst Contr & give more time to production, McCarthy to be DWP [Director of Warship Production] under me. Hannaford to be below McC. Contr said he was quite sure Corps could run this job & intimated if we couldn't he would get in a businessman who could. ...

3 October: Back in Bath. Told Dep Contr [Simeon] of reorganisation scheme, he thinks it wrong to try & run a Bath dept. from London. I can see the difficulty, why I feel I shall be all right on the construction side, on the production side McCarthy will have great difficulty. Told DDNC [Lillicrap] & said he will have to run the dept. in Bath (I mean construction side). [Presumably that meant design.] Told Hannaford who cannot see he is not perfect & wanted to know where he had failed. ...

5 October: ... Afternoon with Contr, Lithgow, W Ayre [committee chairman] & McCarthy. Contr said we are to get busy to build 200 corvettes (120 twin, 80 new SS) on American methods. Later told Contr I should want represent[atives] of E in C & DEE with McCarthy in London, he agreed. At 5 p.m. attended Dep 1st SL's meeting [Kennedy-Purvis], said we could not give them a US design at same displacement & there were features in US design I would not agree to. ...

9 October: In London. Long talk with Craven re prices, I told him I had agreed to waive S/M hull guarantee, he asked me to write Jubb. He had heard of my probable move to London, he said he had refused to come to Admy as part-timer, he said shipbuilders will play the game (he is agin Robin Rowell). ... Gawn came in & talked of his visit to USA, useful but they are not ahead of us in resistance & propulsion.

13 October ... Walsh [D P, Director of Establishments] called, said Wintersgill (late of Blyth) had made a statement against Butt, said I would like to see Sec. [Markham] on 15th. I had already told Butt I proposed him for a bigger job. [Wintersgill and later Butt were accused of corruption, see 24 July 1943.] 14 October: At Contr's meeting, dictated notes. Contr said Goodeve was app[ointe]d Asst Contr for Research & Development (I formed a low opinion of Goodeve but Pringle says he is fine. Perhaps I am wrong [He was. Goodeve had earned a well deserved reputation as a go-getter and problem solver.]). [Goodall's new title was Assistant Controller (Warship Production).] ... Contr's address [presumably to Admiralty staff in Bath] was not very inspiring. ...

17 October: ... Difficult paper from DNE (DC) [damage control] wanting to take over much of DNC's & E in C's work. Got from Mathias [T L] $1.8 \times$ destroyers in operation = destroyers in being [i.e. 55 per cent availability]. ...

19 October: Rushed together notes for this evening's meeting, more particularly US Carriers. Screed from Cunningham (BAD) [= British Admiralty Delegation in America. Possibly Vice Admiral J H D, 4th Sea Lord] saying our aircraft (RN) and our carriers were out-of-date compared to US practice (looked as tho' he had signed what DNAD had put before him). ... I said resistance of new *Ark R.* compared to IAC for underwater attack was 4:1 (I think 8 torps to sink *Ark R*, 2 to sink IAC).

23 October: ... To London. Saw Contr. re new Ark Royals: he said 'Approved to increase beam of CL's & H & W's ships', wrote Johnson & Rebbeck. [*Ark Royal* and *Eagle* ex-*Audacious*.] Contr doesn't like taking away order from S[wan] Hunter & decision re this ship will be given later, wrote Swan. Started work on ideal programme. Saw Contr

re Lithgow helping with the 200 pre-fabricated corvettes, I said 'Fine'. At 1st SL's meeting on Communications & RDF, it looks to me that a fight may come between NOs & scientists who unlike the technicians will not be content to be tools for ever & ever: NOs take on technical work, then drop it & go to sea [a perennial problem in the Navy]. The technicians should be bossing stuff like RDF. Inspected my new room [at the Admiralty Building].

26 October: Long talk with Cotton, he knows about Butt, anonymous letter (he thinks from one of my staff) was sent to Contr saying all Bath staff wanted to go back to London. He told me Admy Bath staff is about 8500 of whom only 3500 came from London. Of this 3500 about ½ are billeted & about ½ have made their homes in Bath. I said hours of work can be longer in Bath because of London travel difficulties. Sent on dockets re Bamford & Miss Mayhew [his secretaries], also Bamford's salary. ...

28 October: Left Bath for London. At Contr's meeting with CMSR [Controller of Merchant Shipbuilding & Repair, Lithgow], DMB [Director of Merchant Building, A Ayre], E in C [Turner], DWP [McCarthy], Bateson [Captain S L, Naval Assistant to Controller], James [probably J H, Assistant Secretary, Admiralty], Lister [possibly Commander F A of E in C's dept] re corvettes (200) mainly CMSR offered to help with mach[iner]y & Dalmuir for fitting out [at the former Beardmore shipyard on the Clyde]: E in C thought former not a great help but latter is. When McCarthy suggested opening another yard, A Ayre said [quite rightly] better man up what yards he has on the Clyde fully: later he talked to me re this which I think we should follow up. ... [Contr] showed me papers re my appt. (no extra pay because an Asst Contr is below DNC!).

29 October: ... Long talk with E in C re destroyers, I said Fleets probably unchanged but intermediates will probably be a new design, he wants to raise [steam] temperature to get higher efficiency without loss of reliability, this means economisers [which heated the feed water before it entered the boiler] heavy weight high up, I said 'Give us the figures'. Saw [movie film] 'In Which We Serve' & got fed up.

30 October: ... Saw Contr re building some corvettes in CMSR's yards on Clyde, fitting out at Dalmuir. Pigott called re last item after seeing Contr, expect he will play, told him about 37' beam of intermediates [destroyers, became 'Weapons'?]. Thornycroft called & we had lunch together. Milne called ready to weld destroyers, said I would discuss at Bath next week. [*Contest* was the first all-welded destroyer ordered from J S White 12 Aug 42.]

31 October: Wrestled with papers & stayed over the afternoon to do so as it is not my intention to work on Sundays in London: journey to & fro takes too much time, I told Contr so yesterday. Got Craven to come in re help from Vickers on S/M design, he will help, dictated notes of our talk. He told me Max Horton is going C in C WA [Western Approaches] [replacing] Noble [Admiral Sir P L H] to USA; Cunningham home [Admiral Sir A B, C in C Med Fleet], Claude Barry FO(S) [Rear Admiral C B]. Hendin is a sick man. C[raven] is going on a Min[istry] of Production triumvirate. ...

2 November: Saw Contr (Dep Contr present) re corvette arm[amen]t, he says ACNS(W) is on the warpath to make them AA ships, he will resist it, they are A/S [anti-submarine], I smiled he asked 'Why?' I said 'DGD' [Director of Gunnery Division, Captain G M B Langley]. He spoke of *Ark R.* I saw Bateson & we told Contr he could change IAC at Walker with an *Ark R.* at S.H. without difficulty, later I showed him letter to this effect from Swan. ... Lunch with A Ayre, he agin Baker [G S], W S Abell, Telfer [E V], Tutin et hoc genus [and all that sort, distinguished naval architects], he says he is prepared to let us build corvettes at Southwick [Pickersgill's shipyard] (told McC[arthy] & Contr). At Dep 1st Sea Lord's planning c'tee, a fight to get 4″ [armour] fl[ight] deck in *Ark R.*

3 November: ... Cleared up papers & left for Bath. Pringle waiting for me at station [presumably both travelling 1st class], he wants to come to London like me & was sounding me what I thought. I said my experience too short yet but my difficulty was going to be to keep in touch with work of dept. at Bath. ...

5 November: At Bath. Dealt with new S/M design (Pamplin back from FOS), put frames inside press[ure] hull ['A' class], left notes. ...

6 November: ... From 11.00-16.15 (with lunch break) Corvette meeting, dictated notes: everybody agreed that the fitting out is the problem. I said again that men like Simons [Clyde shipyard] rep[resentative] are too little for a job of this magnitude: how I long to get W Ayre back on the business: T Edwards & W Reed [Smith's Dock] are too old for something new & big. Told Contr as soon as W Ayre is back & central drawing & ordering office is set up, I must get busy to organise for fitting out & getting the labour &c. At 1st Sea Lord's meeting on torpedoes, not very inspiring AND [Admiralty net defence] was a sorry tale, what material & labour we have wasted on this!

9 November: Wrote Pigott re corvette nos. [numbers] to be fitted out at Dalmuir. ... Pictures up, make room better. [The Civil Service would have a good choice for senior officers' rooms.] Wise called re a shorthand typist,

said I would wait till Monday. ... Saw E in C re machy for transferred Fleet carrier (now at Walker) [*Eagle* before name transferred to *Audacious*] & IAC (now at S.H.) [*Leviathan*], sent him copy of docket. ... At Future Planning C'tee said a 45,000 ton AC could probably have 4″ fl. deck & 4″ over vitals to reduce fire risk. Aircraft should have Diesel engines E in C forecast [diesel fuel less flammable than petrol, but gas turbine also good with kerosene].

10 November: Contr said I must keep him in the picture at Future Building C'tee meetings as Dep 1st SL cannot assume Contr's functions. ... Worked on Creed [inventor of semi-submersible design of Seadrome floating airfield] an awful waste of time. ... James [probably J H] came in re labour statistics, he was useful (use P Br more) [Priority Branch collated statistics].

11 November: ... Meryon [E D, former SCW, now an adviser to Goodall] will see if Scotts can build 6 inter[mediate] destroyers & Clydebank will engine & fit out. ... Bateson came over re 20 knot oilers, told him the difficulty, wrote Rebbeck, Swan, Johnson & Rowell. Butt called, wanted to be WPS southern area. ...

12 November: ... McCarthy & I saw E in C, Perring [Rear Admiral H H, Inspector of Machine Tool Utilisation] & Bentham re machine tools & cranes, agreed to C'tee, saw Contr who will speak Lithgow. ... Had tooth out T.G. A hectic day.

13 November: 1st Lord sent for me re Arrester Gear for MAC ships, told him we should want more capacity, but I was confident we could provide, he then sent for A Ayre, who afterwards came to see me, he denied being the villain responsible for these ineffective ships, got hold of Findlay [Commander J V] in Trade Division who said it was all A Ayre & showed me a docket proposing to cancel the 30 from USA, got hold of DNAD, who said the whole scheme was haywire, Orpen [Commander C I Horton?] of Plans said we were in for 42. Saw Contr who said Provide for 42 independent of Canada. ... A good day.

14 November: Lithgow rang re Harland & W Belfast, sent over their London agent with map of yard, discussed with him, McCarthy & Davies [W J A, Assistant DWP]. Told Davies to see Lithgow before going to Belfast: after further thought I think we ought to use H & W for corvettes. [Four 'Loch' class frigates were ordered.] A spate of papers which I was unable to get at: this paper business is going to be the bane of my new job, so much time goes in meetings & visits to Bath. ...

16 November: Mrs Smith, my shorthand typist joined, gave her a lot of letters which fairly well ate up my paper accumulation. E in C came in to

discuss *Dart*, *Frome* &c ['River' class building at Blyth] agreed I would suggest ASCBS take on responsibility for saying ship can be moved. E in C then spoke of S/M engine situation, he thinks new design will spoil his engine production. ...

18 November: ... In train on way back [from Bath to London] discussed with Contr the programme at Vickers, Walker, they say they cannot do 2 Fleet Carriers, I think they ought to. Dep Contr told me of N African losses, not bad, *Hecla* [destroyer depot ship] & *Avenger* the most serious.

19 November: Back at Admy. Contr. saw me re <u>making</u> Firms fabricate shaft brackets, also somebody following up any delays in dwgs. Talk with McCarthy warned him to be careful what he says to Contr. (I thought his talk in train yesterday about Vickers, Walker, roofing in their destr[oyer] slips was wild). ... At Lithgow's C'tee which did not go well, our side [warships] is hampered by c'tees & depts while his gets busy & orders [merchant ships]. ...

20 November: DDNC (Bath) said 'New Corvette speed might be down ½ knot, must swallow this' [increased displacement]. ... Johnson [H T] rang said '*Implac[able]* is as expected, trouble will be to stop ship hitting other side' [of River Clyde at launch]. Lunch with A Ayre who was pleased with yesterday's meeting, naturally, said I wasn't. Barry (new FOS) called, said Pengelly was doing well, he thinks US should build minelayer cum store carrier S/M. ...

21 November: After lunch with Bateson & McCarthy did 1943 programme for small vessels, left McCarthy to tie up the loose ends. ... Mountain A.S. (M.S.) [J F, Assistant Secretary of Admiralty, Merchant Ships?] rang me re paper for Cabinet on MAC ships, they are still trying to put blame on arrester gear & hoped they had cornered me. I laid cards on table, wrote McTaggart Scott [maker of arrester gear; manufacture of their MAC ship gear design was subcontracted to Vickers-Armstrongs at Barrow and others] that I had now fully committed myself as I had confidence in them. ...

23 November: At Thornycrofts [Southampton]. Train very late. Had a quick look round yard. Very congested, not enough labour, men in sheet metal shop doing work that women could do, while yard outside is starved of men. ... Talk over dates Sir J [Thornycroft] & Donaldson [T, Thornycroft general manager] helpful but Cameron [Norman, shipyard manager] is the hard nut, really he has little vision & go, I thought. They agreed to come up on dates if I could get them 15 shipwrights for *Narbada*'s wood deck [sloop for Royal Indian Navy]. Travelled back with Sir J. & touched him on S/Ms, it would mean a big development of yard.

Churchill was keen to get a fleet of ships capable of landing tanks on enemy shores. At the end of 1940 Woollard and Baker drew up a design of what Goodall called Winettes. But the specification was not well considered, resulting in a 16.5-knot ship 400ft long but carrying only thirteen tanks and twenty-seven trucks. The 5ft 6in beaching draft forward required a complicated extending ramp to allow the tanks to reach shore. These elaborate ships took two years to build. The photo shows *Boxer* (Harland & Wolff's Yard No 1155) on a beaching trial. The three LST Mark 1 proved of limited value so were converted to fighter direction ships in 1944. The American LST Mark 2, which benefited from British experience, proved much more successful although smaller and slower, 115 being supplied to the RN under Lend-Lease. (*Author's collection*)

They had no complaints re plant or supplies (except prot[ective] plating) all labour trouble.

24 November: Undex Panel [Underwater experiments]: useful talk by Pippard [A J S, Professor of Civil Engineering, Imperial College], G I Taylor & Davis, DMWD [Department of Miscellaneous Weapon Development] was represented. ... Lunch with G I who thought we were about level with US on theory but ahead in big scale, they had 3 establishments, a lot of staff & some overlapping. Saw film of auto-gyros & helicopters, work in USA which looks to me a better scheme for air escort of convoys than MAC ships. Saw Contr re Thornycroft, he agreed & orders for 1942 S[ingle] Screw corvettes to new design not using structural engineers [the 'Lochs' were prefabricated, not the 'Castles']. ... Walsh came about a specimen of Butt's handwriting. I said I could not supply without raising

suspicion. [See 24 July 1943.] ... [At 17 lines and 200 words this was one of the longest daily entries in his diary.]

25 November: ...At lunch with A Ayre he gave [me] good dope on contract prices [of merchant ships?].

26 November: ... Callander called re Gunning's design which looks poor to me [possibly triple hull submarine which he designed for Netherlands Navy after the war], said I would join Craven in getting FOS to drop it, he is all for super-charging an 8 cyl T. [class diesel engine] said he should see E in C, he spoke of labour from L[iver]pool in despondent tones. Saw Contr re labour at Belfast being used for new big graving dock, he said 'Get Papers'. Spoke him re Prof. for Turkey, he kept paper to find out who was taking action. [E V Telfer was later appointed Professor of Naval Architecture at Istanbul.] Later he told me *Bruiser* & *Boxer* [LSTs Mark 1] could go back to help CMSR get out 2 merchant ships (he had spoken to CCO [Mountbatten]), wrote E in C Bath. Lunch with Dr (?Raling German Jew, GEC) & Mr Huggett, interesting, made notes. [The GEC company made electric motors for submarines, steam turbines, radar, radios, fans etc.] Tooth out, T.G. [another!]

27 November: Pigott called to see Contr who passed him onto me, he brought Dalmuir fitting out scheme, which seemed to me inadequate. DWP at meeting got Davies & he will go to Glasgow. At Lithgow's meeting with D of C's [Director of Contracts] & C.S.L. [Civil Lord?] repayment for development schemes, an awful lot of piffle from Dale Bussell [Director of Contracts for Merchant Shipbuilding], Mountain & Hughes [R, Principal Secretary of Admiralty?], time wasting: in afternoon Lambert [Rear Admiral D S Lambert, Paymaster Director General?] & Co. had to clear up Perring, Bentham mess. Saw Contr re *Indefat*'s launch he is not going to play 2nd fiddle to L.L. Mt.B [Mountbatten], so I am to go! ... At 1st Lord's inspection of Creed's model (1st L. smoking a cigar & calling 1st SL 'Dudley') 1st SL fobbed it off on to K.P's C'tee [Kennedy-Purvis], 1st L frightened of a press campaign, during talk 1st L was rung up re Toulon Fleet [French Fleet scuttled on 27 November].

28 November: ... Wilfred Ayre back, talking sense, but I do not think even he realises 'the fitting out' problem. Dealt with paper accumulation, the curse of this job, since so much time goes on committees & interviews. Felt rotten all day, diarrhoea, realised the cause was oysters for lunch on 26th & then felt better [there is no such thing as a free lunch!].

1 December: Cleared up yesterday's paper accumulation & was just leaving for Bath when Contr came in. Panic over loss of *Avenger*, apparently one poof & she had gone [one torpedo in bomb room on 15 Nov], said I

would phone him from Bath for his meeting at 16.30. On arrival did this. Gave Bartlett instructions in the coming interview with survivors. ...

2 December: At Bath. Talk with Dep Contr re pumping arrgts in cruisers, also Bucknill Report which with Technical Report has been sent as C.B. [Confidential Book] to Fleet without comment. I must make up my mind whether or not to take this lying down. ... At Models & Mock-ups meeting, dictated notes. With Lillicrap inspected Bridge Model of Hunt Destroyers & gave instructions. ... Discussed Labour with DCW (Ships) [Hannaford] a wetter blanket than ever.

3 December: ... Fraser called re counterflooding, I gave in to counterflood without orders if heel exceeds 6°. Will write him, he wants cruisers with heavier gun than 5.25: he is agin RCNC going into R.N.: I moaned about Bucknill, he advised me to put my views on record. Tobin [T C, naval architect] of H & W called (NBG). Lost key of my safe.

4 December: Key of safe was at dentists. ... John [W G] came in & told him to inspect welding with electrode laid in joint. [A dangerous short cut to fill the gap between bevelled plate edges rather than with weld metal.] ...

5 December: On leave. Moved back into 50 Lyford [Road, his house in London].

7 December (Sunday): ... Contr. has told DUBD [Director of Unexploded Bomb Disposal, Captain L E H Llewellyn] to inspect damaged ships, overlapping bad. DNE (DC), DNC & now DUBD are all doing this job. ... At Future Building C'tee, convinced C'tee that UW protection of light (intermediate) carriers is not bad, got 20 knot oilers back to DMB [Ayre] much talk over Creed Seadrome, all funk turning it down. [Similar concept to today's semi-submersible offshore drilling rigs, with submerged pontoons and columns supporting the deck, less affected by wave action.] Left by night train for Glasgow.

8 December: On the Clyde. After talk with Mathias [J E] went to Dennys where there is a strike of rivet heaters following strike of riveters. Always trouble there, I think difficulty is Russell. Denny [Sir Maurice, chairman] has many other irons in fire & cannot manage Russell, probably men regard him as the 'grey wolf'. Firm wants more engine fitters. To Clydebank [John Brown], launch of Indefat[igable] went well [launched by Countess of Milford Haven]: this firm wants more ironworkers [working in steel but the nineteenth-century term had stuck]. What a gain it would be if there was more interchangeability between firms. This firm is not bad, Skiffington [Donald, shipyard director at Clydebank] may be a bully &

a bluffer but he gets things done. They are gradually getting more aggressive on welding. Went to Lord Aberconway's dinner party, Grant & Mathews [of John Brown, Sheffield] great on new armour.

9 December: To Fairfield for talk with destroyer firms, Stephen [Murray], Denny [Maurice], Barr [George of Fairfield], Yarrow [Harold] & Miller, McNeill [James of John Brown], Hutchison [of Scotts] & R Rowell [of Hawthorn Leslie]. Result good: they all swore they were working like a team (!). Then talk with Stephen [building *Ocean*] and Barr [building *Theseus*] re light carriers, must follow this up with all the L. Carrier firms. Had a look at *Implacable* launching arrgts, tides are higher than anticipated, feel all that can be foreseen has been provided against. To Yarrows, this firm is good I think, but somehow we <u>must</u> get along with wiring [fitting electrical cabling] earlier. Then to Dalmuir to look at corvette fitting out basin. Had long talk with

(Sir) Harold E Yarrow (1884–1962), son of the company founder Alfred, proved as capable an engineer as his father, whom he succeeded as company chairman in 1922. During the Second World War there was a steady output from Yarrow of warships and their machinery, giving Goodall no cause for concern. Like many of his contemporaries he was also involved in professional institutions, national associations, hospitals, banks and good causes generally. His son Eric ran the company after his death. (*The Shipbuilder*)

FOIC [Troup], hope I have choked him off sending *Manxman* [torpedoed off Algiers 1 Dec] to Stephen.

10 December: To Scotts. Rain pelting down. This firm is hopeless. Their lay-out in my opinion is too old-fashioned, they are thinking too much about building merchant ships after the war. Newton says their engine side is very weak. Hutchison would not agree he has too many berths & too little fabricating space. Must think about getting S/Ms away from them for fitting out. To Fairfield, launch of *Implac[able]* went well. H. M. [His Majesty] looked fit & the Queen as lovely as ever beautifully dressed in with a most becoming purple gown [?]. As expected I was well out of the limelight but if anything had gone wrong or if this ship meets an *Ark R.* fate I shall be in the limelight then: how the Board can expect to get a

DNC worth his salt beats me. Had a talk with Lithgow re his ship des[ign] c'tee. Very nice dinner party afterwards.

11 December: Talk with E in C re Scotts & Denny. … Later Craven called & with Contr's agreement I told him of Scotts & asked what he could do. He will send Johnson [W, engine works manager at Vickers-Armstrongs, Barrow], I wrote Greig [of Scotts]. McCarthy very disappointed at attitude of small firms over pre-fabricated corvettes, told Contr who will think it over. I said I want one man not a c'tee responsible for production. Wash out the firms who are ½ hearted. Lithgow rang re cranes & machines, got hold of McC & Butt & pressed latter hard to do i.e. get out orders. …

12 December: Bassett came up, wants to put *Manxman* to HL, after pressing for other firms, I had to agree, subject to Contr accepting deferred N[ew] C[onstruction] dates. [*Manxman* was repaired with new port set of machinery at Hawthorn Leslie to May 1945.] Troup has a letter to put 14 LCF(L) [Landing Craft Flak, Large, converted from LCTs Marks 3 and 4] to Clyde firms, I agreed he can sound them & must report how they affect new constr. before they are actually placed. [LCF(L)15 onwards were converted by regular Clyde shipbuilders and shiprepairers, most in 1943.] … McCarthy came in to discuss corvettes, he thinks he had better

Manxman was one of the class of fast minelayers first ordered in December 1938. Although reputed to be capable of over 40 knots, 35 knots was a more realistic sea speed fully loaded. After being torpedoed in the Mediterranean on 1 December 1942, she lay at Gibraltar before arriving in the Tyne for repairs on 7 July 1943. Her damage required the replacement of her port set of steam turbine machinery (made by Parsons as Contract No 404) as well as refurbishment of her starboard set by Hawthorn Leslie, who also undertook the repairs. She is seen leaving the Tyne in July 1945 ready to join the British Pacific Fleet. (*Author's collection*)

be the <u>one man</u> responsible for production, I did not object but it will keep me overloaded much longer.

14 December: At Contr's Liaison C'tee re 20 knot oilers, DMB & I agreed that best proposition was to ask USA offering to supply machy. ASCBS called re Belfast & Bogie [F G, Warship Production Superintendent, Belfast], said I must go there. Later agreed with Contr that I should go after him. With Butt saw CMSR re C.Laird's cranes & altered docket so as to get a move on. Lunch with CMSR [Lithgow], Ayre & L[awrie] Edwards [Director of Merchant Ship Repairs DMR, previously of shiprepairers Middle Docks], talked 20 knot oilers & corvettes. With DWP saw Contr suggested McCarthy should be the one man responsible, he agreed, told him of cranes for C Lairds. Troup placing LCM(F) [he probably meant LCF(L)] & Bassett placing *Manxman* at HL. ...

15 December: At Bath, saw all ADNCs, ex Woollard & Cole & Offord, got Bartlett busy on Avenger class bomb room alteration. ... Saw W'son re Varley [X craft] & Thornycroft also new design. ... At Dep Contr's New Constr meeting, a most unhappy one. Hannaford harping at length on ships going back. Dep Contr holding forth on no more labour & all our 'target' dates being unrealistic. ...

16 December: ... Saw Woollard who does well, showed me the LCT as gunboat design [LCG(L) converted from LCT Mark 3]. Left by 16.18 [train] tired out.

17 December: Sir S Pigott called, told him of breeze between Bateson & Skiffington. W Ayre with McCarthy on corvettes. McC enthusiastic. Sir J Thornycroft called re Northam bridge [upriver from the Southampton shipyard] told him to send me copies of letters. Contr rang re Turks underwater welding, said D of D the man to stir. Bateson came up saying Pigott was furious (mem. To keep my mouth shut in future). ... Wrote Craven & Greig re 'S' Cl. S/Ms going to Barrow to complete. ...

18 December: ... Rang Craven, told him to send Johnson [W] to Scotts, he said finishing their 'S' boats would not affect his output at Barrow. ... At 1st SL's meeting on Fleet Air Arm, much too long. Dreyer on 'Myself & how I did it'. John DGNDP [?] said DNC had too much say in AC design, I expostulated. [Not surprisingly, how do you design an aircraft carrier without major input from the Admiralty's chief naval architect?] ...

22 December: Continued meeting with H & W. They adamant that they cannot contribute to money for new welding plant. ...

23 December: Sent Xmas message to RCNC in UK & Home waters. ...

25 December: Xmas Day. On leave.

28 December: Back in office after 3 days grand rest. No newspapers, no BBC T.G. Contr spoke of Hannaford. P.M. [Churchill] is kicking up a dust because *Vanguard* is not going fast enough & Contr thought this a reason for getting H[annaford] here to talk to him. … Showed Contr letter from Scotts agreeing to transfer 2 S/Ms to Barrow, he sent it to Dep Contr [Simeon] to arrange [*Sirdar* and *Sea Rover*]. …

31 December: At Bath. Sent out letters re *Bellona* & *Implac*. With Johnson [H T] & Sherwin [C E, constructor] went into *Essex* gun mtg disposition, new *Ark R* as good, could be better if we had to provide less in the bridges, then *Implac's* 2nd mast. … Discussed training of shipwright apprentices with DDNC Bath, must do something.

Memoranda 1942

A very trying year for me personally. The Bucknill C'tee was an obvious political move to make me the scapegoat for the *Prince of Wales* disaster, the C'tee confined their attention entirely to the material side & made a bloomer over application of Job 74 [test section of battleship] results to *P of W*. Wake-Walker admitted in talk that they had been told to confine their remarks to *P of W* & ship construction. An eye-opener that a Judge of the High Court could be so influenced. When the 1st report failed to put the blame on me entirely, the C'tee faded out. I think it wise to let it alone until everybody can take a calmer view & then protest, it will most likely bob up again in the Naval debate [in Parliament]. Then Fraser went at which I was not sorry, he being too much for gold lace & weak on labour & sticking up to 1st L & Staff, but instead of Simeon [Deputy Controller] Wake-Walker was appointed. He went off at once at half-cock & got Bath (& me) upset. Much too impetuous. I get on better with him now I am in London. It has again been a difficult year satisfying demands for staff. The ships have had a better year. *Indom.* took a hammering well, as did *Edinburgh* & *Trinidad* tho' finally lost. Shipyard managements show war weariness & the old men are feeling the strain.

1943

1 January: Honours, Skinner OBE but Corps badly treated again: most disappointing after my special efforts. Sent congratulations to Controller [Wake-Walker], Ayre &c. … Hannaford called re *Vanguard* & depressed me. … Walsh came up to know what I want to do when I reach 60 on 18/4.

2 January: … I told him [Controller] I should be 60 in April, did he want me to stay on? He said 'Yes'. I said that DNCs who had stopped after 60 had not stopped in the best interests of the Service & I wanted to go 6 mos [months] before he wished it. He said I might stay on as AC(WP). I said whom he had in mind as the next DNC? He said he hadn't thought about it. I said I thought Lillicrap who was already 55.

4 January: … After lunch to USA film of underwater expts, must discuss with Offord [D E J, to be Superintendent of Underwater Experiment Works, Rosyth]. Had to leave at 3.30 p.m. for A Ayre's meeting on giving up tramps for corvettes because W Ayre & Co don't want bridge builders on the job. [An interesting comment since when Burntisland started its new shipyard, they used structural engineers to fabricate the steel parts until their own workshops were ready.] I get depressed it looks as tho' the hidden but steady opposition to pre-fabrication is gaining ground. Anyhow we shan't see much from that this year.

6 January: Got Rebbeck [Sir Frederick] on phone. A long tirade from him about welding, evidently he is not an advocate. He agreed to 50/50 on cranes. [Three new ones for Berth 15 at Belfast for aircraft carriers?] & I agreed to push his main scheme for 100% Ad[miralty] contribution. I had previously seen Contr who agreed to my remarks re cranes 27, 28, 29. … Dr Montgomerie [James, Chief Ship Surveyor, Lloyd's Register of Shipping] called re anonymous letters about Curtis of Totnes, accusing his man Robertson [J M, LR surveyor] & my man Scott [C, constructor] of malpractices, said I knew nothing about it but would talk Hanna[ford]. …

7 January: Meryon called, told him of Fleet Destr[oyer] orders & sent paper on. He against D of C [Jubb] said S[wan] Hunter had extras running into thousands outstanding for months while they had had to fork out for a trivial rebate! ... At SYD C'tee meeting [Shipyard Development Committee set up in Nov 1942], H & W went thro' easily but there was a fuss over Robb [shipbuilder at Leith], in the end the main scheme was app'd [approved]. ... After meeting, Mountain showed me a paper in which 1st L [Alexander] said merchant ship output was not to be reduced for corvettes. [It had become necessary to use merchant shipyards for building corvettes to achieve the numbers required.]

8 January: Craven rang, can send 50 men at once to Scotts to take over the 2 S/Ms, rang Greig who said 'No obj[ection] but I can't find accommodation for them', got hold of [W] Johnson [of] V-A who said he could do that. ... ASCBS [Wake] had meeting yesterday (said A.L. of A.I.), [priorities] *Bellona* 1st Sept, then *Indefat[igable* aircraft carrier at John Brown] then *Implac[able* carrier at Fairfield]. ... 1st SL's [Pound] meeting went well but discussions disappointing, younger men would talk afterwards but not in front of big-wigs.

11 January: Saw King [Rear Admiral F V, Deputy E in C] re BAD Wash[ington]'s message on speeding up Escorts [fifty had been ordered in the US in Nov 1941]. ... To Bath. Arrived sneezing, had headache all day, took a sleeping tablet.

13 January: ... At Contr's NC [New Construction] meeting (Dep Contr [Simeon] had piped down on P Br & corvettes, like all NOs in front of superior officer). Contr

(Sir) Frederick E Rebbeck (1877–1964) was a brilliant engineer who became chairman of Harland & Wolff in 1930, keeping that position right up to 1961. Like the former chairman Lord Pirrie, he was an autocrat reluctant to delegate. He had made his name establishing H & W's diesel engine design and manufacturing capacity, the company licensing the successful Danish Burmeister & Wain engine, becoming managing director at Belfast in 1919. He steered the company through the difficult financial years of the 1930s following the crash of the associated Royal Mail Group. During the Second World War, Goodall felt he had too many businesses to manage effectively. In addition to the shipyard, engine works and electrical department at Belfast, there was a shipyard at Govan, engineering works at Finnieston and Scotstoun and repair works at London, Liverpool and Southampton, employing some 50,000 workers during the war. (*The Shipbuilder*)

put *Implac* back. Went thro' Stirling design [special craft for detonating pressure mines] & signed. ...

14 January: Back in London. First Lord chucking a spanner into the mach[iner]y over orders for 1943 Fleets [*Malta* class aircraft carriers] he is scared of P.M. [Prime Minister], drafted yarn with James after seeing E in C. ... Pigott [Clydebank] called, he is willing to build the T[win] S[crew] corvette prototype [*Loch Fada*].

15 January: ... Meeting with Reed [of Smith's Dock] &c on S.S. corvettes [single-screw 'Castle' class], dictated notes; at lunch he wanted me to take on a new design that would be something like a corvette for the war but convertible into a fishing trawler after, decided not to bite, can't afford to interfere with production. [Several 'Flowers' were converted to mercantile use after the war, rather than 'Castles'.] Went thro' Inter[mediate] Destr[oyer] Sketch Design rather lavish and one careless mistake, sent note to Lillicrap. [Became 'Weapon' class.] Told Contr stability of inter ACs [aircraft carriers] good with 2 comp[artmen]ts flooded. Saw Contr re aux[iliary] ACs he said 3 only instead of MAC ships, also we can go ahead to order corvettes from merchant builders.

16 January: ... Baker called, said he could send sketch designs to CCO in USA; told me of LCI(L) [Landing Craft Infantry, Large] & I wrote Bath to let me know trial results. ... Bamford out sick now for 2 days. [Goodall relied on his now private secretary F O Bamford to manage his voluminous paperwork.]

18 January: A[ir] R[aid] warning 04.45-05.45. Spoke Sir J Lithgow re steel, he said my action to get 4 weeks stock & a bigger allocation would do no harm, sent docket to Hopkins [C J W, now Director of Contract Work (Supplies)] & told him to go ahead. Sir J L up against H & W not contributing to cost of welding scheme. ... Contr came up with silly minute from P.M. about building stuff like dredgers in barge-builders yards & using merchant yards so freed for corvettes! ... FBC [Future Building Committee] talk very useful re aircraft of the future [heavier, impact on carrier design].

19 January: ... Bateson came up to talk MACs & Escort Carrier lifts. ... Shook up Mrs Smith for her typing errors. ...

20 January: At Newcastle. [Goodall must have got the overnight sleeper train.] Attended Shipyard Control C'tee meeting where I spoke of U boat successes & need for more Escorts. Then to Hawthorn Leslie, Rowell [H B R, chairman] so clever he bores me. Then to Swan Hunter C S Swan [Sir Charles, chairman aged 73] in his dotage. Made notes. Dined

with Callander [Sir James, managing director Vickers-Armstrongs, Barrow] & Rowell very interesting talk on 'After the War' 'Workers of the World Unite', exterminating Germans.

21 January: ... To V-A [Vickers-Armstrongs] High Walker, talk with Callander & Swan about labour, didn't get far but when going round the yard Swan opened out, wants interchange of trades & payment by results, he will take up with other Firms on the Tyne. To Armstrongs Low Walker [former Armstrong Whitworth shipyard, became Shipbuilding Corporation (Tyne)] met Graham [presumably the yard manager], all right for corvettes [actually only built merchant ships during the war].

27 January: At Bath. ... Went into new 4.5″ mtg [twin Mark VI mounting] for destroyers & got CIGM [Chief Inspector Gun Mountings, Rear Admiral B W Greathed] & McLaughlin [Captain P V, Naval Ordnance Dept] & 1 other over, said it meant big alteration & we would say later if it was possible. Then went further into Inter Fl[eet] destr, big reasons for greater size are machy [in two separated units boiler plus engine room] & arm[amen]t (more amm[unitio]n); knocked out the block of oil amidships.

(Sir) Charles Sheriton Swan (1870–1944) was the son of Charles Sheridan Swan, one of the founders with George Hunter of the Swan, Hunter company. Merged with the neighbouring Wigham Richardson shipyard in 1903. The company was the most versatile British shipbuilder, also owning Barclay Curle on the Clyde and Wallsend Slipway & Engineering. He became chairman in 1928; with sound finances, it survived the Depression. Goodall felt that Swan was losing his grip under wartime pressures and should have given way to a younger man sooner. (*Swan Hunter*)

29 January: ... Object to Swedish DNI [Director of Naval Intelligence] visiting naval firms on Tyne. [Sweden was neutral but supplying Germany; perhaps Goodall was worried that information might get to the Germans.] ...

1 February: ... Called on 5th SL (Boyd) [Rear Admiral D W, Fifth Sea Lord & Chief of Naval Air Equipment] made some notes & sent to Bath, most important is (shall we go to open hangar?) ... With NA [Bateson], Meryon, (Kingcome [Rear Admiral J] & King [F V, both Deputy Engineers in Chief] present when we talked machy) discussed points of 1943

prog[ramme]. Made notes & told DCW (Ships) [Hannaford] to place order for 2 Fl.(inter) destroyers with Whites. [*Celt* and *Centaur* ordered 3 Feb, became *Sword* and *Scorpion*]. CMSR [Lithgow] apparently turns over Neptune yd to us [Swan Hunter's western Tyne shipyard].

2 February: ... Baker called, with Sanders [W G, Deputy Director of Naval Construction in London] & him I discussed anti-landing craft weapons. ...

3 February: Kingcome came in, said if Vickers Barrow cannot take machy for V-A Walker 'Battle' [first mention in the diary of this destroyer class name] it must go to Parsons but they will be late. Held corvette meeting, felt McCarthy & Davies are not getting down to the fitting out problem, adjourned till tomorrow. Attended S/M meeting. Williamson's [L C, ADNC and submarine designer] proposals are good & were accepted, minelayer cum store carrier, new design dropped for W'son to investigate converting old S/Ms. ...

4 February: Finished corvette labour meeting: my notes were scrappy & it took me a long time to dictate report. Told DWP he was worrying too much about new schemes & more slips [building berths], he should digest what he has bitten off (Lord knows it is a big chunk). Attended 4th SL's meeting

Lawrence C Williamson was the chief constructor in charge of the submarine design section from 1938, where he remained throughout the war, having also been in the section under Johns from 1931. He was promoted in 1938 to ADNC then Deputy DNC in 1944. Submarines were always regarded as 'different', their design and operational features being more demanding than surface ships, as any mistake could result in the loss of a whole boat and its crew. He had been the RCNC armour expert in the 1920s. Goodall was relieved that the loss of *Thetis* was not due to any failings of the submarine section; he had a high opinion of the abilities of this dedicated bachelor. (*The Shipbuilder*)

[Fourth Sea Lord, Rear Admiral F H Pegram, Chief of Supplies & Transport] on disposal of surplus gear. I am all for his point of view, but he is too fond of the sound of his own voice, afterwards I pressed him to get surplus gear out of ships as well as yards, he said he would. ...

5 February: ... Forbes [now an ADNC] back from USA thinks our closed hangar is right & armour should be on flight deck, but we should have accommodation just below flight deck & bigger lifts (3 in No.) also

The Admiralty allowed Thornycroft to build two 'Hunt' class to their own design. The unique hull form featured a pronounced flare and knuckle forward to reduce wetness, and a longer forecastle providing more space and better accommodation. Both *Brissenden* (nearest) and *Brecon* were docked in Palmers Hebburn 700ft drydock from 28 May to 7 June 1943, before deploying to the Med. (*Author's collection*)

believes double hangar necessary, in size we must 'think big' both for ship & aircraft. …

6 February (Saturday): … Got going on Honours, rang Stansfield for 3 more MBEs & 3 BEMs. Found typist had gone & the Pool girl was away 'at tea': told Bamford I must have a typist in every Sat. afternoon.

9 February: … Sir John Thornycroft called, asked him for more draughtsmen. He spoke of *Brecon* & *Brissenden* [Thornycroft-designed escort destroyers] weak torp. tube supports. …

10 February: Arrived Carlisle 06.45. Prelim talk with Hopkins & Bartlett [now an ADNC]. … Left at 15.45 for Barrow: stayed at Abbey House. …

11 February: At Barrow. With Callander, Ormston, Johnson [R S] & Williamson discussed S/M programme. Can do 16 A's a year, could fabricate for 5 more, but not provide engines or fit out, could do latter if more labour. But I noted they had a lot of joiners (youngish men) doing aircraft work that could be done by women. They will stop U's [submarines] when present order is complete & concentrate on A's.

Agreed to *Urchin* date [destroyer] coming forward. Looked at *Empire Charmian* [heavy lift ship], *Spartan* [cruiser] & *Vandal* [submarine]. Also new S/M slips. Left by night train.

12 February: Back at Admy. Meryon called, told him Swan H. should go ahead as tho' their destr. was not being transferred. ... WPS Glasgow [J E Mathias] phoned, Stirling Craft will affect new naval construction. Contr said 5th SL wants 34 knots new Ark Royals, also at [Admiralty] Board Meeting position of petrol tanks in Light Carriers was criticised. ...

13 February: ... Sent Contr draft letter of commendation to Vickers re X craft [Vickers-Armstrongs at Barrow had built *X.5–10* very quickly]. Note from Cabinet to report on 20 MAC ships, sent to Hopkins. ... A lovely day, like Spring.

15 February: ASCBS called re Belfast, Ferguson's jetty & steel cum wood furniture. Contr came up with letter from Pigott re Dalmuir [fitting-out base on Clyde for escorts], got Davies along, he & C E in C [Civil Engineer in Chief] man will go to Glasgow Thursday. ... At FBC (Boyd 5th SL late CO *Illustrious* held forth) very interesting as he has been to sea in *Saratoga* [USN carrier], dead against cafeteria [messing] for our service but I had to leave at 17.50. ...

19 February: Craven called, showed him my yarn re high profits, he agreed with small modifications, said *KGV* was cheapest of the 5 [battle] ships, *P of W* made about ¾ of profit of *KGV*, *D of Y* [*Duke of York*] the least & that about ½ of *KGV*. [No figures were given but the profit on *KGV* was probably about £500,000 on a price of about £3.3 million for hull and machinery.] ... Johnson [R S] called, wants more money for welding & more for salvage vessel [*Salveda*]. ... Meryon called with high profits yarn which I had loaned him, advised wiping out ½ para[graph] (re Est[ablishment] Charges down) this I did. ...

20 February: ... E in C also spoke of 6″ monitors of which Contr wants particulars, later Lillicrap gave me a rough estimate. ... Sent in my removals claim (Bath to Admy). Contr was horrified at size & cost of 6″ monitors, he had a little sketch of enemy coasters but they apparently are all guns, no endurance & low speed instead of our 15 knots. [They were never built, converting tank landing craft to LCGs was a better proposition.]

22 February: ... Contr came up & says 1st L spoke of these ships [light fleet carriers] & the time they were taking. He was concerned about the Fleet Carriers, couldn't we build something wanted for this war. 1st Lord's speech introducing Navy Estimates, draft came here for remarks, a very

poor affair showing a wrong perspective of the Navy & its work, I just tickled up Contr's part that I did not like. Later Dep. 1st SL said 'Have a good go' & I saw Contr. He was not so keen on chopping it about. 5th SL was very hot. At FBC good talk on Carriers, I have to put up a paper on closed v. open hangars. ...

23 February: ... Contr said C in C 'X' [Expeditionary Force?] wanted small fl[oating] docks [for LCTs?], I suggested concrete, he told Vice C[ontroller] & I promised Bath should send Vice C dwg of the concrete fl. dock [AFD.33] building near S'ton [Southampton]. Talk with [A] Ayre about H & Wolff, he thinks Rebbeck no good. ...

24 February: Arrived Turnstile House 09.15, left 09.50 arrived Hendon [airfield] 10.20: many formalities, fitting flotation jacket and parachute. Left ground 11.05: arrived Belfast 13.10. All afternoon spent listening to Rebbeck, blitz, effect on efficiency, rise in production, costs on hull side, couldn't accept Jubb's welding [plant] conditions, had a scheme for improving fitting out, which he thought could be tied up to welding & he then would pay 40% of latter, showed me a draft letter which I said I should like to sleep on. Firm fussed over conversion of LCTs [tank landing craft] to LCGs [landing craft, gun] much overtime & disorganisation if date has to be kept. [H & W converted nine, LCG(L) 10–18.]

25 February: At Belfast. Saw FOIC [Flag Officer in Charge, Rear Admiral R H L Bevan] he said H & W a lot of rogues, his position unsatisfactory he has to go to them as a supplicant [the only shipbuilder in Northern Ireland], spoke of LCTs to LCGs, I said I would go into that. Back to H & W, looked over ships at Musgrave Yard [the southernmost yard with largest slipways], Minotaur [completed as cruiser Ontario for Canada] will have a job to keep her launching date [actual 29 Jul 43]. Meeting to discuss completion dates, I noted Bl[ack] Pr[ince] cruiser] might come forward, made notes (later sent signal to Admy re LCTs & to DCW (Supplies) [Hopkins] re machining of rudders of minesweepers). Went on board Mutine (M.S.) [Algerine class minesweeper] a jamb in LL sweep generator room, but CO was happy [Lt Cdr N E Morley]. Met CO Thruster [Mark I tank landing ship] & agreed to pay him a visit.

26 February: Round yard with Rebbeck, then dictated draft letter re fitting out facilities, their structural shop looked good. But the yard is so big, Rebbeck should have a deputy Gen[eral] Man[ager] he said 'Name the man', I said that was his job. Inspected Thruster in dock, damage from grounding aft not serious but rather mysteriously it has put shafts out of line, CO [Lt Cdr R E Baldwin-Wiseman] not impressive. To Unicorn [maintenance aircraft carrier completed 12 Mar], Capt [Q D]

The *Algerine* class minesweepers were designed by Rowland Baker in 1940 to correct the shortcomings of the *Bangors*, notably by increasing the length which went up from 180ft to 225ft overall to accommodate all the new minesweeping gear. The first sixteen were ordered from Harland & Wolff, including *Algerine* herself seen here, which had steam turbine manufacturing capacity. Most of the others had the simpler steam reciprocating machinery, including those built in Canada. (*Blackman collection*)

Graham, rather boring lunch party, Sir V M Hale & a US general, CO more fussed about galley, thinks ship all right but windage area big [flight deck 50ft above waterline]. Inspected minesweepers on slips. Went thro' *Bl. Prince* & must get E in C [Turner] & DNO [Bevir] to see if they can come forward. Saw Unionmelt [welding] machine working. Had a farewell talk with FOIC.

27 February: Rebbeck phoned me at hotel, he had pondered over fitting out schemes & wanted me to forget all about it as he couldn't face the cost. I asked about welding [facilities], he said he would go ahead but would not agree to Admy conditions. Blair [Atholl, H & W engine works manager]

The American Unionmelt automatic welding machine could do butt welding of flat plate seams. The welder is refilling the flux hopper which protected newly-deposited weld metal, which was fed from a coil of wire at right. (*The Shipbuilder*)

took me for a short walk thro' engine shops, in my opinion he is the best of the bunch. Left ground at 12.50, landed at Hendon 14.40. To Admy, revised my notes of visit & sent to type, skimmed thro' papers. DWP & I had a talk, he is up against H & W corvette dates.

1 March: Saw Contr re visit to H & W, he thinks he will get on to McKenna [Reginald, chairman of Midland Bank] as Midland Bank practically own the place [after collapse of Royal Mail Group in 1930]. ... Waded thro' paper accumulation. DMS [Morse] rang up peeved at decision to put back minesweepers for LCTs, told him about 2 weeks delay all through. NA [Bateson] said Vice Contr peeved that H & W is not to build MTBs, said 'I not guilty'. ACNS(W) [McGrigor] said Creed meeting a fiasco & deferred. [Plan for semi-submersible Seadrome floating airfield.] ... Agreed to 2 quad tubes in inter fleet [destroyers] as alternative to 1 and full DCh armt. ...

2 March: Contr in flames about rudders of minesweepers being bottlenecks, calmed him down, nevertheless it is bad that nobody locally tackles such a matter energetically & it is left to me to find it out & get busy. [A fair point.] Held monthly corvette review, things going better but still slow & no sign of hitting the target's bull nor even an inner [shooting analogy]. ...

3 March: At Bath with a bl[oody] cold in the head. Long talk with Simeon re Rebbeck also destroyers he has had RA(D) [Rear Admiral Destroyers, now Rear Admiral I G Glennie] there who is agin big destroyers (but what will he give up?). Simeon is putting up to out all gyro-stabilisers [anti-roll] & depend on remote power control for guns: I said this was discussed & it was thought RPC would get overworked without gyro-stabilisers. Saw Dep E in C re *Black Prince* accel[erated], building S/Ms at Belfast & destroyer programme. ... Mathias [T L, ADNC] said Inter Destr Design could be ready end of April. Firms could have [hull] lines now. ...

4 March: ... Back at Admy 15.15. Contr came up. We had heart to heart talk over Corps personalities, I backed Lillicrap as my successor. Contr said Hopkins very capable but impossible to work with. He agreed with me University entrants were most desirable [rather than shipwright apprentices?]. ...

5 March: ... Jubb rang over bother with Henry Robb, who won't commence his scheme until definite & satisfactory financial arrgts have been made, phoned Robb who finally agreed to go on subject to finance being settled at meeting with Contr next Friday, fixed up meeting. Saw Jubb who spoke of provisional prices being too low [in the absence of tenders from shipyards, contract payment instalments were based on percentages of a provisional price] from technical depts, said I would

write DCW (Ships). I also spoke of H & W, he said their costs were high, he would say nothing about Rebbeck. ...

6 March: ... Contr came up re H & W's fitting out arrgts, told him I had had talk with Jubb, I thought an acc[ountan]t's investigation might help us to gauge efficiency. Bailey of H & W [probably J S Baillie of their London office] called & explained welding dev[elopment] situation, left me copy of letter, said C E in C [Whitaker] was asking for plans &c, I said he should visit Bath & then let me know if he doesn't get the matter put right, he asked what I thought of H & W. I said I was disappointed with output from such a big place [workforce then about 24,000] now that blitz troubles had been overcome & thought there should be more delegation of authority. ... At Club 1st SL introduced his son CO *Lauderdale* [Lt G D Pound, 'Hunt' class escort destroyer] wrote DDNC Bath [Lillicrap] to visit ship.

8 March: ... At FBC ... discussed the 5.25″ Cr[uiser] design, the 8 gun won but I feel sure there will be a rumpus over the reduced speed. Walsh rang that the wretched Butt business will come to a head on Thursday. [Butt was accused of revealing tender figures to a shipbuilder before contracts were placed, see 24 July.]

9 March: Contr fussed over clash between Stirling & MACs at Denny [*Empire Macdermott* and *Empire Macandrew*], phoned Mathias [J E] to go there. Swan has written that Stirling [*Cyrus*] will affect L[igh]t Carrier [*Albion*] I said Swan said it would affect laying down but not completion. ...

10 March: Contr in a stew because we have given CL [Cammell Laird] an estimate for building labour that is 5000 short. He wants statement why *Indefat[igable]*'s complement has gone up by 240 [but it was not Goodall's job to specify complement, only to try to provide accommodation in the ship], phoned Dep Contr & Lillicrap, they are seeing to it, wired [sent telegram] Pigott. Mathias rang that Stirling at Dennys [*Cybele*] puts back MAC ships as Russell [E W, managing director Denny] told Ayre. ... W J Holt called with design for an inshore escort, not bad sent it on: asked him to see what he could do on similar lines for a monitor. ... Scrambler gone wrong [device to distort phone calls to prevent eavesdropping; presumably much used by Goodall owing to the confidential nature of many of his phone calls]. ...

11 March: To Min[istry] of Production re Creed, Lyttelton [Oliver, the Minister] sleek & getting fluffy, you can picture him kissing babies for votes. Alex[ander] smoked first a fat cigar then a pipe. You can picture him posing as the independent working man & getting votes. Awful waste

German pressure mines laid in shallow water were a threat that could not be countered with conventional minesweeping gear. The Stirling craft was developed in great secrecy as a counter, 360ft long, 60ft broad and 30ft deep. This lattice structure with buoyancy chambers was to be towed over suspected mines, which if detonated would dissipate much of their force through the open structure. Denny erected *Cybele* seen here at Dumbarton from material fabricated by Arrol and Motherwell Bridge, launching on 16 November 1943. She and her sister *Cyrus* from Swan Hunter were deployed in Seine Bay after the D-Day landings. (© *National Maritime Museum, London G11240*)

of time, Min of Prod will sum up his views, I know we have not finished with Creed yet. Langley (DGD) came up, we came to some agreement on screed for Fl.ACs [Fleet aircraft carriers] & I sent this to Dep 1st SL. RA(S) [Rear Admiral (Submarines) C B Barry] called spoke of Welman [one-man submarine], showed him Cole's reports on anti U/B [U boat] weapons. ...

13 March: To Whites. Weather cold & passage in boat from Portsmouth to Cowes stirred up my nose. Work looked pretty good. Welding work is getting on but not as fast as I had hoped. Milne said he could take the two destroyers (*Centaur* & *Celt*) as 1943 design. Not much room in [White's] boat [building] dept for bigger craft. ...

19 March: ... Contr came up & held a small meeting re corvettes, more at expense of 100,000 tons of merchant ships, saw A Ayre at lunch, he

very fed up & gloomy, said our organisation rotten, no boss to allot priority, still other interested parties they must put up with it (Stirlings a grievance). Meryon called, gave him cost particulars & asked for help, told him details of Butt affair. …

20 March: Dep Contr called after inspecting corvette bridge mock-up, which went well, he thinks this should do for frigates. He said *Grenville* wardroom (Swan Hunter) had gone wrong somehow, luckily he saw it in time. Contr phoned re 'Bel' boat [*Empire Viceroy* with three 120-ton derricks] at Barrow. *Georgic* [Cunard White Star liner bombed at Suez 14 Jul 41, returned to UK Mar 1943] at H & W (corvettes in lieu). After talk with McCarthy & King [F V] had a meeting with Contr engines & boilers are now the limiting factor in increased frigate output (assuming we get the labour for fitting out). …

23 March: … Dep 1st SL sent for me while Mt.Batten gave tongue on Habbakuk [planned floating aircraft carrier made of ice]. Mt.B excited & nervous: I said very little, feel the whole thing wants careful investigation before I express an opinion. …

24 March: Contr decided Stirling to stay with Denny at expense of destr[oyers], phoned Mathias. [Much of the Stirling craft structure was fabricated by structural engineers so should not have been a great drain on the shipbuilder's resources, as little outfitting and no machinery.] Pigott called, told him of Stirling, discussed Clydebank layout, told him approx dimensions of new *Ark R*. [*Malta* class] begged him to keep an open mind on welding as he said shipowners against it as it will cost more & they don't want the saving in wt [weight] unless it saves them money. Contr app'd placing orders for 6 Inter. Destr. With Davies worked out labour for 21 more frigates at expense of 100,000 tons merchant ships, sent to Contr, who says 'No more labour, our 12,000 all right'. Got busy on Hendon Dock [fitting-out base for escorts at Sunderland] & other SYDC schemes, rang Stanley, also asked him to see if his records showed what Butt did with Blyth in 5-6/39. [An order for two boom defence vessels was placed.] Lunched with Mrs Phillimore's TU [trade union] people, 1st L. isn't the only Labour man who is vain & complacent.

25 March: Dippy's draft of High [warship] Prices arrived. Worked on it & sent to Sec [Permanent Secretary of Admiralty Sir H V Markham] & copies to E in C & DEE. T.G. [Thank God] … McCarthy phoned, Ormston wants frigate dwgs: phoned O. & told him scheme for frigates at Barrow was off. McCarthy said he was expecting to drop Alloa [proposed escort fitting-out base on the Forth], told Contr. …

26 March: To Haslar with Fowler [Sir Ralph, Operational Research], Darwin [NPL] & DSR [Wright]. In morning saw S/M expts & 72' MTB also a dumb [not under power?] turn & cavitation tunnel [for testing propellers]. DSR thought square stern of *Ark R* would be bad for flow over after end of flight deck. I must take this up. Darwin thought some strain-meters he has at NPL would help us, Gawn will take this up. Fowler felt we should press on with variable pitch propellers. Lunch at Blockhouse [submarine base in Gosport]. Then to Horsea [island in Portsmouth harbour with lake for testing free running models and torpedoes] steering of *Ark R*. with bow rudder only is not good, rudder too small [for emergency use if main rudders damaged]. Everybody agreed we should have better facilities for steering tests. Tea at C in C's, met Ad Supt [Clarke].

27 March: … Contr came up … He is bagging Lord Reith [former Director General of BBC, later an MP and now a Captain RNVR] … A lot of paper flowed in while I was away yesterday, including a letter from Wallace [Brown Brothers, Edinburgh], re Robb, who is in trouble for using Govt timber for his private work without licence [they were building three cargo ships], phoned Wallace who said Govt auditors had put Cantlie [AS Rosyth] on Robb's track. Wallace wants me to squash the charge because of the public scandal & effect on Robb's work. Spoke Contr who brushed it aside.

28 March (Sunday): After sleeping on Wallace's letter, wrote to say it would be improper for me to step in. Robb should see Cantlie, confess & beg for mercy.

30 March: … McCarthy wants to requisition Blyth [shipyard], left with Contr. Contr told me what had happened re H & W, he has had a heart to heart talk with Bailey [Baillie]. Thornycroft & Barnaby called re Habbakuk. I was quite frank & said we must play but if B. is convinced the scheme is impracticable he must say so. … FOIC S'ton [Southampton, Vice Admiral Sir J M Pipon] called, said scheme for using [dry?] dock at S'ton for [building] corvettes was dead. Left for Bath.

31 March: … *Dasher* [escort carrier lost 27 Mar due to internal explosion] gave instructions to get on with dwgs for A's & A's [Alterations & Additions] to petrol stowage. … ASCBS rang up that Vickers want to put *Swiftsure* [cruiser] back 3 mos. for dynamos & hangar alteration. With Woollard, Williamson & Lillicrap went into docking *Belgol* [oiler] in 2750 ton fl. dock. [Her light displacement about 2,500 tons, and weight per foot run slightly higher than a destroyer in a 380ft long dock, so probably safe if no cargo on board.] …

2 April: ... Discussed with Watson the frigate pre-fab situation, he will go to Glasgow next week. I think McC[arthy] has been too slow in setting up his progressing organisation. Talk with Cole on anti U-boat weapons [Squid mortar?]. ...

5 April: Wrote McCloghrie [G, ADNC] & Stantan [A G W, ADNC Canada] re standardisation of Brit, US & Canadian escorts. Letter from Merrington arrived Sat [3 Apr] re a Constr[uctor] Lieut Cdr. for training shipwrights for C.O. craft [Combined Operations], wrote DPS [Director of Personal Services, Rear Admiral H T C Walker] asking that in future such a paper be referred to me. ... Letter from Billmeir [J A, shipowner] re buying Blyth, saw A Ayre & James & decided to do nothing. ...

6 April: At Newcastle. Saw FOIC [Maxwell] who wanted to know about Blyth & *Manxman*, told him what I knew. He said Turnbull at Blyth was doing well & corvette labour was shaping well. [Not true, Blyth was well behind in completing its ships.] To H[awthorn] L[eslie] looked at *Diadem* [cruiser] & *Savage* [destroyer with new twin 4.5in mounting]: Rowell thinks he can build the new larger Lt. Carrier [*Hermes* class] but I am to send him more definite particulars. After lunch to Hendon Dock, met

'S' class destroyer *Savage* on completion by Hawthorn Leslie in June 1943. She is sporting the first twin 4.5in Mark IV mounting forward (later fitted in the 'Battles'), hastily converted from a spare Mark II for *Illustrious*. Her two aft 4.5in are the first two single Mark V mountings, built by Vickers-Armstrongs at Barrow as Reg Nos 1 and 2 under contract 400G at £6,867 each excluding guns. The other seven 'S' class had the 55° elevation 4.7in Mark XXII mountings. In other respects she was typical of most of the wartime Emergency destroyers, with the same hull form and conservative 40,000 shp machinery to expedite production. (*Author's collection*)

Harry Hunter [of North Eastern Marine Engineering], bitter bleak spot in north wind, spray sweeps over basin from sea in SE gale. ... To Pickersgill [shipyard] where I was favourably impressed but must get on to C E in C & IMTU [Inspector of Machine Tool Utilisation]. To Clarke Chapman [marine equipment maker at Gateshead], Woodeson [W A, Chairman] gets on wonderfully considering his age [74], but why are we still building seaplane cranes? [They were used for boat handling after aircraft facilities were removed from cruisers.] ...

7 April: At Newcastle, to Vickers Walker. Hendin looks very groggy, this yard is obviously missing his vigour. He & Swan still say they will launch the first carrier in Aug [*Vengeance*]. A lot of talk over *Swiftsure*, it seems to me that they couldn't keep Dec. anyhow, as first it was dynamo alt[eratio]n, now we say 'All right, don't alter the dynamos' & they say it is the hangar altn [she was originally designed for aircraft, now removed]. Must leave to ASCBS, later Allcock [F B, Superintending Electrical Engineer, North East] came to see me & said Pomeroy had refused to go to Bath to fix up. To Swan H, old Swan apologised for writing to Contr re Stirling & resulting delay. To Neptune, *Pretoria Castle* behind, corvettes coming on. [Normally Neptune yard never built warships as its founder John Wigham Richardson was a Quaker.] In evening had talk with ASCBS who thinks it is a mistake for McCarthy to browbeat.

8 April: Back in office. An abominable paper accumulation. Saw Contr re Blyth & Billmeir, passed latter's letter to him. Contr passed over report that new Can[adian] Tribal is weak, told him they are stronger than old Tribals, some B.F. [bloody fool] has been forcing her too much. ... Saw King [F V] re machinery of *Haida* [Canadian 'Tribal' now preserved at Hamilton]. Contr spoke of H & W, he will get Rebbeck here. I drafted a letter for him. Contr says we are to build more frigates at the expense of 93,000 tons of merchant ships. ...

9 April: ... With John [W G] went into crane situation [shipyards adopting more welding allowed more prefabrication, hence needing to lift heavier units at the berth]. Took chair at SYDC meeting, everything went well till we reached cranes, however we decided what to do. [The committee was dissolved in July.] ... Went home v. tired.

12 April: Received Pension Papers. At FBC discussed 5.25″ cruiser, design voted good [but it was never built] but Langley annoying wants still more changes. .... Contr sent for me re frigate steel, situation is bad & I must get it right, spoke McCarthy but he took the line 'DCW, nothing to do with me'. ...

13 April: At Bath. Discussed steel situation with Hopkins [DCW] preparatory to Contr's meeting next Friday, arranged for meeting with steel control & frigate people re steel for pre-fabricators. Had talk with Dep Contr who wants to alter Battles to get in 3 twin mtgs. Discussed with Lillicrap, Mathias [T L] & Vosper [A J] type 275 [gunnery radar] in Battles, new twins for[war]d & 3 twin design, annoyed by M's & V's lackadaisical attitude. At Dep Contr's meeting on NC got dates of *Diadem* & *Apollo* [fast minelayer] put forward but Swan H's 2nd Lt Car [*Leviathan*] goes back. ...

14 April: ... Reith [with Combined Operations] saw Lillicrap, Hopkins fears he is out to make a job for himself. ... Asked DNO when new mtg would be in supply, he said Dec '44. [The first 4.5in Mark 6 went into *Saintes* in 1946.]

16 April: ... Barr called re two apprentices being bagged by us. ... Hopkins, Le Maitre [A S, Principal Assistant Secretary], Bateson, Reith, Parnell [? J W, constructor] & I to Contr's meeting on steel. Contr is heading for trouble over his target dates. [Operational staff needed to know when new ships would become available, unrealistic dates were not helpful.] Johnson [R S] sore because Contr says we must employ more women, also says we shall stir up a hornet's nest if we tackle H & W. ACNS(W) [now Rear Admiral W R Patterson] came in re 12 commandments for WT.ness. [watertightness] ... 1st SL's meeting on A/S warfare, I consider everybody was claiming to have done v. well & I don't think so e.g. Hedgehog & elevating & depressing oscillator [depth-finding sonar].

17 April: ... Bailey [Baillie] of H & W came to see McCarthy (away) & saw Davies [W J A], he (B) wants D. to go to Belfast before Firm comes here: I thought this might be dangerous so saw Contr who thought it might do good. ... King came in to get 2 new design Battles at Fairfield & none at Stephen. Barr agreed so altered minutes of meeting & told Mathias [J E]. James brought up screed re H & W I made marginal notes & returned it. Started working on 1st Lord's Trade Union delegation paper. ...

18 April (Sunday): AR warnings about 13.55-14.10, 22.20-22.40. 60 today. To my joy I now feel that I am free. I have always felt that I undertook to serve till I was 60. I have now come thro' nearly 7 years as DNC & have had to deal with more difficulties than I think any of my predecessors have had to tackle. Inadequate staff. Unexpected losses of good men by death (Hill, Bailey [both in *Thetis*], Bryant [air raid], Palmer [H H?]). A corps of old men & youngsters with far too few between the ages of 30 & 45 (in 1939). The old men are feeling the strain, most of the

youngsters are doing well but inexperience is against them. A 1st L. & 1st SL with no consideration for the RCNC. A pleasant but weak Contr followed by ?

19 April: ... Presided at meeting with Steel Control to consider steel for frigates particularly & naval ships generally. ... [Contr] sketched out to Davies the H & W situation preparatory to D. going to Belfast tomorrow. I said Rebbeck held a card we could not over-trump viz Belfast labour (mixed with religion & politics). [At that time H & W were employing at Belfast about 13,200 in the shipyard, 8,900 in the engine works and 1,900 in their electrical department, the most in any British shipyard, with a preponderance of Protestants.] ...

20 April: Held corvette & frigate meeting: labour situation is bad: it is sticking out a mile that presently we shall have these ships ready to be fitted out but insufficient labour, then other new construction will be thrown out of balance badly. ... Sanders described to me expts at Teddington [National Physical Laboratory towing tank] on Habbakuk, he couldn't say who sent the form. McCarthy & Walsh talked staff, latter naturally doesn't like McC having unpaid ass[istan]ts [Meryon? retired shipbuilders?] but he can't get decent paid ones for us! ...

21 April: E in C came in re fitting turbines & double reduction gear in 2 frigates for trial, talked with McCarthy, then told E in C I would suggest 2 at H & W, phoned Watson to know what was the highest speed we could get out of frigate size. [Length and hull form put a practical upper limit on speed.] ... Wrote Beatty (C E in C) [W D, Assistant Civil Engineer in Chief] re McT Scott [MacTaggart Scott, maker of catapults and auxiliary machinery, Edinburgh] & Hendon Dock. At Habbakuk meeting, a gang of amateurs have been messing about, now they are getting cold feet & we are brought in. ...

22 April: ... Saw Contr re stabilisers & Habbakuk, told him my feet were getting cold over fitting out labour for frigates, I feared hull & machy would be ready but not labour for fitting out, then ships will be sent to naval yards to be fitted out at expense of other warships & the whole naval programme be thrown into confusion. Contr wants labour particulars of H & W, phoned Hannaford. Craven called, I said I was uneasy about the naval yard [Vickers-Armstrongs, Tyne], he promised the 1st Lt Carrier would be launched to date [*Colossus*]. Meryon called, said Scotts don't want to take another 'Weapon' [five ordered in Apr 1943, none completed] wrote Greig. ... Went thro' LCG(M) [Landing Craft Gun, Medium] dwgs, not very good, got Baker to get altered.

23 April: Good Friday. Sir M McAlpine [civil engineering contractor] called with a team & a design of reinforced concrete seadrome; like all the others thought has only been given to a crude hull; Contr turned papers over to me to write report. Woollard came in & I gave him Habbakuk papers to read as he will have to help me. Davies back from H & W, I was not very pleased with result, he saw Contr. Sent on paper backing E in C on Lt Wt [light weight] Diesels. [Did this result in the Deltic engine?]

24–26 April: On leave.

27 April: Talked with McCarthy re setting up Admy schools to train women for fitting out frigates: then met with Contr who did not bite hard, said he had no fears for Clyde where fitting out labour would be plentiful after *Cey[lon]*, *Bell[ona]*, *Indefat[igable]* & *Impl[acable]* are finished! ... With Contr went to fire-fighting demonstration at Haslar, truth is I was not very impressed; men knew exactly what was coming & what to do, very different to the real thing in a ship. ...

28 April: ... Baker came over loss of two LCG(L), can do nothing till I get full report but these ships are really barges & if sent to sea in very bad weather, the worst may happen. [*LCG(L).15* and *16* had been swamped off Milford Haven 26 Apr.] ...

29 April: Told Bogie the facts behind today's meeting with H & W. At 11.00 to Contr's room, CMSR [Lithgow] & DMB [Ayre] there and all the H & W party: Rebbeck on his best behaviour. Contr said Firm must organise a separate Repair Est[ablishment] & take on more frigates at expense of minesweepers & merchant ships. CMSR said they must take on *Georgic* [rebuilt May 1943–Dec 1944]. ... At lunch, Rebbeck said in future communications to H & W were to come from Contr only, not CMSR (Contr confirmed this). Later I told Contr firm had promised a L [hell] of a lot, we should have to see they lived up to it. He told me of Workman Clark yard for LCTs, fabricate in N. Ireland. [The shipyard at Belfast had closed in 1935.]

30 April: At Bath. Discussed with Dep. Contr petrol stowage of Biters [US-built escort carriers with petrol stowage not meeting RN standards], stabilisers in 2 Battles, frigates. With Lillicrap, Bartlett & Mitchell [A] went into design of Lt Carriers, in middle message came that calculations said GM [metacentric height: a measure of a ship's stability] was not 6 but 4.3 ft! This shakes me & shows what troubles we have with dilutees. Dictated notes. After lunch went into new *Ark R.* design with L[illicrap], B[artlett], Sherwin & Lackenby [H, assistant constructor]. Agreed midship lift out of court as stress is too high. [The flight deck was the upper flange of the hull girder, so making an opening in it near midships

would increase stresses.] Two designs to be investigated, one with single, other with double hangar, 5 screws. ...

1 May: Saw Contr with copy of H & W report, he app'd, cancelling minesweepers [nine *Algerines*] & ordering frigates. He gave me letter from FO(S) [Barry] re X craft for USA, saw Craven who said he would play, wrote him & Barry & Lillicrap. Craven gave me some of inner story of Bevin [Ernest, Minister of Labour] & Rebbeck, said former is out to find an excuse for not supplying 12,000 for frigates & latter must be watched to see he keeps his promises. ... Saw Baker re Workman Clark's old yard for LCTs. He told me of findings of inquiry into loss of LCG(L)s. [In building up the superstructure in the tank deck to mount the guns, a well had been left at the forward end which flooded easily, plunging the craft.] Contr said I ought to be able to get dr[aughts]men from H & W, wrote Rebbeck. Dealt

(Sir) Rowland Baker (1908–83) was one of the RCNC's most talented designers. As a young constructor, he had made a success designing sloops and minesweepers. Goodall put him in charge of landing craft design in 1940; his LCT designs proved eminently practical. As Superintendent of Landing Craft, he also oversaw production, largely by structural engineers. Appointed a Commodore by the RCN, he was responsible for that Navy's post-war designs. Success in programme management on the RN's first nuclear submarine *Dreadnought* led in 1962 to him being given the responsibility (and resources) to take the four Polaris submarines from ordering to completion in only five years. This notable achievement (impossible today) was recognised with a knighthood. (*D K Brown*)

with Fin[ancial] Sec[retary]'s [Hall] paper on allegations of Ass[istan]t Overseers Ring.

3 May: ... 1st L wants a draft reply to Sir R Clarry [R G, MP for Newport] re scamped work at Lobnitz. [Minesweepers *Hound* and *Hydra* had been criticised, including defective bilge keels.] ... Got ready for FBC when discussion was on Dep Contr's scheme to modify 1943 Battles, it was agreed 1st 21 should be repeats, last 5 new design preferably with 3 twin mtgs. Hopkins called, said he had said no twist in frigate shaft bracket palms [connection to hull], wrote Lillicrap to ensure production & design sides speak with one voice.

4 May: ... Lord Reith came up & had a long talk on Admy organisation, I said he should go round to shipyards & see what they thought of the way Admy worked, he objected as it would look as tho' he was spying. He has made up his mind I am not an AC [Assistant Controller] for Warship Production.

5 May: ... Cancelled my proposed visit to Glasgow this week, which instead of being easy (Contr away) has been most fierce; I am all behind. FO(S) called, said our S/Ms are doing well in Med. [Helped by Ultra intelligence on enemy ship movements.] Could we slide over from U's to S's at Walker, wrote Lillicrap. Tobin & Pounder [C C, H & W engine designer] called re dr'men from H & W, promised to do something. ...

6 May: E in C came in to discuss high profits & D of C putting up his prov[isional] price estimate. I advised we should not press D of C that we would give up estimating if he disregarded our figures. R Rowell called, said thank you for getting a move on *Savage*, we will now keep our date. ... He suggested Caledon for frigates with turbine double reduction machy. Got H Main [Henry, managing director, Caledon shipyard in Dundee] in & he took it on, reported to Contr. [*Loch Tralaig* and *Loch Arkaig* ordered 2 Feb.] ... Capt (E) Jameson called back from Washington, said Americans much perturbed over torpedoing of N[orth] Carolina, torp set to shallow depth [torpedoed abreast forward turrets 15 Sep 42]. Lt. Lawrence [presume RNVR which most LCT officers were] called back from his passage across bay [Biscay?] in TLC Mk IV. [Flimsy and not very seaworthy.] ...

7 May: Locked myself up in a room in Arch Blk [Admiralty Arch block spanning The Mall] & finished Island [?] aircraft carrier, sent it to ACNS(W). Started on RCNC into Navy [an ongoing theme of Goodall's which never came to pass]. Prepared for Board Meeting. 1st L gets my goat, sitting in the red leather throne with Barnes [Sir J S, Deputy Secretary, Admiralty] on one side & Markham on the other crouching like little dogs on watch. I felt 1st L was airing off to impress me. He remarked on absence of many Sea Lords & said regular Board Meetings so scantily attended were lacking in authority. He talked of corvette & frigate from Staff point of view & said he should be informed earlier of the military characteristics of new designs. He thought complements too big [continually going up as new equipment like radar was added]. After much guff like that, the designs were approved. He knew nothing about a Squid [A/S mortar] but preferred a 4″ gun HA (in a ship specially designed for A/Sub!). [Goodall clearly had a low opinion of his political chief; Alexander remained as First Lord for nearly all the war.]

10 May: ... With E in C, Hannaford & Dippy went into High Profits, H. still unhelpful. Then to Sec's meeting, much talk which did not get us any further, D of C was right in insisting we cannot explain *Unbeaten* satisfactorily without running [down] dockyard. [Vickers-Armstrongs' price from Barrow records was £175,054, cost of hull & machinery £95,491, profit £76,563 i.e. 77.7 per cent on cost. Total cost to Admiralty including Admiralty Supply Items £220,000. *Una* at Chatham was ordered at the same time and completed ten months later at a total cost of £232,000. Excluding ASIs her cost would have been about £187,000 or 90 per cent more than *Unbeaten*, and that is without including a 'profit' margin, which dockyards did not charge. When the Admiralty assessed whether tenders from shipbuilders looked 'fair and reasonable', DNC, E in C and DEE with D of C compared the figures with similar vessels built in dockyards, and if they were broadly similar, they accepted them. V-A would have known dockyard submarine prices which were published in the Navy Estimates, so could pitch their tender a little below and still make a huge profit. They had been making high profits from submarines from the earliest days, admittedly from building them very efficiently. The reason for the high costs of dockyard newbuilding was not explained, but their material costs would have been broadly similar to those of shipbuilders, so it must be due to much higher labour costs and overheads. Perhaps if dockyard managers found themselves with surplus labour or overrunning costs on modernisation jobs, they booked some of the labour costs to new building rather than to repairs.] I said I thought now we had could estimate within ±5% but must check this. [Before the war, the Admiralty had no access to shipbuilders' books, but they took such powers during the war, so they had a better idea of shipbuilders' actual costs.] Dep Sec wants hull cost of 'S' Cl. at Chatham [*P.228* and *P.229*]. Got Sanders to go tomorrow to DFSL's [Deputy First Sea Lord] meeting on more AA guns. At FBC Simeon came & wielded heavy stick which resulted in all NOs piping down (including DFSL) & leaving me to fight the battle on 3rd mtg in Battles [became *Darings*]. I said it was more than an A & A, we had only said it 'looked possible'. DFSL will write C in C about torp mtg out & we have to work out the design.

11 May: ... *Diadem*'s date goes back after I had persuaded Firm to bring it forward: I have to take up with Rowell. With Lillicrap, Bartlett & Mitchell discussed Lt Carrier, particularly WT subdivision: decided on twin rudders & more cut up aft [to reduce turning circle]. ... Talked S/M battery containers [resistance to depth-charge explosions?] with Pamplin & welding pressure hulls at Chatham. [Weight saved by removing riveted overlaps and stiffener flanges allowed the pressure hull thickness to be increased so giving a deeper diving depth.]

Submarines were drydocked before handing over to install and check all underwater fittings and give the hull a final coating. Palmers Hebburn reinstated their Jarrow drydock in 1941; *Uther* was the first submarine docked there, from 26 May to 3 June 1943. She was completed by Vickers-Armstrongs' Walker yard on 15 August. (*Author's collection*)

13 May: Back in London. ... Letter from Swan re strike at Cleveland [Bridge, who were fabricating sections] putting back Stirling [*Cyrus*] & therefore Carrier, phoned Stanley to see if Swan could do Cleveland work, told Contr. ...

14 May: ... Milne of White's called, red hot against Paterson of Boilermakers [trade union], told him we don't care what we pay if we get a good return, he must prove that Paterson is hindering production. He said he could, went with him to Contr who rubbed in the same: he said a Trade Dispute is dealt with by Fin Sec, he can only deal with production. I fear White's welded destroyers are going to be slow [i.e. late; five 'C' class on order]. ... With Offord to Ord[nance] Board meeting, before that went into Undex Works [Underwater Experiment Works] & 'Selling Shells to Simple Sailors' an OB screed showing up Hadfield & Firth Brown [Sheffield makers of shells].

Diadem was one of the five *Dido* class cruisers ordered in September 1939 which were completed to a modified design, removing her fifth twin 5.25in mounting and increasing anti-aircraft weaponry. Delivery was planned for February 1942 but with construction suspended in 1940 due to other priorities and delays to her machinery, she was the last to be completed in January 1944. Seen here leaving her builders, Hawthorn Leslie were paid £712,145 for hull and electrical and £412,063 for machinery (total £1,124,298), excluding ASIs such as armament, armour and electronics, resulting in a profit of £74,201 (7 per cent of cost). (*Author's collection*)

15 May: S I Hill called before leaving for Kilindini [Constructor Captain for Eastern Fleet]. ... Contr came up, showed him photo of D.E. [destroyer escort] from USA with very corrugated side, he took it away, said he would show to 1st L. ... Wrote Grant [of John Brown, Sheffield] as I should like to see him re armour research in light of attack on shell makers. Copy of cost of Chatham S/M looks queer to me. ...

18 May: ... Reith came up & talked RCNC into RN wants to go for a much bigger thing viz. all navy technicians in one RN body. Held Corvette & Frigate meeting, most talk over nature of contract for ships built in one place & fitted out elsewhere. Later Contr agreed that separate contracts were impracticable & that 2 sloops given up at Chatham for 2 frigates need not proceed. [Two *Black Swans* were completed at Chatham after the war and two cancelled.] ...

19 May: ... At Struct[ural] Eng[ineers] C'tee on Habbakuk, a lot of talk about properties of material. At end Southwell [R V, structural engineer]

raised question whether it was really a practicable engineering proposition e.g. propulsion problems. ...

20 May: In Glasgow, at Denny's, firm came forward on some dates & will take 2 Weapons [*Rifle* and *Spear*, later cancelled]. ... Inspected hydrofoil boat (not a convert). To Yarrow: no grumbles except labour being taken away for frigates. To Clydebank, Mrs Eden [Beatrice, wife of Foreign Secretary Anthony Eden] launched *Nairana* [escort carrier converting from Port liner]: told Pigott no good saying workmanship in *Bermuda* [cruiser] bound to be 1st Cl. because ship built at Clydebank. *Vanguard* hopeless & *Bellerophon* suspended looks bad. Inspected frigate bridge [for *Loch Fada*]. *Nairana* won't keep her date. ... Inspected US LSTs looked good but very elaborate [being refitted]. ...

A classic shot from the extensive John Brown collection of photographs now at the National Records of Scotland, Edinburgh. This view of the cruiser *Bermuda* (also on the jacket) shows her at the east wharf of the fitting-out basin in June 1942. Her forward triple 6in Mark XXIII mountings had arrived in May in coaster *Empire Jill* (registered numbers 37 and 38, Vickers-Armstrongs contract 351G placed in September 1938, price £68,680 each excluding guns). The 6in director has yet to be fitted, although the lantern for the Type 273 surface-warning radar is being installed forward of the bridge, a less than ideal location. The shipyard diary records Yard No 568 leaving for trials on 7 August. The destroyer alongside is *Milne*, transferred from Scotts on 31 December 1941 for completion following that shipyard's production problems. (*UCS*)

21 May: ... To Scotts, Greig seems better with Pearson [possibly A W, assistant manager Greenock torpedo factory]. Inspected *Royalist* [cruiser], she looks all right for date. Pre-fab mast & galley are a step forward (*Serapis* [destroyer]). To Fairfield, a no. of bleats from Barr (i.e. steel concession upsetting orders, labour to frigates, *Bellona* gun mtgs), asked ASCBS to hold a meeting. Inspected *Bellona* & she is certainly well on. Barr cannot take both a Lt Carrier & a big Fleet. To Stephen [adjacent shipyard] inspected *Ariadne* [fast minelayer] well on, firm cannot take a new design Lt Carrier. [Light fleet *Ocean* had been ordered but *Hermes* class too big for them.] Dined with John Stephen [J G, director] & had interesting talk on shipyard practice. Must keep in touch with him.

24 May: O. Bellasis called on return from Washington, I scent trouble in comparison between US & British destroyers. ...

25 May: ... Went to Public Accounts C'tee meeting, the whole afternoon was spent on other matters than high profits which will be taken on Thursday. Atmosphere that of a Court with Exchequer & Audit counsel for prosecution, chairman Judge, rest of C'tee jury. Treasury counsel for defence on the whole. Whitaker [F A] got a ragging from [George] Benson, Labour member for Chesterfield over cost of [Bath] headquarters & Wrennery for C in C WA [Western Approaches, Derby House in Liverpool]. Nobody said that P.M. intimated this work had got to be done hey presto & damn the expense. ...

26 May: Saw Sec [Markham] re pts that might arise at PA C'tee tomorrow. (Be conciliatory except with Benson, don't use term 'ring' [cartel]). ... Visited Dam[age] Control School, Capt agreed to Mason [H R] going but was sceptical about Thorpe [T, constructor]. Heard officer speak who had been in *Barham* when torpedoed & in *Naiad*, badly burnt, his face & hands had been treated by plastic surgery. Heard Gunnery Officer of *P of W* [McMullen] who of course blamed us, said 90% of dam. control depended on design & workmanship & only 10% on officers & men!

27 May: ... Worked on High Profits & attended PA C'tee, got thro' fairly well till it came to S/Ms, I was then in for a roasting but Ch'man [Sir Assheton Pownall MP] stopped Benson & we adjourned till Wed. week. I thought Hurcomb [Sir Cyril, Ministry of War Transport] put up a poor show over the Porter frauds [a boiler scaling company from Liverpool who had been putting in claims for fictitious employees]. ... Butt committed for trial: what a disgrace. [See 24 July.]

28 May: Corvette contract meeting with Hendon Dock & builders on [River] Wear & nearby. ... Builders emphatic they would not make one

comprehensive contract [they would only be responsible for hull not fitting out] & I gave in. E in C & DEE won't get the trouble but DNC may. … Ramsay Moon [structural engineer] called, wants John [W G] to be chairman of Locked-up Stresses Sub-C'tee, said I could not spare him: we canvassed everybody else & I rang Ayre but he would not bite. Merrington called, told him he ought to have kept Mountbatten from going wobbly over Habbakuk: he apologised for trying to commit me with DPS to find a constructor for training: he looked ill. Mann [H R, constructor] called not very confident of himself in Fleet, talked of expense, fact is he is keen but his wife isn't (I guess). [Constructors attached to ships were in uniform, so could have high mess bills.]

29 May: Held Frigate & Corvette meeting of Clyde firms to settle contracts: less matey crowd than NE Coast, but we reached agreement. Fleming [W Y F, chairman of Fleming & Ferguson] a bluffer who squirmed as soon as I tried to pin him down. Hancock [probably J, Assistant Secretary Admiralty] came in re green labour for firms giving up labour for frigates & said they will not ask for enough. C[hief] of Staff of Force H [Captain J M Howson] called for a Constr Cdr. [Commander], said I could not supply nor could D of D [Talbot], he thought he might get one out of Home Fleet. Finished week v. tired.

31 May: … Lunch with Craven who told me of changes impending at Walker & Barrow. I spoke of insufficient berths for new Ark Rs [*Malta* class] & cooperation with Canada: also told him of my fears on armour research. Saw Contr 1st time for several days, told him what I had been doing (PA C'tee, Habbakuk, frigate contracts) he gave me several pts. he wants examined, notably Lobnitz not getting enough steel. Left for Bath. Told Contr E in C wants to place orders for [machinery for] Battles & Lt Carriers, he agreed to 1st but wants complete picture of 2nd. [Eight of latter ordered 12 Jul 43.]

1 June: … U boat down off West of Scotland (2nd lost on exercises). [*Untamed* sank in Firth of Clyde 30 May owing to incorrect use of the Otway speed log. Salvaged and rebuilt as *Vitality*. First sub lost was *Vandal*.] …

2 June: At Bath. With Cole discussed US & British destroyers and BDEs [British destroyer escorts], Cdr Millis USN was present, showed him the snorter from C in C Med [Admiral Sir A B Cunningham], gave Cole general directions. … Honours list out Joughin [J C, CBE] & Sims [A J, OBE] but DNC dept. scores another duck. [Both were constructors but neither was based in Bath.] I fear Bath staff is getting very disgruntled (outburst from Williamson). …

3 June: Presided at meeting to consider Fighter Direction arrangements in Light Carriers, DAWT [Director of Naval Air Warfare & Flying Training, Captain J P Wright] created a good atmosphere by explaining reason for alterations. Firms agreed to do without delay. ... With E in C lunched with Sir G Nelson & directors of English Electric re armour welding, reversible & v[ariable] pitch propellers (hydraulic). At Habbakuk Dep 1st SL walked very delicately (Mt.Batten was there). Ralph Freeman [civil engineer] good & definite: every time difficulties are pointed out, new schemes ½ baked are rushed up to close the breach e.g. trunks outside for access to nacelles [propulsion?]. ...

4 June: At Birkenhead. Talk with Johnson re High Profits, Shipw[righ]t Prize. Then looked at scheme for new Fl Carrier on No.6 slip, the only practicable one: the truth is that in any yard one Fl & one Lt Carrier in the same year is overloading. Had a good walk round, [all] welded S's looked all right [first *Subtle* laid down 1 Feb], a lot of pre-fab is going on but J. says it is costing more than the old system tho' permitting greater production. I thought he ought to move cranes on east side of No.6 farther east. After lunch talked prog[ramme] with Peake [H S, PSO], Hamilton [J, shipyard manager] & McMenemy [W H, engine works manager], don't think *Ark R* will launch Dec '44 [actual 3 May 50]. ...

5 June: Back in office. ... 1st L after Contr re reply to C in C Med criticising Battles. Talk with Contr he thought Lillicrap should go to USA seeing he is my probable successor. I said I had fixed Cole [to go to US] & L. couldn't be spared. He gave me papers re *Georgic*. Stuff pouring in over cost of dockyard built ships. Bogie called, Baker came & we discussed building LCTs in N. Ireland. McLaughlin's price excessive & scheme halved [presumably a potential contractor]. Saw Contr who agreed we tell McL. this, get alt[ernative] tender from Chapman [steel fabricators in Belfast] & get Smith & Pearson busy at Warrenpoint [also steel fabricators in Belfast, Warrenpoint Shipyard set up for them later in 1943]. Bogie said H & W cannot do a big *Ark R*.

7 June: Phoned Lillicrap about going to USA instead of Cole, he agreed Cole is the man for destroyers & to my suggestion that he should go afterwards. Told Contr asked L. to send me ratio Armament Weight/ Stand[ard] Displacement for Battles & previous destroyers: armt wt. to include incidental to armt [includes supports, hoists etc as well as the gun mountings themselves]. This arrived in time for FB C'tee. ... Went to Sec's meeting re High Profits, they all seemed convinced I was for it next Wednesday. ... Had a good say on C in C Med's tirade against Battles, D of D backed me up. ACNS(W) has to frame answer, I have to give a part. FBC accepted that only 6 Lights can be built. [Finally only four.]

9 June: … Went thro' High Profits stuff. Attended Public Accts C'tee, I got badly mauled over S/M costs & *KGV* as I expected. I think I made a tactical error in giving figures for actual rise in costs 1937-40 & saying what I assumed rise would be. [DNC had overestimated the anticipated increase in costs between contract signing and delivery several years later, which would have to be reflected in the shipbuilder's tender price; and also the shipbuilders' overhead rates, which had reduced following the big increase in orders with rearmament. The result was that shipbuilders' costs were less than expected so profits higher.] I got in no counter-attack on Benson & in fact came away depressed. Truth is I had a bad case over submarines. [Benson put no fewer than 130 questions as reported in the Committee's report of evidence, which although searching were fair. Fortunately for Goodall, the true reason for very high prices (and hence profits) was not raised, that the warship shipbuilders had a price fixing cartel. While the Admiralty suspected such from the bunching of prices tendered, they did not investigate, believing the resulting prices to be 'fair and reasonable'.] …

10 June: … Ad[miralty] Undex Works has opened [that day at Rosyth, later became Naval Construction & Research Establishment]. … Meryon asked me to call Kyte who was on his staff in '39, said Butt had been to see him to remind him he got tender figs. over phone from him. I told Meryon I understood tender figs. were seen only by him [he was then Superintendent of Contract Work] & me and sometimes senior officer if we wanted to consult him.

11 June: … Adam [J L] called, in difficulty about giving locked-up stress data from USA, I promised to square. Called John [W G] in & Adam gave interesting account of American welded ships' cracks. [Brittle fracture arising from low temperatures, hard spots in structure and unsuitable steel.] Told Contr my confidence in welding was not shaken.

13, 14, 18–24 June: On leave.

25 June: To Bath. … Reported to Contr on [dry]docks in UK for new Ark R's. Sent on docket re larger lifts in *Ark R*. Read adverse reports on Fairmile D's from Med. Fear A B Cunningham is losing balance.

26 June: Went into designs for Bailey Bridge ships & wrote CCO. Hickey [now ADNC] told me of Sea Lord's discussion on 5.25″ cruisers. Sanders told me of SL's discussion on Battles, said to Mathias [T L] & Lillicrap that if only Bofors [A/A guns] right aft, the cut-up need not be altered. Went into Light Carrier design, structural sections bad, both L. & Bartlett said trouble is draughtsmen's stand[ard] very low especially in this section. …

29 June ... Barry called (didn't like the look of left side of his face ?slight stroke) showed him my report to Contr on more S/M production & advised him to get paper. Lunch with Craven & son, talked Naval Yard (S/Ms & ACs): new scheme for contracts: accountants on my staff: more S/Ms at Barrow. ...

30 June: Talk with James about staff for Finance Section, he thought actuary type was what we want: a good idea, he will see what is possible. [After criticism from Parliament, the Admiralty needed better control of shipbuilders' costs and prices.] Bateson came up & we went into '43 A. Carrier possibilities: I said I thought it was overloading Fairfield to give them an Ark R. repeat plus a light. Phoned Barr who will let me know his views, he wanted help for Oerlikons in *Implac*, phoned Lillicrap. Bogie will say on Sat. if H & W could take a 2nd ship. ...

1 July: W J Holt called. I sent him to Vice C with paper that he should go to Gib[raltar] in *MTB 674* [Fairmile D]. Vice C came up, he discounted C in C's moan & said he was attacking Board policy, intimated we should keep out of this battle. I said D Fairmiles had certainly shown one weakness (plywood frames) & Holt should go to Gib only & put [dock]yard wise. Vice C agreed. DNO rang re armour & A[rmour] P[iercing] shell coordination, he is not happy over Goolden [Commodore F H W, Naval Assistant to Fourth Sea Lord] he will come & see me. ... At Univ[ersity] candidates interview, educational standard is lower but we must accept this as Honours courses are not permitted: getting too many Welsh into Corps: dictated notes. ... W Ayre told me frigate [prefabricated] pieces coming in well, he promised Research reply to INA [Institution of Naval Architects] very soon. ...

2 July: Talk with Contr re Honours, he said he had asked for a larger allocation to Admiralty Civil Servants. Sir A Grant called, wants a standard shell for testing armour & a standard plate for testing shells. I said danger was we should get into a rut & soon find the plate that could deal with the standard shell & no other: what shell would enemy use? ... Talk with Vice C about CCO's organisation, he said CCO's party was in a state of chaos unless something were done we were heading for disaster: I saw draft instructions & see a Red Light. Spoke Contr re Ayre's visit to Belfast, told him I hoped he would not upset the separate Repair Staff scheme.

5 July: ... Dorling [Vice Admiral J W S, now at BAD Washington] said the DNC party is doing well but is overworked. Saw Contr who app'd ordering the 8 Lights and a repeat *Ark Royal* (Fairfield) [*Africa*], told DCW(S) [Hannaford]. ... I told him I had seen CCO (he always looks ferocious when CCO is mentioned). ...

6 July: ... Discussed C & D Cl. cruisers with Sanders & Bassett [G A, Deputy Director Dockyards] who then went to Staff meeting to decide what should be done with the poor old crocks. ... To film of launch of *Tirpitz* & destruction of French Fleet at Toulon: 4 [launch] ways used, rudders rather like old *Invincible* [battlecruiser].

7 July: ... Discussed with McCarthy extended S/M & destroyer programme for Far East War, can we use the pre-fab organisation set up for frigates? Spent most of day working on open-sided v. closed hangars of ACs, left in peace for this & enjoyed it. Langley came in re rearming *N[elson]* & *R[odney]*, wants to see dwgs ...

8 July: ... Saw Contr who said 'Order 1943 Fleet Carriers'. Did so. [*Malta*, *Gibraltar* and *New Zealand* ordered 15 Jul] ... Lunched with Ward (D of S's man in USA) [L, Deputy Director of Stores] he gave a gloomy picture of American attitude to us: King [Admiral E J, Chief of Naval Operations] very anti-British. ...

9 July: ... Mason (CL) came in & told me of meeting to comb out certificated engineers from shipbuilding firms for manning merchant ships: gave me a pain, I said I thought it better to call up everybody & then sift them rather than give AROs [recruiting officers?] a quota. Told Contr also saw him re Clydebank's frigate, he agreed this must be built as a prototype & this might mean ship more slowly built than if Clydebank did more [of the] work [itself]. Amusing letter from Barr showing Clydebank v. Fairfield spirit. [John Brown regarded themselves as superior to and more productive than Fairfield.] DWP had to report frigate progress to 1st L, looks as tho' U-boat war success is going to be traded [?] on already. [By this time it was apparent that the U-boats in the Atlantic had been mastered.]

10 July: ... With him [Stantan] saw Bateson re converting merchant ships to LSIL [Landing Ship Infantry, Large] in Canada by Jan 1 '44, I said could not be done in the time. Dep Contr called re *Untamed* loss apparently due to improper use of log. ... Contr rang didn't agree with signal to C in C Med re Battles compared to US design. ... C E in C says [fitting out] wharf at Cowes will be 4 mos late, wrote Milne.

13 July: At Bath. ... Trouble over W/T huts for frigates & corvettes [prefabricated]: not satisfied with McCarthy & Hopkins explanation. ...

14 July: Contr's NC meeting, everybody complaining of insufficient labour. D of D wants to limit new constr[uction] stringently in order to modernise old ships. ...

15 July: Letter from Sec. on High Profits, saying I have exposed new flank! Wrote DNO re mtgs for *Vig[ilant]* & *Vir[ago]* at SH & Thorny (*Undine*s). ... Watson & Sears called after FBC sub c'tee meeting, said they can do a 39 knot MTB & a 29 knot big fellow. Had Contr as my guest at Shipwt's lunch [Worshipful Company of Shipwrights]. 1st L. there made a happy little speech, praising everybody but DNC. ... Sent instructions to cancel U's & order A's at Walker [five 'A' class submarines replaced eight 'Us'] & order armour for *Bellerophon* [at John Brown, became *Tiger*] to start Sept. ... Contr showed me docket re honours, didn't look hopeful. ...

16 July: *Indom[itable]* torpedoed by aircraft off Syracuse [whilst supporting Sicilian landings] abreast port boiler room: not too bad so far. [Repaired at Norfolk Navy Yard Aug 43–Apr 44.] Ship recently fitted with extra AA guns & yet cannot keep off a torpedo carrying plane. [Apparently she did not fire at the attacking aircraft.] *Cleopatra* torpedoed by S/M. [16 Jul off Sicily, repaired Philadelphia Navy Yard 24 Nov 43–18 Oct 44.] After all we must expect such happenings with a big concentration of ships in enemy waters. Capt Kahn [?] Free French called, escaped from France via Spain, very great on using a torpedo against U boats, made great do over leaving me his proposals, he wants to go to Bath to see our designs, rang Ad King (PNLO) he out [Vice Admiral E L S, Principal Naval Liaison Officer]. ...

17 July: ... Contr told me of yesterday's Board Meeting, 1st Lord is jibbing at the Lt Carriers, told Contr we had ordered them! Dep 1st SL inquired whose idea the Lt Carrier was, told him Fraser's [previous Controller]. Spoke Lillicrap re overseers with welding experience at Cowes. Worked on O. Bellasis' visit to USA & ACNS(W)'s insinuation that US ships are the cat's pyjamas compared to ours, annoyed at Goodeve's remark.

20 July: G. Brown [Greenock shipbuilder] came, DWP present at long talk re his yard, he agreed it started as small show badly equipped but is now being brought into better condition. I pressed him to do less himself & take on an ass[istan]t: he thought a 'personnel' officer would relieve him a lot. ... Showed Contr letter from Johnson [Cammell Laird] complaining of withdrawal of skilled men, he grunted. Lithgow was there & Contr told him we were going to take Blyth [shipyard] over.

21 July: At Newcastle. Saw FOIC who spoke of situation at Blyth, he was convinced that merchant ship output on Wear would fall owing to men going to frigates & corvettes [inevitable]. Talk with Rowell re pre-fabbed destroyers, he held out little hope of cooperation & pushed the question on to machinery [Hawthorn Leslie had their own engine works].

Escort and Merchant Aircraft Carriers (MAC ships) supplemented the few front-line carriers, some being provided from the US and some converted in the UK from merchant ships. Among nine Shell tankers converted to MAC ships was the Dutch *Gadila*, completed by Smith's Dock on the Tyne early in 1944. Her tanker superstructures have been removed and hangar, flight deck, island and defensive armament fitted in their place. *(Author's collection)*

To V-A Walker. Ormston wants to cancel *Tiger* [cruiser] to build more S/Ms. *Swiftsure* a sad sight, stopped amidships owing to late machy parts [her machinery contract was with Vickers-Armstrongs at Barrow]. U Cl S/Ms going back owing to late delivery of motors & generators. To Blyth, Turnbull doing as well as can be expected but a shipyard manager is necessary. Looked at *Pretoria Castle*, Capt Bell Davies [Vice Admiral R] seemed satisfied. Looked at frigates & corvettes at Neptune, and *Rapana* MAC ship beautiful welded flight deck. [Shell tanker being converted by Smith's Dock, North Shields.] *Fancy* [minesweeper] at Hughes Bolckow all behind on electrics. [Shipbreakers brought in to fit out Blyth hulls.]

22 July: To Hendon Dock, getting on all right. Long talk with H[arry] Hunter re staff, told him J. Br. would coach up his under managers on frigates. Base could be used for fitting out S/Ms with some addition e.g. battery charging shed. Visited Austin's (Mr Dugdale) [F W, managing director of Sunderland shipbuilder] bomb just missed corvette berth. To Hawthorns talk with Johnson [possibly H T] & Rowell about destr. output, R doesn't want *Tiger*. If destroyers of less speed, rate of output could be increased. Instead of light carrier, firm wants destroyers but no hurry. To Reyrolles [electrical equipment manufacturer at Hebburn] fed up with inability to grasp essentials of quick production, must have a go at DWP & Hopkins & Watson. Stanley in trouble over his contingent acc[oun]t, said he must square up this weekend or call in somebody from DNA [Director of Naval Accounting?] ...

23 July: Saw Contr re *Tiger*, he does not want *Tiger* cancelled, I could consider moving the order to Portsmouth. ... Pigott called, can take 115′

During rearmament, merchant shipbuilders were brought in to build minor war vessels. Blyth Dry Docks & Shipbuilding had built only one small vessel between 1930 and 1936, so the yard began tendering for Admiralty contracts. The yard manager Charles Wintersgill bribed the Admiralty Warship Production Superintendent, North East, Charles Butt, to reveal other shipyards' tender prices. They were then able to submit higher prices but still undercut the other yards, so increasing their profits. Although the report of Butt's trial in 1943 described the vessels as minesweepers, it is much more likely that they were actually the cheaper and earlier boom defence vessels. Blyth built twenty-four in all; the photo is of their *Barcross* completed in 1942. In 1951 she became the South African Navy's *Somerset*, then a museum ship at Cape Town in 1988 before being scrapped in 2020. (*Blackman collection*)

5½″ [fleet carrier breadth]; he will help Hendon Dock. Talk with E in C re Parsons capacity to feed V-A Walker [their normal machinery supplier], he scouted the idea it was insufficient [Parsons did not make boilers], also destroyers of less power with machinery designed for rapid production. Wrote D of D to inquire if Portsmouth could take *Tiger* [they already had *Hawke*, never completed].

24 July: ... Butt sentenced to 3 years P.S. [penal servitude] for taking bribes & 1½ years for breach of O.S. [Official Secrets] Act (to run concurrently). What a disgrace for the RCNC.

[The account of the trial was reported in *The Times* from 22–26 July 1943. Charles James Butt, 55, of Sion Hill Place, Bath, was accused of conspiracy at Leeds Assizes under the Prevention of Corruption Act. Butt was Warship Production Superintendent, North East Area from about 1936, and until recently Superintendent of Labour & Materials on a salary of £1,400 p.a. He was accused of giving Charles Wintersgill, manager of the Blyth Dry Docks & Shipbuilding Co Ltd, information on prices tendered to the Admiralty for minesweepers. Blyth had tendered for two ships at

£61,250 each. Butt told Wintersgill that this was the lowest tender, the next lowest being £11,000 higher. Butt advised him to say that there was a typing error in the Blyth tender, with a 1 instead of a 7, so it should have been £67,250, still £5,000 below the next lowest, so Blyth would receive £12,000 more than originally expected. Blyth were allowed to amend their tender, showing the Admiralty a newly-doctored cost estimate, and received the order. Although the report said 'minesweepers', the typical price for those was about £120,000 and Blyth's first, *Peterhead* and *Blyth*, were not ordered until July 1939. It is more likely that the figures applied to boom defence vessels which had a price of about £60,000. Blyth's first three, *Barbarian*, *Barbette* and *Barbican*, had been ordered in February 1937, so it possibly referred to these. Or it might have been Blyth's first of the slightly smaller 'Net' class, *Bayonet* and *Falconet,* ordered in February 1938. It was reported that Butt had received £60 in 1936, the year Blyth restarted shipbuilding after the slump, and was being paid initially £50 per ship (Blyth had received twelve Admiralty orders in 1937 and 1938), then £25 per month. As a key witness, Wintersgill said that he had paid £1,500 to Butt in £1 notes, i.e. more than Butt's annual salary and equivalent to nearly £100,000 today. Wintersgill was himself then serving a sentence of 5 years in Durham jail for bribery (no honour among thieves?). Butt was sentenced to 3 years on the bribery charge and 18 months on the Official Secrets charge, to run concurrently. Robert Stanley Dalgleish, a shipowner and former Mayor of Newcastle, was managing director of the shipyard and was also charged with bribery and was sentenced to 15 months, less than Butt on account of his age (71) and alleged poor health. He was also fined £1,500, on the grounds that he must have authorised Wintersgill to make the payments to Butt. Shipyard accounts typically recorded such payments as 'commission', commonplace when legally used to pay shipbrokers as middlemen when a shipowner placed an order. Sion Hill Place in Bath has expensive Georgian houses.]

25 July (Sunday): 7 years as DNC. This last year was better on the whole, W-W. [Wake-Walker] is more amenable & I am happier in London where I am in closer touch with what is going on. Also app[ointment]t as AC(WP) indicates the Board thinks I can get things done. Reverse side of the picture, trouble with DCW, high profits investigation & above all the scandal about Butt who let the Corps down badly.

26 July: Talk with Contr re Blyth. 1st L against requisitioning. Contr peeved that Army want our LCT capacity for bridges. …

28 July: … With DDNC, Bessant & Vosper went into Battles. I hate that single [4.5in] gun vice a Bofors, twin O[erlikon] & 4″ S.S. [star shell] gun & think the design much worse for the change. Decided <u>not</u> to increase

beam. Looked at new design, 3500 tons [full load displacement] ridiculous for a destroyer. ...

29 July: ... Craven called, said I did not know Mrs Butt's circumstances, for deserving cases RCNC Ocs [officers?] had a whip round but Butt had let RCNC down badly. Craven promised to get busy on welding at Walker [for all-welded 'A' class submarines]. He spoke of Parsons capacity & said E in C was giving Vickers the machinery for new big carrier. [*Gibraltar* ordered from Walker 12 Jul with machinery from Barrow.] ...

30 July: ... It is heartrending that we cannot settle down to a building plan. No sooner do we key up firms & get them busy on something than we have to butt in, stop that & get them busy on something else. ...

3 August: ... Ayre asked me about Palermo shipyards & docks, said I would find out. [With Sicily now under Allied control, presumably to add to maintenance facilities.] ... P.M. thinks war with Japan will be over by end of '46 but Chiefs of Staff think '48.

4 August: Contr came up re R[einforced] C[oncrete] fl[oating] dock, said he would hold a meeting on Aug 8. He wants to rush it: I repeated I must have time to investigate stability. Later his sec[retary] rang me said Maunsell [G A, reinforced concrete designer] was re-designing because Contr wants less draft. [The docks were intended for landing craft.] ... Yesterday I showed Contr report from US N A [Naval Attaché] that US had had to reduce armt of destroyers for stability reasons. Read 1st L & Sec on shipbuilding after the war. ... Discussed Mrs Butt with Walsh & docketed agreeing to B's discharge but suggesting back pay to Mrs B.

5 August: Wrote Stanley & DCW re *Edgar* dates [light fleet carrier building at Walker, completed as *Perseus*] also DCW re *Defence* [cruiser building at Scotts]. ...

6 August: ... Ad. Burrough [Vice Admiral Sir H M, Force H] called (much thinner) he is disappointed that nothing has been done re RCNC into RN & blames W-W. Got hold of Freidenberger (A.D. of P.) [Captain W H G, Assistant Director of Plans] re depot & repair ships, then talked with DMB who will bite if they are 'Red Ensign' ships. ... Dunstan [M C, constructor] called on way to Lisbon, gave him lines on which to work for installing Oerlikons in Portuguese destroyers & sloops [British-built in 1930s]. Read FBC's report on naval aircraft of the future [much bigger]. ...

7 August: Bateson came up to discuss depot & repair ships, brought a formidable list. ...

9 August: ... Went thro' Weapons & new Battles Staff Requirements, re latter Naval Staff is the limit, having decided that present Battles are too big, they draw up requirements for a ship that is bound to be much bigger as they want much more stuffed in. Contr thinks 2 twin 4.5s but DFSL says 3, I have to see what I can do on 2750 tons [standard]. ...

10 August: Mark-Wardlaw [Rear Admiral A J P, Combined Operations HQ] rang re Merrington going to Reith [now Director Combined Operations Material DCOM]. Held meeting in DMB's room on Depot Ships &c for Far East. DMB helpful. D of P put all the cards on the table. With Forbes & Harrington [J W, constructor] dictated notes. Both are dubious about satisfactory ships being turned out by DMB in the time. But we can't do them in the time without an L [hell] of an impact, I rubbed this in. ...

11 August: To Min. of Production, impressed with statistical information they have collated. ...

The 'Loch' class frigates, ordered early in 1943, incorporated all the lessons learned in the U-boat war. They were designed for prefabrication with units built largely by structural engineers, incorporating many straight lines, which were restricted to only 2½ tons due to shipyard lifting limitations. The first of the eight ordered from Swan Hunter & Wigham Richardson's Neptune yard was *Loch Morlich*, seen here in August 1944; they also built her engines, under both hull and machinery contract number 1784. As the founder of Neptune yard John Wigham Richardson was a Quaker, it built no warships during his lifetime, and after that only during wartime. She became New Zealand's *Tutira* in 1949. Neptune's last three were cancelled in November 1943, by which time the U-boat menace had been largely mastered. (*Author's collection*)

12 August: At Newcastle. FOIC concerned about dispute between shipwrights & boilermakers on pre-fab frigates: both claim the job & threaten a widely spread strike if matters not settled in favour of both! [So much for unions claiming to do all they could to assist the war effort.] Later visited Neptune where work on *Loch Morlich* was at a standstill & *Loch Shin* will be delayed [both frigates]. ... At Wallsend & C S Swan grumbling about good men being taken away & replace being ullage [empty space]: also very sore with Jubb. He criticises N. Hunter [Norman, shipyard manager who was an advocate of welding] which I think is unfair. Stirling a big job. *Vengeance* launch Jan '44, to keep this firm will have to employ more men [actual 23 Feb 44]. To Pickersgill, old man very interesting [Chairman W J, aged 71] extension looks behind. To Crown [Sunderland shipbuilder] some cobbled work aft, must write Montgomerie [LR surveyors were helping oversee warships in merchant shipyards].

13 August: At Smith's Dock, Middlesbrough. Looks to me that jetty extension won't be ready in time [to fit out 'Castle' class corvettes]. *Hadleigh Castle* looks good, mast lkrs [lockers?] obscure junction boxes, told Kimberley [A E] we must not alter RDF offices. Mast rivets look to me too few at cross stays [on lattice mast; Goodall's eye for detail]. Firm fussed by D of C, first they could get no money for corvettes built for France (Admy said it was a matter entirely between Firm and French [who were occupied by the Germans, while the RN had benefited from the extra corvettes]); now Admy want to know if Firm will waive extras for these French ships. Reed wants to shorten *H. Castle* bilge keels, I said 'No' [corvettes rolled badly at sea]. Discussed with Stanley *Diadem*'s gun mtgs, apparently the GMO [gun mounting overseer] is the difficulty. Train late. Didn't get home till after midnight.

14 August: Mitchell [E H] (India Fl. Dock) called, says American machinery bind [?] with his hustle gets across Braithwaite [contractor for *AFD.23*]. Sec sent up yarn for PA C'tee, my first impression is I don't like it: saw Sec & Jubb [both Markham and Jubb had been witnesses at the Public Accounts Committee]. ...

15 August: ... Contr wants screed to refute 1st L's arguments against 1943 Light Carriers. Gave him a story, I then spoke about the Depot &c ships for Far East & said there should be a directive from high authority as to work to be set back if all these depot ships are required as his depts could not take on this addition being already overloaded. ...

18 August: Contr held meeting at War[minster Road, Bath] Huts [new offices] on Battles, he weakened in opposition to 2750 tons, I am to

write screed to give up stand[ard] displacement [as the measure of ship size, which had been brought in by the Washington Treaty]. E in C held out hope of saving say 50 tons of oil if we gave him 25 tons [more] for machinery w[eigh]t. [That would put up standard displacement by 25 tons with more efficient machinery but bring down deep displacement by 25 tons owing to less fuel, an overall benefit.] *Nelson* & *R* rearming, looks like 4.5s or American 5″ [it never happened]. ... At NC meeting, I have to visit Scotts to read the Riot Act [the shipbuilder had a poor production record throughout the war]. Amos Ayre rang, he is worried because we have not told M[inistry] of W[ar] T[ransport] we are after their ships for Far East. ... Lillicrap senior [DDNC's father was a retired constructor] called, looking wonderfully well for his age.

19 August: Back at Admy. ... Johnson of CL called, said he is going on with extension for slip to take new Fl Car. [*New Zealand* ordered 15 Jul.] ... A Ayre came up from 1st L, who wants him to look into LCTs & LCG(M)s (in Heaven's name Why?). [Merchant ships were Ayre's remit not warships.] ... Talk with Ayre re H & W, he thinks Rebbeck is taking notes & will counter attack some day.

20 August: Told Vice Contr & Contr that I had sent Ayre dwgs of LCTs & LCG(M)s: said we could take care of this, we didn't want DMB to do it at expense of Rep[air] & Depot ships. ... Ormston called with proposals for re-modelling Walker Yard for welding, he said steel output per week was roughly ½ that of Barrow with same no. of men [what an admission of poor management]. ...

21 August: Got Contr to sign docket to go ahead with the pilot mtg. Battle at H Leslie [*Saintes*]. ... Yesterday Lillicrap phoned me Butt was appealing, I told Walsh. ... Sanders came over re Habbakuk I & III, I saw Contr who said 1st SL is in Canada would know I was not in it: wrote to Sec. of C'tee to say I had not been consulted & could accept no responsibility. ...

23 August: ... Went thro' Habbakuk I & III with Sanders, wrote Stantan & McCloghrie, Rivett [David, probably of CCO] came over & apologised, promised to send a message to Quebec [Pound was at the Quebec Conference] to say I had not been consulted: nobody who knows anything about an aircraft carrier has been [an astonishing oversight, as aircraft carriers are very complex vessels]. This C[ombined] O[perations] party will land us in the ditch unless the High Ups take more care. Saw Contr who said he wanted to keep out of Habbakuk altogether, so I did not do anything with McAlpine. ...

24 August: To Robb [at Leith] getting on well with extension: workmanship looks average, but still that mixture of riveting & welding aft that I don't like. To MacTaggart Scott, extension a bit behind but not much. To Brown Bros, a fine show, roll-reducer for Fairfield Battles [*Camperdown* and *Finisterre*] well on but it looks a heavy box of tricks for a destroyer. To Rosyth, a few words with Hudson [G, MCD at Rosyth dockyard], he said Pound [F J A, Rosyth Dockyard] not thorough but Craggs [E F, Rosyth Dockyard] splendid, McCallin [E, Rosyth Dockyard] is coming on. Undex looks a bit of a mess but progress very good, a fine spirit there. Offord thinks we cannot protect against a torpedo with shaped charge & must accept a comp[artmen]t knocked out as we are already accepting it for a CNC [Contact Non-Contact] torpedo.

25 August: To Burntisland, said to be most efficient yard for building cargo ships, it is laid out for that & that only. Yard rather cramped, the shop capacity for the small no. of slips [four] is impressive. I was surprised at so much hand riveting & W[ilfred] Ayre's arguments against pneumatic. To Dundee for Caledon, a fine show, Main a goer, corvettes going strong [*Carisbrooke Castle* launched 31 Jul], fitting out well organised. I think we could build destroyers there. At Burntisland the frigate [*Loch Killin*] is coming on well. Whiting looked after me well, he is a great acquisition. … To Glasgow.

26 August: Last night a long talk with FOIC [Troup] at first Pringle there in trouble over elect. labour for *Indefat.* & *Implac.* Agreed to wire asking for *Nairana* or *Enterprise* [refitting at Dalmuir] to be postponed for *Indefat.* [at John Brown]. FOIC thinks labour on Clyde getting more & more difficult. To Denny, their exptl MTB [experimental hydrofoil 109] has its teething troubles, I said I would write FOIC Greenock [Vice Admiral Sir R A S Hill]. Stirling coming on. Their extension approved [welding shop?]. To Clydebank labour troubles here. Dalmuir looks good, we must plan to use it more. Frigate not as far on as Burntisland. [*Loch Killin* was launched 29 Nov, *Loch Fada* 14 Dec.] They will help with frames for BDVs [boom defence vessels]. To Yarrow, a fine spirit here, Weapons engine bearers look poor: extension in hand. To Stephen, Light Carrier going slow [*Ocean*], Pitcher [manager?] rather small minded, they still hanker after a merchant ship in lieu of '43 Lt Carrier.

27 August: To G. Brown, he has done nothing to get more help [see 20 July entry, which suggests Goodall used his diary as an aide memoire]. A hole & corner yard [called Siberia locally on account of its distant and exposed position] but work didn't look too bad. [They were building frigates and corvettes.] To Scotts, first a talk with Greig, then PSO [R K Wood] and EO [Engineer Overseer, Cdr G B Forsyth], then a full meeting

John Brown's fitting-out basin late in 1943, with *Indefatigable* nearly ready for preliminary trials. On the west side of the basin is the Canadian destroyer *Algonquin* launched as *Valentine* and cruiser *Euryalus* in for a ten-month refit (as E.R. 1703) which included converting her 5.25in mountings to remote power control, 'X' and 'Y' being brand-new mountings from Vickers-Armstrongs' Barrow works. (*UCS*)

with Greig, Pearson [A W?], R. Brown [director of Scotts], Benson [F W, general manager], WPS [J E Mathias] & Wood. Got no change out of it whatever. Unfortunately a strike had started that morning & the atmosphere was 'You see what we are up against'. Can't do better, in fact dates are going back still more, can you take away 2 destroyers?! [Scotts' 1950 commemorative book is self-congratulatory despite their consistently poor wartime performance.] To Fairfield to listen to more talk about labour difficulties. *Implac.* depends entirely on elect. work, apart from that she is well on [completed 28 Aug 44, 20 months after launch]. Battles [four on order] back on account of shaft brackets. *Theseus* [light fleet carrier] coming on now, but a hard job to launch by proposed date [actual 6 Jul 44].

28 August: Back in office. ... Talk with Hancock on my visit: he will see what can be done to stop the feeling that the war is over, what can be done re housing at Greenock [much bomb damage], whether Westwood

[William, Chief Industrial Adviser and trade unionist] will visit Greenock. Sanders came over, says Habbakuk I & III are dead, II to go on. Evans [Vice Admiral A E?] wonders what will happen with Mt.Batten [now] C in C S.E. Asia, how is Somerville [Admiral Sir James F, C in C Eastern Fleet] affected?

30 August: Saw Contr re last week's tour: he agreed Scotts not bad enough for drastic action, seemed satisfied with his visit to Belfast, spurred firm on re *Audacious* [*Eagle*]. ... Woollard & Baker came in, talked on training for teachers of Nav[al] Arch[itecture], LCTs converting to LCGs situation at Findlays [LCT builder on Clyde], Baker's organisation. Craven called wants 2 U's cancelled and an A ordered in lieu [at Walker], non-committal about Scotts [dog does not eat dog?]. Meryon called, he will inquire whether Stephen & Denny could help Scotts with *Cretan* & *Crown* [completed as *Bergen* and *Oslo* for Norway after the war].

31 August: A quiet day. Cleared up papers. Saw E in C re his meeting to discuss how naval machy can be improved, S/Ms at V-A Walker, deferring ships at Fairfield. ... Saw [Contr] about requirements for 1944 as a <u>whole</u>, we are dealing with it too much in penny numbers e.g. minelaying S/Ms, depot & repair ships, cable ship and everybody can't have all they want. Left for Bath.

1 September: ... O. Bellasis dropped a brick by saying US destroyers were deficient in stability & strength: this made Cole's job difficult: he was not able to compare <u>completed</u> US & British destroyers. [Cole, now an ADNC, was chief destroyer designer who had just visited USA] ... Held SO's [senior RCNC officers] meeting, everybody seemed full of beans. Drafted letter of appreciation for work during the 4 years of war. Curphey [E S, constructor, Assistant Director of Dockyards] called, not very fit, says dockyards dept. much too much under gold lace [uniformed officers]. ...

2 September: At Bath. Got Murray of Lloyds [H C, North East area overseer from Lloyd's Register] in re workmanship at Crowns, wrote Montgomerie. ... Barnaby called, told him he was being used as a tool to sidetrack me, he thought he should resign from Habbakuk, I agreed. ... With L[illicrap] & Hickey & Andrew [W R, cruiser designer] went into Cr[uiser] design, decided to exp[erimen]t on form of stern & rudders, also flare of bow.

3 September: Attended a service of dedication after 4 years of war. Looked round Quad [quadrangle of Admiralty building] with its bomb scars & thought of Sunday Sept 3 1939 when A[ir] R[aid] warning sounded, messengers ran along corridors blowing whistles & we all went to ground

complete with gas masks for about 1 hour: it was a false alarm! We have been thro' a lot & learned much since then. A good service but the band conductor was too slow. Contr held a meeting to consider more LCTs (Davis [W J A Davies?] attended) later I discussed with him & Baker, sent latter to Bath with instructions & proposed higher priority. ... DMB objects that we have bagged a slip[way] of his at Birkenhead [probably for six LCTs about to be ordered from Cammell Laird], wrote DCW & Peake.

4 September: ... Phoned Scott re Stephens over to help by taking over *Lapwing* [sloop], wrote both firms, Mathias [J E] & FOIC. ...

6 September: Gawn called, reviewed work at Haslar, discussed Denny's exptl MTB ... Merrington called, gave interesting acc[oun]t of what he saw in N. Africa and Sicily [landings]. He said the various types of landing craft did well, which I had guessed as we had not received a storm of howls & complaints. ... Many bombers passed over London for Europe this night [Stuttgart raid].

7 September: ... Labour position looks increasingly difficult: saw Contr who said call-up is only 180,000 & 2nd Sea Lord's [Vice Admiral Sir W J Whitworth, Chief of Naval Personnel] requirements for RN alone are 190,000! DWP had to clear up Squid fittings, Asdic [sonar] & Plotting Office, brass said to be unsuitable. Contr rang re LCTs. Got Baker busy, he will go to Glasgow tonight, try to stop the fuss over Findlay's riveters & sound Lobnitz [probably about converting more LCTs to LCFs]. ... Capt Hickling [H, British Admiralty Delegation, Washington] called re machy for LSTs: said *Glasgow* did well & repair in USA was good [at Brooklyn Navy Yard May 42–Aug 42]. Saw Sec. over High Profits, he is reasonable but what about Jubb? Goodeve called re Overlord, Habbakuk, SAPC [semi armour piercing capped shells].

9 September: Funny but feeling flat instead of elated over [surrender of] Italy, too many think the war is over whereas I think we have a long hard row to hoe yet. Pigott called, will think again over paper by McNeill to open symposium on W.T. [watertube] boilers for merchant ships [standard for warships]: said Denny had approached him re McNeill taking Nav. Arch. chair at Glasgow [University; but Andrew Robb was appointed in 1944 – still Professor when I went there]: electricians out at Clydebank. ...

10 September: Discussed with DWP capacity for NL Pontoons [Naval Lighter, causeway pontoons for LSTs] & inquired if he thought Contr realised shipbuilding pot was so full it could take no more: he thought yes, but Contr was booming off to the last minute interference with new naval constr from LCTs, Depot Ships &c. Later Contr told me he hoped to get

Canada to help on the Depot Ships. Contr sent for me in a L [hell] of a fit over LCTs getting Priority I, said he had only intended it for Material! Baker had bounced him!! I was to clear up a complete bloody mess!!! I went away, thought he might cool off later. Got Baker in, drafted a yarn, saw Vice Contr then he, Baker & I went to Contr (after lunch) & it boiled down to writing explanatory letters to DBCs & WPSs. ... To dentist.

11 September: Wrote Stephen, Scott & Mathias re transfer of *Lapwing*, also wrote Denny to ask if he could take on LCTs. [Many LCTs Mark 4 had been completed without engines, which now needed to be installed as Davey-Paxman diesel production had built up.] Bogie called, went thro' H & W programme, must get John [W G] busy over welding of *Audacious* &c, everybody appears to be going his own way. ...

13 September: Held meeting of firms to consider more LCTs. Firms said we were inviting a stop thro'out shipbuilding industry. [The extra LCTs were urgently needed for D-Day.] ... Cochrane and Cook Welton [& Gemmell] the biggest grumblers [these Humber shipbuilders were busy on naval trawlers]. ... After lunch DWP took meeting & we ought to get 12-20 LCTs from them. [This must refer to the smaller builders, as the larger builders built the bulk of the additional seventy-three Mark 3s] ... Left FBC at 17.50 to go to Bath, glad to get into train to rest.

15 September: Contr NC meeting. All depts. spoke of labour shortage. Contr said there was no hope of more labour for Admy work. I gathered that when P.M. returns [from the Quebec Conference] the whole subject will be discussed and we may definitely be told to stop certain work. Spoke Dep Contr, Contr & D D of D [Bassett] re 2 frigates for Brigade HQ ships, they agreed 2 Rivers due for refit be taken in hand at Royal Yards, took action [*Waveney* and *Nith*]. ...

17–23 September: On leave

24 September: ... Dunstan back from Portugal, he took off the 40mm AA mtgs [1930s model, not Bofors] as they were no good. Merrington called, said Mt.Batten (SAC) [S E Asia?] wants him. Phoned SAC who confirmed this, I said Somerville had Pengelly [H S, now Constructor Captain] but SAC said he would be for Fleet while Merrington would be for Landing Craft, he would send me a signal after seeing Merrington. I agreed & told M. to take some leave. ...

27 September: ... Contr wants us to get busy on a LST [Landing Ship Tank] design using frigate capacity [with a reduced threat from U-boats, escort construction was being cut back]. He wants me to organise the Far East requirements, agreed his Sec should send dwgs to Canada via Ross

[Canadian official?]. For Repair ships he is going to take LSTs [US-built Mark 2s]. Contr spoke of Lillicrap becoming DNC, I said I should have raised this question soon myself. My double job was very heavy especially in winter. I was for Lillicrap going to USA straightaway. Hancock came up, there is going to be an inquiry by M. of L. [Ministry of Labour] into Scotts: the housing situation at Greenock seems incapable of improvement. ...

28 September: ... Saw Goodeve re Habbakuk & Butterworth: we were both puzzled over DFSL's cryptic message to BAD that Bernal [J D, scientific adviser to CCO] & Rivett were British (but not Admy) Technical Representatives. We saw DFSL who said Mt.B. had held a pistol at his head on Sat. morning before he left for Chequers hence this message. I put on the paper that I agreed to McCl[oghrie] & a NO from BAD being authorised to speak for Admy on practicability but Bernal & Rivett should not be so authorised. DFSL thinks US Navy will straighten matters out. Fact is nobody has courage to tell Mt.B. or P.M. that they are being led up the garden path. ...

29 September: ... With Capt. Goolden (OB) [A C, RN retired, Ordnance Board] for Sheffield. After dinner at Guest House with Grant, Goolden & Sykes [possibly a metallurgist], when Grant had gone, had interesting talk on Shells & Armour. Goolden said shells for last war (pre Jutland) met Staff requirements so had always been accepted that shells would burst on plate. ...

30 September: At Sheffield. Before ATC [Armour Technical Committee] meeting I held forth to armour firms, indicating they must get on with research if they are to stop the critics' mouths. ATC went well, Sykes did not make the impression I had hoped. I think also a prophet in his own country, he felt rather weighted down. Hatfield's [sic, Hadfield, specialist steel maker] attitude was 'Youngster, you can't larn [teach] us anything'. I was left to consider accepting a harder plate that would crack. After lunch, walked round works with Crease [Captain T E of the Shipbuilding Conference] & Burrell [? H J, Contract & Purchase], latter wants more staff. Home late, very tired.

1 October: Pigott called, said I might get his slip alteration thro' on 60/40 [cost] basis but doubted 100: he will think & let me know. He says labour troubles will persist until dramatic action is taken with 1 or 2 of the bad agitators. Voting at meetings should be by secret ballot not show of hands. [It took another 40 years before the government brought in such a measure.] Bogie came preparatory to H & W meeting. At Contr's H & W meeting I felt Lithgow will not be happy till Rebbeck is ruined: certainly R. is difficult but wants managing without L. butting in. ...

The new corvette *Morpeth Castle* in the Tyne in July 1944. Her hull had been launched by W Pickersgill & Sons Ltd on the Wear on 26 November 1943 (No 262) but fitted out at Hendon Dock, leaving Sunderland on 15 July. Her standard 2,750 ihp triple-expansion engine had been made by George Clark at Sunderland (No 1346). Longer and more seaworthy and armed with a Squid ahead-firing mortar in 'B' position, the 'Castles' were much more effective than the 'Flowers'. She worked up at Tobermory in August ready to join Escort Group B.4 based at Londonderry. (*Author's collection*)

2 October: Dealt with Clydebank berth alteration [No 4 to take *Malta*], Pigott having agreed yesterday to pay 40%. ... Kimberley called from *Hadleigh Castle* trials, OK except draught on bridge. [RN wind deflectors were poor compared with USN.] ...

4 October: Contr spoke re (LCTs cannot get a decision but we must order materials): (he was forming party M of W T, CMSR & himself to consider shipbuilding & repair programme as a whole): (for Far East he hoped Canada would help but had not heard from Ross yet): (he agreed Clydebank No.4 slip should be modified). ... Worked on Depot Ships for Far East: do not see yet how with these & LCTs & LSTs we can save shipyards from serious disorganisation. ...

5 October: Pound goes, not before it was time [he was in poor health and overworked]. Cunningham [A B] comes in: he has not had a lot of Admy experience & a good C in C does not necessarily make a good 1st SL, vide Beatty. How well will he get on with Alexander & Winston? Latter worked Pound to death. [Literally, Pound died on 21 Oct.] Spoke Contr re Scotts, he is prepared to consider transfer of *Lark* to Stephen & *Cretan* to John Br. but not to take away 2 Weapons & give them to Whites. Wernher [Major General H A] rang re Mulberry, found out what this is from Contr [artificial harbour] M.Br. [Military Branch] came up re

The fitting-out basin at Scotts of Greenock, about September 1943. Nearest is 'S' class destroyer *Serapis* (later the Dutch *Piet Hein*) with *Shark* outboard (later the Norwegian *Svenner*). Across the basin is newly-launched sloop *Lark*, with an 'S' class submarine barely visible outboard (probably *Strongbow*) and at the end of the jetty probably *Spiteful*. (*National Records of Scotland and University of Glasgow Archives & Special Collections, Scotts Shipbuilding Co Ltd collection, GB248 GD323/3/12/14/20*)

Habbakuk but I refused to alter the remarks I had docketed [presumably to say that the Emperor had no clothes]. ... Contr agreed to Scotts Priority being S/Ms, Destr, *Defence*.

6 October: Contr came up, doesn't want to convert [liners] *Alaunia* & *Ranpura*, too long & takes up dockyards, thinks we are boneheaded when we say merchant ships of tramp type cannot be converted to fleet repair ships. [Too slow and with deep cargo holds rather than internal decks.] ... Got further on maintenance ships for Far East, Lenaghan [James, Dept of Merchant Shipbuilding], said 'C' type [standard cargo ship] unattainable but Liberty ships likely. ...

7 October: Before frigate meeting asked Contr if depts should be told of Plans proposal to cancel last 40, he said 'No'. ... Interesting report from USA showing they are not happy over freeboard of their carriers [they were not plated up to the flight deck forward as were the British carriers]. ... W Ayre called, outlined Shipbldg Research Organisation,

thought Mech[anical] Eng[inee]r should be Director, I wanted Naval Architect but could not name a man. He also spoke of post war plans for mercantile marine about 5,000,000 gross tons, owners will work together, no *Queen Mary*'s, he has written Markham about naval prog[ramme]: he said Blyth negotiations very slow, we must exercise Time & Patience. Greig called, got Hancock over who spoke of M. of Labour inquiry, hostels & unskilled labour from Eire. ...

8 October: I went into Fleet Repair Ships. Phoned Dep Contr [Simeon] who is working on same lines. Really Contr first gives him the job, then gives me the same job. So I sent my report to Contr thro' Simeon. ...

9 October: Contr spoke twice of *Alaunia* versus a Merchant Tramp for Repair Ship for the Far East. I said work as a whole would be less if we had *Alaunia*. He wants P[orts]mouth to rearm *Rodney*. The pros & cons are evenly matched. ... With McCarthy went over firms who might do Far East ships. Contr says CMSR thinks 65 'C' type for us. ...

11 October: ... FOS called told me of X craft & one damaged by explosion of her own charge 3½ miles away, said I didn't believe it. He will send me particulars. ... In Bath train Sears told me of MTB situation: he is a good fellow. ...

12 October: ... Wrote Controller re X craft & men who did the work. [*Tirpitz* attack on 22 Sep.] Thank you to mine. At NC meeting Binnie (DSD) [Commander W A C, of Director of Signal Dept] a beastly nuisance, actually I howled him out as a liar over gear for *Termagant*. [Denny's had complained of late delivery of equipment for this destroyer.] ...

13 October: ... At NC meeting I slipped up over *Victorious* rudder, this shows how impossible it is to keep in close touch with all that goes on at Bath. With Lillicrap & Woollard went into LST design & Mulberry, also NL pontoons for the Li-Lo [design of artificial harbour floating breakwater, superseded by steel Bombardons], with Mathias [T L] & Bessant & L. went into new Battle design with 3 twin 4.5s [became *Daring* class]. ... In new Battles I am not prepared to go to USA [design] stresses yet, must wait till welding is a uniform practice in our yards. ...

14 October: ... Baker came up, got him to give me particulars of LSTs &c wanted for Far East. Held meeting on ships for Far East: went well Sir R Metcalfe (for M of W T) [Director of Sea Transport] & Mr Kidd (for D of ST) [H, Principal Technical Officer] helpful, also DMB & DMR. I can see the solution if America helps. Johnson of CL called & left dates for A Carriers at Birkenhead, these are governed by fact that he cannot take 2 carriers into the [fitting-out] Basin at the same time so the 1943 Fleet will not complete till mid 1949! [*New Zealand* later transferred to Harland

& Wolff.] Asked him what he thought of giving up 1943 Light, he didn't want to [*Hermes*, later cancelled]. ...

15 October: ... Contr called me down to meet Mr Howe, Canadian M. of Supply [C D, Minister of Munitions & Supply] who said Canada could do 14 acc[ommodation] & 24 maintenance ships for Far East. Later I got out docket to tell BATM [British Admiralty Technical Mission, Canada] to go into this. Contr also told Howe he would ask if they could cut off last of Algerines [minesweepers] & Castle cl. corvettes. ...

16 October: Letter from Hall [V W, overseer at Fairfield] with bitter complaint against Fairfield on finish of *Bellona*, must speak Barr on Tuesday. ...

18 October: ... Examined photos of *Richelieu* [French battleship] after repair in USA, asked DDNC (L) [London, i.e. W G Sanders] to get particulars of new armament & if possible damage from our attack [at Dakar in Sep 1940]. ... Letter from DCW Mathias [J E] fussing about priority at Scotts i.e. S/Ms first being agin orders, wrote priority not the right word. Prepared for FBC meeting, interesting on Navy of the Future (all Aircraft Carriers in next war will be islands) also Aircraft Transport should come under dept [Admiralty] not Air Ministry. DFSL said 1943 Fleet Carrier app'd, but not Lt [carriers] yet, still we are to go ahead (& land 1st L in a mess?) ...

19 October: Held Lt Carrier meeting. Went well, firms [five] more amenable to bulk orders [for fittings etc]. Swan & Vickers want to do more welding, we have specified no welding where vibration likely nor in way of lift openings [stress concentrations]: I did not know this: afterwards had talk with Johnson [of CL] who spoke like Skiffington [of John Brown] in his opposition to welding: must go into this with Lillicrap. ... Spoke Barr re report from ASCBS re unsatisfactory finish of *Bellona*, he said labour was defeating him. ...

20 October: Baker came up re inconclusive meeting yesterday re LSTs: phoned Lillicrap to discuss turbo-electric [as in destroyer escorts] with E in C & DEE: later E in C came up & said turbo-electric out of question in time: told Baker to take paper to Bath & tabulate what could be done with General Motors Diesels from USA [as in LSTs Mark 2] & with frigate engines [steam reciprocating]. E in C will inquire about engines from USA. Ormston called, wants the third A [sub] also would like cranes hastened, says he can finish *Bellerophon* [renamed from *Tiger*] to time [at V-A Tyne], he is getting more work out of less men now he has cleared out ullage. Agreed with DWP to try *Port Quebec* [auxiliary minelayer to be converted to repair ship] at John Browns. Thompson DEE [J C,

Smith's Dock of Teesside had been prolific builders of whale catchers before the war. When their design of *Southern Pride* was selected as the basis for the 'Flower' class corvette, her four-cylinder triple-expansion steam reciprocating engine was uprated from 2,300 ihp to 2,750 ihp. The high pressure cylinder was 18½in bore, intermediate 31in and low pressure 38½in each with a stroke of 30in, at 185 rpm. Two LP cylinders kept the bore size more manageable as well as giving a better-balanced engine. In twin screw ships the engines were 'handed' i.e. rotated in opposite directions to suit the propellers and manoeuvrability. At the aft end was the coupling to the propeller shaft and the eccentrics operating the valve gear. The engine was fitted in 189 British-built 'Flower' and 'Castle' class corvettes and in 134 'River', 'Loch' and 'Bay' class frigates and LST3s, making 457 engines completed. To expand production from 1943, fifteen land-based engineers were brought in to make the engines which were ordered by the Admiralty and allocated to shipyards as hull production required. Similar engines were built in Canada and USA. (*Author's collection*)

Superintendent of Ships Electrical Equipment] back from Belfast, says later ships will suffer thro' firm cracking on with *Minotaur* [cruiser *Ontario*]. Saw Metcalfe D of ST. He is oily, is he slippery? ...

21 October: ... Trafalgar Day & Dudley Pound died this morning: also E M Kelly [author]. Reed called, said joiners were back & working

properly pending decision re pay for asbestos lining. [Probably insulation for Arctic.] Sutherby called re getting *Impero* [incomplete Italian battleship] for bomb expts: I said most unlikely but agreed bad policy to oppose on the ground. We should press for account of loss of *Roma* [Italian battleship on 9 Sep] & full particulars of *Impero*, also could we get more information on behaviour of CS [control surface?] bombs & 2000 lbs AP without using a ship which will mean a lot of work. Slattery [Captain M S, Ministry of Aircraft Production] came & interesting over new types of aircraft, unfortunately he was placed away from me at Shipwrights lunch. Sinclair, Sec State for Air [Sir Archibald] stammers a bit & spoke awful tripe. ...

22 October: ... Saw Contr re LSTs, he spoke DCOM [Reith] & said for 7″ of draft he would not give up use of frigate machinery. [The steam machinery was heavier than the equivalent diesel.] ... Met new 1st SL [Cunningham] at club very pleasant. ...

23 October: Bogie called, said H & W not getting the labour necessary for their programme, left notes, he will see Contr tomorrow re priorities. Wrote Lord Chatfield [President of INA] agreeing to run Policy C'tee of INA. With DWP [McCarthy] & SLC [Baker] worked out distribution of work between Gt. Britain & USA for Far East: had typed & gave to DWP for Controller tomorrow. SLC came to a stop against CCO on LSTs (frigate machinery), even with frigate machinery (ordered for ships [frigates] now cancelled) we can't keep date for 40. ...

25 October: Lillicrap called, I went thro' pts with him preparatory to his USA visit, he will see Goodeve re Habbakuk. ... With Lillicrap & Offord discussed expts to compare British & US destroyers resistance to distant explosions: also D1 & N. steel for thick bkd [bulkhead].

26 October: Slayter [Captain W R] called, told me of damage to [his ship] *Newfoundland* [torpedoed 23 Jul near Malta, under repair at Boston Navy Yard from 27 Aug 43], stern hit by torpedo, then steamed at 22 knots, rest of stern cut off & crossed Atlantic like that without rudder, supports to Y turret all right by tilt test. He is going to be Chief of Staff to C in C H[ome] F[leet]. ... Saw Contr re prog. He says 4 last Lt Fleets of 1943 will be cancelled [actually not until 1945], he doesn't want LSTs done at expense of 1942 Lights & big carriers, he will think about new *Ranpura* [repair ship] & 2 of new LSTs being repair ships. At Pound's funeral, well done, Crossing the Bar sung beautifully.

27 October: ... Late last night Sears & Gawn called re meeting on engines for MTBs, perturbed that Roy Fedden [aircraft engine designer] is going into hull & armament said I would see R F. ... Told DWP to go into LST

possibilities in warship yards, later he gave me result, said Staff begged that destroyers left alone. ... Meeting attended by CMSR, Metcalfe, Vernon Thompson [Chairman of Union Castle Line] & others. D of ST blew off steam on lines [that he] could do nothing till discussion on highest level with USA. Dictated notes. The landing craft situation also looks grim. Spoke DMR & DMB re victualling standard for converted merchant ships. [Another example of Goodall getting involved in peripheral matters.]

28 October: Pigott called, knew nothing about *Port Quebec*, got DWP busy. He thought firm would go 50/50 on cost of altering No. 4 slip [and probably adding bigger cranes]. Told him Bevin gunning for Skiffington. At Contr's meeting on Far East, Hurcomb tiresome, in the end he withdrew objection to our approaching Canada, & also agreed to the 11 PFC ships [partially fabricated Type C]. I have to get out LST programme: later went thro' this with DWP who is optimistic, but agrees we cannot promise by Nov '44. Pigott took away LST dwg: phoned Lillicrap who agreed best if J Br[own] would work out design. ... Public Accts report out, I get it in the neck.

[The Report from the Committee of Public Accounts was sent for publication on 13 October 1943. In the section headed 'Large Profits on Warship Construction', it spelled out the high profits on warship contracts placed before the war – averaging over 30 per cent on hull and machinery costs for a sample of thirty-two ships. It criticised the Admiralty (and by implication Goodall) for confirming that the tender prices were 'fair and reasonable' when checked against previous contracts and shipbuilding costs in dockyards. The Admiralty had overestimated the rise in costs of materials and labour resulting from rearmament and had not allowed for the lower overheads per ship resulting from the much higher workload at shipbuilders, so did not think that the tendered prices were greatly in excess of their estimated costs. Goodall had admitted in his evidence that the Admiralty had assumed some collaboration existed between the warship builders before they submitted their tenders as the various companies' prices quoted were suspiciously close. But the Admiralty was not aware just how high the comparative dockyard costs were, especially for submarines, and thus just how high the profits would be, given the shipbuilders' much lower costs. As the report said 'Your Committee are forced by the evidence to the conclusion that the knowledge possessed by the technical departments of shipbuilding costs in the private yards has proved gravely inadequate'. This was fair criticism but had been overtaken by events as since 1941 the Admiralty no longer asked for tenders but paid the shipbuilders their costs (as ascertained by Admiralty accountants) plus a modest profit margin of about 7 per cent. But these high profits did enable the remaining fourteen warship builders to survive the 1930s – Palmer and Beardmore had been liquidated in 1933 – so that they were in a position to build the warships the Admiralty so desperately needed once war broke out.]

29 October: ... Saw Contr who asked if South Banks [probably coal-burning 'Tree' and 'Dance' class naval trawlers] could be converted to burn oil. Watkins got busy with DMB & I answered 'Yes'. ...

30 October: ... Hall called re refusal of *Bellona*, went carefully thro' sequence of events. Came to the conclusion that Fairfield is deficient in subordinate officers, Hall will send me distribution of Fairfield officers, he thinks *Implacable* will go back e.g. only one foreman carpenter on ship, quite too big for 1 man since workmen sit about waiting to be told [what] to do.

1 November: ... [Ayre] suggests hard chine for LSTs & says For the love of Mike call them something else. [They were then called Transport Ferries to avoid having to pay the high wages that landing craft workers were getting.] Saw Sir Roy Fedden & told him I was disappointed that c'tee to produce an [MTB] engine was first concerning itself about designing the ship. Fedden stuck to his point that he must have a complete picture: came back & dictated a memo. [It is one thing to understand the requirements and the desirable features, quite another to design the vessel itself.] Contr came up, he thinks if DMB takes on any LSTs he should cut free from us [Admiralty] & go on his own. I said I proposed to use frigate organisation, told him of Fairfield discussion on Saturday [30 Oct], also said I was troubled because so far we had not done a damned thing on Far East requirements, only talk & paper.

2 November: At Bath. ... With Woollard & McMurray [M, constructor] looked up LST dwgs (I call them Seasacks), simplified a bit. Gawn rang & gave disappointing speeds for a lot of parallel middle body, looks as tho' we must give that up [it simplified construction] but might cut off bilge corner.

3 November: ... Discussed quick rolling of DE ships of Captain class [US-built destroyer escorts]. I think extension of bilge keels forward would better conditions. With Watson & Bartlett discussed Carriers, said *Africa* [aircraft carrier on order at Fairfield] must be welded like *Ark R*: decided better to have 1″ trans[verse] bkds & wider hangar than 5″ [armour] on lower hangar deck, make latter 4″. On way back in train DNO's deputy [Captain K L Harkness] said they wanted Denny-Brown roll reducers re-instated. W'son says CL very upset about *Thetis* decision [on widows' pensions?] I agree 'Where is British justice?'. AR warning about 19.35–19.55.

4 November: Craven called, on high profits I said I had been made the scapegoat & firms had let me down, he insisted their estimates were bona fide. [That was disingenuous: their <u>cost</u> estimates may have been accurate, but that did not stop the warship builders conniving to increase the tender <u>prices</u>.] ... Found a hullaballoo on re LCTs [Mark 3s], Cabinet decision we must build them in shipyards [as opposed to structural engineers]. Craven says Contr angry with him because C. told P.M. shipyards would build them without a strike!

5 November: ... [Contr] said O. Bellasis had been in to grumble at slow progress in *Euryalus* at J. Brown [refitting to include RPC for her 5.25in guns] he thinks firm is playing off repairs against new constr. [The yard did find that repairs were a disruption, having to take men off new building, but it was for the Admiralty to determine priorities.] He told Bassett that he or I must go into this. I said I could see no hope of Scotts doing better with their present labour. [Brown was completing some Scotts' ships.] Contr showed me P.M's minute to 1st L on prog, it looks as tho' all the long term projects will be knocked out & the Post War Navy will be completely weak in Carriers. ...

6 November: Adam (B.C.) called after visit to USA & Canada: his talk made me gloomy, says workmanship appreciably worse than it was when he was there 12 months ago owing to over-rushed output. DE frigates building at Kaiser Walsh, Providence RI, especially bad. He attributes welding troubles to bad steel, poor design, poor procedure, insufficient oversight (e.g. no proper arrgts for [welding] current regulation) rather than locked-up stresses. [Evidently high American shipbuilding output came at a price.] Letter from DCW(S) [Hopkins] re poor American steel, too bad for LCTs, I & S Control [Iron & Steel allocation body] say there will be delay if we insist on British steel: arranged after talk with DWP & Baker for meeting next Wednesday. Sent Dep Contr draft reply to Canada for machine tools. Contr said he is going to USA & Canada soon & taking A Ayre & Bateson, wants legends [warship characteristics] &c, wrote Bath. ...

9 November: ... Told DWP Contr is anxious to have plan for turning over corvette capacity we don't want to DMB. Cleared up at last the paper accumulation which has been dreadful this last week & week-end. ... Contr's Sec[retary] told me Far East Fleet all held up pending full discussion with USA (war & merchant ship side).

10 November: ... Gawn & Sears called after meeting, Fedden is still messing about on hulls. Williamson rang, work at Cammell Lairds welding on A class [submarines] bad & programme will get a set-back. [They only completed their first, *Affray*, in May 1946.]

12 November: Gave Contr rough report [on Far East ships]. At his meeting he went thro' it and it was generally accepted. I have to consider building 2 new ships for Repair Ships vice *Alaunia* & *Ranpura*, also take up again LSDs [Landing Ship, Dock] for NL Pontoon ships. For Fighter Direction, consider *Prince Robert* [ex Canadian ferry]. ...

13 November: Held meeting with DMB, DWP & firms who have had corvettes cancelled [seventy frigates and corvettes cancelled], agreed on dates berths would be available, DMB then told firms what would be ordered from them. King [Constructor Captain I E] called from Med. very interesting: evidently he has done well for the RCNC & himself: I know from 1st SL that he found the right way to his right side [when Cunningham was C in C Med]. Told him of LSTs for Taranto [Franco Tosi shipyard]. ...

15 November: ... Spoke DMB re LSTs he wants frames square to

Ivor E King had been at Bermuda Dockyard before the war, then moved to Portsmouth Dockyard. He made his name as Constructor Captain to the Mediterranean Fleet under Cunningham from 1942. In 1945 he returned to Sheerness where he had been in the 1930s, one of the smaller dockyards and no longer building ships. By 1959 he was Director of Dockyards. Constructors serving with fleets wore uniform (as here, with grey between their gold rings) and tended to use naval parlance even in civilian life, going on 'leave' and using the 'heads' (WCs). (*The Shipbuilder*)

keel [for simpler construction, but with designed beaching trim by the stern, they would not be vertical] he also thinks he could turn corvettes we don't want into merchant ships [five were completed as convoy rescue ships], sent note to McCarthy. Dealt with Fairfield Yard & putting back *Bellona*. [Although 'completed' on 29 Oct, she spent the next three months working up and presumably rectifying deficiencies.]

16 November: With Williamson, Pamplin & John discussed bad welds in *Subtle* (S cl. at C Lairds) [launched 27 Jan 44] inspected radiographs [X rays of welds which showed up faults], some are certainly very bad: but W. & P. have wind up badly [a deeper diving depth was approved for

welded submarines as they had thicker pressure hulls]: personally I expect a no. of welded ships doing well at sea have slag in the welds: trouble here is that these ships are S/Ms & some of the radiographs show cracks: decided on action & wrote Johnson [R S]. Talk last night with Bassett who agrees Dockyard Dept. policy has been wrong & unsound owing to Talbot relying on [naval] engineers' advice (e.g. depot ships v. land establishments). ...

17 November: At Bath. W'son wanted a decision whether we should cover up welded butts of U cl. I said 'No' as some of these ships have dived to 300ft (welded butts, riveted seams) & they are all right. [Design diving depth 200ft.] ... Spoke E in C re Roy Fedden, he wants to give R F his head, I said I could not let my people waste any more time on him.

18 November: Pigott called re *Port Quebec* [arrived Clydebank 5 Dec, renamed *Deer Sound*], Contr wants further simplification. I said I would stick to decision to alter No. 4 berth. We had some talk about cutting down naval work, he fears effect on men. ... Johnson [R S] called, we discussed welding & he seemed prepared to do what is wanted: he thinks he talked Bevin over! Meryon called with Ideal '44 prog. looks poor, told him of Manpower trouble. Re latter Contr came up & was less gloomy than yesterday. ...

22 November: Hullaballoo over Habbakuk, Dep 1st SL [Kennedy-Purvis] sent off message (personal) to BAD backing (from Staff point of view) Habbakuk cum Tentacle [plan for a floating airfield of concrete or linked ships]: this was result of meeting at which I was not represented, such a scheme bristles with difficult problems & the productive capacity absorbed would be prodigious & time (from inception) 2-3 years (apparently Bernal & Rivett pocketed Dep 1st SL), Goodeve & I saw Contr, who saw D 1st SL. We then saw D 1st SL. Later at his meeting G. & I said Admy & particularly Contr should be in Habbakuk or out but we would prefer out. D 1st SL said he was going to have his small c'tee as a Post Office, nothing to do with Contr. I said then he must have a technical adviser other than Bernal who was not qualified. Gave D 1st SL a message to say H. cum T. had not been examined technically. ... DTM [Director of Torpedoes & Mining, now Captain A F de Salis] rang re rotten US torp[edoe]s in *Vict[orious]*. [The aircraft carrier had been loaned to USN.]

23 November: ... Had long talk with John about welding. I am really worried over attitude of certain people in the dept, they have no belief in welding & are frightening others: I must speak Lillicrap as soon as he returns [from USA] as being absent from Bath when the demon lives I cannot exorcise him. ...

24 November: ... Morrison [John] & Angus [John] (H & W) called & gave account of progress at H & W Belfast: according to M. everything is fine (he is like S[outhern] Irish for blarney), after he had gone, dictated notes: they are evidently striving to improve but blame slow progress on Unions. ...

25 November: ... Contr rang re LSTs in Canada, said it would not be till New Year that we should have detail dwgs ready for steel orders, told Packham [J M of Canadian Vickers] this also. ... Also sent Vice C. W J Holt's screed about maintenance, Vice C said MTBs will not go east till maintenance organisation is working. ...

26 November: Dep. Contr called, *Port Quebec* fixed up all right, *Implacable* extra accom. investigated, cannot get in more without adverse effect on efficiency. Pigott called, said he had gone into 'hate against Skiffington' & Police had told him that a Communist cell had been formed in Clydebank Yard, hence the trouble, Jubb had agreed 50/50 on No.4 slip. ... Millis called, he said US Navy had not used radiographs, one of their welded S/Ms had been heavily depth-charged & press[ure] hull stood it well. ...

27 November: Captain Haeberle [F E, USN Bureau of Ships] called with Millis. He is over on landing craft & ships & seemed to be 1st class. He said they had to strengthen fore end of their LSTs owing to coral reefs in Pacific. ...

30 November: ... With Hopkins & Somers [Frank, managing director of Walter Somers, forgemasters of Halesowen] discussed forge defects at S's works: he thinks forge will hold out, if it doesn't we must rely on ESC [English Steel Corporation] & Darlington [Forge], not happy but cannot justify labour for new press at S. ... Phoned Woollard, must use frigate W/T offices in Transport Ferries. ...

1 December: Held meeting on corvettes & frigates, a sorry subject now we have been cut. ... King [I E] called, would rather go back to Med than transfer to Overlord: we discussed Transport Ferries at Taranto. ... Re Bucknill report on loss of *P of W* [*Prince of Wales*] Offord sent me case of tanker with two torpedoes from air attack close together, this disproves DTM statement that 2 torps. wouldn't hit as closely as they did in *P of W*. ...

2 December: Worked on papers US ships in Pacific. Discussed with Galcon [? Secretary's department] arrgts if depts had to leave London because of Huns' secret weapon [V1 flying bomb]: then attended Contr's meeting: what was said of weapon left me cold. I said I proposed to stay; later with Sanders & McCarthy decided who should stay with me and where others

should go (worried about N. [his wife Nellie whose proper name was Helen]). [V1 attacks did not start till Jun 1944.] ...

3 December: ... Captain Laing [M B, attached to Saker, Admiralty establishment in Washington] who has been with USN in S W Pacific came & told Sanders & me all about it, he was enthusiastic over USN material especially guns, fire control, stereo-rangefinder, machinery & electrics. Ships are most elaborate & must have been very costly but they do their stuff. I wonder to what extent he is like me after my spell in USA [at the end of] last war i.e. swept off my feet by American enthusiasm & boost of American stuff. He is convinced battleships are by no means finished & with carrier fighters & good HA armament & control they will see aircraft off every time (I doubt it). Americans have suffered most losses by torpedo [this was before kamikaze attacks]. ...

4 December: Milne of Whites called, still held up for crane, he wants to keep a slip free for Overlord [for *LCT.7034*]. I agreed & said I would tell Contr. ... With DWP worked on destroyers prog. & drafted docket to transfer 2 Battles to H[awthorn] L[eslie] from F[airfield] & 2 Weapons from Scotts to F. ... Baker came to see me after visit to N Ireland on LCTs, he thinks Warrenpoint good, he will try to get parts from Whessoe [steel fabricator in Darlington] sent to N Ireland, told him to be hot on Transport.

6 December: Lillicrap returned (T.G.). D of N [Director of Navigation, Rear Admiral W G Benn] came up, wants to alter bridges of 1942 Lt [Fleet] Carriers: after full discussion by FBC & a mock-up accepted, along comes a young officer & all goes into the melting pot again. Attended weld demonstration, Ferguson & Harris [possibly both from Dockyards] both agreed our welds were very bad, *Graph*'s no [?] good [captured U boat]. At FBC Laing [who] held forth, a lot of time wasted on accommodation & mess decks; 5th SL said US ships are hotels, ours a miserable attempt at homes. ...

7 December: At Bath. Held meeting on Manpower shortage, came to agreement & drafted report to Controller. ... With Steed [F H, ADNC] & Watson went into work on Far East ships, not going badly but we <u>cannot</u> get a decision. With Watson & Bartlett went into AC question, *Indefat.* has come out heavy (John Brown!). D of N's bridge scheme is hopeless, Contr has turned right about & now asked Staff for all the alter[atio]ns they can think of!

8 December: ... Went thro' Transport Ferry dwgs & design, the form looks dreadful with its corners instead of curvature but only ¼ knot is lost. ... With Cole went into BDEs as A/A Monitors & Troop Escorts, he says as HQ ships the conversion is going to take 4 mos. ...

9 December: DWP out sick, also Miss Mayhew [his typist]. ... Answered letter from Mrs Butt (really only an acknowledgment). ...

13 December: ... Walsh called with draft instructions for me as AC(WP) & Lillicrap as DNC [presumably clarifying areas of responsibility, as Goodall up to then held both posts]. Asked him about Butt, Mrs Butt, said 'Make my letter official', I did so. Walsh & I agreed that Admy could not employ Butt [after he came out of prison]. Walsh said DPP [Director of Public Prosecutions?, Sir E T Atkinson] was being put [?] on WPS Newcastle's loss (£455) of travelling expenses. ...

14 December: ... Lillicrap not elated at becoming DNC. ...

15 December: At Bath. Held meeting on dynamo power for Transport Ferries. ... At Contr's NC meeting. At conclusion Dep Contr tackled Contr on habitability, which C. rather brushed aside. With Lillicrap & Shepheard [V G, now ADNC, later to become DNC] discussed AP shells, said in my opinion the primary function should now be to defeat decks [implies oblique impact]. With Lillicrap discussed staff questions (Smithers [D W, overseer at Clydebank] to Overlord). Lillicrap agreed to change (DNC) taking place on 22/1/44.

16 December: Bateson in a fandango because Cabinet had referred back

(Sir) Victor G Shepheard (1893–1989) was a constructor who served as damage control officer of the battleship *Agincourt* at Jutland. After various overseer roles in the 1920s, he took over sloop design in the early 1930s, before being appointed Professor of Naval Architecture at Greenwich 1934–9. Back at the Admiralty during the war, he was involved mostly with battleships, becoming an ADNC in 1942. In 1951 he was appointed as the last DNC with the full authority of his predecessors. By the time he retired in 1958 he had seen the Royal Yacht *Britannia* and the *Porpoise* class submarines into service, and the last of wartime construction programme completed. He became a director of shipbuilders William Denny & Brothers in 1959. Goodall regarded him as safe pair of hands with wide experience. (*The Shipbuilder*)

Trans. Ferries because estimated cost was £550,000 per ship (I haven't given an estimate so don't know who produced this figure). Phoned DCW who said Trevan [S N] last night gave a snap of 475,000 (silly fool). H. [Hannaford?] makes it 425,000 which seems a bit high even then.

[Goodall was quite right to doubt these high figures, which suggested the fairly basic LST would cost almost as much as a 'C' class destroyer hull and machinery, and double that of a much larger 10,000-ton deadweight cargo ship. Actual prices were about £250,000 for a UK-built LST, roughly 40 per cent more for a Canadian one.] Held S/M welding c'tee, everybody keen to get the ships right, we shall succeed but it will mean delay to programme. ... At ACNS(W)'s meeting on alterations to Carriers, Staff want the moon, it looks as tho' we shall have to provide more accommodation in 1942 Lights. M. Stephen called, told him of Trans. Ferries, he doesn't want them. [They actually got *LST.3028* and *3029*.] A v. thick day.

18 December: Paper arrived approving Transport Ferries. Got Packham in & discussed how best to get Canada going quickly. I drafted message to BATM, luckily before it was sent off Bateson told me Contr sent one last night: C. & his office do bad staff work by not telling others of action taken. ... Found out M.F. [Military Finance?] gave the ridiculous £550,000 for cost: they will get themselves in a mess by cutting out technical depts. ...

23 December: At Whites, Cowes, with John [W G]. Welding in shop good, but yard very congested as quay is cluttered up thro' crane not being at work yet. John said we could do no more to buck up Butters [Glasgow crane manufacturer]. ... Other apparent difficulty is the weather, it rained like smoke and all welding in open was impossible for a long time. Firm said they always dried seam before welding. [The Admiralty overseer should check that such things were being done.] ...

24 December: ... E in C worried over follow-on orders for Trans. Ferry machinery but Contr said he could not say as CCO wanted re-design to give up frigate machinery & get more speed. [They were designed for 13 knots, the most that the 5500 ihp steam reciprocating engines could provide.] Message rc Court of Inquiry into capsize of *Chasseur 5*, phoned D of D(L) [Director of Dockyards, London?] if Portsmouth would send a constructor. ... Told DWP of coming change (Lillicrap DNC) & sent note to Walsh. ...

27 December: Bank Holiday. On leave. Sinking of *Scharnhorst* broadcast.

28 December: ... Wrote Fraser [Admiral Sir Bruce Fraser, former Controller] re his successful action against *Scharnhorst*.

29 December: McMurray came & I went thro' firms re alterations to Transport Ferries. Held meeting, a very big one. Warship firms jib at the job: H & W gave very poor dates: H L want to be let off 2 & V-A W [Walker] off one. Later went thro' H L situation & we must agree to 2, also V-A W to 4. Then with H & W pressed them for 4 by April [presume

1945 as 1944 impossible], they will phone Belfast (this done by putting back 3 frigates). Ormston thinks he can do *Colossus* by Aug [completed Dec 1944] & H & W think they can keep date for *Glory* [completed Apr 1945]. Told McCarthy to tot up the no. of TFs we can now get by April.

30 December: Merrington called, interesting on Dodecanese failure [German capture of Leros in November], chaotic administration in S. Italy, typhus in N. Africa. He wants to go to Overlord, phoned Lillicrap who said he had not yet taken action to appoint Smithers, asked him to phone C in C East[ern] Fl[eet] if we can keep M. J E Mathias called with Scotts Labour Inquiry report. ... M. said Barr in a fair stink over Admy letter [presumably of criticism] received after *Bellona*. Angus & Bogie called, told them (after phoning Contr) to keep dates for *Glory* & *Warrior* even at expense of *Minotaur*. ... Greig called, swore his pressure hull welding will be all right. ...

31 December: Press Division phoned, BBC wants me to broadcast on 'Ships we have Built'. Said All right, told Contr who looked down his nose as tho' he thought he should have been asked to do it. Contr wants yarn of how we are building TFs & what is involved if we repeat US design & get US engines. [Not practicable: LST2s were slower, of prefabricated welded construction and with different auxiliary equipment as well as diesel main machinery.]

Memoranda 1943

A better year. Have managed to hold the RCNC together and got over the threatened DWP split. [Possibly to hive off Directors of Warship Production to the Ministry of Production.] Hopkins able but difficult. Staffing his Production Organisation & Undex has been very difficult. On top of this requests for more RCNC for Operations & Maintenance have shown clearly that Post-war Corps must be larger & that we must take our place in Operations & Naval Organisation, C in C Med, S C SEA [Supreme Commander, S E Asia], C in C H F [Home Fleet] (a convert) all have written to say RCNC should be in RN. Yet somebody stonewalls & nothing is done, altho' C in C Med has become 1st SL. Butt affair a bad blot on Corps record. High profits investigation is going to be used to boost Secretariat to D of C unless technical depts play together. Habbakuk has been & still is a pain in the neck. Getting Undex work going after a bad start with Goodlet has been a fine achievement. H F successful action. *Scharnhorst* has sent up our stock, so has King in the Med. Firms on the whole are not improving, to wit Clydebank, Fairfield, Scott. But V-A Walker & Whites are better now than at the beginning of the year. Labour has been very difficult e.g. over pre-fabricated frigates.

1944

1 January: Honours: Lillicrap CB [Charles S, Companion of the Bath, about to become Director of Naval Construction] (something good for RCNC at last), Swan a knight [Charles S, chairman of Swan Hunter & Wigham Richardson, died in December]. RCNC in dockyards draw a blank (a damned shame). ...

3 January: Contr[oller] wants particulars of Italian underwater protection, I will send a signal to C in C [Med]. Told him my scheme for converting two 1943 L[igh]t Carriers into FAA [Fleet Air Arm] Maintenance Ships, he is hoping for much from USA. ... Mr Waymouth of BBC came re broadcast which is Overseas not Home, must be done this week. ... Sanders came in with heavy frown because he had not got an Honour.

4 January: Baker [G S, Superintendent of towing tank at National Physical Laboratory, Teddington] called, wants Haslar expt [experiment] results for his propeller investigation: phoned Gawn [R W L, Superintendent of Admiralty Experiment Works, Haslar] who does not trust Baker (neither do I). Wrote B. I would give him particulars but he must not publish nor criticise in public. ...

5 January: ... Worked on broadcast & finished first draft: much too long & dull in the middle. Took it home & N. [his wife] chewed it up. ... Merrington [Constructor Captain A J] called, sent further message to C in C E F [Somerville] to persuade him to release M. for Overlord. Contr came up re X craft at Vickers, told him they must go on [six XE craft were ordered on 13 Jan].

6 January: Contr pressing for whole Trans[port] Ferry picture [Mark 3 Tank Landing Ships]: said he may want me to go to USA in his place (Damn!). ...

7 January: ... Rayner [L W A, aircraft carrier designer] called & said in carriers there is welding plant but [naval] shipwrights don't know how to use it & don't care. ...

8 January: Fardell (D of P) [Commander G E of Plans dept] came up re 1944 Prog[ramme]. Went thro' this very quickly with McCarthy [S A, Director of Warship Production]. ... Annoyed by remark from D A/S W [Director of Anti-submarine Warfare, now Captain A Pritchard] on new destr[oyer] docket that Thorny[croft] can do what we can't (damned nonsense), sent paper back to Sec[retary] FBC. ...

11 January: At Bath. With Hickey [F, ADNC, cruiser and floating dock designer] & Lillicrap discussed stability of *Hobart* [Australian cruiser]. ... Went into *Bermuda* report & wrote Pigott [Sir Stephen, managing director of John Brown shipyard at Clydebank] re workmanship. All welded fore end of *Tiptoe* [submarine building at Barrow] thro' 160 lb/sq in press[ure] test satisfactorily T.G.: wrote Barry [C B, Rear Admiral Submarines]. Discussed possible cancellation of U's & T's [submarines] to get more A's. From CIGM [Greathed] got dates for *Zest*, *Zodiac* & *Peacock* [two destroyers and a sloop building at Thornycroft, Southampton].

Being short of anti-submarine escorts, the USN ordered 100 frigates based on the British 'River' class. Twenty-one were allocated to the RN, named after British colonies, all built by Kaiser-Walsh at Providence RI. The first, *Anguilla*, is seen shortly after her arrival in the UK in January 1944. While built all-welded much faster than the British-built ships, it was at much higher cost, about $2.25 million each (£560,000) excluding Government Furnished Equipment compared with about £240,000 for the British 'Rivers' which *included* ASIs. Much of the difference was in labour costs, not just wage levels over double UK but also higher man-hours. (*Blackman collection*)

12 January: ... With Mathias [T L] & Lillicrap discussed Squids. I like dwg [drawing] with Squids & 3 sets of torp[edo] tubes but it means a bigger ship. Inspected dwgs of [US] Maritime Commission frigates ['Colony' class, based on British 'River' class], told DDNC [Deputy Director of Naval Construction, L C Williamson] to see the first to arrive is carefully inspected [*Anguilla*]. ...

13 January: ... Pigott called, told him about possible suspension of *Malta* [design of new fleet carrier not yet finalised]. ... At 1st SL's meeting on programme, 1st SL [First Sea Lord, now Admiral of the Fleet Sir A B Cunningham] talked against all our new ships, too big & not enough in them! [Incompatible to put more equipment into a smaller ship without sacrificing other features.] All sat dumb except 5th SL [Boyd]: D of P [Director of Plans, now Captain G Grantham] wanted to upset the TF programme, 1st SL has a lot to learn about designs: what troubles me is that the Naval Staff will walk back on their previous requirements. ...

14 January: ... W Ayre [Sir Wilfred, chairman of Hall Russell and Burntisland Shipbuilding, brother of Amos] called, can't do TFs at Hall Russell [Aberdeen shipbuilders. *TF.30* (*LST.3030*) was ordered 12 Dec 43 but not completed as a LST] (we are in a pickle). ... Contr wants me to get a push on LCTs & LCG(M)s [tank landing craft and Landing Craft Gun (Medium)], had talk with Baker [R, Superintendent of Landing Craft SLC] & Vice Contr [Vice Admiral Sir F T B Tower] will see if Hendon Dock [fitting out base in Sunderland] could take LCG(M)s. [It did]...

15 January: ... Noted censor's cuts [to his broadcast]. ... Contr app'd [approved]. C.E. [possibly civil establishments] peeved at the rush, they remarked on the fee! [probably modest]. Went to BBC, gave talk, had to do last part again as it was just too long. Heard first part, didn't sound like my voice but it was certainly what I said. Here & there 'r's' were 'w's'. ...

17 January: FBC at 15.15. Programme for 1944 reviewed. Destroyer designs discussed ['G' class?], also 5.25″ cruiser. ... On battleships Gunnery Division favoured continuing 14″ guns on ground that quick & frequent hitting with 14″ at early stage of action will lead to success rather than a few heavy plonks from 16″: I think they are right. All the same on psychological ground with other powers having 16″ I think we should. ...

18 January: Got up early intending to go to Yeovilton but started sneezing so violently that I gave it up & went to bed. Sick. Heavy cold.

20 January: Back in office. Contr asked if big Fleet Carriers could go into more [dry]docks here if Flight Dk were unarmoured. I said 'No', beam

wanted for underwater protection. ... Callander said could only build 1 TF at expense of 4 T cl. [submarines]. [Possibly in terms of taking up a single slipway, not in terms of cost as one LST cost the same as one 'T'.]

21 January: Mitchell [A] brought up docket, report & drawings for 1943 Lt. Carriers, went thro' carefully, altered description a little and added 'Qualifications'. Then signed my last Board Dwgs [as DNC]. First was for a China gunboat [*Scorpion*]. What a change! Controller invited me to lunch. He is thinking of setting up Industry Panel, at first I did not bite but later said I thought a Shipbuilding Panel might be useful. I said One thing I had not done & that was to get RCNC into RN, he said he had kept the papers as he did not want this question to complicate his scheme for straightening out electrical & signal mess. My last day as DNC. Wrote Dep[artmen]t & RCNC. AR [air raid] warning about 20.50-22.20. Heavy gunfire.

22 January: .... First day as AC(WP) only. Nice letter of appreciation from Their Lordships. Cleared up long outstanding letters from Yarrow & Thorny. re their destroyers going back on account of late delivery of [4.5in] gun mountings &c. ...

24 January: ... Stevens of Canada called & lunched with me, interesting talk on contracts in Canada. MWS [Ministry of Wartime Shipbuilding?] deals with business and they have a Treasury man in the yards. ... Lillicrap called after seeing Contr, Sec. [Permanent Secretary to the Admiralty, Sir H V Markham] & 1st SL, he sent thro' designs as I don't want to tell 1st SL tomorrow anything he disagrees with. 1st SL is most against the Weapons 4″, too small. ...

25 January: ... Had lunch with 1st SL & gave some of my views on warship designs, he sticks to the belief that we have swung too much to AA armament & endurance. He said 'there won't be an aircraft carrier afloat in 20 years' time, they will all be islands'. I said I thought battleships were dead! We are poles asunder. Told Contr & wrote Lillicrap. ... Contr sent for Vice Contr & me re Far East Requirements for CO [Combined Operations] ships. Went into it with Baker & left him to work it out.

26 January: At Newcastle. Attended FOIC's [Flag Officer in Charge Tyne, Rear Admiral Sir W G C Maxwell] meeting re labour for LCTs. ... To Neptune, 3rd frigate [*Loch Cree/Natal*] held up for [prefabricated] pieces: work looks good. They have demarcation labour troubles (sounding pipes plumbers, suction pipe fitters, if 2 pipes combined whose?). At Wallsend [Swan Hunter's eastern yard] held meeting on *Vengeance* [light fleet carrier to be launched 23 Feb] and *Superb* [cruiser launched 31 Aug

43] & *St Kitts* ['Battle' class destroyer], inspected V. & S. Firm will have a job to finish V. in Dec. At Walker [Vickers-Armstrongs' Naval Yard] inspected *Colossus* [carrier launched 30 Sep 43], firm should keep date. ... Inspected yard re necessity for another crane at west end. ...

27 January: To Hendon Dock, work is going well. We <u>must</u> use this place more, it is well laid out & H[arry] Hunter [manager and a director of North Eastern Marine engineering company] is a go-getter, this means sending LCTs & LCG(M)s there & getting more labour in. At present firms are refusing to play because corvettes & frigates have lost their priority. To Tees Side Bridge [landing craft builder at Middlesbrough], found Peat [W B, managing director] speaking to Baker re taking up more energetically salvage vessels [lifting craft], inspected yard & steel fabricating shops, then held meeting Peat, Fletcher [F S, general manager], Jenkins [yard manager?], WPS [Warship Production Superintendent, North East, H Stanley], Lascelles [PSO]; they will do 2 salvage vessels to complete July-Aug [Lifting Craft 23-28 had been ordered in May 1943], 3 LCG(M)s to complete in April [1944], push on structure of 3 LCG(M)s. I will take 2 away to Hendon Dock & perhaps the 3rd. Home 11.25 pm.

While the merchant-ship builders brought in to build more frigates, corvettes and LCTs ordered in 1943 could build the hulls, they lacked the outfitting facilities such vessels required. One outfitting facility was set up at Dalmuir on the Clyde managed by John Brown and one at Sunderland managed by North Eastern Marine, which had nearby engine works. This latter was at Hendon Dock, which is seen on 30 April 1944. The 'Castle' class corvette is probably *Amberley Castle*, launched by Pickersgill, with another two out of shot. Four Mark 3 LCTs from Furness on the Tees are fitting out, *7101* to the left completed the next day plus *7102–7104* (Yard Numbers 379–382), the latter having arrived on the 28th. (*Author's collection*)

28 January: ... Sir H[arold] Yarrow [chairman and managing director of Glasgow shipbuilders] called, all his destroyers will go back because we have been unable to deliver guns for *Caprice* & *Cassandra* & he wants 10 weeks between consecutive destroyers. ... Pigott called, admitted marine turbine designers have not progressed & we are now forced to get land turbine designers in. [Pigott originally came to John Brown as a turbine designer for American Curtis.] ... Contr wants us to give Rebbeck his welding shop extension. ...

29 January: ... [Contr] gave me big ship programme & said I could now get busy, 2 b'ships [battleships!] & in slow time, 2 of 1943 big carriers. ... Wrote Lillicrap a chatty letter re the week's doings. McMurtrie [Francis, editor of *Jane's Fighting Ships*] came up by arrangement with Press Div[ision]. I gave him particulars of Lillicrap's career & showed him My Lords' letter of appreciation, said I was most proud of Illustrious class. ...

31 January: Press Div phoned, BBC want me to do a Home [Service] broadcast on Friday Feb 11. ... Lunch with Craven [Sir Charles, Industrial Adviser to Ministry of Production but still involved with Vickers-Armstrongs] he says Sec [Markham] is getting at him to round down on prices [of warships?] as a favour. ... I asked him if he thought it was time to consider post-war shipbuilding here and in Dominions. He said 'Yes' & agreed Dominions should have a share. ... Mr Robson of Findlay's [landing craft builders on the Clyde] called & talked for 2 hours. I nearly went to sleep but stuck it as I want early LCG(M)s from him. ...

2 February: ... Contr came up with a dreadful screed from Winston who has not learned *P of W* lesson & is still all out for battleships: gave Contr notes. Baker called re LCTs & LCG(M)s, pressed him to keep types at firms down to 2: told him of possible extra demand on fabricators. ... There is now a pro battleship set back in the Admy.

3 February: Tickled broadcast up: James [J H, Assistant Secretary to Controller] phoned then sent a messenger for 2 copies of the script. ... Stephen [Murray, chairman of Glasgow shipbuilder] called, wants to put back a destroyer to get on with merchant ship, said my answer was 'No' but I should have to consult DMB [Director of Merchant Shipbuilding, Amos Ayre]. ...

4 February: ... Contr wants to force welding on destroyer builders, I said 'be careful'.

5 February: ... Baker came up to discuss problem of keeping LCT firms in production till they can slip into [the bigger] LCT8's; this is really Vice Contr's baby. I wrote him a note giving my view that it is better

to go on with LCT4's even if they prove redundant. [The flimsy Mark 4s would not be suitable for a Far East war without strengthening and tropicalisation.] ...

7 February: ... Higham (M. Branch) [?J D, Principal Secretary, Admiralty] came up, told him no hope of getting *Superb* in Oct '44, he will propose some older ship [for Canada] that has not got all the new fire control gadgets. [Cruiser *Uganda* was transferred in Oct 1944 after refit in USA.] Lillicrap came, said he couldn't staff all the new designs & cruiser will not be ready till next year. I told him LCT8 badly wanted. ...

9 February: ... Bateson [Captain S L, Naval Assistant to Controller] came up red hot about USA's red tape & Admiral King. [Ernest, Chief of Naval Operations, no friend of the British.] ... Cdr Burnie [?] USN called, he has bluffed our officers into shutting up over quick rolling of Captain class [destroyer escorts]. [Why? DNC experience could probably come up with a solution.]

10 February: Bassett came up re deferring *Port Quebec* at Dalmuir [fitting-out facility managed by John Brown] where berthing space is urgently required. ... Saw Contr about deferring *Dunkirk* ['Battle' class destroyer]. I wanted to agree to Stephen's proposal because it helps the firm and removes a bit of DMB's justifiable grievance against us, Contr agreed. Went to broadcast rehearsal, James [Godfrey, presumably BBC producer] is very different to Waymouth; W. flatters, while J. criticizes very much; anyhow his criticism turned the talk from dull into lively, we cut a bit.

11 February: Saw Contr re Far East Train: I said I thought it was now all clear except for Hull Repair Ships, Aircraft Maintenance Ships & Coastal Forces Workshops & Parents. ...

12 February: ... Tuesday (Contr going to the party at Buckingham Palace following his son's wedding which was attended by Princesses E[lizabeth] & M[argaret] R[ose].) [Lieut Christopher Wake-Walker married Lady Anne Spencer, aunt of Diana, Princess of Wales, on 10 Feb.]

14 February: To Bath by early train. Went to Repairs & Conversions meetings as well as New Construction. At latter I said what I knew of 1944 Prog. & its effect on 1943 Lt Fleet Carriers. E in C [Engineer in Chief, Vice Admiral Sir F R G Turner] does not want to cancel *Monmouth* at Fairfield. ... E in C also worried about new dates of A Cl. S/Ms, said I would go into this, also told him there were only 20 S/Ms in the '44 Prog. & even those had been queried. ...

15 February: At Bath ... At Contr's NC meeting he spoke of message just in from BATM intimating Canada is fed up with the way they have been

messed about over Fleet Train [and] is doing nothing & cannot give us Victory ships (this is due to M of WT [Ministry of War Transport which included merchant shipping] stonewalling because Contr tried to put a fast one over him (and we are at war!) ...

16 February: ... Champness [E L, managing director of ship repairers Palmers Hebburn] called re getting an Admy grant to help with University training in nav[al] arch[itecture] on NE coast, said I would discuss with Lillicrap & let him know further. Then Champness opened out on HL's *Triumph* overlapping his quay [Hawthorn Leslie's yard was adjacent to Palmers, so presumably concern after the carrier's launch in Oct 1944] (was this the real object of his visit?). I said we had put it to FOIC & I felt must back up his proposal. ...

17 February: Ormston called [J Maurice, managing director of Vickers-Armstrongs shipyards], he will take more TFs but not Scotts' 2 Weapons, b'ship should go on No. 2 but O. was not certain of max. beam he could work to, I must get him on paper. [*Lion*'s keel had lain on their Berth No 2 since Jul 1939, as she was only suspended not cancelled; destroyers were built on either side of her keel.] ...

Wake-Walker's son Christopher at his wedding to Lady Anne Spencer, the aunt of Diana, Princess of Wales, on 10 February 1944. Also present were the Princesses Elizabeth and Margaret, with W-W and presumably his wife. (*IWM A21693*)

18 February: ... Saw Contr with proposal to send no more messages to Canada till after meeting of Cabinet on Feb 28, he agreed. Ayre [Amos] told me he reckoned conversions 4-5 mos [months]. Longer job than str[aight] merchant ships, I have been more optimistic. [P V] McLaughlin (late DDNO) [Assistant Director of Naval Ordnance] captain of *Spartan* when she was sunk [bombed off Anzio on 29 Jan] called, he seemed still rather nervous, & fears blame for losing ship. It looked to me as tho' his Admiral was at fault, a ship at anchor without a smoke screen within reach of shore-based aircraft, fighter protection can't do everything yet (& never will?). ...

19 February: ... Opened ball for Andrew Laing Lecture [prestigious annual lecture to North East Coast Institution of Engineers & Shipbuilders in memory of the late managing director of Wallsend Slipway & Engineering, machinery builders for the 1907 *Mauretania*] by writing to Gawn, Offord, Shepheard, Forbes, Cole & John [W G, Superintendent of Welding Development]. M. Br [Military Branch] panicking for paper re P.M. [Prime Minister] wanting *Vanguard* by mid '45: wrote Pigott a hastener ...

20 February: Sunday, AR warning about 21.40-22.45. Gunfire heavy, one bomb unpleasantly close to 50 Lyford [Road, Goodall's house near Wandsworth Common].

21 February: ... On arrival at office found my windows gone, bomb at corner of St James Park on Sunday night. Worked up for Undex Panel meeting. DTM [de Salis] spoke on CNC torpedo as weapon enemy is using. I thanked Panel for help & begged it should take more practical & less theoretical line on Sub-panel. ... Saw Reith about ASCBS [Admiral Superintendent Contract Built Ships, Vice Admiral St A B Wake] doing transport ferries [as opposed to M of WT], he said Dep Contr [Deputy Controller, Vice Admiral C E B Simeon] had agreed, dictated letter & told DWP [McCarthy] to sign. ...

22 February: At Newcastle. Held meeting re 4 LFCs due to complete this year. Dictated notes. [Presumably Goodall took his private secretary F O Bamford with him.] ... To H Leslie, *Solebay* launched, interesting talk with Lord Sandwich, launching arrangements look light but do the job all right. Yard far too congested, this firm should never have had *Triumph*. LCTs back because riveters went slow, they are now back on piecework. [*LCT.7074*, now preserved at Portsmouth, was launched there 29 Mar.] Told Rowell [H B Robin, chairman of Hawthorn Leslie] Contr was upset that his dates were going back as much for LCTs & TFs. What about sending TFs to Hendon Dock, he didn't seem to like this.

23 February: To Blyth. Considering state of affairs when Turnbull [William, general manager and director of Blyth Dry Docks & Shipbuilding] took over, he is doing well, trouble here is the lieu rate [hourly pay rates], a long established practice & trades will not go on piecework, also firm is not in Federation [Shipbuilding Employers Federation]. Corvettes ['Castles'] have gone back owing to J S White being behind with machinery parts. [The diary says J S White, with engine works at Cowes, but it seems strange that a firm 300 miles away would be given the contract to install the machinery, especially as they no longer manufactured steam reciprocating machinery. Possibly the company was White's Marine Engineering at Hebburn only 15 miles away who did make such machinery. The escorts' actual engines were ordered by the Admiralty from a variety of general engineering manufacturers around the country, and supplied to shipyards from a general pool.] Parts for pre-fab frigates come together beautifully. To Swan Hunter, *Vengeance* launch went off well [that day]. Looked at *Barfleur* [first 'Battle' class], still think firm may complete by June but it is going to be a scramble.

(Sir) H B Robin Rowell (1894–1981) was the son of Sir Herbert Rowell, chairman of shipbuilder and engine builder Hawthorn Leslie. He had been with the Royal Flying Corps in the First World War, before becoming a director of Hawthorn Leslie in 1922. He managed the shipyard in the Second World War, becoming chairman from 1943 to 1965. Goodall had a generally favourable view of Rowell, despite his reluctance towards the end of the war to take warship orders which might delay the company's return to merchant shipbuilding. (*The Shipbuilder*)

[She was notionally completed in Sep 1944 but delayed to Jan 1945 by late delivery of her armament and director control tower.] Talk with Swan & N[orman] Hunter re *Adrias*, can do. [Greek escort destroyer ex-*Border* mine damaged on 22 Oct 43 so having a new fore end built, although repairs were not completed and she was scrapped in Nov 1945.] Later FOIC asked who was going to take Sir Charles place [as Chairman], he is getting very infirm. I suggested Morison from Neptune [director Thomas Morison, but not from any of the founding families]. R. Rowell came to hotel & said he had thought better of Hendon Dock for his TFs. [*LST.3016–3018* were later sent there to fit out.]

Hawthorn Leslie were not keen to build tank landing ships, hoping to keep the berths for merchant ships, but they had to take three hulls, albeit to be fitted out at Hendon Dock. This view about September 1944 shows at left *Transport Ferry No 16* (later *LST.3016*) on Berth No 6 and *TF 17* on No 5. *TF 18* was completed after the war as the mercantile *Rio Minho*. The term 'Transport Ferry' was used to forestall shipyard workers claiming the higher wages that the landing craft builders got. (*Author's collection*)

24 February: ... Letter from Pigott saying he can't launch *Vanguard* before Dec, but can complete Dec '45. ...

26 February: With Hall [V W, Admiralty overseer at Fairfield] & DWP went into Fairfield organisation; agreed McLachlan [shipyard manager?] overloaded; nos. supervising platers, drillers, welders & caulkers look insufficient. ... Contr told me there was witch hunting by 1st SL because KGVs vent[tilation] was not good enough for Far East (Contr was to take the blame, he would not have DNC & E in C singled out!!) [Fair, it is not the latters' job to specify the ambient conditions in which ships are to operate, they supply the appropriate ventilation.] ...

28 February: ... P.O. [Private Office First Lord, A V Alexander] sent paper re not enough work in west Canada & this when M of WT is stopping Fleet Train work there! ... Contr sent for me, in a stick as result of message from Troup [Vice Admiral J A, FOIC Glasgow] about work at John Brown's, wants to take away *Port Quebec* [*Deer Sound*]. Troup is a trial, he did not consult WPS [J E Mathias].

29 February: Sick. Cold. Got a chill on Feb 21 when office &c were so draughty, no glass in windows. Fought the blighter thro' the week & thought that I had won. ...

1 March: Crawled in at 10.30, lunch in office, left just before 18.00. ... Meeting (Cabinet) on Fleet Train which should have taken place on Feb 28 deferred: heartrending. [Decisions were needed on priorities.] ...

2 March: Barr called re Fairfield organisation, had 2 hrs with him, I fear without much effect but he undertook to ease McLachlan & McPherson; he says his big trouble is electricians. ... Barr showed me cost figures of destroyers S H [Swan Hunter] lowest (hull), C L [Cammell Laird] highest (hull) but lowest machinery. ...

3 March: ... Wrote A Ayre & Greig [K E, managing director Scotts, Greenock shipuilders] re TF [LST.3043] going on Defence berth & thus delaying a merchant ship. ... E in C came in, a regular mess over Fleet Train, machine tools [for repair ships] are coming in & cannot be stored. ...

6 March: DNC called. [He remained based in Bath leaving Goodall in London to handle liaison with other Admiralty departments.] Told him of Contr's decision to go ahead on [aircraft] Component and Eng[ine]

Kenneth E Greig (1882–1965) had spent most of his career at Scotts, including managing their Hong Kong subsidiary Taikoo Dockyard. Although a marine engineer rather than a shipbuilder, he became managing director of the Greenock shipyard in 1941. May of that year saw serious bomb damage which severely affected production. Goodall felt that this was used for too long to excuse the continual failings in deliveries during the later war years, with several hulls having to be towed away to other shipyards for completion; indeed the Admiralty was already complaining about late deliveries in January 1941. Greig was the only head of a major Second World War warship builder not to receive a knighthood. (The Shipbuilder)

Repair ships on assumption they will be PF(C) [i.e. converted from standard prefabricated Type C hulls]. ... DWP right that Gibraltar [aircraft carrier] could not go on No. 2 [berth at Walker yard].

7 March: Started A.L. [Andrew Laing] Lecture & wrote Nicol [T S, Secretary of NECIES]. ... Attended Min of Production meeting on steel allocation & transport reduction when Overlord starts [presumably

absorbing much railway capacity]; said shipyards had no stocks on which to live [most steel plates were made to order for a particular size]. ...

8 March: At Glasgow. Breakfast with FOIC to talk about J Br[own] & Dalmuir. ... To Clydebank, inspected *Vanguard* further behind than I thought; then meeting. DEE present [Director of Electrical Engineering Sir James Pringle] agreed can launch Dec. After lunch to Dalmuir, fine show but no labour. ... To Yarrow, *Caprice* was berthed at Barclay Curle [Elderslie repair yard just downstream of Yarrow] as *Cockade* was launched [the day before] & in basin [Yarrow had a covered fitting out basin but restricted in size]. Stayed night at Yarrow's, Lady Y. very nice & wearing quilt, slept well.

9 March: Held Transport Ferry meeting. DMB spurred merchant firms to get on. [Orders for LSTs at warship builders had been placed on 22 Sep 43, but with merchant ship builders on 29 Jan.] They are going to hope DCW(S) [Director of Contract Work (Supplies) C J W Hopkins] will not be forthcoming with supplies (e.g. shaft barrels & rudder posts) [which would give them a good excuse for being late]. After meeting Barr said DEE had been most helpful & he now thought *Implac[able]* would complete to date but Admy supplies would be late. ... To Old Kilpatrick for Findlay's LCTs, really wonderful what has been done without ship builders [they were structural engineers with works in Motherwell] & with wretchedly bad labour [but landing craft yards paid better than regular shipbuilders]. Fitting out at Bowling a trial [cramped harbour a mile to the west] slacking very bad but management is helpless, old Robson struck me as no good. Dined with FOIC & Bassett. Slept well, train 1¾ hrs late.

10 March: ... A Ayre told me there had been some sort of decision over Fleet Train, got Friedberger [Captain W H D, Deputy Director of Plans] who said we are to have 2 Hull Repair Ships & 3 Maintenance Ships (Hull Repair just what we don't want immediately, we were banking on LSTs.) ...

14 March: Back in office. Not too good [recovering from a cold], promised Madam I would go easy. ... Got Fardell up re fast oilers, he said they were not to be mentioned in the Cabinet paper. 1st L was writing a screed on the Fleet Train & was going to put the oilers in (Contr thinks this unwise as it will be another excuse for holding up the Train). ...

15 March: ... Bogie [F G, WPS Belfast] called, gloomy about N. Ireland, took him to see Contr who said that is so but we can't help by worrying over it. B. suggested we might take *Minotaur* away as H & W's trouble is fitting out labour. Talked with Baker (SLC) said I couldn't find it in my

heart to curse Robson, considering all his difficulties Old Kil. does well. ...
Wrote Stephen, Princ[ess] E[lizabeth] will not launch *Cheviot* or *Ocean*.

16 March: ... Wrote Swan, Rebbeck & Barr re suspending work on
A[lbion], *B[ulwark]* & *M[onmouth]*. ...

17 March: Meeting on Vickers Barrow's S/M prog. Then with Callander
& Moss [William, shipyard manager] saw Contr whose threat to 'twist
tail' petered out. Moss confident he can complete *Mars* [light fleet carrier
completed as *Pioneer*] in March '45, also that A cl. pre-assembly will
prove more rapid than he is now estimating. Contr said he would cancel
Threat the last T at Barrow [cancelled 28 Apr 44]. Ayre asked me what
was the use of C.L. Br. [Controller of Labour Branch?]. I said a little
when you want labour (e.g. Hancock [probably J, Assistant Secretary
Admiralty] has promised Callander he will get him some more welders).
Ayre says C.L. no help in disputes. I advised CMSR [Lithgow] should put
to 1st L (copy to Lord Leathers) [Frederick, Minister of War Transport,
former shipowner] his troubles re labour disputes delaying ships for
Overlord. Contr wants notes from me to combat P.M's charge that Admy
have ordered more ships than they can build. ...

The 'A' class submarines ordered in April 1943 were all-welded, not only to speed
production but also to increase diving depth (to 500ft). Vickers-Armstrongs at
Barrow laid out Berth No 2 for erecting prefabricated sections. Seen about April
1945 are (furthest) *Alcide*, *Alderney* and *Alliance* with 16ft diameter pressure hull
units for *Ambush*, *Anchorite* and *Andrew*. (*Author's collection*)

20 March: ... [Contr] asked if he was right in giving priority to A cl. S/Ms at Barrow. I said 'yes', not only were they wanted by FOS more than Ts but once Barrow got into swing production would be more rapid than Ts. ...

21 March: Got S of C [Superintendent of Conversions, K H Watkins] & discussed Accommodation Ships. Then meeting with N A [Bateson], S of C, Kidd [H, Principal Technical Officer, Sea Transport] & Dawson (of D of ST) [F H, Assistant Director of Sea Transport]. Two latter were surprised these 4 ships were required before defeat of Germany, but Bateson rubbed it in that M of WT had agreed to supply ships by required date. ...

22 March: ... Buchanan [G, constructor], Stamp (Fairfield), Melville (V-A, Barrow) & Brown (V- A, Walker) came to discuss conversion of 1942 Prog Lt Fleets to Aircraft Maintenance Ships. ... Afternoon Morrison [John, director and shipyard manager] of H & W Belfast & Baillie [J S, of H & W London office] came re *Warrior* to wash her out. Then with DWP long talk over Belfast situation. I offered to take *Minotaur* away (had Clydebank in mind), Morrison looked down his nose. ...

23 March: Contr's Policy Meeting. I said 'High-ups' should appreciate that labour disputes are affecting operational dates. Morrison called, wants ['Loch'] frigates & TFs taken away instead of *Minotaur*, I said 'Go into this' & let me know dates as soon as strike is over. ... Wrote Pigott re taking H & W's frigates at Clydebank. Barr phoned *Theseus* not wanted as Maintenance Ship, Callander phoned could finish [*Mars/ Pioneer*] mid Jan. ...

24 March: ... Contr phoned, he approved *Edgar* [*Perseus*] & *Mars* as Aircraft Maintenance Ships, phoned Callander & Ormston & Dep Contr. McIntosh (Joint Planners) phoned me re getting more LSTs quickly, told him we were pitting merchant vs warship builders & did not believe the former. ... AR warning 23.25 to 00.55 25/3: gunfire heavy. UXB [unexploded bomb] on [Wandsworth] Common near station.

25 March: Ate up most of paper accumulation. ... Got DWP to write WPSs re helping Harlands with turret planing machine [for *Minotaur's* 6in gun mountings from Vickers-Armstrongs Barrow] & pipework. Contr sent for me re Transport Ferries, Lambe (D of P) [Captain C E] & Nav[al] Ass[istan]t there, they want 34 to leave UK by 1st Dec. I have to say if this is possible & if not, at what cost is it done. Talked with DWP who says 'Quite impossible', told him to arrange for meeting on Wed. with Neptune, Barclay Curle, Barr, Ormston & Stephen; also tell DMB & DCW(S). [Only fifteen were launched by 1 Dec.]

27 March: Fardell came in re *Vanguard*, told him we could not complete by Dec '45 unless it was a 'Named' ship; he indicated Staff would object. ... Letter from Metcalfe [Sir Ralph, Director of Sea Transport] re Notes of my meeting on 21/2 which he proposes to regard as Technical only & wash out date requirements. Saw Friedberger who is apparently a meddler as he is now proposing to alter dates, saw Bateson who got at F. who will give dates to Metcalfe. ... Good screed from J E Mathias re fitting out TFs at Dalmuir, showed Contr.

28 March: ... Contr has TFs on the brain, wants to know if we are insisting too much on Admy practices &c. Bogie called before leaving for Pacific [as Constructor Captain, Eastern Fleet]. Bartlett [J L, ADNC and aircraft carrier designer] called after attending trials of *Indefat[igable]*. Mosquito [aircraft] took off & landed. Island vibration cured, turning

Although a battleship using the four spare twin 15in mountings removed from *Courageous* and *Glorious* had been planned from early 1940, the order for *Vanguard* was not placed until March 1941. John Brown had been earmarked to build one of the 1939 *Lion* class 16in battleships, but as *Conqueror* was never formally ordered (although allocated Yard No 567), were the natural choice of builder for the new battleship, taking over 567. She was built on Berth No 3 following *Duke of York* and *Roberts*. This photo dating from about May 1944 shows a typical Clydebank hull construction scene, with a forest of guy ropes supporting lifting gear. Construction has reached the upper (weather) deck, with the ring bulkhead to support 'X' turret being erected and riveted deck plating. There are about fifty men in view, few of whom seem to be actually working. (*UCS*)

circle 1000 yds, speed apparently not too good, mast has to be moved, we told DRE [Director of Radio Equipment, Captain B W Bower-Smith] it would be too hot where he wanted. [She returned to Clydebank for modifications including machinery 4 Apr–6 May 44.]

29 March: Held Transport Ferry meeting, Barr, Ormston, Morrison, & McLay (Barclay Curle) [W H, assistant general manager] came. No hope of getting 34 by mid Nov, best that can be done is to gain a week or two. Dictated notes & told Contr labour situation getting worse, rivet boys out on Tyne & this has spread to Clyde. Riveters have been going slow on Tyne for several weeks, this is really a stay-in strike for lieu rates. ...

30 March: Contr sent for me re Fleet Train: are all maintenance vessels the same? Said in principle 'Yes'. Did Hull Repair Ship want a boiler for work to go on while ship is under weigh [way]? Said that was news to me, I should have to inquire. Were dwgs all ready for FAA Comp[onents] & Repair Ships, said 'Yes'. Could Fighter Direction Ships be smaller than 15 knot cargo liners. Said I should have to get Bath on that. Phoned Lillicrap on all these points. At Contr's Policy meeting, I said 'Why does Min of Labour spend its time & energy on inquiry into C Laird whose output is good & who have had no labour troubles & leave untouched all the labour disputes'. ...

31 March: ... Held meeting of accommodation ships ([2 for] dockyard [workers] & [2 for] spare crews S/Ms), got complements fixed & also agreed on dates. ... DNC rang me re Fighter Direction Ships, had talk with Todhunter [Captain R C, Deputy Director Combined Operations Material] & DCOM party, no hope of less than 15 knot cargo liner unless Staff come off speed. Gave Contr the 6 firms who by disorganising everything could produce LSTs by mid Nov. Letter from DNC 'all nonsense that Hull Repair Ships want 1 more boiler'.

1 April: ... Saw Contr re LCG(M)s, Tees Side want a lot more riveters, phoned FOIC [Maxwell] & sent letters to Hancock & Stanley.

2 April. Sunday. Double summer time commenced [clocks two hours forward].

3 April: Contr spoke of LCG(M)s, said he would phone FOIC, he thought I ought to take over production of landing craft, I told him I was only concerning myself with these 6 LCG(M)s [Tees Side Bridge had the order for 101–124, all launched in 1944]. (Note. Instructions are my job, does not alter Vice Contr's duties). C.L. sent up yarn that annoyed me re labour situation in Southampton area, is C.L. any use?

4 April: ... Hancock came up while Contr was here, we talked manning Dalmuir. Contr said he must first have it out with Lithgow, said would I see L., I said I would rather leave it to him [they were both on the Admiralty Board] (I funk fighting L.). Contr told me what happened at P.M's Midnight Follies yesterday. [Churchill was notorious for having late-night meetings with an exhausted staff, who did not have the luxury of an afternoon nap.] He thinks he is now going to get the Fleet Train (Bateson thinks Contr too cocksure). ...

5 April: A day of too many callers. Mathias (Glasgow) here full of a grievance against Troup who is undoubtedly a trial. WPS & he drafted a reply to Troup's unwarranted attack on M. ... Pigott called with dwg showing how frigate could be converted to Fighter Direction Ship. ...

6 April: Troup rang re ERO [Emergency Repair Overseers] or WPS taking ships on after they have been handed over, in particular LCT(R) [Rocket] for Americans. ... Sir R Johnson [chairman Cammell Laird] called, wants a push on his [No 6 building] slip extension: spoke of Contr's interference with his labour, said so long as he refuses to employ women we cannot help him: he let out how he keeps his labour quiet (pays more). ...

7 April: Good Friday. Bateson came up re P.M's thirst for more information, found how he had got his figures, sent Contr revised yarn. ... Wrote Rowell re *Manxman* effect on new construction. ...

10 April: On leave. N. had a nasty heart attack.

11 April: A W Watson [ADNC and escort designer] called after *Loch Fada* trials, went well. Baker (SLC) back, fixed up rivetters for Tees Side, we may get a LCG(M) before end of May. [*LCG(M).101* was completed on 22 Jun.] Troup rang 3 times re cutting down fuel [for shipyards], I said we could not agree to shutting down all Saturday, what about Sunday? He said 'That would mean a strike'. [Sunday overtime was paid at a higher rate.] ... Personal minute from P.M. re Fleet Train. Bateson says Fine, I wonder.

13 April: ... Greig of Scotts says he would like to take 2 pre-fab Ts from Vickers, but on working it out it appears to me we gain very little. ... Johnson (C.L.) rang said no objection to small model of S class being presented to Lord Derby [Lord Lieutenant of Lancashire] (torp tubes are not shown). Johnson also on about No.6 slip, said I was having a tussle with M of WP [Ministry of (War) Production]. ... 5th SL asks for open hangar & side elevators in big carrier.

14 April: ... DNO [Director of Naval Ordnance, Rear Admiral C H L Woodhouse who had just replaced Read Admiral O Bevir] sent me

copy of letter to Pigott re delivery of gun mtgs for *Vanguard*, did not look bright I thought. [Harland & Wolff at Scotstoun were refurbishing the four twin 15in mountings from *Courageous* and *Glorious*.] … Vice Contr came up re LST follow-on programme, got DWP in. We agreed that repeat LST3s [first reference to the correct title of TFs] would come out about autumn of '45 while LST4s would not come out till spring '46. [These were designed to be more suited to the beaches in East Asia.] …

18 April: At Bath. … At Dep. Contr's new construction meeting. DNO's towers [director control towers DCTs] putting ships back. After meeting talk with Dep Contr (a) Fighter Direction Ships [F.D.], he won't touch (Contr has ruled they are DCOM's) (b) responsibility for fitting out Fleet Train: Dep Contr wants WPS & Co to supervise, I said 'Careful, if you insist too much DMB & D of ST will say 'Do it yourself' & we shall be using Naval instead of M.S. [merchant ship] labour.' … With Hampton & Kimberley discussed frigates for F.D. ships not practicable. Hampton then showed new Staff Requirements bigger than ever. [LSTs Mark 2 were later converted.]

19 April: … 5th SL wants to alter Fleets [carriers] if he does I fear we shall lose them altogether. …

20 April: Back in office. Pigott called, wanted information re contemplated alterations to Fl. Carriers as he wishes to lay down *Malta* in autumn, told him. … W Ayre called, very pleased with *Loch Killin* [frigate completed by Burntisland 12 April]. …

22 April: … Wrote Dep. Contr re Lochs as AA ships [became 'Bay' class] … Re C.F. [Coastal Forces] parent & workshop ships discussed with DWP building at Lobnitz using M/S [minesweeper] machinery. [Never built.] Makin [J E, Principal Secretary, Admiralty] brought up paper in which Min. of Prod. turns down CL Slip No.6. Damn!! …

24 April: … Wrote screed re H & W's new store to cost £35,000! [about £2 million in today's money]. … Message from BAD [British Admiralty Delegation] giving particulars of Heavy Duty Repair ships USN are supplying [*Assistances*, converted Liberty ships]. D of P (Q) [Captain C C Hughes-Hallett] will take up arm[amen]t which looks unnecessary. …

26 April: … I attended CMSR's meeting, dictated notes, the M.S. side wastes work e.g. mahogany (2 skin) boats by H & W! To listen to CMSR one would think that there is only one ship that can win the war viz *Georgic* [liner still under repair at H & W]. …

27 April: … Contr spoke of ASCBS' phoning, very bad effect on men of commissioning a ship & then having her waiting for K towers [DCT] e.g.

Caprice. … Meeting with H & W got about ½ way thro' they want taken away 6 frigates & 2 TFs. *Audacious* [*Eagle*] is going damned slowly. They left prints of her slip altered for *New Zealand*.

28 April: Pigott called, left another dwg of central lift in *Malta*, he spoke Contr about this (Memo: I must talk to P. less). He is in trouble over delay to *Cambrian* due to late delivery of K tower. [Clydebank were completing her Scotts-launched hull.] He is prepared to take 4 frigates from H & W. With H & W's people saw Contr who was emphatic that [wage] rates in LCT yards [in Northern Ireland] must not be higher than in shipyards, wrote FOIC [Bevan]. …

29 April: Saw Contr re transfer of 2 T S/Ms from Barrow to Scotts, he approved [*Tabard* and *P.343*]. Wrote Greig & Callander & started docket. … Makin phoned, Min of Prod had agreed to CL's No.6 slip: told Johnson he could place contract with MacA [civil engineering contractors McAlpine].

1 May: Got Meryon in & told him of provisional order for 8 Battles & 8 Weapons. Craven will take 2 TFs at Barrow. … Got John's asst. over re Smith's Dock extension, think T Edwards is maddening.

2 May: K towers for destroyers, Contr's has idea to defer 1st ships for several months in order to keep dates for others; DNO called, said dates he has given are not yet firm … Mk VI towers [for control of 4.5in and 4in guns being manufactured by Vickers-Armstrongs at Barrow and Crayford] are also doubtful (this will affect *Barfleur*). …

4 May: Contr came up re Thornycroft building a prototype LCT8. I was agin it, their progress is bad enough already. Later I talked with Vice Contr & told him the same thing, then Baker my reasons: the prototype to be true must be built of pre-fab parts (transport difficulties) it wouldn't be ready until about Jan '45 (Admy supply difficulties) & by that time landing ships will be too far on to alter. Thorny will growl against the machinery all the time [four diesels geared to two shafts]; better a full sized mock up. [Goodall's advice must have been taken as all the LCT8s were built by structural engineers except one ordered later at J S White.] … Davis (DNC Bath) [S M, constructor] called re F.D. ships, told him Contr's idea was to convert [cruisers] *Hawkins* & *Frob[isher]*. …

5 May: Baker (SLC) brought up dwgs of LCT(L) [he probably meant LCT8], they are stoutly built for their size; told Contr I didn't think they could be blown up, so as to disintegrate but would produce obstructive wreckage. I can see nothing better than sweeping for these [beach] obstructions. …

8 May: Letter from ASCBS re K towers in destroyers, he wants to alter some completion dates. Letter from DNO re definite dates for K towers and Mk VI, both are bad. ... Mountain [J F, Assistant Secretary Admiralty] called re arrangements for preventing Germany building merchant ships after G. is whacked & out. I agreed that if they were limited to 250 ft long ships, all big slips &c should be smashed up. I said they must guard against Germany building bigger ships outside Germany. They would need some repair facilities, we would like cranes & shipyard machine tools.

9 May: King [F V] back from Glasgow: still a difficulty in engining H & W (Govan)'s TFs, he will see Barrow re engining the 2 TFs they will take from Belfast, then Belfast may engine all 4 frigates going to Clydebank. Thornycroft called re inclining [measuring stability] *Peacock* [sloop]. I phoned DNC & then T. said it was [destroyer] *Zest*, he is a trial. ...

10 May: Got hold of Bassett who pleaded 'force majeure' over *Newfoundland*, wrote FOIC [Troup] & Mathias [J E], latter to attend conference & then report effect of repair on new constr[uction] at Scotts. [*Newfoundland* had been partly repaired at Boston but needed further refitting in UK.] Vice Contr came up, 1st SL wants a turntable in LSTs, said he should send it to DNC thro' DCOM, wrote DNC asking him to give effect on production. ... Went thro' DWP's proposals for [shipbuilding] berths & agreed, told him CMSR wanted to order a C.P.R. [Canadian Pacific Railway] ship from Fairfield! (Has CMSR got 1st L in his pocket?) ...

11 May: Reith came up with paper re turntable in LSTs, he opposes & asked me to do the same without referring to Bath (rang DNC (at lunch) got Woollard [ADNC] who agreed) put on remarks & sent to Vice Contr. At Policy C'tee meeting, dictated notes. I observe at these meetings Contr shows desire to pull me down [too knowledgeable about too many subjects?]. Merrington [now with Overlord staff] called, says Beach Obstructions now the worst headache, otherwise things look good [for Overlord]. He inquired about RCNC into RN, told him it was now DNC's fight not mine. [Merrington was a constructor in uniform so would be aware of the RN's attitude to RCNC.] ... Pamplin [G W, submarine designer] called after deep dive on 1st all welded S [*Subtle*, designed for 350ft diving depth compared with 300ft for riveted submarines] result good.

12 May: FOIC Glasgow rang re *Newfoundland*, I said I would see Contr, saw him & phoned (i) FOIC to say he must report what can be done in the time & how much longer would be required to complete all A* items & how this would put back new construction (ii) Bassett who is

still optimistic that ship can finish in time (iii) WPS who will see if destrs' could be put back instead of TFs. ...

15 May: ... Discussed with DWP, SLC & then James priority for landing craft (post Overlord). ... Touched Ayre on Fast Oilers, he says 'they're not merchant ships'.

16 May: AR warning about 00.45-01.30. Looked at Fighter Direction Ships rough dwgs: *Hawkins* should do (accommodation difficult). *Boxer* [LST Mark 1] would not give full W/T efficiency. ... At Repairs meeting *Newfoundland* will put *Defence* [cruiser later completed as *Lion*] launch back about 10 days, said 'I would accept'. ... Dep Contr went thro' destr. programme as affected by breakdown in supply of K towers & we agreed to dates. This K tower business is a scandal, scientists designing unpractical gear, firms promising impossible dates.

18 May: Back at Admy. Capt Mainguy [E R, R Canadian Navy] called re *Minotaur*, told him I could say nothing definite re Mark VI tower dates but it looked as tho' completion date would go back: told Contr & wrote Dep Contr (met DEE who said he would need 2 mos for these towers not 1 month as for fitting Ks). ...

19 May: Thornycroft called, said he could do a LCM (welded) [landing craft mechanised, 21 tons] if it did not put back destroyers (told Contr). Said he was late in asking for 15 ton cranes, he would have to design an all-welded destroyer in 5 ton lifts [too small to allow much prefabrication]. [Goodall followed this up with a letter to Sir John on 29 May advising him to adopt welding if they were to have a future building light craft after the war.] ... Sent DMB copy of my letter to Stephen saying he can do 2 merchant ships. Bassett came up, has 3 cruisers to place [for refits] & wants to put one to Belfast, I demurred but agreed to Fairfield & Stephen. [Goodall would have charts showing the planned output of each shipyard and its building berths allocation.] Rang Pigott to send welders to Fairfield. ...

20 May: Contr sent for me re programme, said carriers to go slow, I said Clydebank could go on with a liner. ... Harland & Wolff's labour figures arrived, not very helpful, rather typical of Morrison everything all right (except) on the night. ... Spoke Contr re Vickers Barrow, he said CMSR can have a slip, but must <u>not</u> use it! ... He did not think converted frigates would do as MTB parent ships, anyhow we only want two now not four. DNC called, told him of Thornycroft's attitude to welding, he said *Malta* is to have open hangar.

24 May: Dorling [Vice Admiral J W S, BAD Washington] called, looks fluffy, actually I suppose we are all thinner & don't notice the change till

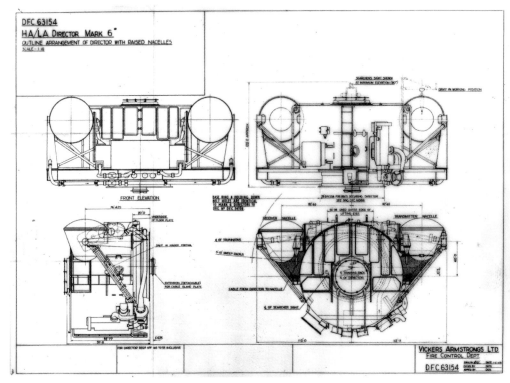

The Mark VI director control tower was a completely new design to control the HA/LA armament of cruisers and destroyers. This 12-ton director (completed overweight) incorporated Type 275 gunnery-control radar and could use remote power control for 4in, 4.5in and 5.25in mountings. Designed by Vickers-Armstrongs at Crayford, the directors were also built at Barrow, but subject to continual delays. Intended for delivery in mid-1944, the early 'Battle' class and some 'Ch' class destroyers were completed without directors, which only appeared in numbers well into 1945. Goodall became frustrated at DNO's and Vickers-Armstrongs' inability to give realistic delivery dates, so that ships otherwise complete were not available for full operations for months, tying up crews and shipbuilding resources which could have been diverted to more productive use. (*Author's collection*)

we meet somebody from a land flowing with milk & honey. He said if M of WT had played when Bateson was in USA, we could have got all the Fleet Train from the other side (was Leathers piqued or acting for vested interests?). Received screed re Mk VI towers, situation worse than for K towers. …

26 May: Baker came re taking on LSTs, told him to shout at once if he felt he was overloaded, wrote Vice Contr. Admiral Mills (USN) called, his talk was very interesting tho' rather bumptious, he is a great believer in the cruisers with 12″ guns [*Alaska*s] as necessary to accompany Aircraft

Carriers in a Task Force, they must not take on battleships (I don't see the need for us to have such expensive ships with a secondary role. What we need most is good carriers). ... Wrote Reith re LST programme: Mills said this month they are completing 50! We hope to do 45 in a year!!

27 May: ... Contr back from Barrow, they spun a yard that *Minotaur*'s [3] K towers would be ready in Aug! (DNO says Nov.) [completed as *Ontario* May 1945] also that Ormston could do a Bel [heavy lift] ship. Contr gave me Bassett's proposals for bringing cruisers up to date, new construction is going to be badly mucked up particularly at Belfast, Clydebank [*Tiger*], Stephen, Scott [*Defence*] & Fairfield [*Blake*]. ...

30 May: ... W Ayre called re [Shipbuilding] Research Ass[ociation]. I said we wanted a portable shipyard tool to test welds. ...

31 May: Bateson came up re Australia building a cruiser & destroyers: I was for a Lt Carrier & new Battle, he for a cruiser & old Battle. ...

1 June: Smithers [D W, overseer at Clydebank] called: *Vanguard* meeting showed that 5.25″ hoists are likely to hold ship back. ... Pigott, Skiffington & McNeill called, they didn't seem very concerned about *Vanguard* but about a £¼ million scheme for yard cranes, said I should have a job to get this thro', they must make a good case i.e. essential for building *Malta* & all welded ships. ...

2–11 June: On leave.

5 June: In Honours List N G Holt [now Constructor Captain, Home Fleet] has a CBE, otherwise RCNC draws a blank as usual. Disgusting. The only way a Corps man can get an honour is to be at sea & so qualify for the Naval List not Civil. Anyhow we have shaken off the insult of an OBE to a Chief Constructor or ADNC. [A Chief Constructor's rank was equivalent to a RN Captain.]

6 June: Last night (at Moor Court [hotel near Stroud]) noise of aircraft was terrific. It sounded like aircraft towing gliders at a low height. Overlord had started.

12 June: At Bath. ... Discussed Mk VI towers with DCW [Hannaford]. He has new dates for towers & ships. Said firms should have dates they will get towers & we should not tell them date of completion of ship. They may find they can fit towers in less than the 5-6 weeks DEE says will be required. Dep. Contr gave a talk on Overlord & how it stands at present. We got ashore with less loss than I expected. ...

13 June: ... *Warspite* mined on way north to changeover worn-out guns. What a story the history of that ship would make. [One of her

former gunnery officers Captain Stephen Roskill did indeed write such a history.] …

14 June: At Bath. Contr's meeting very short. Afterwards I held a short meeting with E in C, DNC & DEE re placing firm contracts for 1944 Programme in view of possible application of Break Clause [cancellation] during construction of these ships. Dictated yarn & sent papers to DNO to ask if he agreed: really I ought to have invited him to the meeting. …

15 June: … Then went to Contr's meeting re Australia building a cruiser & a destroyer. DNC & I rubbed in that we did not think Australia had sufficiently good constructors. Afterwards DNC & I talked of possible men from here but I doubt if Australia would make the job sufficiently attractive. … AR warning about 23.40-09.25 of 16th. Bursts of gunfire about every ½ hour during the whole period.

16 June: … Bamford came in to say they had a bomb near his place, house damaged. [The first V1 flying bomb had hit London on 13 Jun.] … King [I E] in Med says US welded ships do well when torpedoed. [Riveted ships would experience greater leakage through distorted structures.] …

17 June: … Phoned DNC re fast [20-knot] oilers, he will give me approx. dimensions when Crawford [J B, constructor] calls on 19th. Then went into situation with DWP: looks as tho' HL [Hawthorn Leslie] is out (slip too small); it will take too long at V-A Walker & Clydebank. At H & W and SH it could only be done at expense of merchant ships. AR warnings 15.53-16.20, 16.50-17.00, 17.15- after that they were so numerous I gave up recording. Went home via Cl[apham] Junct[ion] got there shortly after a bumble bomb had dropped on to St Johns Hill [nearby]. Prelim[inary] warning that we may have to move to Cricklewood [north-west London].

18 June: Sunday. Last night was very hectic. Almost continuous gunfire, a lull & just chance of sleep when there would be another burst. The day was practically one long 'Alert'. In the evening it was obvious that order had been given not to fire at bumble bombs. This order held during the night & everybody was much refreshed on Monday morning: this morning all were tired out.

21 June: A noisy night but we slept well. Bumble bombs near house but no damage so far, touch wood. … Milne of Whites called … concerned that altho' he has spent roughly 2/3rds of a destr. [labour] on Overlord repairs, he will be kicked for destroyer dates going back. …

22 June: … At Contr's Policy meeting, another cut in shipyard labour forecast, I said 'Ridiculous'. Contr annoyed & ticked me off: but here from one side the Govt is reducing the possibility of carrying on with our

present prog[ramme], while on the other the Navy is filling up the plate (e.g. fast oilers). ...

24 June: ... Saw Seal US(L) [E A, Under Secretary, London] re contracts for 1944 destroyers & *New Zealand*. He was not satisfied but wants some way to tell firms they can spend money so far but no further till they get the order; this might do for *New Z*. He agreed with me that the solution is for Govt to say when Germany goes out, we shall go on with so & so and when Japan goes out with such & such. ...

27 June: ... At British Shipbuilding Research Ass. Curious to note the general desire for research & contrast it with the opposition when Darwin [NPL] started the idea. The Dir[ector] of Res[earch] Dr [S Livingston] Smith [formerly of National Physical Laboratory] will visit Undex. ... Thorny. called re prototype LCT8, a sheaf of moans, I said 'That settles it, I must go somewhere else' then he piped down. Rowell called, said he does not want a fast oiler, fears we are going to earmark his best slip for a cruiser & prevent him building a liner. ...

28 June: ... A day of many alerts, 2 Bum Bs passed over Admy causing fittings in my room to vibrate.

29 June: A disturbed night, many Bum Bs, some burst near enough to shake house. ... Held Transport Ferry meeting, biggest problems are labour at Dalmuir & general dearth of riveters on Clyde. ...

30 June: ... Pigott called, happy about *Vanguard*, confirmed labour for Trans Ferries at Dalmuir, said *Bermuda* [cruiser refitting by John Brown] will not upset new construction. I said he could take a merchant ship (short term). Wood D of S [E S, Director of Stores] called re Anglo Saxon [Shell] tankers, I must see DMB. Bum B burst at Regent Palace Hotel blew my windows open, made staff nervous for rest of day, continuous blowing of whistles [alarms] nerve racking: had difficulty in getting home. Bum B near Wandsworth Common station [the nearest to his house] upset train service. Wrote Stanley to sound Swan, Rowell & Ormston re a prototype LCT8. ...

1 July: Slept fairly well but Bum Bs seemed to be going off frequently & regularly. ... A bad night, Dr Clarke's house in Bolingbroke Rd knocked out; Bolingbroke Hospital evacuated.

3 July: A bit like chewed string after 2 bad nights running. Saw Contr re *Aorangi* [troopship], he app'd she should go to Fairfield, also re *Hermes* [Cammell Laird] going slow & *Mon*[mouth, Fairfield] normal so let CL get on with *Ark R[oyal]*. He did not seem very smitten with idea of MAC ships [merchant aircraft carriers] for Far East Amenities, so I didn't press

it as it means more conversions & getting the ships from M of WT. ... Admiral Doyle (Australian Navy Board) [Engineer Rear Admiral A B, Third Naval Member] called & we lunched together, talk on carriers, he said AAF [Australian Air Force] strong & Navy too small to go in for new type. He agreed with me a 15,000 ton cruiser is difficult to justify. ... Bateson gave interesting talk on desirability of abolishing all coloured stripes. [All RN officers except executive branch had coloured stripes between their gold rings to denote their specialism e.g. engineers purple, supply white. Eventually abolished in 1955, except the medical red which is an international requirement and grey used by RCNC when in uniform.]

4 July: ... Worked on accuracy of NID [Naval Intelligence Division] reports re Jap destroyers. Rang DNC for possible length of new battleship, he thought we ought to cater for 845' overall, rang Johnson [R S] (away & McMenemy [W H, engine works manager] answered) who confirmed that they proposed to lay b'ship down on 4 slip, which could take ship 770' overall & without much disturbance 810'. [Cammell Laird's February 1939 order for *Lion* class *Temeraire* was only suspended not cancelled.] ...

5 July: A quiet morning but after about noon quite hectic, I flopped on floor twice. ... DMB says Combined [Operations] Staffs wanted 8 Bel boats [heavy lift ships], Bateson pulled them down to 2 by end '45, can we build them at V-A Walker, phoned Ormston & Craven who agreed. ...

6 July: Letter from King (Med) [I E] also one 2 days ago; he has tackled Dondona (Italian DNC) [Emilio, Generale del Genio Navale] for design information. ... Lunched Tower [Vice Controller, but to become FOIC Southampton] who goes next week, he is very loyal but let out a thing or two about Wake-Walker. Held Harland & Wolff meeting, both DMB & DMR [Director of Merchant Ship Repairs, Lawrie Edwards] insistent that it will pay everybody to get rid of *Georgic* as soon as possible.

8 July: ... Watkins back from *Montclare* [converting to submarine depot ship at Southampton] has arranged for more supervision, men not working well, if they did ship could finish and trials by end August. Discussed with DWP the paper on P. Branch [Priority] estimating efficiency, he still hankers after a big production Dept embodying all Contr's supply departments, which I don't think would work; he made a good point that in wartime when Govt controls industry we should have an organisation that more effectively controls, in other words 'Bureaucracy to Build Ships'. This doesn't work badly for merchant ships but warships are a greater complication e.g. I have been let down worst since being AC(WP) by DNO (K &c towers). ...

9 July: Sunday. Last night was bad. A Bum B in Tilehurst Rd broke 2 of our windows & damaged ceiling, also a crack is showing in side of house: this was about 21.45 of 9th, another near at about 23.30. Many went over. ...

10 July: Got Meryon in re Seal wanting dope to chivvy inefficient firms, then Craven came, latter agreed firms must play but thought it a tactical error for Contr to tackle Denny first. ...

11 July: At Bath. ... At NC meeting, Dep. Contr's said *Colossus* &c must have [centralised] messing alterations, this will put them back 2-4 weeks. ... All Mk VI towers are back – a ghastly muddle. Dep Contr held small meeting, looks as tho' *Ontario* & *Superb* should finish without towers & builders of destroyers ['Battles' and 'Ch' classes] be consulted which they would prefer: finish ships & bring them back for towers or spin out the building time.

12 July: ... At Contr's meeting, I have to take up with FOICs possibility of restoring some overtime & still keeping the required [shipyard] fuel economy (10%). Contr decided *Ontario* & *Superb* should leave with only 1 instead of 3 Mk VI towers each. [They were finally completed with three, for controlling 4in guns.] ...

13 July: With Ayre & McLeod gave evidence before Lord Hankey's C'tee on university trainees for shipbuilding industry after the war. Said strength of Corps 1935 – 121, May '39 – 138, May '44 – 280, in my view should be 500 after the war. Ayre impressed C'tee with dark days ahead of shipbuilding & unlikelihood of men out of Army getting good jobs in it. Rebbeck called, I had already heard that he had met CMSR & DMB, told him we had concluded indirect labour too high, he said he would be glad to see ARP [air-raid precautions] & firewatchers reduced but that was N of Ireland last [*sic*] moreover these men could not be employed in yard (I didn't believe this of all the men). He thinks he can finish *Georgic* in end Nov-beg[inning] of Dec. & *Glory* end Dec. Says T Ferries going well. Phoned DNC to see that Rebbeck has no excuses re *Aud*[*acious*] & *Centaur*. ...

17 July: ... Gawn called, he, Offord & Woollard came to DTM meeting on counter to pressure mines. I think DTM has been most remiss, 3 years ago we raised the question of the possibility of such a mine. He insisted on *Cyrus* & *Cybele* [Stirling craft] (brutal solutions) [as expendable, *Cyrus* was wrecked 21 Nov 1944] would not think of the 'Cascade' [?] now we are faced with the mine & are at our wits end to know what to do. ...

19 July: ... Many alerts & Doodle Bugs [Goodall now using that name] about today. Grocers Hall got one so [Worshipful Company of] Shipwrights lunch there tomorrow is off. ...

Centaur taking shape on Berth No 11 at Harland & Wolff's Belfast Musgrave yard on 15 October 1946 looking aft. The deck beams forward are at hangar deck level (No 3), 48ft above the keel. The foremost bulkhead is at Frame 10, with watertight compartments ahead. Most of the forward compartments will house messes, bathrooms and stores. Further aft but below deck 6 are the forward aviation fuel tanks. The forward boiler and engine room are in the centre between bulkheads 85 and 112 where the starboard side frames angle out to support the island. The frames midships and aft extend up to flight deck level, typically spaced 3ft apart. Despite the welding of plates and stiffeners, there is little prefabrication, a limitation imposed by the original tower cranes with a capacity of only about 10 tons. (*HW.9614, National Museums NI, Ulster Transport Museum Collection*)

20 July: ... Evans [Vice Admiral A E, BATM] says he is certain Canada means to pack up on a Canadian Navy as soon as war is over. Ambridge [from Canada] wants to go on building merchant ships after the war but the Canadian Govt will be far too anxious to develop its natural resources & run industries that will make not lose money. ...

22 July: DWP back from Belfast, very satisfied with the visit. He thinks H & W are efficient, the trouble is on the merchant ship side (this was my first impression but I changed, personally H & W's people can lay on the Blarney & at first this has an effect). Firm agreed to all dates including *Warrior* if they can get electricians. ...

23 July: Sunday. Just after 06.00 a D. bug fell on No. 62 Lyford which has just disappeared. We [No 50] had back door blown in, 2 ceilings down & several cracked, nearly all the windows out. Glass & dust everywhere. ... N. had a slight cut on forehead. Dr Clarke turned up about 07.00 & dressed it. Wardens & in fact all services fine. RAF men turned up & got busy repairing roofs &c. Took a sleeping draught but a bad night. ...

24 July: On 'compassionate' leave. RAF mended back door. Most of rooms cleared of glass & plaster from ceilings & a number of windows filled in with fabric. A moderate night. Slept better.

25 July: Back in office. ... A quiet day & house looking respectable again. ...

26 July: About 04.15 a D. bug came down on the Common [Wandsworth] opposite about 120 yds away: crater thus [diary sketch 8ft deep]. All fabric out of windows, some more glass gone, more tiles off, plaster partitions between rooms down or cracked. Took another day's compassionate leave to clear up. Henry rang to say sister Flo is sinking [Goodall's sister Florence]. Slept well till about 01.15 of 27th when siren went, after that I dozed. With windows gone the D. bugs can be heard more distinctly. [Wandsworth seemed to be a target area although few military targets (AA guns on Common?); prison nearby.]

27 July: With E in C went thro' report on what had been done to raise efficiency of warship builders & marine engineers. ... Letter from ASCBS re *Ocean* finishing before *Theseus* [she did]. ...

28 July: ... Phoned DNC re *Cockade* [destroyer] & reason for altering Oerlikon armt 3 times. Contr gave me paper re fast oilers, phoned DMB to see if he could give me facts about USS *Cimarron* but he hadn't anything reliable. To dentist. A rotten night, many D. bugs over, some went off near, loose trap hatch jammed down & bell started ringing. About 23.45 policeman walked in, we had left a light on.

30 July: Sunday. Morrison shelter arrived. Got it up with Jackson's help. Frightfully crude work. Bed not too comfortable but I felt more secure. One D. bug during night sounded quite close.

31 July: At Contr's meeting on oyster [pressure] mine; a dreadful exhibition of Admy incompetence. DMS [Director of Minesweeping, now Captain J H F Crombie] appeared entirely ignorant of Admy procedure, DTM almost as bad; 2 years ago I told de Salis sweeps of some sort were the solution. But No he insisted on *Cyrus* & did nothing else & he still harps on this most wasteful way of sweeping mines after all our experience with Bordes [anti-magnetic mine sweeping vessels]. ...

1 August: ... DWP worried that DMB have ordered 2 Bels from V-A Walker: I agreed we could build 2 there but I have a notion I asked DMB not to order more than 1. [They were completed as *Empire Athelstan* and *Beljeanne* with three 120-ton derricks.]

2 August: ... DNC came in, said Contr at Bath yesterday was gloomy about Rocket Bombs & thinks London & most Admy will be evacuated end August. Contr also spoke of the app[ointmen]t of the new Dep[uty] Contr[oller] (Production) his job will be to look after production of all bits & pieces [presumably not ships]. A worse night than any for ages so far; many D. bugs near, got very little sleep.

3 August: A host of callers. Thornycroft: told him no hope for welders from North. Watt USN (son of late Chief Constructor) very pleasant and talkative, in charge of landing craft & ships, wants to reduce No. of types. Inquired about a faster LST, said they were against turntables in LSTs. ... Merrington very interesting on his experiences in Normandy [attached to Allied Naval Commander Expeditionary Force (ANCXF)]. The 3 days gale was a great trial [which destroyed the American Mulberry harbour and damaged many ships]. ... [Contr] said if Rocket Bombs got busy he wants me to go to Bath not Cricklewood. ... -

6 August: Sunday. A D. Bug cut off when nearly overhead (about 13.30) but travelled a good ½ mile before bursting. ...

8 August: Held meeting re *Westernland* [destroyer depot ship ex-liner *Regina*, refitting in London]. Drafted covering report to Contr suggesting 'Do we really want her now, as she can't be ready till end '45.' ...

10 August: On leave, shut up house, saw N. to Paddington for Plymouth [where they had married in 1908]. Came to office, stowed personal gear. ... Slept in Citadel [substantial Admiralty extension] bunk, a blessing to hear neither sirens nor D. Bugs. *AFD.23* sunk [at Trincomalee] a major disaster, don't know why, design all right as it was a repeat of the Singapore [floating] dock.

11 August: ... This ink is vile. [Very faint in diary, Admiralty issue?]

12 August: ... Jubb [E C, Director of Contracts] & Seal are still messing about over transfer of *N. Zealand* to H & W [fleet carrier originally ordered from Cammell Laird]. ...

13 August: Sunday. D. Bugs near Admy about 07.45. Gardened at 50 L[yford]. ...

14 August: Saw Contr re *Westernland*, he agrees finish machinery at G[reen] & Silley Weir [Thames ship repairers] & then take ship away. Re *Southern Prince* [auxiliary minelayer converting to accommodation ship] he wants me to get E in C to agree to take her; discussed this with Bateson, we agreed that if *S. Prince* is taken we should send *City of Paris* [Ellerman liner planned for accommodation ship] to Australia. Friedberger wants to wash out 4th accom ship because he says D of D [Talbot] cannot man her. Doyle came in when I was with Contr & confirmed he would take an accom ship in Australia. ...

Ship repairers had a heavy workload in the Second World War, repairing war-damaged ships and undertaking conversions as well as regular ship maintenance. Escort destroyer *Vanessa* was hit by a bomb in her forward boiler room on 19 June 1941. She was completely rebuilt in that area by Green & Silley Weir at their Blackwall yard on the Thames from 1 July to 15 April 1942. As well as rebuilding her hull amidships, she was reduced to two boilers as a long-range escort with additional oil fuel tanks. (*Author's collection*)

15 August: At Bath. ... Discussed with Williamson & Hickey [floating dock designer] *AFD.23*, both think it must have been caused by pumping out the ends. [The later inquiry showed that this was correct. The newly-completed dock (Goodall's 1941 diary discusses ordering this dock in India) had collapsed at Trincomalee when lifting its heaviest ship to date, the battleship *Valiant*. A full account is given in the World Ship Society's publication *Warships* No 148. Although at 39,000 tons she was close to her maximum displacement, in theory she could have been lifted by the 50,000-ton lift dock. But that weight was heavily concentrated towards the centre of the dock: *Valiant*'s keel length was 544ft in an 855ft long dock, giving a weight per foot run above the designed load. Neither the inexperienced dockmaster nor his superiors had troubled to read the operating instructions for this brand-new dock. The dock was built of seven bolted sections, the centre three pontoons deeper than the end four. Instead of pumping out each of the sections evenly along the length to keep the buoyancy of the dock matched with the weight of ship and dock as the instructions advised, the dockmaster let the water from the ends which had flooded the dock down drain into the centre sections before

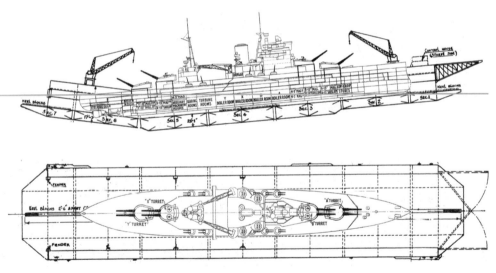

An inexperienced dockmaster, unsupervised by the senior constructors at Trincomalee, had not read the dock operating instructions, despite needing to lift by far the heaviest ship to date in the new *Admiralty Floating Dock 23*. *Valiant*'s displacement was 39,000 tons which, although less than the dock's nominal lift capacity of 50,000 tons, was concentrated heavily over only 544ft in the 855ft-long dock. An incorrect pumping sequence to lift the dock was used, draining the end tanks into the centre tanks, so stressing the dock well beyond its capability. The result was as shown, the dock collapsing into a V-shape, damaging the battleship's aft end, before sinking on 9 August 1944. (*Ian Buxton*)

pumping out. This caused an excess of buoyancy at the ends, and an excess of weight in the centre, so not surprisingly the dock collapsed into a V shape. This serious negligence on the part of all concerned put the only British battleship and carrier drydock in the Indian Ocean out of action as it sank to the bottom of the harbour and was not salvageable. The accident happened on the night of 8/9 August and the whole dock had sunk by the morning; no photographs are known to exist. *Valiant* was badly damaged and had to be sent back to the UK for repair, which was never completed; she was scrapped in 1948.]

16 August: Contr had meeting with DNC & D of D re *AFD.23*. There is to be a Public Inquiry. I said 'So much the better'. At Contr's meeting he decided *Southern Prince* should be accepted & converted here, *City of Paris* to return to trade for the present & be taken over later, probably converted in Australia. Plans said *Aorangi* not now required! With DCW(S) [Hopkins] discussed Dep Contr for Production, I said 'Make him your servant', also discussed steel & move from London. ...

17 August: ... Told DWP not to use the word Priority re Loch class frigates. [The U-boat threat had substantially reduced.] ...

18 August: ... Wrote Johnson re No. 6 slip at Birkenhead & told DWP I should not tell Seal that *Hermes* will be laid down on No. 4; he would only butt in and mess things up. ... Flo died just after 4 pm.

21 August: I started a docket re orders for 1944 Weapons & sloops. ... Bateson came up re A Cl S/Ms, said Manpower cut on RN is going to reduce No. of S/Ms that can be operated in Far East. We shan't want any A's in 1944 prog & can cut down those of 1943 prog. Bateson also said Naval Staff had asked for *Menestheus* [Blue Funnel cargo liner] as an Amenities ship, where we could convert her I don't know (might do her at G & S Weir after clearing *Westernland* out). [She was actually converted by West Coast Shipbuilders, Vancouver 17 Jan 45 to 28 Jan 46.] ...

22 August: Doodle Bugs Kensington way last night, I couldn't get west of St James Park on Underground. ... Wrote CMSR re honour for W Ayre. ...

23 August: Attended Flo's funeral. DNC called, told him my advice to look into loading of fast oilers. He deprecates D of S bossing this job but agrees D of S has staff and DNC doesn't. ... Told him Dep 1st SL [Kennedy-Purvis] was asking for my yarn on the Cruiser thro' the Ages. ... Pigott hinted that fitting LSTs [existing Mark 2s] for tropics will react on frigates then transport ferries then *Vanguard*. ...

24 August: ... Abbey bells rang for Liberation of Paris in heavy thunderstorm. ...

25 August: At Newcastle. DSC [possibly K H Watkins, Superintendent of Conversions] fell on my neck says 'Priorities must be reasonably arranged, he is driven dotty because everybody rushes round saying his pet has 1st priority'. ... To Walker, electrics in *Colossus* show signs of bad planning. *Perseus* date impossible. TFs behind. To Wallsend *Barfleur* could have kept her date if it hadn't been for the Mk VI tower delay. [It was finally shipped on 29 Nov with the ship leaving the Tyne on 25 Jan 45. She had run her full power trials on 14 Sep, her notional date of completion.] Looks as tho' *Vengeance* will keep her date. To Neptune TF looks grand but electrics are going to fix the date. ...

Henry Robb (1874–1951) was a manager at the Ramage & Ferguson shipyard in Leith when he decided to set up on his own in 1918. Starting at first to repair ships and build small craft, he took over other Leith shipyards when they closed, enabling him to build bigger ships in the 1930s. During the war the Admiralty asked him to build escorts and naval support vessels, but Goodall knew he wanted to get back to building merchant ships as soon as possible. (*The Shipbuilder*)

26 August: ... Talk with ASCBS who has fixed up destroyers but is concerned about Barrow's *Pioneer* (? Building new house on flight deck [maintenance carrier]). To Hawthorn Leslie, *Triumph* looks well advanced [launched 2 Oct] & could finish earlier if electrical labour were available. *Armada* ['Battle' class destroyer] well ahead but again Mk VI tower is holding ship back badly. TFs not well advanced and I didn't like the look of the welded plate at turn of bilge to all these TFs, the prop[ulsive] coeff[icient] is going to be low as flow to propellers is poor. Robb [Henry, managing director of Leith shipbuilder] & Whiting [W R G, WPS East Scotland] came to lunch & after much opposition Robb agreed to do *Salverdant* [actually built as *Reclaim* by Simons] but not *Restful* or *Solway* [both cancelled]. Left by night train.

28 August: A.L. Lecture, all photos have now arrived so I can get them off to the Censor as soon as I get time to go at it carefully [his paper included photos of welded ships], but I find the D. bugs make it difficult to give concentrated attention, e.g. this afternoon we had them & the typist wanted to go when the 3 bells rang. [Flying bomb attacks reduced in September as launch sites in France were overrun, though they were still launched from aircraft.] ...

The 'Battle' class destroyers were designed to have their main armament forward and a large anti-aircraft armament aft. *Armada* from Hawthorn Leslie was completed in July 1945 with two of the new twin 4.5in Mark IV mountings (weighing 43 tons each shipped by the *Titan II* floating crane in June 1944 six months after launch), four Dutch Hazemeyer twin 40mm mountings, two single 2pdr and two 20mm, and one 4in Mark XXIII mounting for star shell plus two quadruple 21in torpedo tubes (with eight Mark IX** torpedoes) and sixty depth charges. Her completion was delayed by late delivery of the new Mark VI director. (*Blackman collection*)

29 August: Prepared for Clyde visit. Pressed DWP to get busy over *Zodiac* & *Cavalier* [destroyers], latter completes next week (ex guns & tower) & it is not settled where she is to go. [Their K DCTs were not fitted until mid-1945.] Vice Contr [now Vice Admiral H C Phillips, based in London] phoned that salvage vessels will be badly wanted very soon to clear Channel ports, found DWP had discussed with Contr who seemed apathetic, told DWP to get Whiting to spur on Alex Hall [building four coastal salvage vessels at Aberdeen]. SLC came up re landing craft affected by Lifting Craft at Tees Side. Told DWP to get DNC to take up if he finds lagging a serious bottleneck (lagging [insulation] for Far East could be put on later). ...

31 August: At Glasgow. Meeting with FOIC on Priority, he aired off & really criticised D of D: example of trouble Ad[miralty] wire to fit LSTs & LCTs for tropics by certain date & stop frigates at Clydebank, frigates kept at Belfast. LSTs don't arrive, when they do they have no instructions what to do. After meeting went to Fairfield, *Theseus* very backward [launched 6 Jul]. Back to lunch with DSC, Lithgow there, we talked of A/S frigates

A busy fitting-out basin at Fairfield's Govan shipyard about April 1945. Nearest are three 'Battle' class destroyers, (R-L) *Camperdown*, *Finisterre* and *Cadiz*. Astern are LSTs Mark 3 *3037* (inboard) and *3038*. Across the basin is the carrier *Theseus* which although looking nearly finished is still nine months off completion. Goodall was critical of the Fairfield management and the lack of supervisors to plan and organise outfitting work effectively. Barclay Curle shipyard at top left. (*Author's collection*)

to finish this year, he helped a bit. Went to Stephen, their TFs are better than Fairfields & *Ocean* [launched 8 Jul] looks all right for April. Went to H & W Govan, their 1st TF is the best so far [*LST.3041*]. ...

1 September: Held TF meeting, disappointing, dates are going back particularly of those at merchant yards. Firms are looking to Admy supplies as the excuse, actually the reason is lack of labour particularly riveters. To Connell [Clyde shipyard] a queer mixture of ancient & modern, both TFs behind. To Clydebank, long meeting on manning Dalmuir, much time wasted on separate scheduling of Dalmuir Basin (Troup dead against calling it J. Browns [the managers], labour situation doesn't look frightfully difficult. ... Had a look at *Vanguard* launch date now looks good.

2 September (Saturday): Went to Lithgows Greenock [shipyard at Port Glasgow], work there is rough, not a rivet being driven, riveters won't

A view of the old fitting-out basin at the Denny shipyard in Dumbarton in March 1944. The sloop is *Hind*, one of the fourteen *Black Swan* type Denny built. The destroyer hull on the nearest slipway is *Zenith* and the escort carrier in the main fitting-out basin is *Empire MacDermott*. (NMM G11378)

work on Sundays so rivet heaters won't work on Saturdays! Result no riveting either day. To Scotts who have just had a month's strike of riveters. *Defence* launched [that day], she started at once but was slow to pick up speed. Destroyers looked good. To Dennys [at Dumbarton] had a good look at TF [*LST.3035*] which is coming on, destroyers Z [*Zebra* and *Zenith*] looked all right. Long talk with [Maurice] Denny about 1944 Prog orders, I said they should not have 'Break Clause'. Denny wants a lot of warships cancelled so that he can get on with merchant ships when cease fire in Europe.

4 September: At Newcastle. Big meeting with DSC on shipbldg labour requirements generally and electricians in particular. Agreed Thompson [J C, Superintendent of Ships Electrical Equipment] & Allcock [F B, Superintending Electrical Engineer, North East] to see local ETU [Electrical Trade Union] leaders, then Board (not Contr) to visit Newcastle after approach to Min of Labour. ETU say they will not have dilution. ... To Neptune to see TF launched [*LST.3019*]. Hancock broke the bottle of wine. ...

5 September: Back in office. With Hancock saw Contr who was in the usual rush & flurry, so all we talked about was labour. Afterwards Hancock, Newall [probably P S Newell, Assistant Secretary who may also be working with labour controller] and I drew up for Contr a short memo to say we want another 4000 in shipyards now. Contr did say he would oppose cancellation of pukkah warships on Europe Cease Fire [ECF]. ... Craven called, he knows about 1943 A's being cancelled. I said I proposed to leave only 2 at Walker & let that yard give up altogether, he agreed. I said also I want to keep skilled S/M workers in 3 yards and Chatham. [The submarine builders were Vickers-Armstrongs at Barrow, Cammell Laird and Scotts.]

6 September: Contr sent for me & N Asst [Bateson] and told us to put up to him proposals for enabling firms to go all out on merchant ships when ECF sounds. ...

7 September: ... Went to 50 Lyford to meet surveyor who said only one bit of damage was structural. ... Met Somerville [appointed in charge of BAD, Washington] he looks well & stouter but said the climate in Far East has nearly killed him.

8 September: ... Craven rang evidently in hope that he could save all A's at Barrow. DWP could get no help from DPS [Director of Personal Services, now Rear Admiral H R G Kinahan] to send destroyers on trial & then keep till towers arrive.

9 September: Wrote DNC, E in C, & DEE re turning last three Weapons at Scotts into 1944 design ['G' class]. Finished A.L. Lecture & sent to Controller for approval. ...

11 September: Contr came up, he had read my Priority List proposals & was ready to put back *Glasgow* & *Belfast* [cruiser refits] & later FAA repair ships. ...

13 September: At Bath. Craven rang to alter yesterday's arrgts for cancelling S/Ms at Walker, he wants all 6 cancelled there & one at Barrow so that S/M party at Walker can concentrate at Barrow. I agreed. [Walker never started their 'A' submarines, for which they were relieved, not having built all-welded boats before.] ... At NC meeting Dep Contr railed against comforts in TFs ... With DNC discussed prop. coeff. of TFs & LCG(M)s (latter too heavy, bad miscalculation).

14 September: ... I went to Empire [Hotel, Admiralty offices] to meet Rogers the new Dep Contr for Production, nice fellow & all very friendly. ... Left at 3.15 pm & met N. at Bristol, she very tired & worn, we got to Moor Court all right. ...

15–20 September: On leave.

22 September: In Glasgow. With FOIC & Greig went to Fairfield. FOIC wanted to know how many A's & A's he should do to *Bellona*. I said 'None'. ... Got thro' Scotts, Clydebank, Stephen & Fairfield post ECF: all firms are greedy. Barr said he had 7 orders in his pocket. Pigott said owners haven't made up their minds (both spoke to me privately). ...

23 September: To Denny & cleared up that programme. Russell submitted 2 weeks for LCT launching ways too much but means to take it out of us for other reasons (LCI(L))s. To Yarrow & had a look round. Yarrow said nothing about a merchant ship prog, he could take more Weapons. ...

24 September: An alert about 21.45, first I had heard since my return to London from leave. Doodle-bug went over from east to west. I didn't hear the bang as it must have gone well to the west.

25 September: ... Meryon called, told him how I had got on in Scotland on the question [ECF]. He said Lady Craven died suddenly on Sunday morning & shipbuilders meeting for tomorrow on this subject was therefore postponed [Craven would have been there]. Told DWP I did <u>not</u> agree to risk delay on our TFs in order to provide Canada with bits. Saw Vice Contr on the awful mess we are in thro' Staff wanting everything for the Far East at once. ... H & W are putting back *Glory* 5 mos! ... Posted A.L. Lecture T.G.

26 September: Mitchell [E H] called; said although *AFD.23* was badly handled, he estimates that dock should have stood the bending moment & suspects poor design of detail where deep [centre] section amidships joins narrow [shallow] section at ends, this is where dock broke [not surprisingly at a discontinuity; there were also high shear forces at the break point. Mitchell was at Trincomalee at the time.] ... Ayre phoned, V-A Barrow want a merchant ship if I can agree to cancel *Aurochs* instead of *Anzac*. Phoned Barrow & got Moss, talk too secret so I rang off & wrote that if they want ironwork they should get on with TFs. ...

27 September: ... Rowell called & I went thro' Haw. Les [ECF] he will write me after reviewing machinery situation [HL had their own engine works]. Met Tristram Edwards who said Smith's Dock were easing off! W[illiam] Reed is retiring. Interesting talk with Rowell who said RCNC men are not good in outside industry owing to ignorance of finance & business. [Yet RCNC men later became managing directors: John Starks at John Brown, Sidney Dale at Denny and Derek Kimber at Austin & Pickersgill.] ...

28 September: Johnson [Cammell Laird] called, went thro' ECF, he wants to stop *Vimiera* & *Somme* ['Battle' class destroyers] now, but I said he

The cramped nature of Thornycroft's Woolston yard on the River Itchen is evident from this aerial view of August 1939. In the north yard (left side) is the minelayer *Latona* (an early war loss) and two small Turkish minelayers. The engine works and meagre fitting-out facilities (no proper quay and limited craneage) are in the centre. In the south yard the Brazilian destroyer *Jaguaribe* is nearly ready for launch (but taken over the following month to become the RN *Highlander*). Fitting out are three destroyers, (from outboard to inboard) *Kashmir*, *Kimberley* and *Juruena*, soon to become RN *Hesperus*. (©*National Maritime Museum, London G8079*)

could only go slow (I am hoping to turn these into 1944 design [*Daring* class]). Mountain came in (Cabinet crisis!). Vickers Barrow want a licence for a merchant ship at once or they will have to sack men! Was this right, I said 'No'. M. pumping me for information to stymie CMSR; then Lithgow [CMSR] rang me, I said Vickers had plenty of work to wit TFs, if they had labour they should get on with that. Then Craven rang me in a hell of a temper, I was a Presbyterian Baptist &c. Did I trust him? I tried to get him to see that with Contr telling M. of Lab[our] we must have more men, we couldn't at same time agree we were putting men out of work. Cr. cooled off & said he would write me. ...

29 September: To Southampton. Interesting talk in train with *Queen Mary* officers who had just brought Winston back; some good stories of W. [She had arrived in the Clyde on the 27th bringing Churchill back from Quebec conference.] At Thornycrofts, yard is not up-to-date. To make it so it wants sweeping clear & laying out all afresh e.g. engine

shops lie between slips! Good workmanship. Firm always in trouble with labour partly I think because Paterson (Boilermakers) is too cute for Donaldson [now one of three joint managing directors] who is too much of a gentleman. CO of *Zodiac* very interesting about *Sandpiper* [river gunboat handed over to Chinese 1942]. To Cowes [by ferry or launch]. Inspected radiographs of welds, better than first welds at other yards. Milne wants a Battle [*Grafton* and *Greyhound* had just been ordered] & a riveted LCT [*LCT.4128–29* ordered 28 Oct].

30 September: At Cowes. Had good look at *Contest* [first all-welded destroyer], they are taking pains. Saw the X ray apparatus at work, the weld just taken (a Unionmelt deck seam & long[itudinal]) was perfect. One bkd was buckled a lot. Then to *Craccher* [completed as *Crispin*] thought one OB [outer bottom] plate was too rigidly held along edges for welding the butt. Looked at shop work. Fus-arc [welding machine] a white elephant so far. Women get 94/6d a week, men £6 [120 shillings] so as soon as possible women must be sacked & men taken on, tho' women's work is very good. To Haslar. Gawn's film not good [for Goodall's lecture], Offord's good, the latter is a good propagandist, the former a true scientist. Slides all right. Very crowded train back to London [Saturday evening].

2 October: Piles of tripe awaiting me. … Craven apologised handsomely for his bad language on 28/9; he said 'You were the gentleman I was the shit'. His wife's death has shaken him it was so sudden. … INA Policy C'tee meeting very interesting [Goodall was a Vice President] on Education, Patents & the 3 Inst[itution]s getting together more [with North East Coast Institution of Engineers & Shipbuilders and Institution of Engineers & Shipbuilders in Scotland]. …

3 October: … Rebbeck called re Europe Cease Fire at Belfast: fairly reasonable (what a boaster).

4 October: Shook up Private Office [1st Lord] again on S/M cancellations. … Dep Contr rang re *Agamemnon* & *Men[estheus]*; if they were to be Red Ensign time would be taken up discussing with Owners &c [different manning and accommodation if White or Red Ensign] …

5 October: Sutherby [F S, chief constructor] called, finds it difficult to be WPS [Warship Production Superintendent, Belfast] and PSO [Principal Ship Overseer]. I said he must not try to be PSO of all ships, all he can do is to keep watch over his PSOs & see they do their job. Thorny. called re his layout for all welded destr's, advised him to see Jubb. T. doesn't think much of American all welded frigates which he saw at Portsmouth. … Fardell came up, I got him to show me statement of ships for Far East, with this we can put our house into order (or rather sequence) can D of D? …

6 October: H & W (Belfast) people to meeting. Dictated notes. Morrison after his illness still the same optimistic Blarney stone. Stephen called, wanted the ECF to start now for *St Lucia* ['Battle' class destroyer ordered 23 Apr 43 but not yet laid down] as he could get a merchant ship order now; I said 'Sorry No' & gave him an Aide Memoire. ... Wrote Barr re dates for Fairfield's destroyers, particularly *Omdurman*. Discussed with Stephen amalgamation of Lloyds [Register] & B.C. [British Corporation; Murray Stephen was chairman of its Technical Committee]. I was non-committal. [The two classification societies did merge in 1947.]

7 October: ... Difficulty about *Khedive* [escort carrier] going to H & W London & thus putting back *S. Prince*, wrote Bassett. ... Got home for weekend. AR warning about 20.10-20.30.

9 October: ... Worked on ECF. Wrote Rowell & Johnson who both want too much & the best in 2 conflicting worlds. ... Wrote Callander if he could accelerate launch & del[ivery] dates of TFs [*LST.3044* and *3045*]. Told DWP that M of WT should do reconditioning of ships returning to trade but we should be chary about promising them staff.

10 October: ... Merrington called, said if only we could use Antwerp. [The port and its repair yards had been captured on 4 Sep but the Germans still held the mouth of the River Scheldt.] DWP brought in copy of message from D of D to FOIC N. Ireland [Bevan] more or less forcing *Trouncer* [escort carrier] with 3 mos work (so he says) on H & W. I saw Vice Contr who knew nothing about it. I saw Bassett who defended his action in a torrent of words. I told him he was not straight (he was not honouring the undertaking he gave at my meeting on May 2). ...

11 October: A day ruined by many callers. ... Young Swan [Sheriton C; chairman C S died in December] with Turnbull & McPherson [Thomas, director of Wallsend Slipway & Engineering, a Swan Hunter subsidiary] called re ECF. In general they agreed to my scheme but don't want a fast oiler [they were already building *Hyalina/Olna* for Shell] & want a 1944 Battle as prototype [*Daring* was ordered 24 Jan 45]. Stantan [A G W, Constructor Captain based in Canada] called, looked very tired after his flight, gave general picture of Canadian situation, thinks they will say 'Yes' to Amenities Ships, he wants more staff. Contr back says Canada cannot be a shipbuilding country after the war but we must keep a nucleus that could develop. Mottershead [F W, Principal Private Secretary to the 1st Lord] phoned, 1st L had decided *Ontario* goes back 6 weeks & *Glory* 6, phoned WPS.

12 October: ... Contr agreed to cancel 3 Weapons at Scotts & alter 2 Battles at Fairfield to 1944 design [one completed as *Delight*], also

suspend 4 Lt Carriers. [*Arrogant, Momouth, Polyphemus* and Cammell Laird's *Hermes*, allowing Barrow's *Elephant* to take up the name.] ... Contr told me 1st L thought June '46 too early for date after which ships will not come into Far East war. ...

13 October: Attended Vice Contr's meeting re using Antwerp; Treasury fellow very sticky about [foreign] exchange, wants only work done there that Belgian Govt will pay for. ...

14 October: ... Ayre [Amos] said 1st L had told M of WT we were releasing liner ships. M of WT was hoity-toity, wanted Ayre to say which ships & where; Ayre said 'Would I tell him?' I said I couldn't, all I was doing was mapping out a plan on a policy that at present was only Controller's. I could not give this plan to Ayre for M of WT who might chuck it at 1st L & this would be the first 1st L had seen of it. ...

16 October: ... Held Priority meeting, nobody was prepared to be reasonable except DWP, got Staff to put back *Truncheon* [submarine building at Devonport]. ... To Bath via Stroud, accident at Paddington much confusion, finally motored down. ...

17 October: ... At Repairs meeting, Dep Contr tackled Far East requirements. Afterwards I said I thought it was wrong to take in a ripe old ship like *Rodney* for 18 months; labour could be far better employed. [The Americans were also refusing to take elderly British warships in for refit.] ...

18 October: At Bath. Contr came into DNC's room while I was there re salving fl. dock XXIII. I was for giving it to a private firm e.g. Critchley [G R, Liverpool & Glasgow Salvage Association] but DNC & Contr thought Dir. of Sal. [Rear Admiral A R Dewar] should do it (not very different as D of SV has got in outside people for the war). ... Contr said ships ready before end Aug (not end June) '46 should be reckoned as in Far East war. ...

19 October: On leave. Brought N. back from Moor Court (rather worried about her health). [Presumably with the reduction in flying bomb attacks, Goodall thought it safe for her to return to London.]

20 October: ... Grant called, he is retiring [Sir Allan J, director of John Brown, Sheffield]. Nowlan [H J, Assistant Civil Engineer in Chief] came over re Birkenhead No. 6 slip, wrote Johnson [R S]. Ayre wrote re Vickers now not hastening licence for N.Z. ship, replied that TFs had highest priority. All morning went on shipbuilding after war (Mountain is rushing 1st L & it is a case of the blind leading the blind). ...

21 October: ... With Bamford read proof of A.L. lecture & sent to Nicol. ... Wrote destroyer builders re dimensions of 1944 Battles [*Daring* class]. Trafalgar Day.

23 October: Dealt ... also with Scotts cranes for building S/Ms. I am not on a good wicket here. ... Vice Contr said he was coming up re Air Sea Rescue [boats] but he didn't. ... Talk with S L Smith [BSRA] at lunch re education for shipbuilding, he says universities are only manufacturing draughtsmen [he seemed to be confusing them with colleges producing such].

25 October: Johnson [R S] & John [F O, director and naval architect] called, worried because CL have had a letter cancelling the old *Temeraire* contract & he wants to know if that washes out the 1945 Battleship, I said 'No'. [Astonishing that the Admiralty was still considering building new battleships as late as this.] ... Told Johnson Contr app'd his slip arrgts if he would finish *Somme* by end Aug '46: I said he would. [Optimistic as she had not even been laid down.] ... Message from Canada they can do *Aga[memnon]* & *Men[estheus]*, phoned D of ST who said they didn't want them as troopers but don't tell Contr till Lord L[eathers] agrees (Contr so tactless). [*Agamemnon* arrived at Victoria Machinery Depot 20 Jan 45 for conversion to an amenities ship which was cancelled on 22 Nov 45.] ... King [I E] back from France says things are bad there. ...

28 October: Finished Europe Cease Fire screed & took it to Contr who was fussing for it. I should say he just skimmed thro' as when I saw him after lunch he said he had sent it to type & 1st L would have it on Monday. I said I had said nothing about Finance and Treasury will probably take line that we cannot give the Admy a blank cheque. Contr said the essence of the scheme was a 'Five Year Plan' for the Navy. ...

Standard C class prefabricated hulls for the Ministry of War Transport were allocated for conversion to support ships for the British Pacific Fleet. *Empire Pitcairn* was launched by Readhead at South Shields on 17 October 1944. She was fitted out as an aircraft engine maintenance vessel but not completed until November 1945, as seen here, named *Moray Firth*. After the war she was converted to the cargo vessel *Linaria* for Stag Line. (*Author's collection*)

30 October: ... Maxwell put the labour situation well which fed Contr up, he likes to hear soft words from Hancock. ... I have to tackle DMR re FAA ship at Readheads [Tyne shipbuilder building *Beauly Firth* and *Moray Firth*]. ...

31 October: ... CMSR fussing Contr that there are more slips available for merchant ships than I say. I told CMSR to send Moore [possibly W J, Personal Assistant to A Ayre] over, he came, he wants to count in every potty little slip & take no account of unavailability of labour to work on them, also slips that will have warships on them till end of '45. [Another example of Goodall's practical approach to theoretical proposals.]

2 November: At Newcastle. ... Inspected TFs at Walker, the dates they are giving for completion are ridiculous, *Perseus* also looks bad. Saw the machines that are the cause of the strike [gas cutting?]. To Swan Hunter, said fast oiler [*Olna* ex-*Hyalina*] should go before *Superb* [it did]. To Neptune, their TFs look in a good state. Swan Hunter always go for me over payments, now they say they are in a mess over payments for the fast oiler. [Contract stage payments were the responsibility of Jubb, Director of Contracts, not Goodall.] ...

3 November: First went to Lit[erary] & Phil[osophical Society] to see slides & films rehearsal, a good thing I did, one slide jammed & the film of Undex had 2 bad spots (don't know how they got there); also screen wasn't white enough. [The building was close to the Royal Station Hotel where Goodall was probably staying.] To Readheads [at South Shields]. Their first engine repair ship is behind date, upholstery & stuff like that which doesn't matter is there also no austerity about merchant ship practice! [*Beauly Firth* launched 24 Aug.] To Palmers [Hebburn, a Vickers-Armstrongs subsidiary], Champness said ship won't be with him till Dec! [Palmers were to convert the hull to Admiralty requirements.] Reed [Smith's Dock] yesterday buttonholed me that he couldn't do Gray's 1171 [hull of repair ship *Cuillin Sound*]. I said he must go to Lawrie Edwards [DMR]. To Hendon Dock, going well. Gave A. Laing Lecture (59 mins plus Undex film was good) everybody very polite.

4 November: ... At Blyth there is still friction between Blyth & Whites [machinery contractors], Blyth's 1st TF [*LST.3026* launched 30 Oct] is held up because they can't get engines & boilers in. *Good Hope* [ex *Loch Boisdale*] looked well & CO was very pleased but there may be trouble brewing over vibration. This yard is improving but is very much at the mercy of sub-contractors. Hughes Bolckow is also much better. [Blyth shipbreakers brought in to fit out hulls.]

6 November: ... *Southern Prince* is to go to Canada independently (hope she doesn't get torpedoed but U boats are getting more active). [She was converted by United Shipyards at Montreal 24 Nov 44 to 11 Oct 45.] ... Wrote Jubb re fast oiler.

7 November: Contr gave me paper re 4 distilling ships [for fresh water]; showed it to Stantan who thought Canada could do it. ...

8 November: ... Contr sent up D of P's scheme to cancel a no. of Battles & Weapons of 1943 Prog, made me very angry: result would be shock [?] in marine engineering particularly. ... Mk VI towers still going back (Damn). ...

9 November: Rowell called: can he put a merchant ship on No.6 berth. I said 'Yes' & sent a note to DMB. [Probably Shell tanker *Neara* keel laid 16 Nov.] I gathered Rowell is not worried about future prices for warships as Admy is now committed to paying his Est[ablishment] Charges [overheads] whether high or low. ...

10 November: Greig called, dictated notes, said 100-1 chance that last 3 Weapons would be cancelled: no obj[ection] to him having licences for 3 merchant ships. Yarrow called, said I could give him nothing definite but scheme was to keep him on destroyers. ... Ayre has got some merchant ship orders from Canada: he says Canadian shipbuilding thoroughly inefficient: cost terrific, industry must put its house in order or shut up. Sent Contr yarn re *Tiger* cancellation [cruiser on order at Walker]. Wrote Pigott on how DNC should be treated at a launch [Lillicrap was going to *Vanguard*].

11 November: ... Sent Head of C.L. Callander's letter saying without extra labour he cannot accelerate TFs, met him at Club with Newell, they say Vickers Barrow incorrigible ...

14 November: At Bath. At Repairs meeting D of D gave refit programme for battleships (keeping the old junk alive!). [Goodall had been in charge of battleship modernisations in the early 1930s so knew their state well.] ... 'Is the big gun ship as we know it today dead' (I think it is). ... At New Constr meeting grand scrap between DEE & Binnie [Commander W A C, Radio Equipment Dept] over radar requirements for *Vanguard*. [Goodall's first use of the term instead of RDF.] ... At NC meeting said last 3 Weapons (1943) from Scotts are to be cancelled & *Vimiera* & *Ypres* built to '44 design. [Y was built as *Delight* and V as *Danae* but later cancelled.]

15 November: E in C & DNC agreed to my report to Contr on dynamo (750 kW diesel) in '44 cruisers [6in never ordered]. ... At Contr's NC

meeting he spoke of merchant ship building, I said if *Ark R.* &c went slow there was trouble ahead, the question was not entirely one of clearing slips. ... Told Hancock to watch CMSR transferring riveters from Belfast to Clyde. ...

16 November: Back at Admy. Fardell came up re sloops, walked into him over Naval Staff having no prevision. ... Ayre told me he was going: fed up with Seal & Mountain [civil servants] amusing to see reaction of such a man [successful shipbuilder] to the fetters we have to put up with the whole time. [Plus ça change, plus c'est la même chose.]

17 November: ... Sent Contr list of warships that should be completed for Far East. He then discussed the whole scheme; he very peeved because Board Meeting had been postponed & 1st S Lord was opposed to the whole business as 'killing the Post War Fleet'. I gave him dates when the battleships &c could be laid down if designs were ready. Lunched with ACNS(W) [Patterson] who had had a meeting that day to consider rocket ships [guided weapons] instead of battleships. ...

18 November: Finished *AFD.23* report: Lessons are (i) Dockyard officers must have enough design knowledge of the ships they are using or repairing (ii) promoted foremen are not good enough for the RCNC without some sort of design course (iii) when CE or D of D cuts civilian staff, technical depts should nail them down. At Malta we did not get the staff we wanted for the Fl Dock, everything went all right [Goodall had been the constructor there when ex-German *AFD.8* arrived in 1925]. At Trinco ditto but when everything went wrong, the Constr[uction] Dept got the blame tho' understaffed. I should say owing to loading being too heavy the dock started to leak, pumps were pumping the sea dry [there were probably some loose rivets in the Indian-built dock], then to correct trim, ends were pumped (pumps & pneumercators [indicators of liquid depths in tanks] not altogether satisfactory) add[itiona]l loading was too much. ... Craven died [less than two months after his wife].

19 November Sunday: About 08.30 a Rocket [V2] fairly near Thrale Hall. AR warning about 21.15 but I have given up logging AR warnings.

20 November: ... Fardell came up twice re Board Memo on merchant ship capacity from warships. Staff has been put up by 1st SL to oppose (I think Contr made another of his tactical errors by not taking Staff & 1st SL into full confidence).

21 November: Held meeting on Hull Repair & FAA Ships, went well but it is obvious dates are not going to be kept. However all concerned appeared anxious to do their best. Lunched with Newell & tried to get

into his head some ideas on how to improve Admy organisation (I wonder if he is a future Secretary of Admy) [shown as Under Secretary in 1959 Navy List]. Thornycroft called re his layout: I advised him to write a more concise letter & make it definite that he will pay if Admy will hire the cranes to him. ... At Contr's Priority meeting, he put his foot down at last & of course everybody said 'Aye Aye Sir'.

22 November: ... On 15/11 I sent Pringle a note putting the problem of avoiding somehow or other the spate of electrical work on ships finishing, he called about this yesterday, his view is that if only he got information early enough everything in the garden is lovely. ...

24 November: Pigott called, said I agreed to his merchant ship proposals & he agreed to keep his warship dates. Got Lillicrap moved up for Nov 30 [launch party for *Vanguard*]. Pigott has had a hell of a time with Troup over the business, the Authorities want to take a movie without Pigott [managing director of the shipbuilder] in it (? because other shipbuilders will be jealous). To Craven's Memorial Service, good but too impersonal, only men in choir made singing most effective & appropriate. [Goodall had worked with Craven of Vickers-Armstrongs for over 20 years.] Came away with Meryon who in the lining of his top hat keeps a record of the initials & dates of funerals the hat has attended. ... Ormston called, DEE present. O. stuck out that last minute alterations to *Colossus* were mainly petty but innumerable. O. then saw Contr who said he gave up the shipbuilding industry as hopeless. (Yet they have done a hell of a lot). ...

25 November: ... Sent Contr statement of ships that would be completed in time for Far East War if date were 31/12/46 instead of 30/6/46 (& 31/8/46 for destroyers). ...Saturday afternoon is a blessing as it is then possible to get at a job without interruption.

27 November: ... Ingram [US Naval Attaché?] called with Capt ? Submarines & Cdr Smythe Hull Design section [US] B[ureau] of Ships. Latter wants to see launching arrgts of *Vanguard*, phoned Pigott who agreed. ...

28 November: Sweated on screed for Controller setting out how we were mucked up by M of WT on Fleet Train, especially FAA Repair Ships thereby got pushed into the winter (when light is bad & ships come in with winter damage). ... Fardell came up re Plans Div worrying whether the 20 A Cl S/Ms of 1944 programme were cancelled or not. I said Contr considered then cancelled & we had enough S/Ms on order to keep the machine ticking over. I said also that I thought 1st L should put the warship capacity to merchant ship scheme before Cabinet, he will see Private Office. ...

29 November: ... I asked [Contr] re Bassett's backstairs move to get Destroyer Escorts back into 1st Priority, he said he had always intended this! I then showed him Hughes' [probably W R N, Dept of Dockyards] compromise which I thought good but throwing the whole thing into the melting pot. ... Late in evening 1st L wanted notes on Clydebank before 8 pm [for *Vanguard* launch next day]. Damn him. Sent them & therefore late for dinner.

30 November: Attended Shipwright Co's Prize Scheme meeting. Lord Westwood [William, of Ship Constructors & Shipwrights Association] very interesting on Trade Union practices (tho' a TU official he talks reasonably). ... Message from 1st L to V-A Walker not to use gas cutting machine (strike now 6 weeks old) & this after he wanted to know when Trade Unionists came back from USA why we were not using more gas cutting machines!

1 December: H & Wolff meeting continued: fuss about electricians on repair throwing establishment out of balance & Firm would have to discharge or derate dilutees. ...

2 December: Morris (D of F) [J D, Director of Finance] came up re Thornycroft's yard scheme, gave him answers to Treasury questions. ... Sec. [Markham] sent for me re a constructor on Economic Control in Germany, said it would be difficult but DNC would see him today. DNC called, he was treated well at the launch. Discussed with him Bay Cl. frigate prototype, he agreed, also centralised messing for *Audacious* [*Eagle*], also an ADNC for Germany, also fast oiler under ASCBS [i.e. White Ensign]. ... Started to deal with paper accumulation ... also A Cl. S/Ms for the Dutch [they later got 'T' class]. End of a hectic week. ...

5 December: Pity the journey to Barrow is so tiresome. Vickers S/M construction is very interesting. Moss swears it is going to prove cheaper. Told Callander of the possibility of two A's going to Dutch but could not say if that would mean 2 extra, anyhow Vickers will hold back material for two. Disappointed with TFs. *Pioneer* looks all right but is a fine ship wasted [as a maintenance ship rather than an aircraft carrier]. *Majestic* is very backward. Told Callander he could use No. 4 berth for a merchant ship if he wishes since cruiser design is going to be late. [The New Zealand ferry *Hinemoa* was laid down on it Apr 1945.] Went into labour for TFs. No hope of placing H & W frigates here; suggested they should tackle Chairman of Manpower Board for fitters.

6 December: Left Barrow for Carlisle. Filthy journey. Held TF meeting. Scottish firms did not turn up in force. Russell [of Denny] as usual a nuisance but DCW(S) [Hannaford] being there was very helpful & kept

R. from being too bad. Tackled Barclay Curle possibility of fitting out their 2nd ship [*LST.3015*]. ... Left Carlisle for Liverpool by car, arrived 6.30 pm, journey could have been worse.

7 December: At Liverpool. Talk with FOIC [now Vice Admiral J W S Dorling], WPS [A E Horley, chief constructor] & Duncan Labour Officer about labour for Barrow more particularly. *Ark Royal* is behind, Johnson still says he will launch in Dec [presumably 1946] but I offered to bet Hamilton [James, shipyard manager] £5 [about £300 in today's money] he wouldn't & H. wasn't taking it on. [Goodall would have won as she was not launched until 3 May 50.] Looked at *Venerable*, she will finish all right bar accidents [17 Jan 45]. Destroyers waiting for DCTs are a sorry sight [*Hogue* and *Lagos*] but they would have gone back in any event (labour to *Duke of York* [battleship refitting by CL at Liverpool] & *Venerable*). These destroyers will require *Venerable*'s labour & it would be a big upset if CL took one of H & W's ferries. ...

8 December: Back in office. ... Met Nowlan (CE in C) & spoke to him about C Laird's No. 6 slip, he says Lithgow has made a move. After discussing with DWP, wrote Lobnitz & Yarrow re frigates from H & W. ... Wrote DNC re the proposed new graving dock at Liverpool. ...

9 December: ... Met Hancock, most unhelpful over labour, said Vickers Barrow screwed men down, firms were discharging their inefficients, we had come to the end of our tether. ... Went to Doctor re rupture.

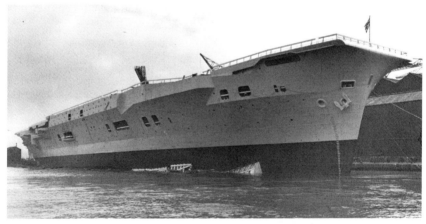

Although *Ark Royal* was ordered in March 1942 and keel laid in May 1943, she was not launched until 3 May 1950, as new naval construction was slowed after the war, both to reduce expenditure and to allow shipbuilders to concentrate on merchant ships. Lillicrap attended the launch as DNC, and probably also Goodall as a director of Cammell Laird. Completion in 1955 allowed post-war developments such as the steam catapult, angled deck and side lift to be fitted. (*Author's collection*)

11 December: Fitted for truss. ... Watkins [K H] said *City of Paris* earmarked & drawings sent to Australia. [She was actually sent to Montreal in April 1945 for conversion by United Shipyards, but was cancelled in September. Reconverted to mercantile by Palmers Hebburn 1947 £750,000.] ...

12 December: At Bath. ... We are likely to get into a muddle over destroyer dates of completion (a) ex towers [*sic*, but probably with] (b) without towers. Gave Kingcome my first shot at revised destroyer programme. ... Fardell gave me D of P's shot at 1945 Programme, a woolly yarn which I altered. Discussed with Hickey Fl. Dock XXIII, he showed me dwgs of connections of sections, I was not too happy. [The dock was built of seven sections, bolted together, so they could be separated for towing or repair.]

13 December: Discussed 1945 Programme with DNC, he pressed for early decision on Battleship Sketch Design & Cruiser Sketch Design, he asked for a prototype S/M in the programme. Contr had motor accident on way to Bath, he went back to London, James [J H] & Bailey [Captain R, Secretary to Controller] in hospital. Bath meetings a fizzle therefore. ... Very foggy & train 2 hours late. Got a good meal at Admy canteen for 1/- [one shilling = 5p]. Did not get to bed till 23.30.

14 December: D of P [Grantham], DD of P [Captain R K Dickson], Fardell & Naval Asst came up re 1945 Programme. I had a go at them about battleships with 16″ guns & cruiser with 6″ (back to the wooden walls) & advocated a prototype S/M & MTB. Also urged we should not suspend 2 Gibraltars [*Malta*s]. ... Backed up Ayre as Chairman of Ad[miralty] [Ship] Welding C'tee after he leaves Admy. A bang (rocket) near at about 17.30.

15 December: ... Contr phoned. Palmer (of H & W Belfast) [probably Charles Palmour, new chairman] was seeing him, had I any points? Said H & W were much improved if only their programme could be kept stable they would be all right. Dealt with proposed CAFO [Confidential Admiralty Fleet Order] saying contractors won't get money from Admy for plant developments (I see no use in it). Lobnitz [H P, director] phoned, he would take on a frigate instead of a LCG(M), saw Baker & said frigate must go before LCG(M). [*Loch Ard* completed by Lobnitz as *Transvaal*.]. ...

16 December: ... Thompson [J C] called, back from H & W Belfast, only 200 elect[rician]s for naval & merchant repairs, looks bad for new constr[uction]. Wrote FOIC re *Loch Ard* & firm having to do *St Austell Bay* themselves. Phoned Vice Contr re *Dacres* ['Captain' class destroyer escort] going to Belfast for refit & preparation for Far East & docketed engine repairs only (? Bassett trying again to get a fast one past me).

18 December: A troublesome paper to cancel *Lion* & *Temeraire* contracts made me waste a lot of time. Ashton Cross, Morris & Seal are a trial, playing the peace time game of stopping work & progress, thereby money is saved; sent the paper to DWP. Saw Morrison (Ayre's successor) [W McArthur Morison] re a visit from the French to see welding in merchant shipbuilding. Fardell (Plans) came up to discuss '45 programme further: oilers will not be in so I think I must let *Bulwark* [not yet laid down] go on at H & W & stop *Monmouth* at Fairfield. ...

19 December: Worked on Plan for arranging orders so that the Big XIV [warship builders] get a fair share of Post War work, difficult now that *Malta* & *New Zealand* are to be suspended. Discussed with Kingcome who suggested new sloops might go to a firm instead of Chatham, I shall take this up. K. also said Fairfield without *Monmouth* would be in an engineering mess. Thornycroft called & wants 2 Battles. I said I couldn't promise more than one [*Duchess* ordered 29 Mar 45]. He doesn't want the sloop, I said he could lay this down mid '46. He left slip chart & I gave DWP a copy. ... *Tiger* paper arrived, app'd to build to '44 design.

20 December: Rang DNC re new design of sloop, he phoned later to say that he estimated 25 knots meant a length of 340' and SHP 12,000. ...

21 December: At Contr's Policy Meeting. A breeze with Contr over the new dock at Devonport, he said 'It must not be too big.' I said 'For God's sake don't repeat the mistake of building a new dock with insufficient width'. He said 'Ships are too big'. I said and when anything goes wrong it is DNC who is on the carpet for ships having insufficient beam to give good underwater protection. ...

27 December: Cogitated on Destroyer Flotilla for Canada ... *Loch Killisport* has arrived at H & W Liverpool [repair yard]. T.G. Worked thro' most of paper accumulation over the holiday.

28 December: ... Denny wrote re his exp[erimenta]l *MTB 109*, wants to get rid of it. ... Stantan wrote, won't write a paper for INA on warship building in Canada, begged him to reconsider. [John Robson did produce one for INA in 1946 on Merchant Shipbuilding in Canada.] ...

29 December: ... Baily of H & W [J S Baillie] called, wants to lay down a tanker on No. 10 berth (Musgrave [yard]). I said 'No objection' in fact am pleased as the Fast Oiler is not in the '45 prog & *Bulwark* is to be suspended (did not tell B. this tho' I said *Bul.* was a 'go slow' & therefore anything might happen). Bed shook about 10.30 pm, thought it was a rocket but it may have been the earthquake. ...

30 December: ... Vice Contr said Admiral Evans (BATM) was lost, apparently aeroplane came to grief, this is a heavy blow. ... Phoned Stanley

if Walker was getting hard up to employ trades put off by prolonged boilermakers' strike, he said they had transferred 300 [to other yards?].

31 December Sunday: Yesterday I went to see the Mulberry Exhibition at the Civils [Engineers Institution]. Propaganda. Disgusted at the way the work done by the Admiralty has been completely left out of the picture. [The Admiralty had been heavily involved in designing and testing all types of floating structures and breakwaters.]

Memoranda 1944

A year of Ups & Downs. All my efforts to get a steady output of destroyers were wrecked by the inability of DNO & Vickers to produce DCTs in time. The only plan that has come to fruition was the completion of 3 Light Fleet Carriers (Colossus class) before the end of the year [actually only *Glory* was completed by 31 Dec]. The frigate plan fizzled out but the reason was a good one, viz the failure of the U boats to keep up their offensive. The main struggles this year have been for Transport Ferries and the first is completed, not a bad effort. The Fleet Train for the Far East was steadily stonewalled by Lord Leathers with the result that we are now in the mess we tried to avoid, viz a whole lot of completions involving an impossible load on fitting out trades at the end of the year & in the first 6 mos of 1945.

Overlord went better than I expected, one result was that everybody got too optimistic and there is now a feeling of disappointment because obviously there is plenty of fight still left in the Germans. Still when looking back at this time last year the progress has been fine. Then we lived under the threat that with Doodle Bugs & Rockets London would have been untenable by now.

In domestic affairs the year has been sad. Really Flo's death was a blessing. N's health is becoming an anxiety, tho' she seems better now than in the autumn. My double rupture is another warning of A.D. [Anno Domini, Goodall was now 61, his wife 11 years older]. The damage to our home and the refusal of the authorities to let me have it repaired have been a blow.

Lillicrap appears to be doing well as DNC. The firms are all thinking of merchant ships. Labour is getting more & more difficult. Fitters strike at Belfast. Riveters going slow on the Tyne. Shipwrights & boilermakers quarrelling over the pre-fab frigates (then Westwood is made a peer & Hodgson [Mark, of Boilermakers' Society] is knighted!). Now the strike at Walker. Do we really deserve to win wars?

Wake-Walker has toned down. But I think he is a bad Controller (he tried to be too clever with Leathers, hence the Fleet Train mess. He rushed his merchant shipbuilding with warship capacity over the head of Naval Staff who are out now to see that it fizzles).

1945

1 January: Honours. Bassett [G A, Deputy Director of Dockyards] gets a CB [Companion of the Bath] at last. Lithgow [Sir James, Controller of Merchant Shipbuilding & Repairs] CMSR a CBE [Commander of the British Empire]. I wonder if he is pleased. Ditto [Lord] Reith [Director of Combined Operations Material and formerly Director General of BBC] CB. ... Worked on shipbuilding after the war & asked [Amos] Ayre [until recently Director of Merchant Shipbuilding] how he equated merchant ships tonnage to warship [displacement] tonnage. [Although Goodall did not note any figures my rough rule of thumb is that 1 ton displacement of warships then had about the same work content as 6 gross tons of merchant ships.]

2 January: ... Trouble at Southampton over Priorities, M of WT [Ministry of War Transport] stopping refits of LCTs in order to get on with merchant ships. [More of the flimsy LCT4s needed strengthening and tropicalised for the war against Japan.] Told Vice Contr [Phillips] this was my mistake, it was never intended to interfere with Overlord: suggested he phone CMSR

LST 3043, ordered as Transport Ferry No. 43 with Admiralty security designation J.11060, newly completed by Scotts in August 1945 to prepare for deployment out East. Although Scotts installed her machinery as Contract 711 (Hull 634), her two standard frigate steam reciprocating engines were ordered by the Admiralty from A F Craig of Paisley. (*Blackman collection*)

& put LCTs in Priority 1 above merchant ships. ... Said he [Meryon] should speak A Ayre & let him know that firms must have merchant ship orders soon if they are to retain their labour. ... DNC [Lillicrap] said *TF.19* [Transport Ferry or *LST.3019*] had got 13 knots [on trial].

3 January: ... James [J H, Principal Assistant Secretary] said cause of accident [car to Bath on 13 Dec] was Contr's impatience: altho' a thick fog, he was urging chauffeur to push on. ...

5 January: Held TF meeting, gloomy. Blyth [shipbuilder of *LST.3026* and *3027*] and White [machinery contractor] going back badly, had a talk with King [Rear Admiral F V, Deputy Engineer in Chief] who will see if he can get some other machinery contractor to take on Blyth. Walker (VA) [Vickers-Armstrongs' Tyne yard] another black spot [building five]; we may get 20 by end of April [actually only eight]. TFs some vibration trouble & air in circulating [cooling] water when going astern. ... Talk with Stanley [H, Warship Production Superintendent, North East] who says feeling at Walker is due to Vickers being regarded as an interloper on Tyne [the Barrow shipbuilder took over the Armstrong yard in 1928]. Ormston has imported too many Barrow men [Barrow was more productive than Walker].

6 January: Contr phoned CMSR inquiring if H & W [Harland & Wolff] Belfast can do a Flying Boat Depot Ship. ...

8 January: ... To Ramsay's Memorial Service at [Westminster] Abbey (beautiful music) [Vice Admiral B H, ANCXF, had been killed in an air crash on 2 January]. There was a big bang while Padre was reading the lesson, he didn't bat an eyelid.

10 January: Pigott [Sir Stephen, managing director of John Brown] called, promised to get out Connell's TF [*LST.3031* being fitted out by Brown] by end April. ... Attended meeting on reducing strictness of censor on work during war. ...

12 January: ... I was lunching with Dana [R W, Secretary of Institution of Naval Architects] when Bamford rang to say brother Ernest collapsed on London Bridge station & died on way to Guys [Hospital]. After lunch, phoned coroner's office then went to Kingswood, Clarie [Ernest's wife] prostrate, like all of us thought he was in robust health (he would have been 59 on Jan 15).

16 January: On leave. Ernest's funeral.

17 January: In office. ... 1944 Battle orders paper from Seal [E A, now Under Secretary, Admiralty] proposing to place firm orders for first

8, I shall see Kingcome, then Controller. [Eight *Daring*s were ordered Jan/Feb.]

18 January: Meryon called, showed him the 1944 Battle paper. Saw Contr with it & said Admy was speaking with 2 voices (Contr: we will help the industry, Treasury: we must reduce expenditure on warship building). ... Went to Preece's Memorial Service [Sir George, retired Engineer in Chief]. I don't like St Martin's [in the Fields] mem services there, dull & impersonal. ...

20 January: ... SLC [Superintendent of Landing Craft, Chief Constructor Rowland Baker] found from DCOM [Director of Combined Operations Material, now Captain R C Todhunter] that Canadian TFs will come here, that washes out any from Canada being in the 14 required by mid April.

22 January: Fifty years ago today I entered Owens [Dame Alice Owen's school then at Islington]. Wrote Headmaster, good wishes. ...

23 January: Skin under truss [for his rupture] a raw mess. Stayed in bed & sent for doctor. Dermatitis due to wearing truss. Must stay in bed till skin is healed & then probably have an operation.

[Off sick till 12 February.]

13 February: Motored to & from office & had lunch in office. DWP [Director of Warship Production S A McCarthy, effectively Goodall's No 2] sick. Picked up most of the threads, reading the accumulation. Contr said he would send for me but he didn't before 4 p.m. when I left. No use worrying but the production situation goes badly. Mark VI [director control] towers fall back again [and were overweight]. Fairfield is in a mess as usual. Denny blaming everything on TF [they were building only one, *LST.3035*]. The root trouble is insufficient labour & no notion 6 years ago of the great increase in electrical work. [True, but shortage of labour should not prevent the production planners in the shipyards from giving the Admiralty realistic completion dates.]

14 February: ... Worked on agenda for BSRA [the new British Shipbuilding Research Association] must rub in need to collect all war lessons resulting from enemy action on merchant ships. ...

15 February: At BSRA, dictated notes. W Ayre said shipowners were coming round to prices but Anderson [probably Sir Alan, a director] of Orient Line said they were fantastic & orders would not be placed while they remained so (Pilate saith unto Him 'What is Truth?'). [Anderson was probably thinking of how shipbuilding prices fell sharply after the First World War; they did not after the Second.] Champness [E L, managing

director of Palmers Hebburn] told me Sims & Stunden [G J, Constructor at Chatham Dockyard] made a poor show at interview for Professor at Kings College [now Newcastle University]. He agreed Burrill was a poor choice but they just had to appoint somebody. [The Chair had been vacant since 1941. L C Burrill was a propeller specialist and a local man.] ...

16 February: Saw Contr re *Bulwark* [at H & W] and *Monmouth* [at Fairfield] & visit of Sir Basil Brooke [Prime Minister of Northern Ireland]; he thinks we cannot keep N. Ireland going at expense of English & Scottish yards. ... Paper on Lobnitz dock [fitting-out basin?] is getting on but the talk, Talk, TALK. Kingcome [Vice Admiral Sir F R G, Engineer in Chief] came in (Turner going, bad luck. K. proposed as new E in C). ...

Vice Admiral (Sir) John Kingcome (1890–1951) was appointed Engineer in Chief in 1945, Goodall having had many dealings with him as Deputy E in C from 1942. Academically gifted, he had been a member of the Board of Invention and Research in the First World War. Seagoing appointments included Squadron Engineer Officer of the 1st Cruiser Squadron in 1929 and Home Fleet Engineer Officer in 1939, interspersed with time at the Admiralty. (*The Shipbuilder*)

17 February: Contr came up with P Branch [Priority] charts, showing Fairfield particularly in a mess: he seems to think we take no notice of such circumstances, but F. has lost a lot of men during the past year. Hancock [J, Assistant Secretary] & his No. 2 came up to let me know the latest about the labour situation. Admy are asking for 4000 men mainly for repair. (250 electricians for the Clyde). I get windy when I compare the shipyard labour situation with the work in hand for the Far Eastern war. Mrs Smith [his shorthand typist] called looking very well (?clothes & make-up) sorry she has left. Bamford wrote to say he will be out some time. ...

22 February: ... Cooper DA/SM [Captain P F, Director of Anti-Submarine Materiel] called re trials of a new [sonar] dome in *Camperdown* ['Battle' class destroyer at Fairfield]. ...

23 February: Pigott called again, said he wanted a decision on *Trincomalee* now as one or two plates already down [destroyer laid down 5 February].

I said 'Leave present slip arrangements alone as we cannot afford delay to *Trinco*; then if Cunarder is ordered [*Caronia*], lay her down at *Malta*'s slip. *Malta* could lay down early 1947 & complete 1951' [planned new Fleet carrier]. ... Yesterday & today I found short hours I am working [doctor's orders?] a serious handicap.

24 February: ... H & W's (Govan) [Clyde yard] TF *[LST.3041]* at Dalmuir is going back but Fairfield's is coming forward [*LST.3037*]. ... Treasury want to get from Germany imports we can't produce (suggested machine tools, chain cable & ball bearings).

25 February: Stunden called. I wanted his account of the interview for Prof. of Naval Architecture at Newcastle. He was certain that the C'tee's [committee] mind had been made up before the interviews, the professorial side sat 'Mum' except that Hawkes [C J, Professor of Mechanical Engineering and a former RN engineer officer] asked one question. All the shipbuilders' questions were to the effect that he knew nothing about merchant ships [probably true]. I think the C'tee's choice disastrous & hope I may be wrong but I can't see Robb [A M, new Professor at Glasgow University] or Burrill inspiring the coming generation rightly. [Though a somewhat arrogant man, Burrill made a success of the role, getting a good team around him, building new experimental facilities and making Newcastle the top UK school of naval architecture.] ... Attended lecture on Far East campaign, much too long, a pity Americans are so verbose.

27 February: ... I was very annoyed to find Contr had app'd [approved] A's & A's on the Clyde to *Colossus, Venerable* & *Vengeance* [newly completed light fleet carriers].

1 March: Pigott called with Clydebank programme, he has filled his plate with merchant ship orders. ... King [I E, Chief Constructor] now at Sheerness called & described Italian underwater protection, they could not find report on expts [experiments] (largest were 1/3rd full size) to test this type of bulge & the American sandwich & from his guide's remarks he inferred that results did not demonstrate advantage of Italian but the Chief Constructor had patented this & meant to adopt his patent.

3 March ... AR [air raid] warnings have restarted, two last night, two this afternoon [the last V2 rocket fell on London on 27 Mar].

5 March: Contr rang to see if we can let up on LCT work on the Thames area to help merchant ship repairs. [The Thames LCT builders Harland & Wolff, Green & Silley Weir and J Russell were also ship repairers.] Got Baker up who agreed we can; told him to write a yarn, also to suspend work on LCT8s at Cowes [*LCT.4128–29*]. ... Smithers [Constructor

Captain D W, Med Fleet] in Med fears *AFD.24* (cruiser dock) will be a total loss [floating dock which broke its tow and stranded near Derna en route US to Trincomalee]. We are having bad luck with floating docks for Far East. ...

6 March: ... Pringle [Sir James S, retiring DEE] called, as pleased as usual with himself, he is going to Met Vick [Metropolitan-Vickers at Manchester] (very hot about Contr). ...

7 March: ... DNC called, said *Malta* redesign has now to proceed. ... Rocket near 50 Lyford but no damage there I think.

9 March: Capt Ross (Australia) called with Mr Frazer [Norman, Managing Director] & Mr Roe [George, Engineering Manager] of Cockatoo Island [Vickers-Armstrongs shipyard in Sydney] re Battle class they are going to build, they will visit White, Thorny[croft], Stephen, J Brown. ...

12 March: Held meeting on utilising German capacity; weaned [?] up (very much up) ideas and result was a formidable list (DMB [McArthur Morison] useful as Lenaghan [James, ship surveyor, later managing director of Fairfield] had been in Germany shortly before the war). ...

13 March: At Bath. ... Dep Contr [Deputy Controller Vice Admiral C E B Simeon, based in Bath, who was also Director of Naval Equipment] spoke of FAA [Fleet Air Arm] ships going under ASCBS [Admiral Superintendent Contract Built Ships, now Vice Admiral H E Morse] but what he told me of *Derby Haven* [depot ship for coastal forces, ex-*Loch Assynt*] shows

Derby Haven was a 'Loch' class frigate converted after launch to a coastal forces depot ship. She and her sister *Woodbridge Haven*, both built by Swan Hunter, were planned to accompany MTBs squadrons about to be deployed east. (*Author's collection*)

result would be to add to work required. ... At Repair meeting, I think we are doing a lot of work in Royal Yards on old junk, e.g. *Renown*. ... Had interesting talk with Shepheard and Chapman [J H B, Chief Constructor], former confirms my opinion that the all big gun ship is passé, latter that our people in USA should have been in uniform. [The equivalent US Construction Corps officers were.]

14 March: Interesting talk with John [W G] on [Admiralty Ship] Welding C'tee; he will take up in Working C'tee that the ship that goes to sea for prolonged tests will be all-welded. If this is done, my objection to still water expts on all riveted, all welded and ½ and ½ ships with sea tests on only one will go. [A series of full-scale structural tests were being undertaken on recently-built cargo ships and tankers.] ... Admy has to release 30,000 but these will not come from building & repair capacity.

15 March: Boys died at 07.00 [G V, former Secretary to DNC]. Johnson [Sir R S, chairman of Cammell Laird] called (to pump me about cancelling *Temeraire* [battleship ordered in 1939]) said he & Vickers [with order for *Lion*] should hang together. Discussed with SLC LCT4s [building] in London & tail end of LCT8s. ... Vice Contr says he will want a spate of Transport Ferries as LST2s are not being released [Lease-Lent from USA]. ... New shorthand typist turned up vice Mrs Smith. ...

16 March: 1st Lord [of the Admiralty, A V Alexander] wants to know if we can overcome *Vanguard* labour shortage by more overtime. ... Admiral Land [Vice Admiral E S, Chairman of US Maritime Commission] called, looks fit & in fine fettle (not 66 years old), he said Roosevelt had lost weight & was having trouble with his teeth (he must do less himself as he is losing pep). [He died on 12 Apr.]

19 March: ... Canada wants a salvage & rescue vessel on West Coast towards end of the year. Contr wants me to look into possibilities of new construction! I see no hope of getting anything new before end of '47 but will ask DMB. Discussed with DWP points for his Glasgow visit. Told him not to get labour for *Vanguard* mixed up with labour for Dalmuir [fitting out facility managed by John Brown]. He will see Stephen for a cabin in *Ocean* [for a constructor?], also Barr re TFs (we are losing TF.37 from April [to War Office?]). Told King (D E in C) that TF.39 should have machinery fitted by Fairfield [hull from Fairfield, engines from its associated company Rankin & Blackmore at Greenock] before leaving for Dalmuir. [Launched 27 Jun, but not completed for RN, sold incomplete to Brazil and completed in 1951 as *Rio Douro*.]

20 March: ... Rang DCOD [Director Combined Operations Division, Captain J Terry] re Canadian TFs coming here, he explained manning

& taking things East in them governed situation, also if they passed thro' territory of C in C BPF [British Pacific Fleet] he will pinch them! … Yarrow [Sir Harold E, chairman of Yarrow shipbuilders] spoke of getting his son from Army [Eric, a major with Royal Engineers in Burma, presumably to understudy him at the shipyard; he later became chairman, b 1920 d 2018]. I spoke Contr who said 'No hope. P.M. [Prime Minister] had issued a directive', phoned Y. …

21 March: Milne [of J S White] called, complained of his men being taken away for repairs & the amount of repairs he had to do, then on top of this DCW (Ships) [Director of Contract Work, C Hannaford] said he was inefficient because his new construction dates were going back. He said his output for manhours was good & costs low, he was sure the welded ships [destroyers] were going to come out cheaper. Should he try & get merchant ship orders. I said 'Certainly'. …

26 March: … He [W H Wallond, WPS North West] said D of D [Director of Dockyards, Vice Admiral Sir Cecil P Talbot] just back from Med thinks Gib & Malta can't return to S/M [submarine] refits [much of Talbot's naval career had been associated with submarines]. … W'son [L C Williamson, Deputy Director of Naval Construction] at Vickers Barrow last week, says delay in A Cl. caused by finding it better to fit [torpedo] tubes in shop, therefore V. want them earlier [external supplier]. …

27 March: … Contr wanted launch dates for Duchess of Kent [see 8 June]. On same job Barry [Rear Admiral C B, now Naval Secretary to 1st Lord] came up with letter from her adc [aide de camp] planning a joyride, phoned Pigott, Ormston & Swan & sent Barry dates. Replied to letter from Turner [lately E in C] (Camper & Nicholson [yacht builders of Gosport & Southampton] want to go back to commercial work as soon as European war is over!). I answered No & Yes! E in C has landed us in a mess over TFs at Blyth & Walker. DWP has agreed to concentrate on 1st & let 2nd suffer most. Sent Hancock DWP's proposals for getting men from other yards to *Vanguard*. H. said Boilermakers [trade union] were sticking out against another union doing sheet iron work. …

28 March: … Got Baker up re fitting 3 LST3s as Senior Officers ships: besides upsetting our production, it seems dreadful to me to turn ships specifically built for assaults into accommodation ships for administrative purposes. …

29 March: Held Priorities Meeting (Vice Contr, DWP, DD of D (L) [Deputy Director of Dockyards (London), Bassett], Hughes [probably R, Principal Secretary/Priority Officer]. We are departing a little from what CMSR agreed to as there are new requirements for the 2nd Assault Force

[in S E Asia?]. Vice Contr says CMSR can't be trusted; on the Clyde his repairs include a large number of coasters for west of Scotland &c, this work could be reduced. ... We are getting into a most frightful mess owing to repeated deferment of Mark VI towers for destroyers.

30 March: Good Friday. Saw DoD (H) [H presumably Home, if so Talbot] re *Charity* [destroyer building by Thornycroft, completed 19 Nov 45]. He confirms impossible to commission without tower (manning). Wrote FOIC S'ton [Flag Officer in Charge, Southampton, Tower] asking if he could berth her away from Woolston [shipyard, presumably so as not to discourage workers]. Admiral Boris [? constructor] (French Navy) called, looked well but thin, he said the worst of Paris during the occupation was the entire absence of reliable news & information from the outside world, he & his wife had been arrested. ...

3 April: Cole called called with chart of German production organisation (looks cumbersome to me, wouldn't work well here). ... Lunched Barry, pumped him about Contr who evidently is going to stay over his 3 years. Damn. Contr wants me to hold a meeting to consider if by holding back cruiser refits, we can stop Fleet Train sliding back. ...

5 April: Pigott called, very interesting on gas turbine which he saw yesterday at De Havilland's. He has an order for cross channel ship (I agreed to slip) [*Arnhem*] but said he could not put the cruiser back any more [*Tiger*]. ... *Indefat[igable]* damaged by suicide dive bomber. ... Harland & Wolff meeting, they have booked a lot of merchant ship orders on cost [of labour and materials] plus fixed sum for profit [and overheads]. ...

6 April: ... They [H & W] always succeed in convincing me they are first class. I do believe we have pulled them together a lot. ... CMSR is also for high priority for [requisitioned] trawlers returning to trade.

7 April: ... Contr came up re whaling ships [whale factory ships were required to improve supplies of oils and fats] at Furness [shipbuilder on the Tees], told him we must guard against fitting out labour being taken from LCT8s, TFs & *Cuillin Sound* [aircraft component repair ship completing at Smith's Dock]. ...

10 April: P.M. on warpath over merchant ship repairs, says we must take 1000s off new naval construction & put them on repairs. ...

11 April: Talked with Contr re new naval construction vs. merchant ship repairs. Rang DMR who said the trades he wants are mostly fitters, then Dep E in C who held out little hope of getting fitters from naval firms (I really can't believe this as destroyers are going back so badly). ...

12 April: Pigott called with Randall; can do *Diamond* by end of '46, laying down in July [destroyer not laid down until 1949]. ...

13 April: Baker SLC came up re LCT8s, I told him Contr wants to cut at the tail end so he must make certain of the fore end (75 by Feb '46), if his own firms can't arrange fitting out we will help. ...

14 April: ... Contr rang re altering bow doors of LST3s, I should have thought DNC would have taken action but Contr told me to do it. ...

16 April: Rang Friedberger re ships from Germany, he thinks on account of the manning difficulty, it is no good asking for much. ... Ingram [USN, Goodall's guest at Shipwrights' lunch] said DNC has a good film of painting and US ships in Pacific now [dry]dock according to condition of underwater fittings not fouling of bottom. [Ships foul more rapidly in warm waters; a really effective anti-fouling which could last up to five years was not developed until the 1970s.] ...

17 April: At Bath. First A cl. S/M has dived successfully to 600ft (all welded). [*Amphion*: the 'As' were designed for 500ft.] TF bow doors were foolishly below strength of LST2 doors. [A basic procedure in ship design is always to look at previous successful designs.] ... At Repairs meeting it was evident that D of D & Dep Contr & Naval Staff [all naval officers] will try to bring back junk e.g. *Renown* & *Rodney*. ... Dep Contr made remark indicating that suicide dive on *Indefat.* has shaken the advocates of open hangars & unarmoured flight deck. Spoke Watson [A W] re jet propulsion for MTBs.

23 April: ... Blackout ends today.

24 April: Letter yesterday from Stantan re Canadian output of TFs not rosy outlook. Today note from Contr that first 3 TFs from Canada can't be manned! Sent reply to Contr pointing out that if these TFs hang about in Canada, effect will be very bad. ... DWP keen on an establishment for mass production of escort vessels in wartime. I said only hope was to get shipbuilders e.g. W Ayre interested.

25 April: ... Contr talked of using Chatham yard in peacetime to build a prototype of mass-produced escort vessels. Don't think much of this idea, to be done properly it should be clear of a naval dockyard [too many distractions]. ....

26 April: At Contr's Policy meeting, dictated notes. Bassett is going to squirm out of only one cruiser on the Tyne [Palmers Hebburn was the favoured repair yard for cruisers], told him I knew he was going to do the dirty! Johnson [C Laird] called, I said he could build a tanker on No. 6

slip South Yard before the battleship. He showed me his slip chart (would not part with it) but he is filling up with merchant ship orders. He swore he would keep his date with *Somme* [keel laid 24 Feb]. ...

30 April: WPS Newcastle [Stanley] wrote, at Neptune *Woodbridge Haven* [coastal forces depot ship ex *Loch Torridon*] is going back for an Ellerman liner [*Tasso*]. Don't see that matters much but saw Contr as this is contrary to Priorities & if he lets CMSR get his way here he ought to have a quid-pro-quo somewhere else. ... DNC called, Staff is in a fix over new battleship, all they want means an enormous ship (which is what I said 2 years ago). Contr can't go till he finds a successor (Phew). ASCBS called, *Ocean* may be delayed owing to additional new radar fit for night fighters. [American SM.1 was to be fitted at Liverpool.]

1 May: At Edinburgh. To Rosyth. While there phone call from Bassett to AS [Admiral Superintendent, Rear Admiral H C Bovell] asking if he could take *Ocean*. ... To Undex. Offord is doing well but seemed too interested in his gadgets instead of results. To Alloa (Shirley-Smith good I think) [H, manager at Arrol's LCT building yard]. Looked at a LCT8, it is a big job, really a young TF. To Robbs [Leith shipbuilder] & listened to usual grumble about no discipline & men not working, their Bay looked good [*Cardigan Bay* completed 15 Jun]. Is she top heavy? ...

2 May: ... To SMT [Scottish Motor Traction, Edinburgh, building LCM7s] a live crowd & work fizzling out, we ought to use them. Discussed with Whiting a scheme for fitting out LCT8s by SMT at far end of Leith Docks. We must do that. Interesting talk at lunch on Post-war situation & Nationalism in Scotland. SMT motored me to Newcastle.

3 May: In Newcastle. Hendon Dock all right but sad to see frigates waiting for labour. *Mullion Cove* [hull repair ship converting] at Greenwells [Sunderland ship repairer] bad, read Riot Act. ... *Beauly Firth* bad but Champness swears he will keep date [aircraft engine maintenance ship completed at Palmers 6 Jun]. *Solway Firth* worse still, looks more like September [aircraft engine maintenance ship never completed at Palmers, sold mercantile]. ...

4 May: ... To N. Shields. *Dullisk Cove* [hull repair ship converting by Smith's Dock] all right but trouble with compressor vibration. ... *Superb* at Swan Hunter Wallsend going back (electrical labour). ... To Hawthorn Leslie, *Triumph* all right at expense of destroyers. ...

5 May: Back in office. .... Troup rang that [destroyers] *Zenith* & *Cheviot* are being asked (Denny & Stephen) to do extensive A's & A's: builders are refusing & they come on to EROs which is quite wrong. ...

The light fleet carriers ordered in 1942 proved successful and long-lived ships, initially referred to by Goodall as 'Woolworth carriers', i.e. cheap and quick to build, or Intermediate Aircraft Carriers. With DNC's aircraft carrier team busy on the fleet carriers (*Ark Royal* and sisters) the design was worked up by Vickers-Armstrongs at Barrow, capable of carrying forty aircraft at 24 knots. *Triumph* was the largest warship ever built by Hawthorn Leslie at 18,200 tons full load displacement, seen here leaving Hebburn on 15 April 1946. (*Author's collection*)

Interior photographs of British war-built ships are few in number, but Hawthorn Leslie commissioned a series for *Triumph*. This view of her hangar shows its 17ft 6in clear height, fortunately increased from the planned 16ft, which allowed her to stow the larger American aircraft. (*Author's collection*)

8 May: V Day. In office. ... Rang FOIC (Newcastle) re *Beauly Firth* (Ross DAMR [Captain G C, Deputy Director of Aircraft Maintenance & Repair] rang me yesterday, he seemed in a fix). After hearing from FOIC rang Ross that he should cater for ship staying in Tyne till 5/6 June, take in Air Stores & Petrol at Rosyth & do any late A's & A's such as more fire extinguishing at Rosyth. ... Vice Contr rang, convoy system will stop & this will ease pressure on merchant ships [convoys meant delays at marshalling and dispersal ports, as well as speed of slowest ship].

9 May: VE Holiday. Croquet.

11 May: ... W J Holt called (back from Burma) says RCNC is badly represented in India e.g. Mutch [H H, Constructor Commander, former Foreman of the Yard] at Trincomalee instead of a pukkah Corps man. (This is D of D who in my opinion has wasted pukkah Corps staff at home & starved ports abroad thro'out the whole war).

12 May: Hughes came up as he senses a row with CMSR over Priorities. I agreed he should tell Contr what the row will be about. Some firms have sent in curves of numbers employed on ships. I think I have enough dope to make a show at CMSR's committee. ...

15 May: At Bath. ... A full day yesterday as I put into my bag a lot of unanswered tripe; dealt with half of it today. Wrote firms to know what trades they would employ in an ideal world. At Repairs meeting I was staggered to hear it was proposed to put *Cardiff* at Stephen for repairs! [28-year-old cruiser.] ... Contr [Wake-Walker] gave a cocktail party to celebrate promotion to full Admiral: very nice but food on too lavish a scale for wartime.

16 May: ... Contr said CMSR was in a fury over Priorities, serve him right for cold shouldering my meeting (see May 12) & sending a dictatorial note instead of a representative. At NC [New Construction] meeting, Contr said we were all fine fellows particularly the civil side! A pity he doesn't turn those words into acts (Honours for NOs [naval officers] & none for civilians). But we have succeeded in making a different man of him in 3 years, he started (to use Craven's words) 'clever but a shit'. ...

22 May: DWP and Leggatt [Captain W R C, Naval Assistant to Controller] came in to discuss how to be ready with Combined Operations Ships for the next war. I said the main requirement is to have a reserve of fitting out labour i.e. the Naval Reserve should include SRRs(D) [Special Repair Ratings (Dockyard) were tradesmen called up to serve afloat overseas]. The main difficulties are finance & trade union restrictions. DWP back from Glasgow (not a profitable visit). I am afraid he is right & that we shall have

to cancel or suspend some ships that we had hoped we should complete in time for the Far East war. James came up to say we had captured [Albert] Speer (the German Head of all Production i.e. aircraft, ships & army equipment ex artillery). I gave him a list of questions to ask Speer. ...

25 May: ... Went with Heads of Depts to Room 60 WI where Alexander sang his swan song [as First Lord] & we said 'Goodbye'. DNC thought he was genuinely affected but I always feel doubtful of his sincerity; in his remarks there wasn't a word about the technical depts & the difficulties they have had to overcome. [Churchill had just appointed Brendan Bracken as First Lord.]

26 May: ... FOIC writes that *Superb* may suffer from *Newcastle* being in hand [cruiser to refit at Palmers in July]. [*Superb* had already been fitting out for 21 months, but had been launched in only 14. Her four DCTs were only delivered between 28 May and 7 Sep 45. Finally completed on 16 Nov.]

28 May: ... DNC told me the new 5th SL [now Rear Admiral T H Troubridge] is opposed to carriers with open hangars and unarmoured flight decks!! ...

30 May: Contr sent up message that prefabricated S/Ms at Blohm & Voss [Hamburg shipyard] should be seen by DWP. Rang DNC then reported to Contr that Davies [W J A, Assistant DWP], Fulthorpe [H J, constructor] & 3 from Vickers should inspect. ... Interesting report from Smithers on Ansaldo Yard at Genoa undamaged, told DMR. ...

31 May: ... Denny called, told him destroyers could finish end 1949 [two 'Weapons' and two 'Gs' on order] but sloops 1948; was he prepared to give up a sloop [two *Black Swan*s on order], he will write me. I told him dockyards at Hoboken near Antwerp were undamaged & had plenty of labour. ...

1 June: ... CMSR wants labour from LCTs (Tees Side) to go to whale factories. I said not possible unless All Highest says whale factories must be provided & Far East can go hang. ... Also CMSR wants to build gates for Swansea dock at Chepstow [the Fairfield yard there now building LCTs made such constructional steelwork before the war]. Micklem [E R, deputy chairman Vickers-Armstrongs, retired RN Commander] sent me slip charts for Barrow & Walker, asked him to confirm 662ft cruiser can go down on Barrow's No.4 slip. [Currently used for 420ft New Zealand ferry *Hinemoa*, previously 512ft cruiser *Spartan*.]

5 June: ... Merrington [with ANCXF] called, Kiel practically wiped out, Wilhelmshaven almost as bad, Hamburg central gone.

7 June: Perring (IMTU) [Rear Admiral H H, Inspector of Machine Tool Utilisation] with Sinclair & Dep Contr M. Tool Control came re our requirements of machine tools from Germany. I said these were rushed out & magnified to offset Russian demands, they included armour plate rolling mills &c which were not machine tools. ... At House C'tee & INA Council, latter meeting most disappointing, none of the 3 candidates for the Secretaryship were impressive. Really Council wants a £1500 [a year] man & is only offering £1000; if Dana will carry on during summer, we are to try all over again.

8 June: Sent Contr screed re Palmers Hebburn's extension & said if we backed it, we must send naval repairs there in peace-time. ... Contr back from Tyne (D. of York launched *Leviathan*) [*sic*, actually Duchess of Kent]. He was pleased with Hendon Dock. I had another go at him re taking labour from Tees Side LCT yards for Furness whalers [factory ships], he said FOIC believed it a Salvesen ramp [Leith-based operator of British whale catching fleet] & whalers are only required as early to scoop the pool first [before their principal competitors Norway could resume operations?]. I got him to sign he would not muck up LCT construction.

12 June: At Bath. At Repairs meeting Naval Staff said they want *Renown* taken in hand for defects only to replace a KGV casualty if it occurred in Far East. ... At Conversions meeting, Staff said *Solway Firth* may not be required! I said If that is so, say so (but what a shindig Leathers will raise!). At New Construction meeting it appeared that DNO will be late with 4.5″ mountings for Co & Cr class destroyers. Damnation. *Vanguard*'s date is getting very shaky owing to electrical gear being behind.

13 June: Talk with Sims re his visit to Germany. S/Ms were in fitted out sections, not built to jigs & joints were sometimes an inch out [Type XXI]. Their diving depths were not as great as had been reported. They had designed for keeping underwater thro'out a cruise but had not got so far when surrender came. Their latest destroyers were like our new Battles in size (really young cruisers). At Contr's meeting he said we could not have a German destroyer here but must send contractor's representatives out there; told DWP to write firms. I have to see that we are not employing labour on ships that will be too late for Far East war & warn Canada also. ...

14 June: On leave. Birthday Honours. RCNC draws a complete blank. Its treatment by B. of A. [Board of Admiralty] amazes me. How can they expect good recruits? W Ayre a Knight (well deserved) [Burntisland had an impressive shipbuilding output for its size], Barr a CBE (sick I expect).

15 June: Honours Part II out. RCNC another blank. Shirley-Smith OBE, good.

20 June: Milne called, he will look after the party going to Germany to see the latest German destroyer, phoned Thornycroft & Yarrow who agreed. Wrote other firms asking if they wish to send a representative. Phoned DNC who said Vosper [A J] will go as service Father. ...

22 June: Sent to Contr screed on how I fostered liaison with US Construction Corps & particulars of Baker's help to them on LCTs, LSDs [Landing Ship, Dock] & LST2s. ... Interesting lunch with Barry [former Flag Officer Submarines] & Mrs and Lt [J T] Lorimer. Lt L. had been to the Palace to get his DSO for being one of X craft fellows [X.6] who got under *Tirpitz*. He was a prisoner of war, he said ship was dirty, men looked in poor condition, they had no bakery, ship's amenities did not exist, compartmentation overdone.

25 June: Held meeting to answer P.M. on merchant ship repairs (Problem: to spin a yarn that will not lead to further questions). ... Told Hughes that *Daring* should be taken out of Category III (after discussing with E in C). *Diamond* is to stay in Cat III as machinery will not be ready. ...

26 June: Sent to those present notes of yesterday's meeting re Merchant Ship Repairs. James bunged his copy in to Contr & apparently took the line that it was my draft (Dirty work, actually it was his as modified by the meeting. Contr sent for me in flames as he didn't agree with it & James sat mum while I defended it. ...). Contr said he proposed Yarrow as a member on the committee to put RCNC into the Navy, I agreed. (Denny has refused & I'm glad). Started on Prof

The *Daring* class destroyers were ordered in January 1945 to take account not only of wartime experiences but also improved machinery performance. Their steam turbines used higher pressures and temperatures than the wartime-built vessels. Their double reduction gearing allowed for slower propeller revolutions (310 rpm) and larger diameter (12ft) so increasing propulsive efficiency and lowering fuel consumption. This photo shows *Daring* in drydock shortly before her trials in 1952, with her two 3-bladed 6.5-ton manganese bronze propellers and twin rudders. (*Author's collection*)

[M M] Postan's History of Admiralty Production during the war; it is all wrong; wrote Lillicrap. ...

27 June: ... Had talk with Baker (SLC) on labour of Landing Craft. If the Far East war finishes on 31/12/46 we ought to have no labour employed on these craft after August '46 whereas Baker plan goes on till Oct. I must take this up, he says CCO [Chief of Combined Operations, now Major General R E Laycock] will not agree to shut down. Attended CMSR's Output C'tee, pointed out that our charts are estimates & should not be used in Report, said no shipyard labour could be obtained from boat builders & that 1/3rd of LCT men could be used in shipbuilding i.e. 3000-4000, we should commence to reduce in Jan '46.

28 June: To Shipwright Apprentice Prize selection. Very good report on Wood who has already benefited. Best boy from Caledon, next Cammell Laird, next Swan Hunter. Thornycroft sent a good man but he was in his 4th Year, he will get a consolation prize. ... To Glasgow by night train.

29 June: At Glasgow. To FOIC where I found DEE [now H D MacLaren]. Long talk about overtime at Fairfield for electricians: real trouble is vendetta between Barr & a certain shop steward plus Barr's desire to keep down costs. To Fairfield with DEE, looked at *Theseus*, electrical & plumbing work behind, then talk with Barr. We reached a compromise on overtime, I wrote out a statement which was typed & signed by Barr, DEE & myself. Looked at *T.F.38* [*LST.3038*] very good. To Stephen [adjacent shipyard] ASCBS said *Ocean* very bad & dirty. I went round & thought it was not good but not as bad & dirty as he made out. Looked at *T.F.29* [*LST.3029*] she is behind. To Lobnitz [shipbuilder at Renfrew] all quite happy, they have plenty of merchant ship orders. ...

30 June: At Glasgow. Had a good go around *Vanguard* [fitting out]. With six months to go not a turret on board, looks very gloomy to me.

(Sir) Donald J Skiffington (1880–1963) was appointed John Brown's shipyard manager in 1921, continuing in that position throughout the Second World War, during which the yard concentrated on warship building. He was seen as the archetypal bowler-hatted shipyard manager, who Goodall regarded as a bit of a bully, but he got things done. (*The Shipbuilder*)

Firm is pushing on fine but they cannot get much clewed up & compartments locked up. Sinners DNO, DRE [Director of Radio Equipment, Captain F J Wylie], D of V [Director of Victualling, O S N Rickards], DCW(S) [if S = Supplies, Hopkins]. … Looked at target that represents underwater protection for *Malta*, some difficult work. [John Brown was building two, 64ft long, 30ft wide and 49ft deep.] To Dalmuir Basin, inspected TF.31, looked good. A sad sight to see destroyers & TFs lying about, former because of towers, latter because of lack of labour. Wet day. Skiffington [Donald, shipyard director] motored Pigott & me to Loch Lomond, later he dined me & spoke of dry docks for Clyde, he will send me plans. [There were none which could take a battleship, so Clydebank's had to go to Liverpool.]

1 July Sunday: Arrived from Glasgow at home 08.50.

2 July: … Wrote firms that German destroyers were now coming here for technical inspection. [*Z.38* sailed for Portsmouth on 6 Jul and was renamed *Nonsuch*.]

3 July: Looked in at Dunlop War Exhibition, small but very interesting; RAF exhibits the best. Wave damper [for Mulberry harbours] has got boosted in the Press tho' no good compared to our Bombardons. … With DWP & SLC discussed Forthbank (Motherwell yard at Alloa), advised Vice Contr to see Miller [T R, chairman of Motherwell Bridge] & cancel last 4 LCT8s. …

4 July: Yesterday Sutherby reported *Potsdam* & *Patria* [17,000 grt German passenger-cargo ship to convert to troopship *Empire Welland*] are going to H & W Belfast (DMR had suggested Vickers Walker, I said No. What about C Laird & would he tell me work involved). Saw Bassett who knew nothing about it, phoned DMR who said FOIC [Belfast?] had been consulted. Went down to Contr & blew up; to my amazement CMSR had approached Contr who had agreed. I said it was bound to affect *Warrior, Magnificent* & *Powerful*, he said 'No, we shall see.' Contr went up in smoke over *Dullisk Cove* but my counterattack on *Potsdam* &c rather silenced him. Later he sent for me & I told him what I had done in Glasgow. He had evidently phoned CMSR as result of my protest & CMSR said 'Probably only one should go to Belfast'. What I don't like about this is that CMSR mucks up H & W Belfast if possible & L. Leathers is hitting shipbuilding by trying to get for British shipowners German ships on the cheap. … Held meeting with WPSs on getting back to peacetime routine for trials. [Ship trials were much curtailed in wartime, both for confirming required performance and for giving feedback on design.] …

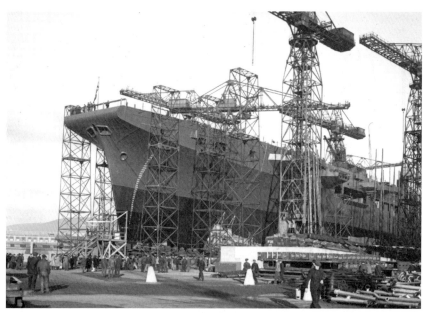

Nine aircraft carriers were ordered from Harland & Wolff at Belfast during the war, although *New Zealand* was cancelled on 5 November 1945. All were built in the Musgrave yard which had been laid out at the end of the First World War. Four of its six berths were used to build large warships during the war. As soon as *Minotaur/Ontario* had been launched from Berth No 10 (the northernmost), *Magnificent* was laid down. This view shows her shortly before launching on 16 November 1944. She was completed for the Royal Canadian Navy in 1948. (*Author's collection*)

5 July: Voted in General Election. ...

6 July: Concluded Harland & Wolff meeting. Capt [F L] Houghton [RCN of *Warrior*] agreed to steam trials before final commissioning ... disappointed at 15 weeks for SM.1 but DEE's rep. agreed this time was necessary. [*Warrior* commissioned for Canada on 24 Jan 46.] ... Mass of paper re cancellation old *Lion* & *Temeraire* contracts. I said new battleships must go to these firms if Cabinet agree they are in '45 Prog.

7 July: A tiresome morning. ... Contr came up & wants me to fix up a launch by wife of his Sec. [Capt N E Denning] ... Worst of all, Troup phoned & as usual took ½ hour for 5 mins talk. ...

9 July: CMSR's Output C'tee: still not clear about numbers of men on Landing Craft: phoned Baker to consult P. Branch & Labour Statistical man. Result 7000 in yards, 4000 in fabricators, 1600 sub-contractors, 1400 minor landing craft, total 14,000: told CMSR 3500 might return to shipbuilding. ...

10 July: At Bath. ... At repairs meeting, it appeared that *Valiant* after much work on her [at Devonport] is going into Reserve! [Her damage from the collapse of *AFD.23* was more severe than at first thought.] At NC meeting talk about reducing amount of painting owing to dearth of painters. Dep Contr rubbed in to Depts that we are building ships to fight Japan, not to have all A's & A's embodied until, when this war is over, we have the perfect ship. Dep Contr said that when a suicide bomber hit flight deck of *Illustrious* there was a fire, when it hit the soft deck of an American carrier there was a damned great hole: yet Boyd [Vice Admiral D W, former 5th Sea Lord] has insisted that *Malta* &c be re-designed to have a soft deck. Also Lambe (CO *Illustrious*) [Captain C E] said at his lecture yesterday 2200 men in a ship designed for 1300 were quite happy. [Now refitting at Rosyth.]

11 July: At Bath. Contr more pious than last month (? getting tired). ... DNO having let us down over Mark VI towers is now letting us down over 4.5″ RPC mountings for destroyers. [While industry was responsible for the manufacturing delays, given previous experience DNO should not have accepted their optimistic completion dates for vital equipment, which meant that shipbuilders used resources on ships that would inevitably be delayed rather than on ships that were not so dependent, e.g. light fleet carriers.] ... Worked on Postan's Production History, a dreadful effusion. Met Tees Side Bridge man: fitters went on strike: they put a boy to watch that a dynamo didn't get hot & then filled in 6 forms (Min of Labour's advice) to make him a dilutee, no fitters being available.

12 July: ... [Contr] asked about Italian underwater protection (1st SL thinks it marvellous because he [Admiral A B Cunningham when C in C Med] torpedoed these ships without much result. [Fewer hits were obtained than claimed and then only with 18in aerial torpedoes which might not defeat a battleship's side protection.] Contr said 'This only proves our torpedoes had little effect'. What a confession from one who has been DTM [Director of Torpedoes & Mining]). ... At Vice Contr's meeting with Denny on *MTB.109* [experimental hydrofoil]. D. like a fool offered to take £6500 (a loss of £5000) & Medd [W, Principal Assistant Secretary] froze on to this. ...

13 July: Saw Contr re converting trawlers at Scotts, he agreed to my draft i.e. no objection but TFs and *Chequers* & 2 CVEs [US-built escort carriers] must not be delayed. ... Wrote WPS Glasgow re *Ocean* conference at C Lairds (see Stephen's responsibilities are not shirked). [She had just been drydocked in *AFD.4* in the Clyde and arrived in Liverpool on 13 Aug.]

14 July: Worked on FO(S)'s [Flag Officer, Submarines, now Rear Admiral G E Creasy] proposals for suspending or scrapping S/Ms building, drafted

a report, sent to DNC, E in C & DEE for remarks. ... Wrote DNC re *Times* article that bow of USS *Pittsburgh* [cruiser] cracked & fell off during a typhoon [on 5 June in Pacific, poor welding]. Asked SLC how many LCTs were all welded & whether any of these had cracked.

15 July Sunday: Very prolonged thunderstorm during night to announce end of double summer time!

16 July: Held Priorities meeting. CMSR not obstructive, his presence quieted Naval side who usually cry for the moon. ... Sir Summers Hunter [managing director North Eastern Marine Engineering] has written FOIC (who has sent it to Contr) a letter stating it is desired to withdraw Harry Hunter from [managing] Hendon Dock.

17 July: ... S. Hunter called, said that their post-war work on Diesels was all behind & he wanted H. Hunter for that. The present No.2 at Hendon Dock was not good enough even if H. Hunter kept a watchful eye on the place. ...

18 July: Stantan walked in about 5.30 pm; left Montreal yesterday about 4 pm. (our time) this world is getting too small. ... Robb [Henry,

'River' class frigate *Croix de Lorraine* was being operated by the Free French Navy when seen here about to enter refit at Palmers' Hebburn yard on the Tyne in August 1944. She had been completed by Robb at Leith a year earlier as *Glenarm*. Originally described as twin screw corvettes (they had two 'Flower' class engines), they were the first RN escorts take account of its experience of U-boat warfare when designed in late 1940. At 100ft longer and 4 knots faster than the 'Flowers', they had much better seakeeping for North Atlantic operations as well as a much larger depth-charge outfit. (*Author's collection*)

chairman] called, no particular reason, his naval work is petering out he said (to date I have built 42 ships for RN in this war, that number would have to be checked). ... Maxwell (FOIC Tyne) called, *Beauly Firth* a pain in the neck, he will think about Hendon Dock. ... Talk with Baker (SLC) on Forthbank fitting out LCT8s & Hendon Dock. ...

19 July: General talk with Stantan on our programme in Canada. Men are leaving shipbuilding & ship repairs & our work is suffering. Two TFs due to finish June '46 have gone back to Oct, but Dewar [C L, President (Canadian) Wartime Shipbuilding Ltd] is moving them from Burrard [shipbuilder in Vancouver] to Davie [in Quebec] & hopes to get them in Oct. Amenities ships are slipping back. ... Left soon after lunch for dentist, tooth out T.G. [Thank God] (the blighter kept me awake half last night).

20 July: ... Newell [P S, Assistant Secretary] called later & we had a grand crack on things in general (Admy organisation, Executive's control of technical matters &c). Stantan wants me to write a letter of commendation on Canadian LST3s, had a go but not very keen, I am disappointed with their output. [Canadian Vickers at Montreal and Davie had done well, completing nine to date.] Skiffington sent plans of wet basin & dry docks on Clyde west of R. Cart. [On south bank opposite the shipyard.] I like them but can see they should benefit J. Brown more than anybody else. Wrote Morrison (H & W) to cut down the 15 weeks for SM.1 [in carriers].

26 July: ... Election Results. What a landslide! Hope we don't get Alexander back. [He was a Labour MP.] ...

27 July: Read carefully papers re an establishment for experiment (involving production) of AP [armour piercing] shell & bombs, backed it up & said <u>small scale</u> armour expts also necessary. ... Perring (IMTU) called, he is leaving, becomes a Director (only) [i.e. non executive] of Whites [shipbuilder], interesting talk on future of this firm & shipbuilding generally. Wrote Clyde Navigation Trust & C F in C [Sir F A Whitaker] re scheme on south side of river. Pigott called, fear Skiffington's work is over [then 65, health?], gun mountings are going to put *Vanguard* back. [The first 15in mounting, 'X', was being shipped that month; the first two 5.25in mountings from Barrow only in Dec.] ... Wrote Winston [no longer Prime Minister], felt I had to: ingratitude more strong than traitors' arms, quite vanquished him?

28 July: Worked on another screed Admiralty Production History (P.05756/45) so far not too bad i.e. it savours less of club chatter of irresponsible and ignorant officers. [It was never published as one of the

official war histories, although parts were included in *Administration of War Production* and Postan's *British War Production*.] Denny wants help over Voith-Schneider propellers (to see ex German E boats). [The propellers had vertical blades which could be adjusted to thrust in any direction.]

30 July: Worked on S/M programme & proposed cancellations; can't get original paper so can do nothing till I know Staff views. Got paper on Dutch [transfers], piles of talkie-talkie, a first class example of the evil of mixing up a number of subjects in one docket. ...

31 July: ... Bamford wants to retire, I didn't press him to stay, he has served me splendidly & really is worn out. [Bamford kept a diary (also in the British Library) but it only discusses his domestic doings, not his Admiralty work. He was the same age as Goodall, who he referred to as The Chief.] ... Went to Chinese reception, talked to some of the young constructors; these Chinese want to spend too long at school.

1 August: ... Johnson of CL called, very upset as he has had a snorter from Admy telling him to do what he is told (i.e. get on with repairs & trawlers). He says nearly all his work is PBR [Payment By Results, i.e. piecework] if he stopped that there would be labour trouble also a lot of his men charged to new construction are on repairs (he hasn't the clerical staff to sort them out). [Cammell Laird's shipyard, engine works and repair yard were all on the same site at Birkenhead, so men could be interchanged. By its very nature, labour required on repair work is unpredictable.]

3 August: ... Alexander back as 1st L. Damn. ...

4 August: ... DSC Newcastle says shipwrights supplied to V-A Walker for TFs are being used on *Hercules*, as Admy says this ship must be launched in Sept [actually 22 Sep by Lady Cripps, wife of the President of the Board of Trade]. (Actually firm wants slip to push on with merchant ships. I am sick of Ormston). [Cargo liner *City of Hull* was laid down on No 3 berth on 27 Sep.] ...

7 August: Cogitated a lot over refitting Portuguese destroyers at Yarrows, don't like refusing work from abroad, but felt I had to. [Yarrow had built hulls and machinery for five destroyers in the 1930s.] Letter from A C Hardy [prolific writer on ships and a temporary constructor] re Capt (S) Duckworth applying for the Secretary of INA, later Duckworth called, I gave him particulars of the job & wrote Lord Chatfield [President] and Dana. D. looks a likely candidate but is 49. [He was later appointed.] Ingram phoned, Cochrane [Admiral E L, Chief of Bureau of Ships]

arriving on Thursday 9th. He wants to go North, phoned DNC then got Ingram to call, we fixed up a tour & I wrote FOICs &c. Contr's Sec rang, he will try to fix an official lunch or cocktail party. Barr is snowing me under with bleats about labour for *Theseus*.

8 August: Stephen phoned, *Ocean* has a crack in LP [low pressure turbine] casing, can't ship be accepted subject to this defect which could be made good while ship is at CLs; saw E in C. [It was].

9 August: Held S/M meeting. FO(S) wanted decision now to suspend a number, I wanted a decision now to cancel or scrap a few. We compromised pro tem. ... Cochrane & party called; almost his first words were 'Thank God we should soon have a hard deck carrier out in the Pacific' [*Midway*]. I dined him & had most interesting talk. He agreed with me that brittleness of mild steel did not account for fracture of welded ships which were of 'rank bad design'. He thinks capital ship of the future will not be that carrying a 'heavy rifled gun'. He believes in big carriers.

10 August: ... FOIC Tyne's paper on repair facilities on this river after war is getting scant sympathy. I must put in a counter stroke. Told DWP to be ready with (a) chapter & verse on trawler interference with warships for Far East (b) proposals in event of Far East war coming to an end. ... Then to lunch when I read Japanese offer to surrender (one condition only). Met VCNS [Vice Chief of Naval Staff, now Vice Admiral Sir E N Syfret] I asked 'Is it Peace?' He said 'I am trying to find out'. Went to Vice Contr's room & he held a small meeting. I was for doing something (at least stopping overtime) but Vice Contr said Staff had decided we must wait till it is seen if Jap Central Authorities control Army in Manchuria, S E Asia & atolls. With DWP & SLC started on proposals if surrender comes about.

11 August: Vice Contr said the one proposal from 1st L. yesterday was to cancel the 2 Arks just ordered. ... Ingram's sec. phoned that Cochrane had been recalled (Priority) & was leaving for Washington tomorrow. Phoned Dorling, Maxwell & Troup [all FOICs] & wrote firms. ...

12 August: Sunday. At church Rector said it was his duty as a Christian to protest vehemently against use of atomic bomb by USA & GB. Wrote him asking if Christ's teachings forbade us to resist evil by force. If his answer was 'Yes', he should have said so before. But if 'No' he was only quibbling.

13 August: Contr came in. I saw him re action if surrender comes; I had fairly well interpreted his views. He said action to use light carriers for trooping was being considered [they were]. He gave me Plans paper on

post-war fleet. I dictated extracts with DWP (a grim outlook). ... Dep Contr thinks we shall be forced to cancel a number of destroyers & it would pay the Navy if Admy took initiative instead of being forced into it by Treasury. Smithers & his Commodore called, they want more work for Italy (hopeless now). Italy is getting restive because we won't let them build for themselves (if we did they would come to us for coal & steel).

14 August: ... [Dep Contr] agreed with me that Plans paper on the post-war fleet is nebulous & dangerous. I told Contr this & he bristled! I said the economy birds will say e.g. 35 cruisers, right you've got more than that already, scrap *Defence*, *Blake* &c. ... I drafted proposals, showed them to Eames (D of P) [Commander W E J, Plans] who agreed & sent them on. ... Eames says we shall want a lot of minesweepers. ... Dep Contr is not so fussed about the atomic bomb & says there should be a counter. Sent congratulations to 1st SL on his peerage.

15 August: Japan surrendered. I did not know till this morning & as it was wet I came into the office, fortunately as Contr called a meeting to consider the building programme, particularly in Canada. ... Leggatt then saw Naval Staff & they whittled the programme down a bit more, particularly on maintenance ships (I think the Naval Staff is crying for the moon & will be brought to earth with a jar). Had a general talk with Stantan who leaves for Canada tomorrow. It is interesting to recall the meeting in Contr's room [then Fraser] on 3/9/39 (Sunday) to consider the war programme and compare it with the meeting today to consider winding up. I am the only one who was at both meetings.

16 August: VJ Holiday.

17 August: Leggatt phoned re building programme. I said I should like to keep Battleaxes ['Weapons'] & G's [*Gallant* class] rather than Bay Cl. frigates. Attended 1st Lord's meeting, a lot of blether & little guidance, dictated notes. Waldock [C H M, Principal Assistant Secretary] said Dutch want a cruiser, which do I think better 'Turn over *Mauritius* or let them have *Sheffield* pro tem & build one for them later?' I said 'Sell *Mauritius*, they wouldn't get a new cruiser for 5 years'. [In the event the Dutch completed in 1953 the two cruisers ordered in 1939, *De Ruyter* and *De Zeven Provincien*.] Told Contr also that Venezuela wanted to negotiate for warships and I had agreed. [Two destroyers were ordered in 1950 from Barrow.] ... Told Contr I wanted to retire at end of Oct; he was very polite & said 'Discuss rearrangement with Lillicrap'. ...

19 August Sunday: To St Pauls for Thanksgiving: Daimler broke down & we drove up in a 9 HP Morris. Some of the NOs behaved as tho' this was an international match at Twickenham. ...

20 August: James came up re his visit with 1st L to M of WT. I told him what I hoped would be agreed viz no more than present number of trawler reconversions, minesweepers high priority, M of WT to name their urgently required ships. We then went on to cancellation procedure, brought in DWP & Head of C.L. [Controller of Labour?] & agreed Heads of Depts could write direct to firms. Wrote Pigott, Press & photographers can attend launch of *Talavera* (CNI agreed [Chief of Naval Information Rear Admiral R K Dickson]). ['Battle' class destroyer launched at Clydebank 27 Aug.] ...

21 August: Held Priorities meeting which went off well; all agreed to settling broad principles leaving Hughes to put them out in detail. ... Staff want 95 LCT8s finished, I bet they don't get 50. [Actually only thirty-one were completed for RN.]

22 August: At Bath. ... At Repairs meeting I got impression that work is proceeding on a lot of junk (*Renown, Valiant*). At New Constr meeting

'Battle' class destroyer *Talavera* was launched at Clydebank on 27 August 1945 as Yard No 617. She was cancelled on 1 November and her incomplete hull towed to Troon on 26 January 1946 for scrapping. The Admiralty reimbursed John Brown with £275,567 for work done, much of that for machinery, about half the final cost. This photo is of her sister *Barrosa* launched as No 615 on 17 January 1945 from Berth No 6. She was completed in February 1947, taking longer than usual for fitting out as the yard gave priority to merchant ships after the war. (*UCS*)

Dep Contr went thro' lists & said what was to be done. I have to take up *Vanguard* finishing electrical trials at Clydebank & docking later, also destroyers more particularly Battles. Discussed with Lillicrap what will happen when I go, he proposes to come to London, a good idea. ...

23 August: ... Sent on paper re A.C. [alternating current] electric installation in 1944 cruiser & Battle destroyer. [Four *Daring* class were built with A.C., the other four with D.C. (direct current).] Saw Vice Contr with my request to retire on Oct 31, then took it & covering letter to Controller to Contr's secretary. Milne called, told him LCT8s were to go on & I was hoping to save his destroyers, but I advised him strongly to get commercial work. [*Scorpion* and *Dainty* were the only two of the seven on order to be completed.] ...

25 August: Told DWP I hoped to go at end of October. Dep Contr came, I called in E in C, DWP & SLC and we flagged out procedure for cancelled ships. London (?ACWP [i.e. Goodall or successor] or DWP) as soon as cancellations are known will inform DCW (Bath) & he will start action with D of C [Jubb] &c. When ship [assumed already launched] has to be taken away, WPS will inform DCW who will start action with DoD(H) [Director of Dockyards (Home)]. I pointed out that supply depts should be told the principles on which they should go re removing gear, Dep Contr thought this should be limited to confidential items (fire control e.g.) & stores. I agreed but advised that D of C & MF [Material Finance] should know as there might be awkward questions re selling a ship for a mere song when it had brand new machinery on board. Dep Contr said he would issue a directive.

26 August Sunday: Rector had another go on the atomic bomb & I sent him a counter again, challenging him to a public debate. [Probably not taken up as no mention in his diary.]

27 August: Bassett came up re *Newcastle* in the Tyne, he won't budge. Showed him letter from Stanley re Hendon Dock for reconverting trawlers, he will send Jackman [W H, Chief Constructor] to see if he could use it. ... Perring called, he is in civvies & inquired about Whites; I told him I hoped to keep them going but was uncertain about the Weapons, they ought to get foreign orders. [Milne, who had been manager of the Dunkirk shipyard before the war, later got a batch of orders from France.]

28 August: Sent draft letters of commendation to firms that built landing craft. [Structural engineers like Tees Side Bridge had performed very well.] ... Wrote Micklem & Johnson re S/M cancellations [at Barrow and Birkenhead]. ...

30 August: … Staff want to keep a flotilla of Battles with US fire control [eight with Mark 37 directors were retained]. … Dined with Murray Stephen who said there would be heavy discharging if we cancelled *Dunkirk, Malplaquet* & *St Lucia*. [Only *St Lucia* was cancelled, with *Malplaquet* completed as *Jutland*.]

31 August: A small world: met today Driver [probably E F, civil engineer in Dockyard Dept] & Treagus [H A, Victualling Dept] who were both at Malta when I was (1925-7). DWP peeved at Dep Contr's memo re cancelling ships, fact is Simeon doesn't think much of him & probably dislikes him. … Simeon & Leggatt came in, we had a long yarn, Simeon wants to cancel drastically on financial grounds, I want to go moderately or the shipbuilding industry will be discharging finishing trades heavily & we shan't get them back. …

1 September: Ayre sent me graph of merchant shipbuilding labour forecast, which should be useful at Contr's meeting next Monday. … FOIC Tyne has accepted *Cuillin Sound* & suggests ship be used for training air mechanics. …

3 September: Got ready for Contr's meeting. Contr didn't seem much improved by his leave, more jumpy than before; curious to notice how he & Simeon react on one another, I thought Simeon was very restrained. [W-W had just been appointed C in C Med Fleet]. Contr agrees *Vanguard* should have high priority. …

4 September: Sent letters to Big XIV [warship builders] re cancellations & drafted letters to the few minor firms. …

5 September: … Sent docket to D of P re cancelling S/Ms (all 3 firms want to keep too much but I propose to get the bulk of the cancellations away before tackling these few). … Johnson [C Laird] called & was very calm over cancellations (the old blighter has his pocket full of merchant ship orders). Took him down to Contr who confirmed what I had told him (very funny). J said W-W's sister was quite nice so different to her brother).

6 September: … The Naval Officer is not a production expert nor even a technical one but as a figurehead he receives attention because he represents the 'user'. Contr is influenced by 'Jobs for NOs'. …

7 September: … Yarrow called, we had lunch together, long talk over RCNC into RN. On cancellations he thinks destroyer firms are coming off badly. …

8 September: Hancock came up, Govt wants a cut in coal consumption [in shipyards], particularly the good stuff used for gas. …

11 September: At Bath. At repairs meeting a more reasonable attitude over bringing old junk up to date. ... Curphey [E S, Assistant Director of Dockyards] looked into DNC's office when I was working & we had a long yarn. Hill [S I, Acting Constructor Captain, Eastern Fleet] & Mutch are to be disrated to their substantive rank as a result of India Floating Dock disaster [AFD.23]. He thinks this is too harsh; it is certainly severe but they were to blame. [Goodall was right, the two senior constructors were culpable in leaving the lifting of Valiant, which was four times heavier than any previous ship docked, to inexperienced underlings without checking everything and supervising themselves – they had gone to a concert ashore. The oversight by Hill was even more surprising as he had been the constructor in charge of Valiant's modernisation in the floating dock at Devonport in 1939, so would be aware of the problem of matching weight and buoyancy. The modern injunction 'When all else fails, read the instructions' would have avoided the disaster.] What makes me mad is the [Admiralty] Board will punish if the RCNC makes a mistake but for all (& it is a lot) that has gone right the Corps gets nothing.

13 September: ... Pigott called, told him he has blotted his copy book by trying to get Princess Margaret to launch the cruiser [Tiger on 25 Oct by Lady Stansgate, wife of Secretary of State for Air and Tony Benn's mother; Princess Elizabeth had launched Vanguard 11 months earlier.] Contr sent for me & outlined a yarn he wanted me to draft for 1st L re cancellations. 1st L wants to see Chancellor [of the Exchequer, Hugh Dalton] with it on Monday. I said I would do it with DWP as my leave started tomorrow. Went to Special INA Council meeting re a new Secretary. Baker [G S], Telfer [E V], Todd [F H] & Wigley [W C S] [all distinguished naval architects and members of INA Council] obstructed, invoking a Bye-law, result an awful waste of time; poor Chatfield was worn out. I got back about 6 p.m. & Greig of Scotts was waiting for me (he came at 5 by appointment), told him what was going to happen ... Dined at Club. After dinner DWP & I got out the draft for 1st L re cancellations. ... A very thick day [twenty lines in his diary, double the usual number]. ...

14 September–3 October: On leave.

24 September: Controller died suddenly this night. [Overwork may well have contributed to his death (similarly to Henderson in 1939); as well as ships, Controller was responsible for materiel generally, not just ships but machinery, armament, armour and equipment.]

29 September: Bamford phoned me that [Permanent] Secretary [Markham] had written asking me to stay for a month or two until the new Controller was in the saddle.

Tiger, ordered as *Bellerophon* on 19 May 1941, was launched at Clydebank on 25 October 1945, planned to be fitted with three triple 6in Mark 24 mountings. Construction was suspended and her hull with machinery partly installed was towed to Dalmuir on 30 April 1946 to lay up. A new design featuring two twin 6in Mark 26 rapid-firing HA mountings was prepared. John Brown was given a new contract to complete her, still as No 593. She was towed back to Clydebank by *Flying Swordfish* and *Flying Hurricane* on 29 February 1956, with only the two funnels of her original superstructure remaining, completing three years later. (UCS)

1 October: On leave. Came into office on way to Memorial service & wrote Secretary a note suggesting I talk over my retirement with him. 'De mortuis nil nisi bonum' [Of the dead, (speak) nothing but good] but the Parson on Wake-Walker overdid it to put it mildly. Returned to 50 Lyford.

4 October: Back in office. Saw Sec. who raised no further objection to my retirement (he said Simeon had written, I wonder what S. said). Sec. showed me papers Contr proposed Lillicrap as AC(WP) & DNC with no increase in salary. [Goodall had held both posts 1942–4.] ...

5 October: With DWP [McCarthy] went thro' happenings while I was on leave. The cancellations are a muddle and nothing definite has been done yet. The S/Ms I proposed for cancellation have so far not even been suspended. [Perhaps with no Controller, staff were waiting for Goodall to return with his push and grasp of the situation?] Phoned DNC re Production matters of urgency & importance to be brought to notice

of new Controller. [Vice Admiral Sir Charles S Daniel was appointed, latterly with the British Pacific Fleet.] ...

6 October: Wrote D of D (copy to DNC) in reply to his of 3/10 re building a prefabricated escort vessel at Chatham [it was never done]. ... Started clearing out gubbins & sent some drawings to DDNC (L) [Deputy Director of Naval Construction W G Sanders in London]. ...

8 October: ... Read report of delegation of British shipbuilders &c that visited German yards. I must talk with Cole, the delegates think we have nothing to learn re practice but the Germans (thanks to Hitler) have got over trade union demarcation problems & pay a man according to his skill; also they have better canteens & washing & changing arrangements for men, who however do this in their own time. Most yards have apprentices at school during working hours.

10 October: Did a bit more clearing out. What work & problems we had, a lot just ended in paper. At House C'tee meeting [INA], I mentioned my project for a W Froude [William, pioneer of ship model testing] corner in the Science Museum. Belch [Alexander of the Shipbuilding Conference] said 'Tackle the whole question of the shipbuilding & naval architecture exhibits.' ...

12 October: Another day of callers. Perring said Whites are not yet dead sure of the French orders (value of the franc a snag). Pigott said Vanguard's date looks like May '46, he wants her out of the basin in April [she left for trials and drydocking on 2 May]. Pringle had a lot to say agin W-W. Meryon called. McCloghrie called, interesting on American views re atomic bomb & its effect on ships. ...

15 October: Dep 1st SL rang re cancellations (he, wise man, wanted views direct instead of via Vice Contr). I was not called to 1st SL's meeting so I butted in & invited myself. ... Dictated notes of 1st SL's meeting; actually if what he decided finishes cancellations, the industry should get thro' the next 3 years all right. [Smoother transition to building merchant ships. Post-war problems in shipbuilding were more to do with shortage of materials than shortage of orders.]

16 October: Norman Hunter [Wallsend shipyard general manager] phoned in a flurry over Oleander [oiler completed as tanker Helicina in 1946] & River Plate ['Battle' class destroyer]. Re former I phoned Harlow [S, Deputy Director of Stores, whose department ran the oilers] he said decision expected soon & will let me know. ... I told N. H. on phone & confirmed by letter that he can get ship off slip [River Plate had been laid down on Berth No 4. After the partially erected structure had been

Vanguard fitting out early in 1946, nearly complete with 'X and Y' turrets erected and with US Mark 37 directors and boats already in place. Her 5.25in mountings are about to be delivered from Barrow in the coaster *Empire Jack*. The crane to the left is a 150-ton derrick made by Cowans Sheldon of Carlisle in 1906. (*UCS*)

removed, the French passenger-cargo vessel *Foucauld* was laid down. The Admiralty paid Swan Hunter £41,000 for hull work done and Wallsend Slipway £125,000 for machinery, about 27 per cent of the likely final price.]

17 October: Milne called, now wants to save *Sword* from cancellation, told him it was too late. He said he will have to stand men off. ... Drafted new docket on a Production Research & Development yard. ... Wrote to IPCS [Institute of Professional Civil Servants] resigning Vice Presidency.

18 October: ... Thornycroft [Sir John E, chairman] called, told him *Howitzer* ['Weapon' class destroyer] was to be cancelled, he appeared to be very glum but he will be lucky if there are no more. ... Going thro' the accumulated dope, I came to loss of *Prince of Wales*, apparently I have not got the complete story, wrote DNC to ask if can give it to me. ...

19 October: Wrote Offord if he could give me the missing link in *P of Wales* report after Bucknill's first report. ... Mr Johnson of Warrenpoint called, I could not see him, he saw DWP. He could sell a LCT8 to Eagle Oil but D of C has stopped it; all such sales are to be by Admy; we are going to lose a few £100,000s by this policy. ...

22 October: Dep 1st SL sent for me re merchant shipbuilding & naval programme being arranged to give an even load to the industry. He showed me Lithgow's remarks on Hurcomb's [Sir Cyril, Ministry of War Transport] letter to 1st L. I agreed the industry should not be kept in a strait waistcoat by a Govt C'tee & that unions must be brought into any talk on increasing efficiency. ...

23 October: At Bath. Went round saying 'Goodbye'. D of D [Talbot] & I skated over the ice; DEE will back Prod R & D yard. He was interesting on the new 'L' scheme & said fully applied i.e. DEE Dept all NOs was going to be very expensive. [The Electrical Branch of the RN was only formed in 1946, previously being part of the torpedo branch.] DNO [Woodhouse] asked me in the light of my experience what did I think of DNO's dept. I said bluntly he was dependent on amateurs, first rate engineers stuck to E in C where there was the big plum, hence he only got second rates, in other things he was too dependent on firms who since the last war had been reduced in number & had gone downhill. Told Jubb about sales of scrapped ships & of new ships to foreign powers, also cancellations. RCNC Association gave me a nice party but I had to leave early to tune 'Jolly Good Fellow'. Home 22.30.

24 October: ... To Mansion House, Lord Mayor entertained King to lunch; afterwards H.M. as Permanent Master held Shipwright's Court & Honorary Freedom [of City] was presented to Winston; he looked subdued. I had a word with him but he didn't remember my work [Churchill had been First Lord 1939–40 when Goodall was DNC]. ... Read TL's [Their Lordships] letter of appreciation of my work as AC(WP) [no doubt drafted by Markham].

25 October: Discussed Priorities with DWP for 1st L's meeting tomorrow. Suggested to Vice Contr he should hold a preliminary meeting; he said he had already done this with Dep 1st SL (he hadn't invited either DWP or me, such is life). ... [Sir R S Johnson] asked if he could cut up *Somme* & *San Domingo* ['Battle' class destroyers], I said 'Yes'. ...

26 October: Attended 1st Lord's Priority meeting. How I dislike Albert [Alexander] with his 'I this' & 'I that' & the smack of lips & tongue lick before he says what he thinks is funny. He said 'Certainly not' to the proposal from Lithgow that trade unions should be told the priorities. ... Finished clearing up room & went to Foyle's [bookshop] who will buy text books but not Proceedings of Institutions. [At that time each member of most engineering institutions got a free copy of the annual *Transactions*, so there were always a lot on the market.] ...

27 October: ... Wrote DNC re *Albion* [light fleet carrier at Swan Hunter] not getting higher priority, dividing D class 16 ships into 8 to go ahead &

8 to be deferred [these latter were later cancelled] also re-arrangement of areas for WPSs & AROs [Admiralty Repair Officers?].

29 October: … Wrote to firms saying 'What a fine lot they are.' [Well, some, see page 21.] Finished packing up & took all my gubbins home. Wrote to FOICs. DDNC (L) had his party photographed & asked me to join in.

30 October: Wrote love letters to remaining firms & WPSs. Started a round of 'Goodbye' visits. 5th SL jovial but did not impress me. Had lunch with Sec. who pumped me about naval status for the RCNC. I told him what I thought about Production, Navy Estimates not being annual, Research yard for Production. He said he is half Welsh, now I think I understand him better. He told me a good story about Reggie [Henderson, pre-war Controller] 'meekly kneeling upon my knees'.

31 October: McArthur Morison [DMB] called to say Goodbye, interesting to listen to him on the Admiralty & Minister of War Transport [Leathers]. Said Goodbye to 1st SL who was great on RCNC going into RN [but it never happened]. 1st L put me off, then I ran into him in the corridor. He took me by the arm & was very affable, so I only had a few minutes with him. He asked me if I was going into any other concern, I said 'No, my interests are more in the scientific than commercial side of my profession'. Immediately I got back to my office, Johnson phoned to ask if I would join Cammell Laird's Board as a director. I said 'Write what it involves'. Meeting in my room to wish Bamford all the best, he was funny about P.W. [W-W?]. Dep 1st SL fished to know what I should do, he has been asked to join the Radio Trade Association. [Kennedy-Purvis died in May 1946 aged 62.] So ends my active service in Admiralty after more than 46 years.

1 November: My first day of freedom. Letter arrived from Johnson. Yesterday I forgot to say 'Goodbye' to DWP, I kicked myself & wrote him last night. …

2 November: … More nice letters from firms.

3 November: Wrote Johnson accepting his invitation to join Cammell Laird's Board, but asked that the appointment should not be made nor announced till the New Year.

7 November: Called Institution of Naval Architects & went thro' draft membership form. After lunch attended meeting of President of INA [Chatfield], NEC [North East Coast Institution of Engineers & Shipbuilders, Sir Summers Hunter] and Scottish [Institution of Engineers & Shipbuilders in Scotland, Sir Murray Stephen] re affiliation. Two latter won't play, NEC particularly sticky (keep out of our territory, more amicable over distribution of post-war papers [on warship types built]).

11 November Sunday: Dr Clarke vetted me, a good bill except for my feet (skin). He advised croquet before golf & bowls not advised.

14 November: Received from Offord copy of final Bucknill Report on Loss of *P of W* & later of Job 74 trials [a full-scale target before the war]. Letter from Johnson saying one of his directors said there was a recent AFO [Admiralty Fleet Order] prohibiting retired officers from joining a private firm for 12 months after they left the service. Replied saying I knew of no such order but would inquire further.

15 November: ... At lunch [after INA Council meeting] interesting talk with McCance [Sir Andrew of Colvilles Steel] & Lillicrap on atomic bomb: Daniel [R J, constructor] is back from Nagasaki. [His autobiography *The End of an Era* tells of visiting Japan to assess the damage caused. It is critical of many officials and a revealing book.]

16 November: Finished RN on 3/9/39 & New construction during the war down to & including cruisers, left drafts with Lillicrap, he gave me typed part of first instalments [Goodall was preparing two papers for the INA]. He could find no AFO. ...

19 November: Wrote Johnson no order to prohibit me joining Board. Then came letter from Lillicrap enclosing CMD paper saying Admy approval is necessary so I wrote Johnson another letter. ...

22 November: Called at INA. Duckworth's first day as Secretary. ... Interesting talk at lunch, Lord Woolton on Cripps, House of Lords full of experts & you have to be mighty careful when you get up to talk there. ...

26 November: ... Called at Admy & saw Markham, he would not commit himself, said he thought the precedents were in favour but Treasury would have to be consulted & 1st Lord, I must write. Went to Club, wrote Markham a semi-official letter which I left with his sec; wrote & told Johnson what had happened.

28 November: Letter from Lillicrap saying various RCNC men will write papers for the INA. [The 1946 and 1947 *Transactions* have many interesting papers by RCNC staff on Second World War warship designs.]

30 November: ... Received from Paymaster General Pension for 1st December.

4 December: Cammell Laird phoned to inquire if I had yet heard from Markham re my joining the Board; I said 'No, the mills of God &c'.

5 December: At Goodeve's [Sir Charles F, Assistant Controller (Research & Development)] lecture on 'The Defeat of the Magnetic Mine'. Very good, he was not too long & stuck to principles instead of wallowing in

details. But I think he & the Press are too anxious to say that German scientists are no good compared to ours. Actually the enemy gave us a bad time with the magnetic mine & to overcome it necessitated a huge effort & absorbed a lot of our capacity & energy. ... Letter from Johnson appointing me Director 'if &c'.

15 December: ... Received request for payment of Income Tax on BBC fees, apparently they are charging me twice. ...

22 December: ... Letter from Markham re Cammell Lairds; must be patient, apparently Treasury is dubious. [Markham died in December 1946 aged only 49, probably from overwork and a gastric ulcer.]

Memoranda 1945

Finished my service in Admiralty, Thank God. We struggled along fairly successfully with the Transport Ferries and were keeping our promises when VJ Day came: Canada's output was disappointing. The Fleet Train was a fizzle, the fitting out was too much for the merchant ship repair firms and only a few had been completed when VJ Day arrived. The destroyer delays went from bad to worse; DNO's party was hopeless. Turner E in C left invalided & Pringle (DEE) retired. The Light Carriers fell back, V-A Walker being particularly disappointing. The frigates have been successful. I got on well with the plans for turning over shipbuilding capacity from warships to merchant ships, but we were given a date Nov '46 for end of Pacific War; it came in August [1945] and we were not prepared. I managed to keep a good many contracts alive but after I left there were further cancellations, and the outlook for the industry isn't good.

Markham & the Treasury won't give me a decision re joining Cammell Laird's Board. I got on better with Wake-Walker but he died suddenly in September, leaving a reputation he did not deserve. In domestic affairs the year has again been a sad one. Ernest's death in January was a severe blow & Clarie taking it so badly has added to it. N's [Nell, his wife Helen] health is better but she is not strong enough to run the house to which we returned in October with the inadequate domestic help obtainable. Now I have retired more of my time than I like is going in assistance to her and the plans I had made are fizzling. Also my study is too cold for prolonged work with this fuel shortage.

Sources

Primary Sources

The primary source has been Goodall's own diaries 1937–41, 1942–46. British Library Add.MS 52790-91.

Director of Naval Construction correspondence files Vol. 13 July 1940–March 1941. National Archives ADM229/15.

Navy Lists. Published bi-monthly by the Admiralty. Names and postings of naval officers and Admiralty officials. Downloadable from https://digital.nls.uk/british-military-lists/archive/93506066

Secondary Sources

Brown, D K (1983), *A Century of Naval Construction: A History of the Royal Corps of Naval Constructors* (London: Conway Maritime Press).

Brown, D K (2000), *Nelson to Vanguard: Warship Design and Development 1923-1945* (London: Chatham Publishing).

Brown, D K (1997), 'Sir Stanley Goodall', *Warship 1997-98* (London: Conway Maritime Press).

Buxton, Ian (1998), *Warship Building and Repair during the Second World War*. Research Monograph No 2, Centre for Business History in Scotland, Glasgow University.

Buxton, Ian (2018), 'Vickers Gun Mountings Built at Barrow', 4 parts, *Warships* Nos 192–195 (World Ship Society).

Fassett, H G (ed) (1948), *The Shipbuilding Business of the USA*, Vol 1 (New York: Society of Naval Architects & Marine Engineers).

Goodall, S V (1944), 'Some Recent Technical Developments in Naval Construction', *Transactions of the North East Coast Institution of Engineers & Shipbuilders* Vol 61 (Newcastle).

Goodall, S V (1946), 'The Royal Navy at the Outbreak of War', *Transactions of the Institution of Naval Architects* Vol 88 (London).

Johnston, Ian and Buxton, Ian (2013), *The Battleship Builders* (Barnsley: Seaforth Publishing).

Lenton, H T (1998), *British and Empire Warships of the Second World War* (London: Greenhill Books).

Moore, George (2003), *Building for Victory: The Warship Building Programmes of the Royal Navy 1939-1945* (World Ship Society).

The Shipbuilder. This well-produced monthly magazine published in Newcastle was not only full of shipbuilding and marine engineering news and articles and ship descriptions, but usually featured each month a prominent shipbuilder or naval architect with a portrait and brief biography. These have been very useful for fleshing out many of the people Goodall encountered. Copies accessible at Marine Technology Special Collection, Newcastle University.

Statistical Digest of the War (HMSO 1951).

British Shipbuilding Database. 81,000 British-built ships from the mid-nineteenth century to date. Compiled by I L Buxton. Accessible at Marine Technology Special Collection, Newcastle University.

Blackman photograph collection, World Ship Society.

Larrie Ferreiro and Ian Johnston have been very helpful providing additional information and illustrations.

Index

Page numbers in *italics* refer to illustrations.